THE SLIM GOURMET COOKBOOK

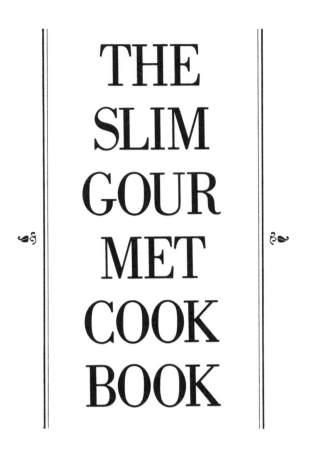

THE SLIM GOUR MET COOK BOOK

Barbara Gibbons

HARPER & ROW, PUBLISHERS

New York, Hagerstown, San Francisco, London

Designed by Patricia Girvin Dunbar

Library of Congress Cataloging in Publication Data

Gibbons, Barbara.
  The slim gourmet cookbook.
  Includes index.
  1. Cookery. 2. Reducing diets. I. Title.
TX652.G52 1976   641.5′635   75–23883
ISBN 0–06–011517–3

78 79 80 81 10 9 8 7 6

CONTENTS

v

THE SLIM GOURMET COOKBOOK

INTRODUCTION:
WHAT IT'S REALLY
LIKE TO LOSE
LOTS OF WEIGHT

Ever wonder what it is like to lose a lot of weight? Not just a few pounds to squeeze into last year's bikini, but a *lot* of weight, sixty, eighty, or a hundred pounds? Let me tell you.

After weighing more than 200 pounds, almost since infancy, it seems, I woke up one bright June day weighing 128. Not that I lost eighty pounds overnight, it took nearly two years, but the realization that I was finally "normal" did seem to strike me all at once. And here are some of the curious things that happened:

I didn't recognize myself for the longest time. I kept running into "me" in mirrors and store windows and wondering who that vaguely familiar person was. It took more than a year before I could begin to spot my reflection—but I got lots of practice, because mirrors began sprouting all over the house. (Previously, the only mirrors in our house were eye level!)

The same "nonrecognition" affects others, too. One day my husband spotted "a young girl in blue jeans" standing on the deck of his boat. He wondered who she was, until he got close enough to recognize his wife's familiar face.

The "fat self-image" is very slow in dying. I still don't walk through narrow spaces or attempt to "squeeze" into tiny chairs for fear that my phantom "behind" will get wedged into an embarrassing spot. Besides picking the sturdiest chair to sit on, I avoid climbing on rickety-looking ladders. And my clothes coming out of the washer always look as if they've shrunk. (When a salesclerk hands me a size nine it always looks like a kid's dress I'll never wriggle into!)

Psychologists say that this distorted body image mainly afflicts people who were overweight since childhood (I was), but not those who became fat as adults. After several years of slimness it gradually begins to fade.

Other small surprises:

Not only did my dress size change, but my shoe, ring, and glove size, too. I went from a size eight shoe to a six. And after my wedding ring slipped off in a swimming pool, I had it resized to a four.

And speaking of swimming, I sank straight to the bottom my first "skinny" summer. The swimming pool's "unsinkable Molly Brown" had lost her built-in lifejacket!

I found bones I didn't know I had. One day I discovered that my ribcage was "growing" and protruding outward, clearly a sign of bone cancer. After a panicky visit to the doctor and finally a specialist, we found a case of childhood rickets or congenital rib malformation, buried all those years under rolls of fat.

I also found that while being overweight can lead to backaches, slimming can, too. For a brief period I was bothered with low back pain while my body adjusted to its new center of gravity.

And something else I never would have believed: both my appetite and tastes in food changed. Eating less is easier than I ever would have thought, because my smaller body doesn't need all that nutritional support. And those crunchy munchies I used to consider "rabbit food" are now both appealing and appetizing. No kidding! Not because it's "good for you," but because it tastes good.

But the best thing about slimming down is that all your other "impossible dreams" begin to seem reasonable. Others who have succeeded in losing weight report the same feeling. A person who's licked a lifelong weight problem feels as if he can lick the world. Why not go back to college or open a business or learn to ski or marry the boss? Why not get your own apartment, a Ph.D., or a divorce? Why not learn to drive or sew or paint or type or program a computer?

Why not?

1
GETTING
STARTED

Forget everything you've ever heard or read about dieting, because today is *your* day to become a Slim Gourmet. Once you do, you'll never have to start another diet, because "Slim Gourmania" is a permanent way of life, a whole new approach to dining and dieting that can keep you healthy, happy, and heartily fed for the rest of your life—without all those unwanted extra pounds.

As a Slim Gourmet cook, you don't give up the foods you love, you simply learn to prepare them without the extraneous calories. And little by little, slowly but surely, the extra pounds will painlessly disappear. You won't go "off" your diet and gain it all back, because you weren't on a "diet" to begin with.

Do Slim Gourmets count calories? Absolutely! Despite the claims of fad diets, calories *do* count. In fact, calories, or the lack of them, is *all* that counts when it comes to losing or gaining. All diets work by forcing you to take in fewer calories than you use up. But there's no reason why the calories you take in have to be in the form of dreary, unimaginative foods or rigidly repetitive meals.

KEEP A DAILY DIET DIARY

What? When? Where? Who? Why?

If you can answer those five questions about the food you eat, you're well on the way to weight control. Taking a close look at day-in, day-out eating habits is the first step in "behavior modification." The idea behind "behavior mod" is to replace faulty food habits with healthy ones, a step at a time.

And the first step is to begin keeping a daily diet diary, in which you keep track of every bite and nibble, no matter how small—and the when, where, with whom, and how come of it.

At the outset, it's not important to diet or cut down; that will automatically follow once your diet diary points up just how many "countless calories" you are thoughtlessly consuming for no good reason.

First, in a notebook with horizontal lines, write across the top of each page, *What, When, Where, Who, Why.* Then, if you need them, draw vertical lines to separate each heading.

Now, write down every morsel of food you eat under the "What" column (use a separate line for each item), and fill in the rest of the columns with the appropriate information explaining the circumstances of that particular eating experience. Nobody's going to see this diary but you, so be honest. Some typical entries might be as follows:

What: 3 slices pizza. *When:* 10 P.M. *Where:* Bowling alley. *Who:* Bob, Ted, and Alice. *Why:* Because Bob paid for it.

What: Half a chocolate doughnut. *When:* 3:30 P.M. *Where:* Kitchen counter. *Who:* Billy. *Why:* Because Billy didn't finish it.

What: 3 scoops cherry-vanilla ice cream. *When:* 10 P.M. *Where:* The den. *Who:* By myself. *Why:* Because I always have ice cream with the ten o'clock news.

Such record-keeping reveals that most fattening foods are consumed, not because it is a regular mealtime, but because certain places, people, activities, and times bring on the imagined need to eat—often in spite of having just finished a meal. Once recognized, you can contrive to avoid these situations. Pick a different bowling alley, for example, or different partners. Or let Ted pay for the pizza. Set out the afterschool snacks and vacate the kitchen; instruct the kids to clean up after themselves so you won't be tempted to. Stop watching the ten o'clock news, or quit buying ice cream, or pick the one flavor you hate.

After you get the hang of it—in a week or so—expand your daily diet diary with one more entry—a sixth column, "How Much?" Here you will keep track of the caloric costs of all food you eat, with the aid of a good calorie counter. Your reeducation now begins in earnest.

HOW TO COMPUTE YOUR DAILY CALORIE BUDGET

How many calories per day can you eat to attain and remain at the weight you want to be? Here's a do-it-yourself guide.

Men

Height (with shoes on) 1-inch heels Feet Inches	Small frame	Medium frame	Large frame
5 2	112–120	118–129	126–141
5 3	115–123	121–133	129–144
5 4	118–126	124–136	132–148
5 5	121–129	127–139	135–152
5 6	124–133	130–143	138–156
5 7	128–137	134–147	142–161
5 8	132–141	138–152	147–166
5 9	136–145	142–156	151–170
5 10	140–150	146–160	155–174
5 11	144–154	150–165	159–179
6 0	148–158	154–170	164–184
6 1	152–162	158–175	168–189
6 2	156–167	162–180	173–194
6 3	160–171	167–185	178–199
6 4	164–175	172–190	182–204

Women

Height (with shoes on) 2-inch heels Feet Inches	Small frame	Medium frame	Large frame
4 10	92–98	96–107	104–119
4 11	94–101	98–110	106–122
5 0	96–104	101–113	109–125
5 1	99–107	104–116	112–128
5 2	102–110	107–119	115–131
5 3	105–113	110–122	118–134
5 4	108–116	113–126	121–138
5 5	111–119	116–130	125–142
5 6	114–123	120–135	129–146
5 7	118–127	124–139	133–150
5 8	122–131	128–143	137–154
5 9	126–135	132–147	141–158
5 10	130–140	136–151	145–163
5 11	134–144	140–155	149–168
6 0	138–148	144–159	153–173

1. Decide your ideal weight. (You probably already have an "ideal weight" in mind, or use the United States Public Health Service "Desirable Weight" chart on page 5 as a guide)

2. Find your "calorie quotient" on the chart below:

Age	Men	Women
20–30	20	18
30–40	19	15
40–50	17	14
50–60	16	13
60 up	15	12

3. Multiply your "calorie quotient" by your "ideal weight"———

4. Now, subtract one-fourth from this total—if you are an "inactive person."*

LEARN THE WORDS: PROTEIN . . . FAT . . . CARBOHYDRATE

Everything edible can be categorized as either protein, fat, or carbohydrate—just as the inedible world can be divided into animal, vegetable, and mineral. But few foods are purely protein, or purely fat, or carbohydrate. Most are a combination, just as your inedible umbrella is animal (bone handle), vegetable (fabric covering), and mineral (metal shaft).

Protein, of course, is "animal" food—meat, poultry, fish, and eggs. But none of these is "pure" protein, because they also contain such nonnutritive and inedible matter as moisture and bone, as well as fat in varying degrees. And the fatter the food, the more valuable protein is displaced.

Protein is also found, along with fat and some carbohydrates, in such dairy products as milk and cheese. (But the more fat, the less protein.) It is also found in beans, but vegetable proteins are less complete, with one exception—soybeans. Soybeans and soy-enriched products are very valuable to protein seekers, and protein is the one food element the dieter simply cannot skimp on.

Fat is either animal or vegetable in origin—both have the same calorie count. Ounce for ounce, fat has twice the calories of either protein or carbohydrate. Some fat is needed in every diet to help absorb nutrients properly, so a completely fat-free diet would be unhealthy. However, Americans have the fattest diet in the world, as well as the highest cholesterol levels and heart-disease rate. The American Heart Association has urged Americans to cut down on *all* fat in their diets, but particularly animal fat, which is believed to raise cholesterol levels.

Carbohydrate, simply speaking, is everything else—fruits and vegetables as well as starches and sweets. In addition to being a delectable and important

* *Important*: Don't attempt a diet below 1,200 calories a day without medical supervision.

source of needed vitamins and minerals, fresh fruit and vegetables are high in moisture and noncaloric roughage.

ALL YOU SHOULD EAT EACH DAY

⋘ Two cups' worth of skim or low-fat milk may be used in cooking, coffee, or beverages. Low-fat cheese, milk puddings, and ice milk can provide part of the quota.

⋘ Six ounces lean meat, poultry, or fish—trimmed of all fat and cooked with a minimum of fat—for protein. Eggs, low-fat cheese, skim milk, soy, and other vegetable protein foods can contribute to your protein quota.

⋘ Two cups or more mixed low-calorie vegetables and fruit (without added sugar or fat). Have a variety every day—some green, some yellow, and some citrus fruits and tomatoes.

⋘ Four servings of carbohydrate foods, such as 1 slice of whole-grain, enriched, or protein bread; 1 cup cold (or ½ cup hot) cereal; ½ cup starchy vegetables or fruit (potatoes, corn, peas, beans, bananas, etc.). Decalorized desserts and snacks can also make up part of this category.

TRIMMING THE FAT

When it comes to fat, you are what you eat. So . . . if you like to trim fat from your figure, start by trimming fat from your food!

Hard or soft, solid or liquid, saturated or not, most fats range between 100 and 125 calories per tablespoon, depending on the purity.

The typical American diet consists of at least 40 percent fat. More than half of what most of us eat is fat. As a result, many of us are putting away 1,500 or 2,000 calories a day in fats alone. Fat is tucked away where it can't be seen. Butter, margarine, salad oil, and the fat that fringes your steak account for less than half of the fat we consume. The rest is buried in canned goods, frozen foods, bakery items, mixes, convenience foods, sauces, snacks, drinks, toppings, and restaurant meals—even in many natural foods that don't seem fatty.

Let's go on a meal-by-meal "fat-finding expedition," and see where these fat calories lurk.

BREAKFAST: Sausage and bacon can be nearly half fat. Lean ham or Canadian bacon is a much slimmer choice. (And have you heard about beef bacon? Now that calorie-counters and cholesterol-watchers have discovered its lower fat content, beef bacon is available in many supermarkets, in both kosher and nonkosher varieties. Raw pork bacon is almost twice as fattening as beef bacon. According to U.S. Department of Agriculture data, the calorie count of bacon is reduced only by about 10 percent when cooked—a lot less than most people think!)

Egg yolks contain fat, and fried eggs can absorb a great deal of cooking fat, so if you must fry your eggs use a nonstick skillet. Toast and hot breads, Danish pastries, packaged squares, and toaster tarts are notorious fat hiders and butter absorbers. The least fatty breakfast choice is protein cereal, fruit, and skim milk.

LUNCH: Many "cold cuts" are as much as one-third fat, except "boiled" ham, chicken roll, and turkey products. Most cheeses are about 30 percent fat, but not the new low-fat, so-called imitation cheeses (they're called "imitation" because the fat is reduced). Watch out for tuna, chicken, and egg salad, packed with mayonnaise. At 110 calories a tablespoon, mayonnaise is one of the fattest offenders. Choose diet mayonnaise instead, only 30 calories. Select water-packed tuna in place of oil-packed—half the calories.

DINNER: Steaks, chops, and hamburgers may be one-third fat or more. Dine on lean cuts of meat, choosing among veal, seafood, poultry, and liver. Avoid grease-soaked, batter-dipped, or breaded foods. Skim the fat from stews, pot roasts, and gravy. Almost all pouch-packed "vegetables in sauce," frozen entrees, canned sauces and gravies, and convenience mixes contain added fat, so be a fine print reader and check the label. Most bottled salad dressings are at least half fat; choose the diet version instead. Cream and sour cream (even the nondairy fakes) are 20 to 37 percent fat; top your potato with onion salt and yogurt. Avoid bread, except for lunchtime sandwiches (if you *must*), and you'll also avoid butter. Remember, margarine is just as fattening as butter (except, of course, for diet margarine).

DESSERTS: The worst offenders are pies, pastries, ice cream, whipped toppings, icings, cookies, and canned and frozen puddings, and most types of cake (particularly pound cake). The least fatty are sherbet, low-fat ice milk, angel and sponge cake (great with fruit), gelatin desserts, homemade custards, mousses, and puddings made with skim milk.

SNACKS: Potato chips, puffs, and cheese spreads are generally one-third fat. Peanuts and peanut butter are nearly half fat. Avoid commercial dips, spreads, and greasy cocktail foods. The safest choices are vegetable nibbles, pretzels, butter-salt flavored popcorn, homemade "sour cream" dips based on plain yogurt or blender-whipped cottage cheese.

SOME MISCONCEPTIONS CLEARED UP

FAT FACT #1: Butter is *not* less fattening than margarine. Nor does corn oil have some miraculous calorie-saving advantage over other salad oils. Most fats have comparable calorie counts: per tablespoon, butter and margarine have 100 calories; salad oils have between 115 and 125 calories, lard and solid shortening have about 115. If you like the taste of butter, you don't have to live without it. Try the butter-flavored salt or butter flavoring you'll find on your supermarket spice shelf.

FAT FACT #2: Diet margarine is half the calories because it's half water. You can make your own "diet margarine" or "diet butter" by whipping it with equal parts ice water.

FAT FACT #3: "No butterfat" doesn't mean fat free. Frozen whipped cream substitutes, spray-on toppings, thaw-and-pour creamers, dried coffee lighteners, sour dressings, and mock sour creams frequently contain vegetable oil in place of butterfat and the calorie count may be comparable.

FAT FACT #4: The vegetable oil in some nonbutterfat products is highly saturated coconut oil, chosen for its long shelf life. But coconut oil is a poor choice for anyone on a cholesterol-lowering diet. Read the label! Any manufacturer whose product is low calorie or low fat won't be afraid to put the full facts on the label.

FAT FACT #5: "96% fat-free" doesn't necessarily mean a product is nonfattening. Other factors may boost the calorie count. Sugared-up fruit yogurt, for example, is double the calories of plain unsweetened yogurt. Look for the calorie count on the label of any product that tries to imply it's calorie wise.

FAT FACT #6: Greasy foods won't keep you warm during a fuel pinch. One hundred calories worth of fat won't keep you any warmer than 100 calories worth of protein or carbohydrate. The only fat that keeps you warm is your own personal body fat. Wouldn't you rather put on a sweater?

FAT FACT #7: Greasy foods won't give you shiny hair or a supple skin. Your complexion and coiffure will probably be better helped by low-fat foods such as fresh fruits and vegetables, which provide vitamins, minerals—and regularity.

FAT FACT #8: Simply adding extra oils to your diet won't lower your cholesterol count—unless they replace animal fats (butter, meat fat, dairy cream, fatty cheeses, etc.).

FAT FACT #9: Eating fat won't make you thin, despite the promise of some fad diets—unless you somehow manage to cut calories at the same time. Ounce for ounce, fat has two and one-quarter times the calories of any other food basic.

FAT FACT #10: Everybody needs a minimum of fat in their daily diet to help the absorption of vitamins, so a totally fat-free diet would be unhealthy —and almost impossible, because fat goes hand in hand with almost all animal protein foods, which we also need to eat every day.

LOOK FOR GOOD PROTEIN BUYS

If every calorie and every penny really count, rely on your "Slim Gourmet Comparison Shopper" to help you find the best protein buys in your supermarket. For the weight-wary shopper, you need the most protein for the lowest cost, and the fewest calories for the most food value.

Here are some tips to remember when shopping for more protein and less fat:

⋘ Don't overfeed on meat. Six ounces (or 60 grams of protein) a day is all you really need.

SLIM GOURMET PROTEIN-CALORIE "COMPARISON SHOPPER"

Protein Source (1 Pound)	Calories	Protein (grams)
Beef rib roast	1,843	57
T-bone steak	1,596	59
Beef chuck	984	72
Flank steak	653	98
Round steak	863	89
Pork loin	1,065	62
Ham	1,100	68
Lamb chops (loin)	1,146	64
Lamb chops (rib)	1,229	55
Leg of lamb	845	68
Chicken (fryer)	382	57
Chicken pot pie	993	30
Turkey (whole)	722	67
Fish fillets	358	75
Fish sticks	798	75
Fishcakes	1,224	41
Tuna (canned in oil)	1,306	110
Tuna (canned in water)	576	127
Sardines (in tomato sauce)	889	85
Shrimp (canned)	363	74
Frankfurters	1,402	57
Bologna	1,379	55
Sausage	2,259	43
Bacon	3,016	38
Eggs	658	52
Cheese (American)	1,805	113
Cheese (Cottage)	390	77

❧ Choose low-fat poultry, seafood, veal, and "variety" meats (liver, etc.) at least as often as you choose beef, lamb, pork, and ham. For each pound of beef or ham you buy, pick up a corresponding quantity of chicken or fish.

❧ Don't pay a premium price for extra fat and calories. The fattest cuts and grades also happen to be the most expensive, even though they offer less protein. "Prime" beef has 5 percent more fat than "choice," which in turn has 6 percent more fat than "good."

❧ Brush up on meat anatomy. Cuts from the middle of the animal are the fattest and most expensive (rib roasts, loin chops, etc.). Front-end cuts (shoulder, chuck) cost less in cash and calories, while the "back end" represents the best calorie bargain of all. Beef round, leg of lamb, fresh or cured ham—all cut from the hind leg—are relatively lean.

◦§ The younger, the slimmer. Veal ("baby cow") has less fat than full-grown beef. Frying chicken has only one-fifth the fat of stewing fowl. A young, small turkey has less than half the calories per pound of a fat, mature bird.

◦§ Frying adds calories. Baking, broiling, and barbecuing subtracts them. Less tender meats can be marinated in wine, citrus juice or other acid liquid, or tenderized with commercial tenderizers before going on the spit or rack.

◦§ Stews, ragouts, pot roasts, and other slow-simmer dishes should be prepared ahead of time, then refrigerated until dinner time so the fat can rise to the surface for removal.

◦§ Turn the liquid into fat-free gravy and serve it over vegetables and modest portions of pasta, rice, noodles, or potatoes to cut down on meat intake and calories.

BEWARE OF DIET MYTHS

Do you pass up the potato and finish the steak? Order a double hamburger and no roll? Skimp on the salad, but not on the dressing? Eat the cheese but leave the fruit?

If so, you're a victim of the "carbohydrate myth," an outdated, century-old diet notion that refuses to die, despite disfavor among nutritionists and other experts. Hardly the "revolution" it is touted to be, the low-carbohydrate diet idea was a bestseller back in 1865 when a sweet-eating stuffgut named William Banting knocked off his largesse of lard by laying off the goodies in favor of a high meat diet. This was back before the medical profession knew anything about cholesterol. Banting-type diets have been periodically recycled ever since, up to and including today.

Carbohydrates, one of the three basic food elements, include not only the nutritionally neutered, empty-caloried sweets, sugars, and starches, but also such valuable items as cereals and other whole grains, rice, potatoes, pasta, breads,* and all fruits and vegetables. Depending on the severity of the diet,

---

* The calorie count in breads depends on which one you use: ordinary white bread is around 65 calories per slice. You can save a few calories, or a lot, with slim-slice or special formula breads—it all depends on how determined a label-reader you are. Gluten bread, for example, is made from a type of flour that needs no shortening and weighs in at 30 calories a slice.

Some protein-enriched breads are only 40 calories a slice—and they're made with part soy flour so they're a nutrition boost as well. Other breads achieve a lower calorie count simply by being slimmer-sliced—but they may not be that much slimmer in calories. Look for the calorie count on the label, and if they don't say, don't buy. Any bread that implies it's lower in calories ought to be willing to print the calorie-per-slice in a nice, neat number that anybody can understand.

A note to barbecue lovers:

Both hamburger and hot dog rolls average around 116 calories each for the soft types (hard rolls are considerably higher: upwards of 160 each). You can slim down the calories even more by pulling out part of the doughy center before adding dog or burger. If you're fresh out of frankfurter rolls, one slice of toasted diet protein bread (at about 50 calories) makes a perfect wienie wrapper!

these foods are restricted in favor of fat and protein foods—meat, butter, milk, eggs, cheese and other animal products.

Most popular of the calories-don't-count plans is the high-fat, low-carbohydrate "ketogenic diet" that claims you can lose ten, fifty, or a hundred pounds on as much as 5,000 calories a day—if you eliminate carbohydrate foods and eat all you want of fat and protein. The diet causes the disordered state of "ketosis," and in this condition you're supposed to experience huge weight losses. The diet has a multitude of fans who swear they've lost eight or ten pounds in a week while eating more calories than ever. Cheese, bacon, whipped cream, buttered steak—it all sounds too good to be true!

The American Medical Association finds the whole idea "incredible," "without scientific merit," and "potentially hazardous," while warning of such possible complications as heart disease, hardening of the arteries, increased cholesterol, dehydration, kidney trouble, gout, fatigue, low blood pressure, and dizziness. The AMA statement provides insight into why such diets seem to work in the beginning, and why they really don't—unless you cut calories. Here are some points:

◄§ Temporary weight loss can be explained by the initial upset in salt and water balance. In other words, it's only water.

◄§ Scientific studies of starving patients show that ketone losses "rarely, if ever, exceed 100 calories a day, a quantity that could not possibly account for the dramatic claims."

◄§ Studies show that two groups *lost the same* weight after twenty-four days, even though one group ate 90 percent fat and the other, 90 percent carbohydrate. But the calories were the same, hence the equal weight loss.

◄§ Low-carbohydrate dieters *didn't lose* any more weight than patients on a "balanced" diet of the same number of calories.

◄§ Successful losers on an eat-all-you-want low-carbohydrate regime actually ate 13 to 55 percent *fewer* calories. That's why they lost!

SOOTHING YOUR SWEET TOOTH

Instead of concentrating on the diet myths that forbid carbohydrates, it would be wiser to avoid, as a rule of thumb, all refined sugars and starches in this category. They have been stripped of everything worthwhile, leaving empty calories.

If the statistics are right, the average American consumes 500 calories worth of sugar daily. Since some people consume relatively little sugar, it's safe to guess that the typical overweight person, and many children, take in considerably more.

◄§ Sugar *is* calories, pure and simple, stripped of all vitamins and minerals, totally devoid of roughage, bulk, or protein.

◦§ Sugar is negative nutrition; sweets tend to displace real food for those with fussy appetites. On the other hand, sugar fails to sustain that full feeling needed by those with big appetites.

◦§ While sugar contributes nothing to nutrition, it's suspected as the root of many modern ills. Among those catalogued by noted British nutritionist Dr. John Yudkin: tooth decay, ulcers, chronic stomach distress, hypoglycemia, diabetes, blood clots, metabolic changes preceding cancer, premature aging, heart diseases, emotional disorders—and, of course, obesity. (Dr. Yudkin details his claims in the book *Sweet and Dangerous*.) *

◦§ Every overweight adult with a sweet tooth has good cause to suspect that desserts and sugar-rich foods contribute to his plight. But the groundwork for his sweet addiction and superabundance of insatiable fat cells was probably laid in infancy and childhood. Instead of mother's milk, babies are fed on formulas of cow's milk and sucrose (sugar), then graduated to sugar-rich commercial baby foods and finally into the typical, sugar-rich American diet, augmented by TV-touted sweets and snacks.

Most Americans could easily cut their sugar consumption in half. Saving 250 calories a day in sugar could add up to 91,250 a year, or the calorie cutback needed to lose twenty-six pounds. That's the amount found in two bottles of sugar-sweetened soda or five or six cups of sweet coffee. Total elimination of sugar is practically impossible, unless you plan to set up your own self-sustaining farm. (Any diabetic can confirm the difficulty of finding sugar-free foods.)

Learn to like foods less sweet . . . gradually. You don't have to give up desserts; you simply make them with less sugar. Here are some tips:

◦§ Home-baked cakes need some sugar for bulk, but the quantity can be cut by as much as half. Experiment! Rely on the natural goodness of apples, pineapples, bananas, raisins, and fruit juices to add natural sweetness to your desserts. Make your apple pie with more apples and less pie.

◦§ Avoid sour or bitter ingredients that need lots of sugar. A little less chocolate, lemon, or coffee in your recipe will reduce the amount of sugar needed.

◦§ Check your supermarket diet shelf for low-calorie or sugar-free desserts, mixes, and canned fruits. Think of imaginative ways to use them.

◦§ A dash of vanilla can heighten the illusion of sweetness. And a pinch of salt is needed for accent, even in artificially sweetened foods. (Most dietetic foods seem bland because they lack salt—for the salt-free dieter!)

◦§ Modern sugar substitutes can be helpful, not only in beverages but also in cooking—as we explain next.

---

* New York: Wyden, 1972.

THE SECRETS OF COOKING WITH SUGAR SUBSTITUTES

With the price of sugar what it's been, lots of shoppers are deciding that the smart place to pinch pennies—and calories—is the sugar bowl. If you're new to using sugar substitutes, here are some tips:

◄§ New ones are coming, but substitutes currently on the market are variations of the same basic ingredient: saccharin. Sweeteners are available under many brand names, and in many forms. Try a variety, to see which suits you best.

◄§ Types include quick-dissolving tablets, concentrated powder in jars or single-serving packets, shake-on liquids, and granulated sweeteners that can be used spoon for spoon in place of sugar. Sweet 'n Low is a granulated concentrate ten times sweeter than sugar. There are also nonconcentrated sugar replacements such as Sugar Twin and Sprinkle-Sweet, which have the same volume as sugar and can be used spoon for spoon and cup for cup in place of sugar.

◄§ Tablet or "pill-type" sweeteners are the least expensive and most convenient for sweetening hot coffee or tea. But for cooking the tablets must first be dissolved in a little hot water. Quarter-grain tablets are the equivalent of 1 level teaspoon sugar. Half-grain tablets equal 2 teaspoons sugar, and one-grain tablets equal 4 teaspoons sugar.

◄§ Keep this kitchen math in mind: 3 teaspoons equal 1 tablespoon, and 16 tablespoons equal 1 cup. Therefore, a recipe that calls for 2 tablespoons of sugar would need 6 quarter-grain tablets of saccharin $(2 \times 3 = 6)$. A recipe requiring 1 cup of sugar would need 48 quarter-grain tablets (16×3).

◄§ Liquid and concentrated powder sweeteners usually include a "table of equivalents" on the label. Check it for how much to use. The granulated types that can be used spoon for spoon in place of sugar don't require any arithmetic.

◄§ Unless your diet dictates no sugar whatsoever, you'll be happier with the results if you combine both sugar *and* sugar substitute in a recipe instead of eliminating sugar altogether. If a recipe calls for 1 cup of sugar, use only ½ cup sugar, and replace the other half with its equivalent in sugar substitute. This method is particularly recommended where some sugar is needed for bulk—in cake and baked goods, for example. Don't be afraid to experiment, but do be prepared for some failures.

◄§ Heat is the enemy of sugar substitutes, so you'll be happiest with recipes that don't require cooking—refrigerator frozen desserts, pies, gelatins, puddings, and the like. Look for recipes in which you can add the sweetener after cooking—a stirred custard, for example, to which the sweetener can be added after the mixture is removed from the heat.

◆§ Yes, you can bake with sugar substitutes, but quick-baking cookies or low-temperature cakes (like cheesecakes) are preferred.

◆§ Fruit and fruit-based desserts are the best candidates. The fruit acids and natural fruit sugar combine very well with today's sweeteners.

◆§ Canning and other high-heat uses are less than satisfactory. Can fruits without sweetener and add it at the table. But sugar substitutes do work well in the freezer.

◆§ Certain ingredients combine very well with sugar substitutes and help eliminate tip-off aftertaste: vanilla, lemon juice, fresh and dried fruit, citrus rind, liqueurs, chocolate, coffee, dried fruit, and most spices.

◆§ Don't try to oversweeten! Once a certain concentration level is reached, additional substitute adds bitterness, not sweetness. As a maximum, figure on 1 tablespoon worth of substitute per serving. In other words, a dessert that serves eight should contain no more than the equivalent of 8 tablespoons worth of artificial sweetener.

◆§ Every time you replace ½ cup sugar with sugar substitute, you're saving 375 calories.

TABLE OF EQUIVALENTS*

Sugar	**¼-Grain Tablets**†	**Granulated Concentrate**	**Liquid**
1 teaspoon	1	⅒ teaspoon	6 drops
1 tablespoon	2½	¼ teaspoon	¼ teaspoon
¼ cup	12	1⅕ teaspoon	1 teaspoon
½ cup	24	2⅖ teaspoons	2 teaspoons
¾ cup	36	3⅗ teaspoons	1 tablespoon
1 cup	48	5 teaspoons	4 teaspoons

* Individual brands may vary: check label for best results.
† There are also ½-grain saccharin tablets, each equal to 2 teaspoons sugar.

WHAT ABOUT OTHER "NATURAL" SWEETENERS?

Did you know that it takes more than 160 calories worth of corn syrup to equal 100 calories of sugar? And that honey has more calories than sugar, but it's sweeter, so you need less?

What about molasses? Maple sugar? Brown sugar? Are these more "efficient" sweeteners than sugar, if you have to count your calories?

The higher price of sugar has caused lots of homemakers to thumb through the backs of their cookbooks for guidance on how to exchange one sweetener for another. The answers they find are often conflicting, and rarely spell out the sweetness comparisons and calorie costs.

Below is a guide for calorie-wary cooks. The comparisons are only approximate. The sweetness level in any given recipe depends on a number of factors: other ingredients (especially acid foods), time and temperature of cooking, and whether the dish is served warm or chilled. Please note the chart is for comparison purposes only; it is *not* a guide for substitutions in baking. Sweeteners are not always interchangeable in cookies, cakes, and other baked goods recipes.

Sweetness Equivalents (*to equal 1 cup of sugar at 770 calories*)	*Calories*
¾ cup honey	770
1½ cup molasses	1,050
1½ cup maple syrup	1,050
1½ cup corn syrup	1,250
1⅛ cup brown sugar	900
9 tablespoons fruit sugar (fructose)	430
13 ounces Sorbitol	1,230
48 saccharin tablets	0

If this chart seems at odds with your cookbook, it's because most substitution guides are concerned mainly with baking and what will work in cake recipes. For example, many guides suggest you replace sugar with equal or lesser amounts of corn syrup, even though the latter is substantially less sweet. The reduced sweetness is seldom mentioned. But if you notice it, you're likely to conclude—erroneously—that corn syrup is less fattening than sugar. But cup for cup, corn syrup is higher in calories. And if you try to match the sweetness level of sugar, the calories will be higher still. If you have to watch your weight, corn syrup is not a very calorie-efficient stand-in for sugar. Honey would be a better choice.

Our chart also includes two sweeteners that aren't generally available in the retail market—fruit sugar (fructose) and Sorbitol. But both are used in commercial foods and dietetic products and we thought you'd like to see how they compare. Intensely sweet, fructose occurs naturally in fresh fruit. Recently, food scientists have found a way to produce it economically from cornstarch. Several companies are trying to resolve labeling hangups with the Food and Drug Administration so it can be made available to consumers.

Sorbitol, on the other hand, is a carbohydrate used in some foods for diabetics, chosen because it is slowly absorbed. Despite the "dietetic" label, Sorbitol is a high-caloric sweetener.

BEWARE THE CAN-OPENER MEAL . . .

If you spend those summer weekends "away from it all" (including your dishwasher, electric mixer, toaster, and well-stocked freezer), beware the can-opener main course, particularly if you're poundage prone. Most are skimpy in meat but overgenerous in fats, starches, and calories. One cupful would hardly make a serving for most vacation appetites, but look how calorie-costly it can be:

Can-opener Meals	Calories Per Cup
Chicken à la king	210–330
Chili	300–500
Baked beans	260–360
Beef stew	180–360
Beef and macaroni	130–495
Spaghetti and meatballs	250–600
Corned beef hash	400–500
Ravioli	200–300
Hot dogs and spaghetti	230–470
Sloppy Joe	280–470
Macaroni and cheese	180–230

Note that these counts are not for a serving or a canful, but one tiny measuring cupful!

. . . LIKEWISE THE FROZEN DINNER

Want a low-cal lunch? How about a "frozen dinner?"

Not the calorie-laden packaged kind that the supermarket has, but a weight-wary full course meal you've made yourself from leftovers. With a little forethought, it's easy to prepare "extras" at dinnertime with future lunches in mind. If you get into the habit of squirreling away leftovers into latter-day lunches, you'll be less tempted to overeat at the main meal.

But whatever you do, don't be tempted by commercial frozen dinners. Most are just too fattening. Calorie counts can vary widely—anywhere from 280 for a bargain-brand turkey dinner all the way up to 680 or more for one maker's beans and franks. And even though all those three-part trays are the same size, it's usually fruitless trying to guess how many calories they wrap up.

For example, fish and chicken are usually thought of as low-calorie, but not when they're all bundled up in a thick overcoat of well-oiled starch! Consequently, frozen fish dinners average around 400 calories and fried chicken dinners can range as high as 600.

Here are the approximate calorie counts for one of the best-selling brands of frozen dinners: meat loaf, 419; roast beef, 414; chopped beef, 447; fried chicken, 600; pork, 460; ham, 366; shrimp, 358; "fish" dinner, 429; "Italian" dinner, 448; "German," 405; "Chinese," 356; "Mexican," 658; veal parmigiana, 492; corned beef hash, 511; macaroni and cheese, 367; three-course frozen dinners, 495 to 652 calories.

But calories aren't the whole story. If you've got a weight problem, chances are that a protein-skimpy dinner will leave you hungry for something else. Like a piece of pie.

With a little forethought and an ample freezer it's easy to pack away your own protein-plentiful calorie-wise frozen dinners. For lunch, here are some easily assembled combinations from "planned leftovers." Make them up in divided trays or aluminum pie tins. Cover with foil and label with marking pens. Then just pop them in the oven, frozen, and reheat for 30 minutes at 400 degrees.

⊷ Broiled or baked split chicken breast and half a cupful of frozen or drained canned peas topped with butter-flavored salt. Uncover the chicken in the last 10 minutes of heating. *Only 230 calories.*

⊷ A 4-ounce raw fillet of sole or flounder, liberally sprinkled with lemon juice and peppered with paprika, plus half a cupful of frozen or drained canned corn with a teaspoon of butter. Uncover the fish before heating. *Only 210 calories.*

⊷ A 3½-ounce slice of your own special meat loaf (lean ground round and no bready fillers) plus half a cupful of canned or frozen string beans sprinkled with nonmeat bacon bits. *Only 200 calories.*

⊷ A leftover quarter-pound lean hamburger covered with instant mushroom-tomato sauce (mix a tiny 2-ounce can of mushrooms, including the liquid, with 2 tablespoons catsup). Fill the vegetable section with canned or frozen sliced carrots with lots of parsley and butter-flavored salt. *Only 290 calories.*

⊷ Cover a leftover chicken breast and two or three stalks of frozen broccoli with a spicy sauce made from ¼ cup sherry wine and ¼ cup low-calorie Caesar salad dressing. *Only 208 calories.*

⊷ Leftover very-rare roast beef (3 ounces) and "candied carrots" (half a cupful of canned or frozen sliced carrots sprinkled with lemon juice, parsley, and two tablespoons diet maple syrup). *Only 200 calories.*

⊷ Franks and sauerkraut: two of the former, uncooked, and half a cupful of the latter, well drained. Sprinkle with caraway seeds. *Only 300 calories.*

YOU'RE IN THE "DIET DOLDRUMS"

You've been at it for a few weeks, and you've lost a few pounds—but nowhere near what you need to. Lately the temptations seem more irresistible, and the lapses more frequent. Even the scale seems to have lost interest, stubbornly stopping at the same old weight, day after day. What a drag!

Watch it! How you handle this crisis will determine whether you go up in defeat or down in victory. Here are some tips for staying on the straight and narrow:

◆ᔕ Contrary to the usual advice, weighing yourself every morning is a good idea—a ritual that reaffirms your commitment to lifelong slimming. Don't be discouraged by inevitable plateaus. Every day you hang in there is one day closer to your goal.

◆ᔕ Chart your future progress. On a sheet of paper note the dates of the next ten or fifteen Fridays. Now write your present weight for the first Friday. Then deduct 1½ pounds and write that weight down for the following Friday —and so on, until you've lost 25 pounds on paper, or reached the weight you want to be. Post this chart in a prominent place (the refrigerator, for example!) and keep track of your actual progress. Don't be surprised if you find yourself ahead of schedule.

◆ᔕ Dress slim. Take in or discard those baggy things that fit when you were fatter. Buy something new, glamorous, and expensive in an even slimmer size and diet down to it. Stand tall and walk slim, too.

◆ᔕ Have something around your finger to remind yourself that you're dieting. Every time you put it on or look at it, the ring or whatever will remind you of your good intentions.

◆ᔕ Add a new dimension to your diet with new foods. Check your calorie chart for all the low-calorie foods you've never eaten before, and try something new every day. Have you ever had rabbit? Escargots? Mussels? Mangos? Kohlrabi? Kidneys? Pomegranates? Papaya?

◆ᔕ Look for an ally to join you in your slimming efforts. Join a diet club or form your own. Having someone to talk with is terrific therapy.

◆ᔕ Lead yourself not into temptation. Avoid fat luncheon companions, fancy restaurants, and dinner invitations—at least until you're secure in your ability to live skinny in a fat world.

◆ᔕ Write your own diet book. In a looseleaf notebook, work out a variety of gourmet menus personally suited to your own special tastes and the style of life you lead. Devise your own "decalorized" adaptations of the fattening foods you love. Collect calorie charts to help you compute the calories—and use an adding machine to speed the calculations.

◆ᔕ Make a list of everything you hate about being fat. For example: having to wear a girdle, wearing dresses instead of pants, not being able to cross your legs, bulging over your belt, huffing when you climb stairs, one-piece bathing suits, the way you look in a sleeveless blouse, being the exception to "one size fits all," watching somebody else get the job, promotion, or date you wanted.

Overweight isn't inevitable for the determined calorie counter who understands his problem. Taking in more calories than you can use up is still the basic cause of overweight. And reversing the process—by whatever means— is the basic cure!

View your condition as a sort of a "calorie allergy," a special sensitivity to excess calories that cause you to break out—in ugly fat. Diabetics, asthmatics, kidney sufferers, and many others have learned to live with their special condition—once they decided that the alternative was unacceptable.

MAKE SLIM THINKING A HABIT: AT THE TABLE

There's no "end" to slimming; it's a whole new approach to eating and cooking that must be lifelong to succeed. But calorie counting needn't occupy your attention forever. Gradually you'll develop new, healthy responses to food. Being slim will become second nature.

For the present, however, rebuilding new habits will take concentration. Here are some tips, for at the table:

⋖ Train yourself to become aware of contrasts of textures, the blending of flavors. Train your taste buds to single out spices and seasonings—the way a musical ear pinpoints instruments in an orchestra.

⋖ Dinner conversation should be light and unprovoking. Avoid the "business lunch," and save heavy decision-making discussions for coffee time. If you must negotiate over lunch, eat sparingly. You won't enjoy the food anyway.

⋖ Are you the fastest fork in the West? Eating too fast means that you habitually shovel in more than you really want, simply because your stomach doesn't get the chance to register "tilt." Eating at a more leisurely pace gives the food a chance to sift down, to the point where that imaginary "appetite control center" can send up the "full" signal.

⋖ Never come to the table famished. Low-calorie snacking isn't necessarily harmful. In fact, many doctors now favor six light meals instead of three squares.

⋖ Don't omit the preliminaries. Soup, salad, low-calorie fruit cocktail or tomato juice are really "de-appetizers" that help take the edge off your hunger before you reach the heavier part of the meal.

⋖ Since everyone has a tendency to rush through rapidly cooling food before it becomes unpalatable, be sure that hot meals are really hot. Foods that cool quickly are best served on heated plates—rare steak, eggs, fish fillets, thin slices of roast, for example.

⋖ Foods that require picking and fussing help halt the headlong race to the finish line—broiled chicken, shellfish, bony meats, vegetables that need slicing.

⋖ Drink frequently with your meals—quaff some water or sip some wine. Lunch with low-calorie soda. Have your coffee or tea with, not after. Liquids, whether in a glass, cup, mug, or soup bowl, help create a feeling of fullness.

⋖ Pause frequently. The longer you spend at the table, the more psychologically satisfying the meal will be.

◦§ Don't eat what you don't like. If you want to treat your family to a dinner they love and you hate, cook two meals and freeze the extras.

◦§ Don't eat when you're not hungry. Don't eat because someone else is eating. Don't eat because it's there. Don't eat because you paid for it. Don't eat because it's free. In short, don't eat unless you really, *really* want to. Make every calorie's worth of food pay its way with enjoyment.

◦§ And once you're finished, be finished. Lay down your knife and unlap your napkin. Don't reach for seconds just to occupy yourself while you wait for your tablemates.

YOUR PLATES ARE TOO BIG!

Check out your china closet and put away all your oversized plates. Six years ago, when I decided that calorie-conscious cooking could be my way out of a 200-pound-plus figure, I decided that for family meals, nine-inch plates are adequate. I now weigh 125 and the fat plates come out for company only.

I went plate shopping in a restaurant supply house—they really know how to make less look like more. I bought 8¾-inch plain white plates with big inch-and-a-half rims. They have an extra-heavy, hearty-meal look that no delicate porcelain can match. The design of restaurant dinnerware is no accident—the dollars a restaurant can save in smaller portions really adds up.

A cut of pie or wedge of cake on a giant seven- or eight-inch dessert plate looks like it calls for a second helping—but it's more than enough if served on a six-inch bread and butter plate instead. A six-inch bread plate that leaves only enough room for a few pickle slices is the right size for sandwiches, too.

Wine glasses can vary anywhere from less than three ounces to over five. (You may prefer fragile stemware, but the heavier carved or cut-crystal types *look* like more.) And speaking of wine glasses—a footed champagne glass makes a dramatic presentation of less ice cream or pudding.

It works in reverse, too. A filling broth served in a super soup bowl can get dinner off to a slimmer start. And toss out those dainty little salad plates and enjoy yours by the hefty bowlful!

AND AWAY FROM THE TABLE

Everybody knows the homemaker who "eats like a bird" and still looks like an elephant—despite minuscule portions at mealtimes. Truth is, she does most of her eating before and after dinner—in the kitchen, not at the dining table. She slices off slivers of roast "to test for doneness," samples the sauces for seasonings, snacks on the appetizers and sips at the soup.

Afterwards she really cleans up—finishing off the leftovers on her children's plates, the unused slices of meat, the half-eaten rolls. She "straightens up" the cake or pie by slicing off the "crooked" pieces. She is a living, breathing garbage disposal unit, unbeknownst to the rest of the family. They really do think it's her glands.

Kitchen nibbling is the occupational hazard of homemakerhood. Trouble is, it's such an insidious habit that most women are unaware they're doing it. If that's your problem, here are some tips to help eliminate it:

When cleaning the table, pick up all the utensils first. Put them in your dishpan or dishwasher before you tackle the food. Then you won't be able to slice something extra without first going to the silverware drawer.

When buying or baking desserts, do it in serving size units—cupcakes or individual custard cups instead of a whole cake or bowl of pudding. It's too easy to slice off a sliver from a whole cake.

Invest in a kitchen scale and measuring spoons and cups. Weigh and measure food every day for a week until you can recognize quantities. Then, don't make leftovers. Gauge your cooking so that there's just enough to serve everybody, and no more.

Chew gum. Not the most attractive habit, but a lifesaver for those who can't keep their fingers out of the food.

Can't beat the clean-up habit? Let the family tackle the table while you read the newspaper. They won't cooperate? Tell them the real reason and maybe they'll be happy to go along.

Learn to make soup or stock from leftovers. Or a compost heap. Or buy a dog. Or face up to the fact that the ultimate waste is to force food on a body that doesn't need it—and throw it out.

Be a once-a-week cook and load your freezer with homemade, portion-controlled, thaw-and-serve meals. That limits the taste-testing temptation.

Never, *never* eat anything standing up. That automatically excludes most kitchen nibbling.

Have everybody sprinkle salt and pepper all over the unsalvageable left-overs, lest they lead you into temptation.

Design your next day's lunch around tonight's remainders and pack them away as soon as possible. Pretty soon you'll be scrupulous about squirreling away scraps.

Plan ahead. Anticipation is part of enjoyment. Knowing that there's a luscious lunch waiting will get you past the coffee break without doughnuts. A delicious dinner in the offing can stave off a four o'clock potato-chip panic.

YOU "EAT OUT" A LOT: TIPS AWAY FROM HOME

If you get to eat in an elegant restaurant only on your anniversary or thirtieth birthday, dining out is no threat to your figure. But suppose you had to eat out twice a day, every day. That's the problem faced by Ruth Melchet, banquet manager at the Promenade Café in New York's Rockefeller Center. Here are Ruth's suggestions for eating out with seams intact:

◆§ Do not allow yourself to become intimidated by the sight of a haughty headwaiter. According to Ruth, "The more demanding you are, the more likely it is that the waiter will consider you an expert diner and respect your wishes."

◆§ Banish the brimming breadbasket! Ask—in fact, *insist*—that it be removed. There's no worse combination than a ravenous patron, slow service, and hot rolls. Nibble on a 25-calorie cracker, if necessary, and wash it down with all the water there is.

◆§ Fruit cocktail? Forget it . . . it's packed with sugar. Order the tomato juice instead, or well-chilled shrimp. Soup? Only the consommé is calorie safe, and better restaurants always have consommé even if it's not on the menu. Ask.

◆§ Dress your salad with a squeeze of lemon and a twist of fresh-cracked pepper. Most restaurant salad toppings are concoctions of incredible richness —don't even be tempted!

◆§ Steer clear of main-course dishes with cream sauces. In a better restaurant, the meat, fish, and poultry are generally kept separate from the sauce until serving time, so there should be no problem ordering yours unsauced. Ask for your fish broiled instead of sautéed—and lavish it with lemon. And remember that prime beef, restaurant style, is even more fattening than the "choice" grade of beef available in the supermarket.

◆§ Vegetables "smothered in butter" are often just that, so order yours plain, and add a hint of butter from your bread plate, if you must. Baked potato is fine unless it's buried under mounds of sour cream. Naturally, you'll say no to fatty French fries, *duchesse*, *rissole*, or *Roesti* potatoes.

◆§ Forgoing dessert altogether is simply too spartan for Ruth, so here's what she does: "I order a small scoop of vanilla ice cream and a cup of hot coffee. I add a spoonful of ice cream to the coffee, turning it into café Viennoise. Then I drizzle a little hot coffee on the ice cream, creating a delightful hot coffee sundae."

WATCH OUT FOR THE SUPERHOSTESS . . .

A long skirt and a trayful of little cheese things are all it takes to turn your dearest neighbor, your own sister, or your best friend into your worst enemy. You've lived on lettuce all month to squeeze into that pantsuit—what does she care? Once your coat is in her closet, you're safely snared in her lair; now her mission is to stuff as many calories into you as she possibly can.

If you are to survive, here is what you must do:

◆§ Do not, under any circumstances, announce that you are on a diet. To do so will make you the prime target of the evening.

◆§ Be a conspicuous taster, and accompany every bite with large, loud compliments—that's what she really wants, anyway.

◆§ Smuggle in some low-caloried nibbles, under the guise of being a thoughtful guest. What harried holiday hostess wouldn't welcome an extra tray of goodies—a pretty platterful of crunchy raw vegetables around a bowl of counterfeit "California dip" (low-calorie plain yogurt flavored with onion soup mix)?

◆§ When wicked little bacon things arrive, announce that you're saving yourself for the marvelous dinner ahead. At dinner tell her you stuffed on her sensational appetizers, or you're reserving room for her lemon meringue pie —you get the idea.

◆§ When cornered, use diversionary tactics. Tactic number 1: "Where did you get that marvelous antique bench?" Number 2: "Quick, a pencil. I must get the recipe." Number 3: "Where's the bathroom?" Number 4: "I think your kitchen's on fire!"

◆§ If necessary, plead an allergy (to calories) and that you break out all over in a rash (of fat). It is not necessary to describe the nature of your allergy.

. . . AND THE SUPERHOSTESS'S SUPERSTRATEGIES

Be prepared to counter these recognized Superhostess Superstrategies:

GUILT: "Your favorite cheese! I took the train all the way into Farnham to get it."

GUILE: "Don't worry about these cheese puffs, they're all air. You should see how tiny they are before they're fried."

NOSTALGIA: "Remember the night you and Bootsie and I swiped a whole case of these pineapple Danishes from the dorm and everybody ate twelve pieces?"

ETHNIC PRIDE: "What true Irishman (Italian, German, Hungarian) can pass up corned beef (provolone, Linzertorte, strudel)?"

VANITY: "I don't care what they say, darling, your new figure is worth a few wrinkles!"

PITY: "Poor little me. If my beef Burgundy was any good at all, you'd have a third helping."

COMPLICITY: "I'll have another if you will."

COMPROMISE: "Let's split it."

2
KITCHEN HINTS FOR THE SLIM GOURMET COOK

BASIC LESSON: BROWNING MEAT THE LOW-CALORIE WAY

Beef stew, sautéed chicken, fried liver and onions, mushrooms in wine, chili, veal scaloppini, fried eggplant are just a few of the hundreds of recipes that first call for the basic step of "browning"—frying in fat just long enough to provide a nicely browned exterior.

Let's see how different cooks approach the same recipe:

Beef stew, for example. Cookbook author James Beard uses 5 tablespoons of fat (500 calories) for his American beef stew. Craig Claiborne's recipe calls for 2 tablespoons (200 calories). But *The Joy of Cooking* advises browning beef in half a pound of salt pork (1,705 calories!). All their recipes use the same quantity of meat—2 pounds of beef cubes. None mentions anything about draining the fat or skimming before serving, and, in addition, James Beard advises thickening the stew with an unspecified quantity of "pea-sized" balls of flour and butter kneaded together.

However, you *can* brown most meats with no fat added! Most cuts have ample fat of their own. Beef stew meat may contain as much as one-third fat. By browning the meat in its *own* fat, you subtract calories rather than add them. Here's how:

First, you must have a nonstick skillet.

Put the meat in a cold skillet. Heat it slowly over a moderate flame. Give the meat time enough to release its own inner fat for browning.

With lean meat, add a tablespoon or two of liquid (broth, soy sauce, wine, water, or whatever). At first the meat will seem to "steam," but then the liquid evaporates and the meat will brown in its own residue of melted fat.

For chicken, poultry, and meats with skin, place the pieces skin side down in a cold skillet. Let the skillet warm slowly, and the pieces will brown in the fat that melts from under the skin.

Really fatty meats—Frankfurters, sausages, bacon, and so forth—have more fat than they need. Puncture with a fork and brown very well, to get rid of as much pound-provoking fat as possible. Blot the meat with a paper towel.

Liver, scallops, shrimp and other virtually fat-free meats and vegetables can be browned in as little as ½ tablespoon of fat or oil. To help spread the fat around, combine the fat with 1 tablespoon of water or liquid (or use 1 tablespoon of diet margarine; it's only half fat). Turn the food frequently over moderate heat. Once the moisture evaporates, the food will brown quickly.

MEAT TENDERIZERS

Meat tenderizer penetrates and softens the connective tissues, thereby rendering a tough chuck steak as tender as porterhouse. Not only will the tenderized steak be more chewable, you'll find that it has shrunk considerably less—and cooks about 25 percent faster.

"No meat additives for me," you say. "If that stuff can soften meat, what does it do to my stomach?" In an age of consumer cautiousness about chemicals, that's a reasonable question. However, most tenderizer is a totally natural ingredient—papain, the enzyme found in the tropical papaya melon.

However, for papain tenderizers to do their work, they must be used correctly. Many on the market are labeled "instant" and advise a quick sprinkle immediately before cooking. I find, however, that they work much better when given time. Allow at least an hour per inch of depth—in other words, 2 hours or more for a 2-inch steak. And there's no harm in allowing several hours or more, because the tenderizing action ceases at a certain point.

Tenderizing stops once meat is either cooked or frozen, too. For that reason, it's best to tenderize immediately after meat is brought home from the market. As I unload my groceries, I stack all meat to be tenderized on the kitchen counter. After applying tenderizer, the meat is wrapped and labeled for freezing. But I don't freeze it immediately; I store it in the refrigerator for several hours or all day, depending on the size and depth of the cut.

Tenderizer contains sodium, so no additional salt should be added in cooking (it can always be added at the table). Also, those on a salt-free diet should avoid conventional tenderizers. (There are salt-free tenderizers available through mail order directly from one manufacturer: Adolph's Ltd., 1800 West Magnolia Boulevard, Burbank, Calif. 91503.)

A round steak, pan fried and served rare, can be every bit as tender as a Delmonico steak (boneless rib steak). But a pound of fat-trimmed round is only 612 calories, while boneless rib is more than 2,000 calories a pound, and nearly half fat. Consider what that sort of calorie-cutting can add up to at the end of the year!

SLIM GOURMET GUIDE TO BEST BARBECUE BUYS

What's more calorie-wise than cooking over the coals? The meat never has a chance to sit in its own fat. The grease—and calories—are consumed by the flames.

Here is our Slim Gourmet guide to the best barbecue buys—the leanest, least-caloried cuts. We also tell you the approximate calorie count per quarter-pound portion (lean meat only), plus the best method for barbecuing each cut.

But first, let's define our terms:

QUICK-BROIL: Broil means close to the coals, or at high heat on an adjustable gas or electric grill.

SLOW-BROIL: Move the grid further up, or adjust the heat down.

SLOW-ROAST: Rotisserie cooking on a covered, revolving grill.

TENDERIZE: Apply commercial meat tenderizers according to package directions.

MARINATE: Soak the meat all day or overnight (in the refrigerator) in an acid liquid—dry wine, tomato juice, citrus or pineapple juice diluted with water. No fat or oil needed.

BASTE: Moisten the meat with marinade while it cooks.

Beef

Flank steak: Tenderize or marinate. Quick-broil, baste. Serve rare, sliced thinly against the grain. *About 225 calories.*

Round steak: Prepare as flank steak. *215 calories.*

Wedgebone sirloin: Quick-broil. Serve rare. *236 calories.*

Round roast: Have trimmed of fat, boned, rolled, and tied. Tenderize or marinate. Slow-roast to internal temperature of 140 degrees (rare). *215 calories.*

Cubes of round: Trim off fat. Marinate, then thread cubes on skewers with vegetables. Slow-broil. Baste. *215 calories.*

Arm steak: Trim off fat. Tenderize or marinate. Slow-broil. Baste. *220 calories.*

Hamburgers: Have custom-ground from fat-trimmed beef round. Quick-broil. *215 calories.*

Pork

Pork steak: Cut from the leg and trimmed of fat. Marinade optional. Slow-broil until cooked through. Baste. *250 calories.*

Fresh ham roast: Have fresh ham ("leg of pork") trimmed of fat, boned, and tied. Slow-roast on rotisserie until cooked through. Internal temperature of 170. *250 calories.*

Pork kebabs: Fat-trimmed cubes cut from leg. Marinate in cider or apple juice, thread on skewers. Slow-broil until cooked through. *250 calories.*

Shoulder roast: Have trimmed of fat, boned, and tied. Tenderize or marinate. Slow-roast to internal temperature of 170. Baste. *240 calories.*

Porkburgers: Have fresh ham or pork shoulder trimmed of fat and ground. Slow-broil until cooked through. *250 calories.*

Cooked or canned ham: Can be cooked as solid roast, steaks, or cut in cubes and threaded on skewers. Quick-broil or roast to heat through. Baste with unsweetened pineapple juice. *215 calories.*

Lamb

Leg steaks: Trim off fat, season with garlic salt and marjoram. Quick-broil. *215 calories.*

Lamb kebabs: Cubes from fat-trimmed leg. Marinate in diluted lemon juice. Season and quick-broil. *215 calories.*

Leg of lamb: Have trimmed of fat, boned, and tied. Slow-roast on rotisserie to internal temperature of 175 degrees. *215 calories.*

Arm chops: Trim off fat. Tenderize or marinate meat. Slow-broil. Baste often. *235 calories.*

Loin chops: Trim off fat. Quick-broil, serve pink in the middle. *215 calories.*

Lamburgers: Have custom ground from fat-trimmed leg. Quick-broil. Baste with pineapple juice, if desired. *215 calories.*

THREE KITCHEN CONVENIENCES TO HELP THE CALORIE-CONSCIOUS COOK

Pressure Cookers

These were all the rage back in Grandma's day, but then they fell into disfavor—partly because of the rising economy and disinterest in "budget" meals, but also because of their ability to turn food into a mass of mush. Overcooking can be a matter of seconds when it comes to vegetables, and the inexperienced or careless cook can easily render a pot roast into a pile of tasteless strings if he or she forgets to set the timer.

In recent years there's been renewed interest in economy foods—chuck steaks, pot roasts, soups, stews, spaghetti sauce, beans, and other fare that normally needs long, slow cooking. And pressure cookery comes to the rescue of dieters, too. The least fatty, lowest caloried, most cholesterol-shy cuts of meat are generally just the ones that need long, slow cooking to create the fork-tender taste and texture everybody loves. The pressure cooker can deliver it in one-third the time.

So—if you have an old, unused pressure cooker tucked away in the attic, drag it out and learn how to use it. Be sure, however, your pressure cooker has the one feature it should have—a nonstick interior, for browning meat without added fat.

Microwave Ovens

Energy from these can zap food hot in seconds instead of minutes, or minutes instead of hours. Here are some diet-wise tricks I've developed with my microwave oven (a General Electric countertop portable):

◄§ Scramble eggs right on the breakfast plate, no fat added. Simply fork scramble and cook in 2 minutes. Lean breakfast ham can be microwave heated on the same plate, no frying.

◄§ Quick-steam low-calorie lobster in its shell.

◄§ Cook fresh vegetables with no water at all. For crunchy asparagus, lay the spears on a paper plate and microwave-heat only until warmed through. Wash, plastic-wrap, and heat corn on the cob. "Boil" potatoes in their own skin, retaining vitamins. No water needed.

◄§ Pop popcorn right in its own heatproof, not plastic, serving dish with no oil at all, but cover it first!

◄§ Freeze your own fresh vegetables in season. Use your microwave oven to "blanch" (quick-steam) washed and sliced vegetables before freezing. The heat kills enzymes that cause deterioration.

◄§ Frozen packaged vegetables can be cooked right in their own box.

◄§ Microwave energy cooks from the inside out, so it's efficient at melting the fat trapped in meat, without evaporation of moisture. "De-fat" franks or sausages by slitting them open and cooking them on layers of paper towel. Bacon, too.

◄§ The microwave makes it easy for a dieter to serve him- or herself a solo meal—meat and vegetables heated on a plate is easier than a sandwich.

◄§ Fish fillets can be poached in a small amount of wine, without losing their shape or inner moisture.

◄§ Soups, sauces, and stews can be made ahead and refrigerated so fat will rise to the surface and harden. At dinner time, lift off fat and reheat your dish in the microwave.

◄§ Make your own frozen diet dinners. Cook extras of favorite low-caloried meals and assemble the ingredients on serving plates. Wrap and freeze for reheating later.

◄§ Baked apple or other low-calorie fruit desserts can be prepared in less than 5 minutes.

The Wok

We may have our electronic ovens and microwave ranges, but the Orientals have a fabulous appliance that cooks a whole dinner for four in ten minutes or less—the wok.

A wok, of course, is a Chinese frying pan. Thanks to its unique design, it can quickly turn out a one-dish dinner for four, including meat and lots of crunchy vegetables, and do it using only one tablespoon of oil. Since most cooking oils weigh in at about 115 calories per tablespoon, any gadget that cuts down on fat is a calorie saver.

Instead of being flat-bottomed like a Western frying pan, the wok is round-bottomed, with high sides. It comes with a round metal stand that fits over the gas or electric burner so it won't tip.

In wok cookery, bite-sized pieces of meat and vegetables are swirled through a minimum of oil and up the steep sides. Because the oil always collects in the bottom, only a tiny amount is needed. You would need three or four times the amount to keep a similar amount of food from sticking in a conventional frying pan.

In addition to cutting calories, consider how wok cookery contributes to retaining all those health-giving nutrients in the foods we eat. Compare how we might normally cook a dinner of steak and broccoli. The steak is broiled or pan fried in one utensil while the broccoli is boiled in water. The broccoli water, and most of the vitamins and flavor, are thrown away. Then, to make the broccoli taste like something, we slather it with calorie-rich butter! The Chinese, by contrast, would cook steak and broccoli together, and all the flavor and vitamins come to the table.

Lacking a wok, you can still reap the benefits of Oriental stir-fry cooking techniques if you have a large nonstick skillet with its "anti-stickery" in good working order.

Now, look what wok cookery can do for leftovers.

Beware leftovers . . . they're nearly always fattening! Or at least they will be, if you follow the usual recipes for recycling yesterday's roast into a new-again meal. To most cookbook authors, the word "leftover" automatically summons up cans of creamed soups, packages of stuffing mix, and heaping scoops of shredded cheese. Not for us weight-wary types!

Oriental cuisine to the rescue! The Chinese or Japanese cook stretches her leftover pork roast or cupful of cooked turkey with lots of vegetables—crunchy, vitamin packed, and low in calories!

There's nothing simpler. In a big skillet or wok (over high heat) lightly toss together bite-sized bits of meat, lots of onions, and whatever fresh, frozen or canned vegetables you have on hand. Almost any compatible combination can be used; many Oriental recipes combine two kinds of meat, or poultry with seafood, so whatever you dream up will seem authentic. Everything is stirred together with soy sauce, seasoning, and thickening, and served up while the onions are still crunchy-crisp.

Dinner is ready in 5 minutes or less—and it all looks as elaborate as a classic from the best Chinese restaurant in town!

Here are some suggestions for your Oriental-style leftovers.

MEAT: Roast beef, pork, fresh ham, leftover steak or chops, turkey or chicken, trimmed of fat and cut in cubes. Pork, beef, or ham can be "stretched" with canned chicken or turkey. Poultry leftovers can be mixed with canned shrimp, tuna, or crabmeat.

ONIONS: Peeled and cut in big chunks. You will need 2 small onions or ½ large Bermuda onion per serving.

OTHER VEGETABLES: Fresh, frozen, or canned. Use a combination or try diagonally sliced celery, broccoli, asparagus, chunks of red or green pepper, shredded red or green cabbage or romaine lettuce, bite-sized bits of green or yellow squash, fresh or canned sliced mushrooms, or frozen green beans.

SEASONING: Soy sauce, 1 to 2 tablespoons per serving. You may also add a generous shake of granulated sugar substitute and a few grains of hot pepper.

LIQUID: Not much needed. A little water, dry sherry wine, or fat-skimmed broth.

THICKENER: Use ½ teaspoon arrowroot per serving. This is the authentic thickener for Oriental dishes; it has the same calories as flour but nearly triple the thickening ability. If you can't find it, use cornstarch.

FAT OR OIL: Absolutely none needed in nonstick skillet.

3
APPETIZERS

⊷ "SOUR CREAM" DIPS ⊶

Once upon a time a very harried hostess stirred an envelope of dry onion soup into a carton of sour cream and started the social phenomenon known as the "party dip." Hostesses have been stirring and guests have been dipping ever since.

Sour cream dips are fattening—and so are cream cheese dips and even low-fat Neufchâtel dips—just compare all the possibilities in the table below:

HOW DIP BASES COMPARE

Eight Ounces	*Calories*
Dairy sour cream	500
Sour half-and-half	320
Nondairy sour cream	380
Low-fat sour dressing	210
Buttermilk	88
Plain yogurt	130
Low-fat cottage cheese	180
Cream cheese	840
Neufchâtel cheese	550
Low-fat "imitation" cream cheese	430
Farmer cheese	305

But by using the recipe for Slim Gourmet Mock "Sour Cream" on page 277, you can skirt the calorie problem in party dips, as the following suggestions prove:

VARIATIONS

California Dip I: Add 1 packet onion soup mix. Stir well and refrigerate 1 hour before serving. *Only 12 calories per tablespoon.*

California Dip II: Even lower in calories. Add ¼ cup minced onion and 2 teaspoons concentrated beef bouillon. *Only 9 calories per tablespoon.*

Manhattan Dip: Add ¼ cup minced onion, 1 tablespoon minced fresh parsley, and 2 teaspoons concentrated chicken bouillon. *Only 9 calories per tablespoon.*

Clam Dip: Add 1 teaspoon salt, ½ teaspoon Tabasco, 1 tablespoon grated onion, and the contents of a 7½-ounce can of minced clams, well-drained. *Only 8 calories per tablespoon.*

Blue-Cheese Dip: Add ¼ cup (2 ounces, crumbled) blue cheese and 1 tablespoon chopped chives or fresh parsley. *Only 12 calories per tablespoon.*

Nippy Dip: Add ¼ cup (2 ounces) shredded extra-sharp Cheddar or American cheese and 2 tablespoons minced fresh parsley. *Only 12 calories per tablespoon.*

Instant Dip: Any packaged "dip mix" in a tear-open envelope becomes low-calorie if you ignore the directions that call for sour cream or cream cheese and use your Slim Gourmet Mock "Sour Cream" instead: onion, horseradish, Roquefort, garlic, bacon-flavored—most add up to only 10 or 15 calories per tablespoon instead of the 25 or 30 they would be with a more calorific dip base.

NOTE: For diet-wise skinny-dippers, use green pepper strips, radish rosebuds, raw cauliflower buds, celery scoops, carrot sticks, cucumber or pickle chips.

◄§ EASY DIPPING SAUCES §►

Oriental Dip: In the blender, whip ¼ cup soy sauce, ¼ cup sherry wine, 1 clove garlic, 1 cup low-fat cottage cheese. *Only 12 calories per tablespoon.*

Zesty Dip: In the blender, whip 1 cup low-fat cottage cheese, 3 tablespoons skim milk, 5 tablespoons catsup, 1 tablespoon horseradish, and 2 tablespoons lemon juice. Add a dash of Worcestershire, Tabasco, and garlic salt. *Only 12 calories per tablespoon.*

Diet Cocktail Sauce: Combine 1 cup dietetic catsup with 2 tablespoons horseradish, 2 tablespoons lemon juice, and 1 teaspoon onion salt. *Only 6 calories per tablespoon.*

Rémoulade Dip: In the blender, whip 1 cup low-fat cottage cheese, ¼ cup skim milk, 1 hard-cooked egg, 1 tablespoon prepared mustard, and 1 tablespoon lemon juice. Stir in 5 tablespoons chopped pickles and 1 tablespoon capers. *Only 12 calories per tablespoon.*

Extra-easy Dip: Empty the contents of a bottle of low-calorie Russian salad dressing into a small bowl; thin it with water if needed. *Only 15 to 20 calories per tablespoon, depending on the brand.*

⊷ APPETIZER SHRIMP ⊱

When it comes to calories, shrimp is a winner! Here's an ounce-for-ounce calorie comparison:

Appetizers or Party Foods	Calories Per Ounce
Shrimp	26
Potato chips	160
Pretzels	111
Most nuts	175
Cheese cubes	105
Cheese spreads	80
Cheese puffs	150
Franks-in-blankets	112
Pâté de fois gras	130
Caviar	80

To save work, look for fresh-frozen shrimp already cleaned and peeled. To save money, do the cleaning yourself.

To cook shrimp: For each pound of shrimp use 1 cup of water, 1 teaspoon salt, 4 peppercorns, and ½ lemon. Bring to a boil and add the shrimp. When the water returns to boiling, cover and simmer over very low heat, 5 to 8 minutes, depending on size. Shrimp may be peeled and cleaned before or after cooking. Chill and serve with the low-calorie sauce or dip of your choice.

⊷ DEVILED EGGS ⊱

1 dozen eggs, hard-cooked
2 teaspoons Dijon-style mustard

⅛ teaspoon cayenne pepper
½ teaspoon butter- or celery-flavored salt
¼ teaspoon coarsely ground pepper
1½ tablespoons minced onion
⅔ cup low-calorie mayonnaise
 6 stuffed olives, sliced
    Paprika

Slice the eggs in half lengthwise and carefully remove the yolks. Set the whites aside. Mash the yolks, mustard, seasonings, and onion with just enough low-calorie mayonnaise to make a smooth paste. Put the mixture into a pastry tube and pipe it into the reserved egg whites. Decorate each with an olive slice and paprika. *Twenty-four eggs, 49 calories each.*

⊷ CHOPPED CHICKEN LIVERS ⊶

1 tablespoon butter
2 tablespoons dry white wine
2 large onions, chopped
3 stalks celery, chopped
1 green pepper, seeded and chopped
2 pounds chicken livers, halved
2 teaspoons butter-flavored salt
½ teaspoon coarsely ground pepper
¼ teaspoon ground cloves
6 hard-cooked eggs, finely chopped
¼ cup diet mayonnaise

Combine all the ingredients except the eggs and diet margarine in a non-stick skillet. Cover and simmer over moderate heat until the onions are soft, then uncover and continue cooking until the liquid evaporates. The livers and vegetables will begin to brown in the remaining fat; stir to keep from sticking. When no pink remains in the chicken livers, remove from the heat.

Chop the liver mixture very fine, or put through a meat grinder. Combine the liver and chopped eggs with just enough diet mayonnaise to hold together. Press the mixture into a round-bottomed bowl and chill several hours. Unmold onto a bed of lettuce and serve with saltines or matzos. *Twenty-four appetizer servings, 80 calories each.*

The Festive Mushrooms

The mushroom is the one luxury food that even dieters can afford. After all, a whole pound is only about 120 calories. No need to peel mushrooms; if the stem end seems a bit dry or brown, simply cut off a thin slice. Fresh mushrooms should be rinsed very briefly in cold water and then drained and gently blotted dry. Then they are ready to cook—or to eat raw, for sliced raw mushrooms are an excellent appetizer or party nibble, much better for you than greasy packaged snack chips.

And when you turn a mushroom upside down, all it catches is calories, in the form of a fattening filling—butter-soaked bread crumbs, sausage meat, rich cheeses, cream concoctions. There's no limit to what the inventive hostess can pack into a mushroom!

But "festive" mushrooms don't have to be calorie disasters, as the recipes below will attest.

⊷ MUSHROOM PARTY NIBBLE ஒ

Large raw mushrooms
Diet French dressing

Slice the mushrooms and arrange prettily on a tray, surrounding a cup of dressing for dip.

⊷ PICKLED MUSHROOMS ஒ

  1 **pound small fresh mushrooms**
  1 **cup white vinegar**
  1 **cup water**
1½ **teaspoons garlic salt**
  1 **bay leaf, crumbled**
  2 **tablespoons sugar**

Rinse and dry the mushrooms. If larger mushrooms are used, cut in halves or quarters. Combine the vinegar, water, garlic salt, and bay leaf in a saucepan and heat to boiling. Add mushrooms and the sugar and boil for two minutes. Spoon into 3 half-pint sterile jars for storage; serve chilled. *Each ¼-cup serving is 18 calories.*

⊷ MUSHROOMS STUFFED WITH SHERRIED TUNA ஒ

  2 **dozen large fresh mushrooms**
  1 **tablespoon butter or margarine**
 ¼ **cup sherry wine**
1½ **tablespoons minced onion**
  1 **tablespoon minced fresh parsley**
  1 **can (7 ounces) water-packed tuna, flaked**

Wash and dry the mushrooms. Remove the stems and chop fine. Put the stems in a nonstick skillet and add all the other ingredients except the caps. Cook, stirring over a moderate flame until the wine is evaporated. Pile the mixture into the mushroom caps and bake in a preheated 425-degree oven for 10 to 12 minutes. *Each mushroom, 25 calories.*

⋲§ CHEESE-STUFFED MUSHROOMS §⋺

2 dozen large fresh mushrooms
½ cup sliced onion
1 tablespoon olive oil
4 tablespoons pot cheese or low-fat cottage cheese
2 tablespoons Italian-seasoned bread crumbs

Wash and dry the mushrooms. Remove the stems and chop fine; reserve the caps. Sauté the stems and onions in the oil, then combine with the cheese and bread crumbs. Stuff the caps and bake in a 425-degree oven for 10 to 12 minutes. *Each mushroom, 15 calories.*

⋲§ EASY QUICHE §⋺

A *quiche* (pronounced "keesh") is French for pie, and the thrifty French women who first made it didn't go to cocktail parties. Their quiches were strictly family fare—a low-cost supper dish that made use of their abundant eggs and cheese instead of the not-always-abundant meat. The Lorraine ladies would roll out a pie crust and fill it with a mixture of cheese, cream, and eggs, flavor it up with onions and herbs, and serve it crusty-fresh from the oven. If some bacon was handy, that might get thrown in, too. If you've been counting calories as you read, you'll notice that the classic quiche is fairly fattening fare, but then the hard-working French farmwives didn't have to worry about their weight!

You, on the other hand, worry a great deal about it, and you don't have all day to pot-watch a double-boiler. So here's an easy quiche that you whip up in your blender or an electric mixer, using such time savers as those easy-to-use bacon-flavored bits you buy in a jar at the supermarket. About the only real work is rolling out the calorie-reduced pie crust, but it's really worth the saving in calories: this crust is only 459 calories, while a packaged or frozen crust may range as high as 738.

This recipe is only 94 calories an appetizer-sized slice; conventional quiche recipes range between 300 and 350 calories a slice, and are so high in butterfat that they're off limits for many people.

PIE CRUST:
½ **cup all-purpose flour**
  Pinch of salt
2 **tablespoons polyunsaturated oil**
¼ **cup cold water**

FILLING:
3 **eggs**
1 **cup skim milk**
½ **cup low-fat cottage cheese**
½ **cup grated Swiss cheese**
  Pinch of dry mustard
1 **teaspoon salt**
  Pinch of freshly ground pepper
¼ **cup minced fresh parsley**
2 **tablespoons bacon-flavored bits**

Blend together the pie crust ingredients. Knead until the pastry forms a ball, then chill well. Roll out on a lightly floured board and line a 9-inch pie pan. Prick the bottom in several places with a fork and brown in a hot (425-degree) oven for 10 to 12 minutes.

Beat the eggs on high speed until frothy. Add all the other ingredients, except the Swiss cheese and bacon bits, and whip until creamy. Line the browned pie crust with the Swiss cheese and 1 tablespoon bacon bits. Pour in the egg mixture and sprinkle the top with the remaining tablespoon bacon bits. Bake in a slow (325-degree) oven for 45 minutes and serve hot. *Twenty-four appetizer servings, 94 calories each.*

⋑ TUNA QUICHE I ⋐

1 **unbaked 9-inch pie shell**
6 **slices (6 ounces) diet cheese**
3 **eggs**
1 **can (7 ounces) water-packed tuna**
1 **can (13 ounces) evaporated skim milk**
½ **teaspoon onion salt**
  Pinch of cayenne pepper
5 **stuffed olives, sliced**
1½ **tablespoons chopped fresh parsley**

Sprinkle the cheese and tuna in the bottom of the pie shell. Combine the eggs, evaporated milk, salt, and pepper in a blender. Cover and blend smooth, then pour over the tuna-cheese combination. Sprinkle with sliced olives and parsley and bake in a preheated 375-degree oven for 40 minutes or more, until set. *Eight servings, 185 calories each.*

⋅§ TUNA QUICHE II §⋅

1 can (4 ounces) refrigerator crescent rolls
1 can (7 ounces) water-pack tuna
¼ cup minced fresh parsley
2 tablespoons minced onion
1½ tablespoons Worcestershire sauce
4 eggs
1½ cups skim milk
1 teaspoon salt

Unroll the crescent rolls in an 8-inch nonstick cake pan. With your finger-tips, spread the dough evenly over the bottom and up the sides of the pan, cutting to fit, so that all inner surfaces are covered with a thin crust. Bake in a preheated hot (450-degree) oven for 7 or 8 minutes, only until lightly browned.

Remove the quiche shell from the oven and spread the drained tuna over the bottom. Sprinkle on the parsley, onion, and Worcestershire sauce, then beat the eggs, milk, and salt together and pour over. Return the quiche to the oven and bake for 10 minutes at 450 degrees. Lower the heat and bake an additional 20 minutes at 325 degrees, until the filling is completely set. Slice into pie wedges to serve. *Sixteen appetizer servings, 65 calories each.*

⋅§ TUNA PIZZA RUSTICA §⋅

1 can (4 ounces) refrigerator crescent rolls
1 can (7 ounces) water-pack tuna
1 package (10 ounces) frozen zucchini or spinach, thawed and
    thoroughly drained
1 teaspoon oregano or Italian seasoning
1 teaspoon garlic salt
    Pinch of freshly ground black pepper or cayenne pepper
3 eggs
1 cup plain tomato sauce
3 slices (3 ounces) part-skim mozzarella cheese, shredded

Unroll the crescent rolls in a 9-inch nonstick cake pan and, with your fingertips, spread evenly, all over the inner surface, cutting to fit. Bake in a preheated 450-degree oven for 7 to 8 minutes, until lightly browned.

Remove the shell from the oven and spread the tuna over the bottom. Top with the drained, thawed zucchini or spinach and sprinkle with the seasonings. Combine the eggs with half the tomato sauce and fork-blend lightly. Pour over the spinach, then top with the remaining tomato sauce.

Return the pizza to the oven and bake at 450 degrees for 10 minutes, then lower the heat to 350 degrees and bake an additional 40 minutes. Sprinkle the surface with the mozzarella during the last 15 minutes of baking. Cut in wedges to serve. *Sixteen appetizer servings, 73 calories each.*

ONION CHEESECAKE

Party time is when Onion Cheesecake really shines. Fresh from the oven and sliced into creamy-golden brown-crusted wedges, it beats out all the more fattening competition on the appetizer tray.

4 eggs
1 cup pot cheese or low-fat cottage cheese
1 cup skim milk
6 tablespoons all-purpose flour
¼ cup minced fresh parsley
½ small onion
1 teaspoon Dijon-style mustard
1 teaspoon salt
¼ teaspoon freshly ground pepper
  Pinch of garlic powder
2 tablespoons bacon bits, chopped pimento, chopped chives, or sliced stuffed olives for topping

Put all ingredients except the topping in your blender and whip at high speed until creamy. Pour into an 8-inch nonstick cake or pie pan. Sprinkle the surface evenly with the topping. Place in a preheated 325-degree oven and bake for 1 hour, or until the crust is nicely browned. (As with all cheesecakes, the crust puffs up, then settles down when removed from the heat.) *Twenty appetizer servings, 39 calories each.*

PRETTY PARTY MEATBALLS

2 pounds lean beef round, trimmed of fat and ground
1 onion, minced
  Salt and freshly ground pepper
3 tablespoons prepared mustard
2 tablespoons Worcestershire sauce
1 tablespoon arrowroot or cornstarch
1 can (10¾ ounces) onion soup, skimmed of fat
1 cup plain yogurt
  Minced fresh parsley

Combine the beef, onion, Worcestershire, salt, and pepper. Shape into 1½-inch meatballs and spread lightly with mustard. Broil until lightly browned on all sides.

Combine the arrowroot and onion soup in a saucepan. Heat to boiling. Stir in the yogurt and heat through, then add the browned meatballs and minced parsley, pour into a chafing dish, and keep warm. *Thirty-six meatballs, 47 calories each.*

⊷ PARTY MEATBALLS IN "CREAM" ⊷

½ cup water
 1 can (13 ounces) evaporated skim milk
 4 slices dark protein bread or whole-wheat bread
1½ pounds lean beef round, trimmed of fat and ground
 ½ cup minced onion
 2 egg whites
 ¼ cup minced fresh parsley
 1 teaspoon caraway seeds
 2 teaspoons garlic salt
    Freshly ground pepper
 1 can (4 ounces) sliced mushrooms, undrained
 1 tablespoon arrowroot or cornstarch
    Butter-flavored salt

Combine the water with ¼ cup of the evaporated milk. Add the bread and mash. Stir in the beef, onion, egg white, 3 tablespoons of the parsley, caraway seeds, garlic salt, and pepper. Toss lightly to combine. Shape into 1½-inch meatballs and brown lightly under the broiler.

Combine the mushrooms, including liquid, with the arrowroot and remaining evaporated milk in a saucepan. Cook, stirring, over low heat until the cream sauce simmers and thickens. Add butter-flavored salt, pepper, and the remaining parsley, then stir in the browned meatballs. Pour into a chafing dish and keep warm. *Twenty-four meatballs, 62 calories each.*

◄§ JANE BENET'S PARTY MEATBALLS* §►

1 pound lean beef round, ground
½ teaspoon ground ginger
¼ cup soy sauce
1 tablespoon polyunsaturated oil
2 tablespoons water
1½ cups diagonally cut celery
3 tablespoons blanched almonds
1 can (10½ ounces) beef consommé, skimmed of fat
5 tablespoons dry sherry wine
2 tablespoons cornstarch
2 tablespoons granulated sugar or equivalent sugar substitute
2 tablespoons vinegar
1 cup fresh or canned sliced baby tomatoes

Combine the beef with the ginger and 2 tablespoons soy sauce. Shape into 1-inch balls. Arrange in a single layer in a shallow pan and bake or broil until lightly browned on all sides.

Combine the oil, water, celery, and almonds in a skillet and stir-fry over a moderate flame until the moisture evaporates and the celery is tender-crisp. Combine the remaining soy sauce, beef broth, sherry, cornstarch, sugar, and vinegar. Pour into a skillet and cook, stirring, over medium heat until the sauce comes to a boil and thickens. Add the browned meatballs and cook, covered, for 10 minutes. Gently stir in the tomatoes and celery-almond mixture and heat through. Serve in a chafing dish with toothpicks. *Sixteen appetizer servings, 78 calories each with sugar; 72 without sugar.*

* Adapted from Jane Benet, *The San Francisco Chronicle Cookbook*, San Francisco: Chronicle Books, 1973.

4
SOUPS

Is soup making a lost art? It shouldn't be. Hearty homemade soup can be rich with flavor and nutrition, yet shy of calories. Easy and economical, soup is a great way to extract full value from bones that might otherwise go to waste. According to the *Wise Encyclopedia of Cooking*, 2 ounces of bone contain more gelatin than a whole pound of meat. This valuable substance adds strength, variety, and thickness to soups, along with tasty, low-calorie nutrition.

Soup making starts in the supermarket, often as a "bonus" for smart meat shopping. Instead of paying a premium price for boneless steaks, stew meat, or fatty hamburger, have your meat fat-trimmed and cut to order from larger bone-in roasts. Don't leave the bones behind or discard them. Instead, store them in a plastic bag in your freezer until you have enough. Have one freezer bag for beef bones, another for ham or pork, another for poultry.

The most important calorie saver in soup making is getting rid of fat. Do it (1) by choosing lean ingredients; (2) by trimming fat before cooking; and (3) by skimming surface fat after cooking. Chill finished soup stock in your refrigerator and all the remaining fat will rise to the surface and harden. Then you can lift it off—and throw the calories away.

In the good old days, every housewife had a soup pot a-simmering on the back of the stove. Today's two-career homemaker may not have as much kitchen time, but she does have such handy helpers as self-timing ranges, automatic slow-cookers, and triple-fast pressure cookers. A roomy freezer means she can make a lot of soup at once and freeze it in meal-sized portions.

For even greater versatility, you can make your own simmered-down soup "concentrate," which can be frozen in small jars. When defrosted, the "concentrate" can be the start of a variety of soups and other dishes merely by varying the ingredients added.

◄§ BEEF SOUP CONCENTRATE §►

1 **pound lean stew beef, trimmed of fat**
Beef bones
1 **quart water**
1 **tablespoon salt**
1 **onion, chopped**
1 **clove garlic**
1 **bay leaf**
1 **tablespoon monosodium glutamate (optional)**

Cut the meat into 1-inch cubes, then, if you wish, brown it lightly in a nonstick pan with no fat added. Add the remaining ingredients, bring to a boil and skim the surface. Cover tightly and simmer over very low heat for 1 hour or more (or 20 minutes in a pressure cooker, following manufacturer's directions). Remove from the heat until cool enough to pick any remaining meat from the bones. Discard the bones and bay leaf.

Chill the broth until the surface fat hardens, then skim it off. Divide the broth and meat into 1-cup jars; cover, label, and freeze. To serve, defrost and reheat to boiling, thinned with water or skim milk, or prepared as described below. *Six cups, 134 calories each.*

NOTE: This recipe can, of course, be doubled or tripled.

VARIATIONS

Quick Beef and Carrot Soup: Combine 1 cup defrosted Beef Soup Concentrate (see above) with 1 can (8 ounces) sliced carrots. Heat to boiling. *Two servings, 100 calories each.*

Meaty Spaghetti Sauce: Combine 2 cups defrosted Beef Soup Concentrate with 1 can (6 ounces) tomato paste and ¼ teaspoon Italian seasoning. Thin with water, simmer 10 minutes, and serve over 4 cups tender-cooked spaghetti. *Four servings, 257 calories each.*

Chop Suey: Combine 2 cups defrosted Beef Soup Concentrate with 2 cups canned, drained Chinese vegetables. Heat to boiling, then thicken with 2 teaspoons cornstarch combined with 2 tablespoons soy sauce. Serve with rice, if desired. *Two servings, 170 calories each; ½ cup rice per serving, 90 calories.*

◄§ EASY BEEF BROTH §►

Spread beef bones on a broiler tray or roasting pan. Bake or broil at highest heat until the attached meat is nicely browned. Sprinkle the bones lightly with salt and dump them in a stockpot, then cover with water and simmer, covered, for an hour or so. Strain the broth and chill, then lift off all hardened fat. You can freeze the extra broth for use in any kind of soup, stew, or sauce that calls for beef stock.

◄§ QUICK CHICKEN SOUP §►

To turn leftover chicken broth into a quick soup, simply skim away the surface fat and add some chopped onion and sliced carrots. (Some chopped parsley and a few tablespoons of white wine would be nice, too!) Simmer, covered, over low heat until the carrots are tender.

◄§ QUICK CREAM OF CHICKEN SOUP §►

2 cups water
2 cups skim milk
4 chicken bouillon cubes
½ cup minced celery
¼ cup minced onion
2 tablespoons all-purpose flour
  Paprika

Combine all the ingredients in a saucepan and cook, stirring, over low heat until the soup thickens and simmers. Add a dash of paprika and simmer for 10 minutes. Whir in the blender for extra smoothness (nice but not necessary); and serve. *Four and one-half cups, 72 calories per cupful.*

◄§ SUPER SOUP §►

Hearty soup is the wintertime counterpart of summer's super salad bowl. You can have soup for lunch or supper any time you want—if you make it ahead in quantity and freeze it in meal-sized portions.

The make-ahead method is ideal for cholesterol watchers as well as calorie counters, because it's the one technique that really lets you whisk away most of the fat. (Nutritionists love soups because you can't lose the vegetable vitamins; they stay in the broth.)

So dig out your biggest stockpot or that old pressure cooker and simmer up a soup the calorie-wise and heart-smart way.

Vary the ingredients and seasonings to make your soup an "original"—but follow these basic rules for a soup that's never greasy:

1. Put about 3 pounds of lean beef or 2 whole chickens in a big stockpot and add 1 tablespoon salt and 3 quarts cold water. Bring the water to a boil and simmer over low heat, covered, until the meat is tender (around 2 to 4 hours). A pressure cooker can cut this time to 1 hour or less; check your instruction booklet for specific directions.

2. Remove the meat and refrigerate the broth. Discard any skin, bones, or solid pieces of fat or gristle. Cut the meat into hearty chunks.

3. When the broth is chilled, lift off all the fat and return the broth to the stockpot. Add the cut-up meat.

4. Now that the fat is gone, add 3 cups of coarsely cut-up vegetables. Simmer for another 20 minutes, covered. Uncover and cool quickly, then package in diet-sized portions, diluting if necessary.

A good diet-sized portion should offer about ½ cup of vegetables and ¾ to 1 cup of broth. Prepared in the manner above, you'll have a one-dish meal that's 300 calories or less.

What about the vegetables? Celery, onions, carrots, and mushrooms are the obvious choices, but don't overlook spinach, lettuce, beansprouts, cabbage, cauliflower, broccoli, green beans or any vegetable you happen to favor. Even if it is an off-beat soup addition. But do avoid calorie-rich corn, peas, beans, and potatoes, as well as rice, noodles, and barley.

Frozen or canned vegetables can be used if convenient; the important point is to remove the fat before adding the vegetables. Vegetables will absorb fat and add to the calorie count.

Flavor up your soup with a little wine, if you like—most of the calories evaporate. Avoid caramelized coloring agents; they're mainly sugar. Use soy sauce for a darker broth.

An easy way to freeze diet-sized soup portions is to apportion the cooled soup into 12- or 16-ounce paper cups and top with aluminum foil. Just tear away the cup and pop your super "soup ice cube" into a saucepan to thaw and reheat at mealtime.

⟋⟍ BEEF AND BARLEY SOUP ⟍⟋

 2 pounds soup bones
½ pound beef soup meat
 2 quarts water
1½ tablespoons salt
 ¼ teaspoon freshly ground pepper
 ¼ cup chopped fresh parsley
 ¼ cup medium pearl barley
 1 cup sliced carrots
 1 cup sliced onion
 1 cup sliced celery
 1 can (16 ounces) tomatoes

Brown the soup bones under the broiler, turning to brown evenly. Cut the meat into cubes. Combine the bones, meat, water, salt, pepper, and parsley in a soup pot. Cover and simmer for 1 hour, then remove the bones and chill the soup until the fat rises to surface. Skim off all the fat. Add the barley and vegetables and cook an additional 1 to 1½ hours, until the meat and barley are tender. *About eight servings, 97 calories each.*

⟋⟍ BLENDER-EASY FRENCH POTATO SOUP ⟍⟋

4 leeks or 3 onions, sliced
1 tablespoon diet margarine
4 potatoes, peeled and diced
6 cups water
6 chicken bouillon cubes
2 teaspoons salt
   Pinch of freshly ground pepper
1 cup plain yogurt
2 tablespoons chopped chives

Sauté the leeks in the margarine in a large nonstick pot. Add the potatoes, water, bouillon cubes, salt and pepper, then cover and simmer for 30 minutes.

Whirl the soup smooth in a blender or put through a sieve. Blend with the yogurt and serve reheated (but not boiled) or chilled, with a garnish of chopped chives. *Twelve servings, 60 calories each.*

⊰ GARDEN SOUP ⊱

1 tablespoon diet margarine
1 leek, thoroughly cleaned
3 medium potatoes, peeled and diced
2 carrots, scraped and sliced
1 stalk celery, sliced
2 tablespoons parsley
4 chicken bouillon cubes
1 tablespoon salt
  Pinch of freshly ground pepper
5 cups water

Melt the margarine in a soup kettle. Slice in the white and tender green parts of the leek and sauté gently for 5 minutes. Add the potatoes, carrots, and celery and cook for 2 minutes more, stirring when necessary to prevent sticking. Add all the other ingredients, cover, and simmer for 1 hour. Serve as is, or puree in an electric blender and reheat. *Eight servings, 56 calories each.*

⊰ MUSHROOM-VEGETABLE SOUP ⊱

1 can (4 ounces) mushroom stems and pieces, undrained
2 cans (10½ ounces each) condensed chicken broth
2 soup cans water
1 can (8 ounces) sliced carrots, undrained
¼ pound fresh spinach, cleaned well and chopped
1 large ripe tomato, peeled and diced
1½ tablespoons chopped fresh parsley
2 tablespoons dry white wine

Drain the mushroom and carrot liquid into a saucepan and set the vegetables aside. Add the chicken broth, water, parsley, and wine to the saucepan, cover, and simmer for 8 minutes. Add the mushrooms, carrots, spinach, and tomatoes, then cover and simmer an additional 5 minutes. *Six servings, 38 calories each.*

Calorie-Conscious Cream Soups

If you have fattening tastes, your favorite soup is probably cream-of-anything! Leave the consommés to the skinnies, we could-be fatties know that there's nothing more inviting than a steaming mug of cream of mushroom or a brimming bowl of golden cream of chicken soup.

Unfortunately, most of those easy-do, can-opener soups have an uncanny affinity for calories—between 200 and 300 per serving, thanks to the starch and fat content. Remember that the next time you run across one of those can-opener casserole recipes that calls for dumping a can of cream soup over leftovers!

Homemade cream soups are so easy to make, why not be the only cook on your block to make his/her own? It's a snap with your blender, and you can cut the calories by two-thirds. You won't have to feel guilty about enjoying these soups; they're packed with milk nutrition, but the fat content is so low it barely counts.

⊷§ "CREAM" OF MUSHROOM SOUP §⊶

- 2 teaspoons butter or margarine
- ½ pound fresh mushrooms, chopped
- 2 cups chicken stock, skimmed of fat, or 2 cups water and 2 bouillon cubes
- ½ cup minced celery
- ¼ cup minced onion
- 2 tablespoons minced fresh parsley
- 2 cups skim milk
- 2 tablespoons all-purpose flour
- ½ teaspoon salt
- ½ teaspoon paprika
  Freshly ground pepper
  Garlic powder

Melt the butter in a nonstick saucepan and add the mushrooms. Sauté lightly. Add the stock, then add the celery, onion, and parsley and simmer, covered, for 10 minutes. Remove from the heat and pour into a blender container. Blend on high speed until smooth, then pour back into the saucepan.

Combine the milk and flour and add to the soup mixture. Continue cooking, stirring occasionally, until the mixture simmers and thickens. Add seasonings to taste and serve. *Four and one-half cups, 90 calories per cupful.*

NOTE: A shake of Worcestershire sauce or a dash of white wine is a nice addition.

◄§ QUICK "CREAM" OF CHICKEN SOUP §►

2 cups water
2 cups skim milk
4 chicken bouillon cubes
½ cup minced celery
¼ cup minced onion
2 tablespoons all-purpose flour
  Paprika

Combine all the ingredients in a saucepan and cook, stirring, over low heat until the soup thickens and simmers. Add a dash of paprika and simmer for 10 minutes. Whir in the blender for extra smoothness (nice but not necessary), and serve. *Four and one half cups, 72 calories per cupful.*

◄§ "CREAMED" TURKEY AND MUSHROOM SKILLET SOUP §►

What to do with the last of the turkey? The old bird still has another meal in it if you're a penny-wise cook. If you're also calorie conscious, you can turn those leftover turkey bones into a rich-tasting soup that only seems fattening—a hearty creamed soup with mushrooms.

The exact calorie count will vary, depending on how much meat you're able to salvage from your holiday bird. The meatier the bones, the better the flavor. (Our calorie estimates are based on about a cupful of meat.)

1 turkey carcass
1 small onion, sliced
1 quart water
½ teaspoon monosodium glutamate (optional)
½ pound fresh mushrooms, finely chopped
2 teaspoons polyunsaturated oil
1 tablespoon chopped fresh parsley
1 can (13 ounces) evaporated skim milk
1 tablespoon all-purpose flour
  Salt and freshly ground pepper

Combine the turkey carcass, onion, water, and monosodium glutamate in a large pot. Cover and simmer for 2 hours (or 45 minutes in a pressure cooker). Strain the broth and refrigerate several hours. (You should have about 3 cups; add water if needed.) Pick the meat from the bones; discard bones and skin. Mince and refrigerate the meat, covered.

In a large nonstick skillet, brown the chopped mushrooms in the oil. Add the turkey meat and parsley, then skim the fat from the turkey broth and add broth to the skillet. Heat to boiling.

Combine the evaporated milk and flour and stir into the skillet. Cook and stir over a moderate flame until the soup is hot and bubbling. Season to taste, pour into soup bowls, and serve immediately. *Six cups, approximately 125 calories each.*

✐ HOMEMADE ONION SOUP ⳾

Flavorful French onion soup, extra thick with onions, afloat with rounds of cheese-topped toast! It's the perfect prologue to any meal, even a diet dinner.

At 76 calories a serving, including the cheese-topped toast, this extra-special onion soup is an extravagance even a calorie counter can afford. After all, with such a glamorous opening course, even the most spartan meal seems sumptuous.

To make French onion soup, you'll need a good beefy broth for a base. If you don't have time to make your own, canned beef broth or consommé is an acceptable stand-in. But be sure to skim away any surface fat.

1 **tablespoon butter or peanut oil**
6 **onions, thinly sliced**
2 **quarts beef broth**
1 **teaspoon salt**
1 **teaspoon monosodium glutamate (optional)**
10 **Melba toast rounds**
10 **teaspoons freshly grated Romano, Parmesan, or Swiss cheese**

Heat the butter or oil in a nonstick saucepan and add half the onion slices. Cook over low heat, stirring with a wooden spoon to break them into rings, until golden brown. Add the remaining onions, beef broth, salt, and monosodium glutamate. Heat to boiling, then cover and simmer over low heat until the onions are just tender, about 5 minutes.

Ladle the soup into a large ovenproof tureen or individual soup bowls. Float the toast rounds on top and sprinkle with the grated cheese (Romano is the most flavorful), then slide the tureen or soup bowls under a preheated broiler and broil until the cheese melts and turns golden brown. *Ten servings, 76 calories each.*

✐ EASY-DO FRENCH-STYLE "STEAK" SOUP ⳾

Have you ever had "steak" soup? It's a great Sunday night supper. Steak soup, French style, is a super supper for two—or four, or six, or more, simply by doubling or tripling the recipe. No matter how many you serve, supper is ready in just a few minutes.

½ **pound lean beef round, trimmed of fat and ground**
    Garlic salt and freshly ground pepper
2 **onions, thinly sliced**
1 **tablespoon diet margarine**
1 **can (10½ ounces) onion soup**
1 **soup can water**
2 **tablespoons freshly grated Parmesan cheese**

Season the meat lightly with garlic salt and pepper, then shape into 1-inch meatballs.

Put the meatballs, sliced onions, and diet margarine in a nonstick skillet. Cook, stirring occasionally, over moderate heat until the meatballs are nicely browned and the onions are soft. Add the canned soup and a canful of water, then cover and simmer for 2 or 3 minutes, until the onions are tender. Pour into 2 soup bowls, sprinkle with cheese, and serve. *Four servings, 292 calories each.*

NOTE: For an authentic French touch, pour the hot soup into ovenproof soup bowls and sprinkle with cheese. Slip them under a broiler for a minute, until the cheese is brown and bubbly.

VARIATION

Italian Meatball Minestrone: Follow the preceding recipe, but substitute a 10½-ounce can of minestrone soup for the onion soup. Season with a pinch of oregano or Italian seasoning, if desired. *Two servings, 345 calories each.*

⋖ MAIN-COURSE MEATBALL SOUP ⋗

4 **stalks celery, including leaves, cut up**
1 **onion, chopped**
2 **carrots, scraped and sliced**
2 **potatoes, peeled and cubed**
1 **can (16 ounces) tomatoes**
2 **teaspoons salt**
3 **cups water**
1 **pound extra-lean beef round, trimmed of fat and ground**
1 **egg**
¼ **cup chopped fresh parsley**

Combine the celery, onion, carrots, potatoes, tomatoes, salt, and water in a large pot. Cover and simmer for 30 minutes.

Meanwhile, mix the ground beef, egg, and parsley. Shape into 1-inch balls, add to the soup, and simmer, covered, for 15 minutes longer. *Four servings, 270 calories each.*

Calorie-Wary Chowders

There seems to be a firmly held belief among cookbook writers that the eastern seaboard is in civil strife on the clam chowder issue. Should it be made with tomatoes? Or potatoes and cream?

If you want to be a Slim Gourmet, I suggest you ignore the cookbooks altogether, since most cram their chowders with unneeded extra calories in the way of greasy slabs of pork fat and gobs of heavy cream. Those hidden fat calories add little to the flavor or texture of chowder.

Here are some Slim Gourmet chowders that are heavy on the clams but light on the calories and the effort. All are made with canned minced clams.

⋖§ EASY MANHATTAN CLAM CHOWDER §⋗

```
 1  can (20 ounces) minced clams, undrained
 1  can (16 ounces) tomatoes, broken up
3½  cups water
 ½  teaspoon dried thyme
 1  tablespoon cornstarch (optional)
 1  cup thinly sliced onions
 1  cup minced celery
 1  teaspoon salt
    Pinch of freshly ground pepper
 1  tablespoon minced fresh parsley
 3  tablespoons bacon-flavored bits (optional)
 6  soda crackers, crumbled (optional)
```

In a 3-quart pot, combine all the ingredients except the bacon bits and crackers. Stir well, then cover and simmer over low heat, stirring occasionally, until the celery is tender. Pour into soup bowls, sprinkle with bacon bits and crumbled crackers, and serve. *Ten cups, 68 calories each with the crackers and bacon bits, 45 calories without.*

EASY NEW ENGLAND CLAM CHOWDER

2 teaspoons butter
1 cup chopped onion
1 can (20 ounces) minced clams, undrained
4 cups water
2 teaspoons salt
Pinch of freshly ground pepper
2 teaspoons cornstarch
2 potatoes, peeled and diced
1 can (13 ounces) evaporated skim milk

Melt the butter in a nonstick saucepan. Add the onion and sauté lightly. Drain the liquid from the canned clams and add to the saucepan; reserve the clam meat. Add the water, salt, pepper, and cornstarch and stir well. Add the potatoes, then cover the pot and cook over low heat for 10 minutes. Uncover, add the evaporated skim milk and clam meat, and cook, stirring, until the mixture simmers. Serve immediately. *Ten cups, 83 calories each.*

BOSTON CLAM CHOWDER

2 cans (7 ounces each) minced clams, undrained *fresh*
2 onions, peeled and chopped
1 can (10½ ounces) cream of celery soup
1 soup can water
2 potatoes, peeled and diced
2 stalks celery, sliced
2 teaspoons dried thyme
2 teaspoons salt
Pinch of freshly ground pepper
Chopped fresh parsley for garnish (optional)

Combine all the ingredients except the parsley in a large saucepan and simmer for 30 minutes. Garnish with parsley before serving, if desired. *Ten servings, 70 calories each.*

CLAM AND VEGETABLE CHOWDER

1 onion, chopped
2 potatoes, peeled and cubed
2 carrots, scraped and sliced

½ cup white wine
1 teaspoon dried dill
  Pinch of freshly ground pepper
1 can (7 ounces) minced clams, undrained
1 package (9 ounces) frozen green beans
1½ cups skim milk

In a large pot, combine the onion, potatoes, carrots, wine, dill, and pepper. Drain the clam liquid into the pot; reserve the meat. Bring to a boil, then cover and simmer 20 minutes, adding a little water if necessary. Eight minutes before the soup is done, add the green beans. Just before serving, add the clams and milk and heat thoroughly, but without boiling. *Four servings, 144 calories each.*

◄§ TUNA CHOWDER §►

1 can (10¾ ounces) condensed cream of potato soup
½ cup skim milk
½ cup water
1 can (7 ounces) water-pack tuna, drained
2 tablespoons minced chives
½ teaspoon salt
  Pinch of freshly ground pepper
1 tablespoon bacon-flavored bits

In a saucepan, combine all the ingredients except the bacon-flavored bits. Heat just to boiling, then garnish with bacon-flavored bits and serve. *Three servings, 161 calories each.*

5
BEEFSTEAK, ROASTS, AND STEWS

The fatter the beef, the higher the calorie count—it's as simple as that. Here's a comparison chart, based on information provided by the United States Department of Agriculture:

Beef Cut	Fat	Calories
Chuck	30%	1,597
Arm	14%	1,012
Flank	none	653
Hindshank	33%	1,311
Porterhouse (with bone)	33%	1,603
T-bone (with bone)	34%	1,596
First cut loin	30%	1,443
Sirloin	27%	1,420
Hip steak	39%	1,869
Short plate	41%	1,814
Rib with bone	41%	1,843
Boneless rib	45%	2,041
Blade	29%	1,647
Round	11%	894
Rump	25%	1,374

Naturally, no two cuts are exactly alike; these approximate calorie counts are based on uncooked 1-pound portions of beef—boneless unless otherwise specified—and butcher trimmed so that no more than ½ inch of border fat remains.

All counts are for USDA "choice," the grade most often found in supermarkets and butcher shops. USDA "prime," usually found only in specialty shops and better restaurants, as mentioned before, is generally about 5 percent fatter, while USDA "good" is about 6 percent leaner, but rarely available. Many heart specialists have long campaigned for a change in meat-grading standards so that leaner beef is more widely available. Early in 1975 the U.S. Department of Agriculture approved changes in the government's "beef-grading standards."

These new changes, the first in nearly ten years, aim at putting more lean beef in the market at lower cost, by reducing the amount of time and grain needed to fatten cattle to marketable standards. Previous standards encouraged overfattening by placing a premium on the amount of fatty "marbling" (the untrimmable flecks of fat found throughout beef). As a result, the meat with the highest fat and calorie content—and the least nutrition—commands a premium price!

Under the new standards, beef under thirty months of age will be able to make the premium "prime" and "choice" grades with a lower fat content than the old standards required. The change also upgrades the requirements for "good," setting up what USDA officials call a "special" uniform grade for beef with less internal and surface fat than that graded as "choice."

Slim Steaks

The average American man's idea of a perfect "diet" dinner is broiled steak and salad—virtuously skipping the potato.

Unfortunately, most such "diet dinners" are far from low calorie. The kind of beef that makes a man-pleasing steak is well larded with hidden fat. The cuts of beef most often chosen for steak contain anywhere from 30 to 45 percent fat—and 1,700 to 2,000 calories per (boneless) pound.

There's one steak, however, that's so low in fat and calories that the weight-wary male can make a meal of it any time with no qualms of conscience—flank steak! Flank is so free of fat that it is only 653 calories per pound.

Flank steak is a tender boneless piece of beef averaging around 2 pounds, and you get twice as many servings per pound as you would with fatty, bony steaks. However, flank steak takes special care to reach its delectably tender potential.

⤆ PERFECT FLANK STEAK ⤇

1. Flank has a definite characteristic "grain" of long meat fibers. The high heat of cooking will cause your steak to shrink and shrivel unless you cut through the surface fibers beforehand. So you'll want to "score" your flank steak in a diamond pattern on both sides before cooking. Spread the steak on

a cutting board and make *very shallow* diagonal slices, about an inch apart—first in one direction and then in the other. Turn the steak over and score the other side, too, with the same diamond-shaped pattern. Both sides should look like the fat on a fancy baked ham. But don't make the cuts too deep—you just want to penetrate the upper layer of the meat.

2. Now, to assure tenderness, sprinkle both sides liberally with meat tenderizer. Add a generous sprinkle of garlic powder or onion salt, if you like, then sprinkle the steak with a little water to activate the tenderizer. Let the meat "tenderize" for at least an hour at room temperature, or all day (overnight) in the refrigerator. Or you can freeze it for a future meal. You can cook flank still frozen or partially thawed for a hurry-up steak that's sure to be rare and very tender.

3. It takes less than 10 minutes to cook a flank steak, even if it's frozen, so be sure to have everything else ready. Flank can be broiled under high heat—or, if you have a big enough skillet, it can be pan fried to perfection.

VARIATIONS

London Broil: Sprinkle with salt and pepper and a dash of Worcestershire sauce, if you like. Broil on a rack in a broiling pan under highest heat, 4 to 5 minutes per side.

Pan-fried Flank: Add a tablespoon of water or red wine to a nonstick skillet. Season the steak and put it in the cold skillet. Heat it over highest flame. The liquid will help melt the few bits of fat clinging to the steak's surface. When it evaporates, the steak will brown in its own fat—about 4 or 5 minutes per side. Steak should be rare.

To serve, cut the steak in thin, diagonal slices, against the grain. A nice, big salad with low-calorie dressing is all you need to complete the meal. *Each 4-ounce serving is 222 calories.*

◄§ FLANK STEAK AUX CHAMPIGNONS ଽ◆

(*Flank Steak with Mushrooms*)

    1 small flank steak (about 1 pound)
      Salt and freshly ground pepper
      Meat tenderizer
      Garlic powder (optional)
    1 tablespoon polyunsaturated oil
    3 tablespoons dry white wine
    1 small onion, minced
  ½ pound fresh mushrooms, sliced
      Minced fresh parsley

Prepare the flank steak as described in the basic directions (page 57), using the salt, pepper, tenderizer, and optional garlic powder. Brown quickly on both sides in a hot nonstick skillet with a minimum of fat (the 1 tablespoon is ample). Add the wine, onion, and mushrooms, then cover and cook for 2 minutes. Uncover and continue cooking until all the liquid is evaporated, stirring the mushrooms until they are lightly browned and stirring in parsley at the last minute. Slice the meat very, very thin, against the grain. *Four servings, 216 calories each.*

FLANK STEAK BORDELAISE

Char-brown on the outside and pink in the middle, lavished with a wine-kissed sauce, flank is the steakiest steak there is!

1½ **pounds flank steak**
  3 **teaspoons polyunsaturated oil**
  1 **clove garlic, cut**
  3 **tablespoons minced shallots or onion**
  1 **cup beef broth, skimmed of fat, or 1 bouillon cube in 1 cup water**
  2 **tablespoons all-purpose flour**
  ¼ **cup dry red wine**
  2 **tablespoons lemon juice**
  ¼ **cup chopped fresh parsley**
     Dash of cayenne pepper
     Salt and freshly ground pepper

Rub the steak with 2 teaspoons of the oil and a cut clove of garlic. Broil it quickly under high heat, 4 to 5 minutes per side.

Meanwhile, make the sauce. Sauté the shallots in the remaining oil until tender, then add the beef broth and stir in the flour. Add the remaining ingredients and continue heating over a moderate flame, stirring frequently, until the sauce simmers and thickens, about 5 minutes. Pour over the steak and serve. *Six servings, 200 calories each.*

SLIM GOURMET ROUND STEAK

This version of round steak is a budget-wise dinner in which beef is browned, then slowly simmered in a thickened sauce of tomatoes, onions, and seasonings. Here's a step-by-step guide to cooking this basic dish the calorie-wise way:

1 tablespoon polyunsaturated oil
2 pounds lean round steak, 1½ inches thick
2 teaspoons salt
¼ teaspoon freshly ground pepper
   Garlic powder
2½ cups canned tomatoes *potatoes*
1 tablespoon all-purpose flour
1 tablespoon cornstarch
1 cup sliced onions
   Water, if necessary

Measure the oil into a nonstick skillet—1 tablespoon is all you need—and brown the meat slowly on both sides. Drain away any oil that remains and sprinkle the meat with the seasonings.

Open a can of plain tomatoes (check the label to make sure no sugar or oil is added) and empty it into a bowl. Stir in the flour and cornstarch (see note below). Cover the steak with the tomato mixture. Add the onions (see note below), then cover the pan with a well-fitting lid and simmer until tender. (Simmer means just barely bubbling—definitely not boiling!) Continue cooking until tender, about 2 hours, depending on the thickness. Uncover and check occasionally with a fork, stirring in extra water if needed.

Before serving, scrupulously spoon off any melted fat floating on the surface (each tablespoon you get rid of is 100 calories down the drain). Or make this a day ahead and refrigerate overnight. Before reheating, simply lift off the chilled fat. *Six servings, 250 calories each.*

NOTE: Cornstarch has 50 percent more thickening power than flour, but by itself will create a clear, jellylike gravy. By combining cornstarch and flour, you get the best of both with fewer calories.

Do not add onions or flour when browning meat, because both absorb extra fat—and calories. Also, unbrowned onions add a more onion-y flavor than those that have been precooked in fat—more flavor with fewer calories.

⋄§ SWISS STEAK ᠖⋄

1 teaspoon meat tenderizer
¼ teaspoon freshly ground pepper
1 pound lean round steak, trimmed of fat
2 teaspoons polyunsaturated oil
1 cup plus 2 teaspoons water
1 envelope dry onion soup mix
1 can (16 ounces) tomatoes
4 carrots, scraped and cut in 2-inch pieces
2 potatoes, peeled and quartered

Pound the meat tenderizer and pepper into the meat, then cut into 4 serving-size portions. Combine the meat, oil, and 2 teaspoons water in a nonstick skillet and brown the meat slowly over medium heat. Add all the other ingredients, cover, and simmer 1 hour, stirring once or twice. Check occasionally and add a little water if necessary. *Four servings, 298 calories each.*

⋖ FLEMISH BEEFSTEAK ⋗

1 **pound top round steak**
1 **tablespoon polyunsaturated oil**
1 **tablespoon all-purpose flour**
1 **tablespoon brown sugar**
6 **ounces beer**
 Fresh parsley for garnish

Trim the steak of fat. Heat the oil in a nonstick skillet and brown the beef rapidly on both sides. Sprinkle both sides of the browned steak with the flour and sugar. Swish the steak around in the pan, first on one side and then on the other, so that the flour and sugar are well-moistened with the pan juices. Add the beer to the skillet and continue cooking over a moderate flame, turning occasionally, until the liquid is reduced to sauce consistency. Remove the steak to a hot platter and garnish with fresh parsley. Pour on the remaining pan gravy and serve. *Four servings, 260 calories each.*

NOTE: To decalorize this dish even further, use one of the low-carbohydrate, low-calorie beers. There are at least four on the market, and the best-known brand is only 99 calories in a 12-ounce bottle, compared with 155 calories for regular beer. (The carbohydrate content is only .02 gram, compared with 13.2 grams carbohydrate for regular beer.) I've made it both ways, and the only difference is in the calories. Cooking with beer is like cooking with wine: the alcohol calories evaporate in the cooking, and all that remain are carbohydrate calories. Flemish Beefsteak is nonalcoholic family fare.

⋖ INDONESIAN CHILIED BEEF ⋗

1 **pound top round steak**
1 **tablespoon polyunsaturated oil**
1 **large onion, thinly sliced**
2 **tomatoes, peeled and chopped**
½ **teaspoon chili powder, more if desired**
½ **cup water**
2 **teaspoons concentrated beef bouillon**
 Salt and freshly ground pepper

Trim the beef of all fat and cut into 2-inch cubes. Heat the oil in a nonstick skillet and add the beef. Stir-fry until browned, then remove and set aside. In the same skillet, stir-fry the onions until soft and transparent. Add the tomatoes, chili powder, water, and bouillon and simmer for 5 minutes. Add the meat cubes and seasoning and cook to desired degree of doneness. *Four servings, 218 calories each.*

◄§ STEAK AND ZUCCHINI, ៛► ITALIAN STYLE

1 **pound lean boneless beefsteak, trimmed of fat**
  Polyunsaturated oil or spray-on vegetable coating
2 **zucchini, sliced**
1 **Bermuda onion, sliced into rings**
1 **cup tomato juice**
½ **teaspoon oregano**
¼ **teaspoon garlic powder**
2 **tablespoons freshly grated Romano cheese**

Cut the steak into 2-inch cubes. Wipe a nonstick skillet lightly with oil, or spray with vegetable oil coating for no-fat frying, and brown the steak cubes over high heat. Add all the other ingredients except the cheese, cover, and simmer about 3 minutes, until the onion rings are tender but still crunchy. Uncover and continue to cook over moderate heat until the steak and vegetables are coated with the sauce. Sprinkle with the cheese and serve. *Four servings, 230 calories each.*

◄§ CHINESE STEAK WITH BROCCOLI ៛►

1 **pound boneless sirloin, trimmed of fat**
2 **tablespoons sherry**
2 **tablespoons soy sauce**
½ **cup beef bouillon**
1 **tablespoon polyunsaturated oil**
1 **onion, sliced**
1 **pound fresh or frozen broccoli**
1 **teaspoon cornstarch**
  Pinch of ground ginger
  Freshly ground pepper to taste

Cut the beef into 1-inch cubes, trimming fat as you cut. Marinate the beef in the sherry, soy sauce, and bouillon for 15 minutes or more, then drain the meat, reserving the marinade.

Heat the oil in a wok or large nonstick skillet and add the beef and sliced onion. Stir-fry over highest heat until browned on all sides, then remove and reserve. Add the broccoli and stir-fry for 2 minutes (defrosted broccoli will cook much faster than fresh). Combine marinade with the cornstarch, add to the wok, and cook, stirring until the sauce thickens and the broccoli is crunchy-tender. Add the meat and onion and cook only until warmed through; the beef should be slightly rare and onion still crisp. Add ginger and pepper to taste and serve immediately. *Four servings, 237 calories each.*

On with the Show: Steak, Japanese–Restaurant Style

The ingredients and technique of Japanese cuisine read like a prescription from the Heart Association—a little lean beef, crunchy vegetables, just barely cooked in a small amount of polyunsaturated oil. No fatty steaks, no creamy sauces, no eggs, no cheese, no butter, no bread, no heavy desserts. (In fact, the only reservation might be the American penchant for dousing each dish with salty soy sauce.) Japanese steakhouse fare is also relatively low in calories, far slimmer than anything encountered at your favorite Italian, French, or American eatery, easy to duplicate at home.

◦§ STEAK AND ZUCCHINI, §◦ JAPANESE-STYLE

1 pound lean boneless beefsteak, trimmed of all fat
2 zucchini, cut in strips
4 small onions
  Polyunsaturated oil or spray-on vegetable coating
2 tablespoons Japanese-style soy sauce
2 tablespoons sherry wine
1 cup tomato juice
¼ teaspoon monosodium glutamate (optional)

Cut the steak into 2-inch cubes. Cut the squash into quarters, lengthwise, then into slender 3-inch lengths. Peel and quarter the onions. Wipe a nonstick skillet lightly with oil, or spray with vegetable coating for no-fat frying, and brown the cubes over high heat. Add the remaining ingredients, cover, and simmer 3 minutes. Uncover; cook and stir until most of the liquid evaporates and the meat and vegetables are coated with a thick sauce. The vegetables should be crunchy. *Four servings, 229 calories each.*

✓ ❧ JAPANESE STEAK AND VEGETABLES ☙

1 pound flank or boneless round steak
  Meat tenderizer or sherry wine to cover
1 large Bermuda onion
½ pound fresh mushrooms
1 small zucchini
1 cup beansprouts, fresh or canned
1 tablespoon safflower oil
1 teaspoon monosodium glutamate (optional)
2 tablespoons Japanese-style soy sauce
1 tablespoon sesame seeds

Slice the steak, against the grain, into quarter-inch-thin slices (easier to do if the steak is partly frozen). To ensure tenderness, sprinkle the meat with tenderizer or marinate it in sherry. Slice the onion paper thin and separate into rings. Slice the mushrooms. Cut the zucchini into quarters, lengthwise, then into slender 3-inch lengths. Rinse and drain the beansprouts, if canned. Arrange all the vegetables on a platter.

Heat the oil until hot in a nonstick skillet. Add the beef and stir-fry 2 minutes, then add all the remaining ingredients and cook and stir until the vegetables are heated through, but still crunchy. Serve immediately. *Four servings, 254 calories each.*

Make Your Own Minute Steaks

Make your own minute steaks—from a sale-priced boneless beef roast. By preparing them yourself, you know that your minute steaks come from that part of the beef with the most protein and least fat.

Here's how:

✓ ❧ MINUTE STEAKS ☙

1 boneless bottom round beef roast
  Garlic or onion powder
  Meat tenderizer
  Salt and freshly ground pepper

Trim and discard all exterior fat from roast. Using a sharp knife, cut half-inch thick slices of meat, against the grain. Sprinkle the steaks with seasoning, then, using a metal-tipped meat-tenderizer mallet, pound the steaks thin on both sides.

To FREEZE: Use only meat tenderizer. Omit garlic, onion, salt, pepper. Add seasoning when the steaks are cooked.

To Cook: Spray a nonstick skillet with vegetable oil coating for no-fat frying or wipe lightly with oil. Cook for about 1 minute each side over a moderate flame, longer if frozen. Don't overcook; the steaks should be still pink in the middle. *Each 4-ounce steak will be approximately 153 calories.*

✑ SKINNY MINUTE STEAKS ੬◉
WITH RED-WINE MUSHROOM SAUCE

```
1   tablespoon polyunsaturated oil
1½  pounds tenderized minute steaks (see page 64)
1   tablespoon all-purpose flour
¼   teaspoon poultry seasoning
    Garlic salt and freshly ground pepper
1   can (8 ounces) sliced mushrooms, undrained
½   cup dry red wine
```

Heat the oil in a nonstick skillet (1 tablespoon is all you need; don't add any more). Pan-fry the steaks quickly over high heat; sprinkle both sides with the flour and seasonings. Add the mushrooms and wine, then cook and stir until the wine sauce thickens and forms its own gravy. Serve immediately. *Six servings, 192 calories each.*

✑ MINUTE STEAKS WITH ੬◉
WHITE WINE AND MUSHROOMS

```
1   pound tenderized minute steaks (see page 64)
    Garlic salt and pepper
1   can (4 ounces) button or sliced mushrooms
¼   cup minced dried onion
¼   cup dry sherry wine (or mushroom liquid)
```

Season the steaks, then combine with the remaining ingredients in a large nonstick skillet over a moderate flame. When the liquid evaporates, brown the steaks for 1 minute on each side. Stir the onion and mushrooms to brown evenly and serve. *Four servings, 165 calories each.*

✑ MINUTE STEAKS PARMIGIANA ੬◉

```
    Onion or garlic salt
1   pound tenderized minute steaks (see page 64)
1   can (16 ounces) plain tomato sauce (no oil added)
2   ounces (4 thin slices) part-skim mozzarella cheese
½   teaspoon oregano or Italian seasoning
```

Season the steaks, then brown for 30 seconds on each side in a skillet over high heat. Pour on the tomato sauce. Top each steak with mozzarella and oregano and continue to cook, uncovered, until the tomato sauce bubbles and the cheese is melted. *Four servings, 225 calories each.*

◄§ MINUTE STEAKS IN BEER §►

Salt and freshly ground pepper
½ teaspoon granulated sugar
Pinch of dried sage
1 pound tenderized minute steaks (see page 64)
1 tablespoon all-purpose flour
¼ cup minced onion
1 cup beer

Season the steaks, then brown for 30 seconds on each side in a nonstick skillet over high heat. Sprinkle the steaks with flour on both sides. Add the onion and beer and simmer, uncovered, until the beer evaporates into a thick sauce. *Four servings, 180 calories each.*

◄§ SKILLET STEAK AND TOMATOES §►

2 pounds cubed beef round "minute steaks" or veal steaks
1 tablespoon olive oil
1 cup cold water
2 tablespoons cornstarch
6 tomatoes, peeled and cut in large chunks
1 onion, sliced
Garlic salt and freshly ground pepper
2 teaspoons oregano or Italian seasoning

Trim the fat from the meat. In a large nonstick skillet, brown the steaks quickly in the oil. Remove the steaks to a platter and drain off any fat from the skillet.

Combine the water with the cornstarch and add to the skillet, along with all the other ingredients except the meat. Cook and stir until the mixture is thickened, then return the steaks to the skillet and reheat. Serve immediately. *Eight servings, 207 calories each.*

◆§ PENNYPINCHER STEAK AU POIVRE §◆
(Peppercorn Steak)

1 or 2 tablespoons whole peppercorns
4 minute steaks (see page 64), 4 ounches each
   Spray-on vegetable coating or polyunsaturated oil
   Worcestershire, Tabasco, or lemon juice
   Fresh parsley for garnish

Use a mortar and pestle to coarsely crack the fresh peppercorns. Or put the whole pepper in a plastic bag and pound with a hammer or heavy (unbreakable) object. Press the cracked pepper into both sides of the steaks, then refrigerate for 1 hour or more.

Spray a nonstick skillet with vegetable oil coating for no-fat frying, or wipe lightly with oil. Brown the steaks quickly on both sides, then remove to a serving dish and sprinkle lightly with Worcestershire, Tabasco, or lemon juice. Garnish with parsley. *Four servings, 160 calories each.*

◆§ SLOPPY JOE STEAKS §◆

   Spray-on vegetable coating or polyunsaturated oil
4 minute steaks (see page 64), 4 ounces each
1 cup chopped onion
1 cup chopped green pepper
1 tablespoon mustard
1 tablespoon catsup
1 can (8 ounces) plain tomato sauce (no oil added)
2 large hamburger buns, split

Spray a nonstick skillet with vegetable coating for no-fat frying or wipe lightly with oil. Brown the minute steaks quickly on both sides, then add the onion, green pepper, mustard, catsup, and tomato sauce. Cover and simmer until the pepper is soft, about 10 minutes.

Put half a hamburger bun on each plate. Top with a steak and sauce and serve, with steak knives and forks. *Four servings, 270 calories each.*

◆§ OVEN-BAKED "BIG FAMILY" STEAK §◆

Your best buy is a super-thick steak cut from the arm (chuck) or the leg (round). The most expensive steaks have the least lean meat! A chuck steak contains 77 percent lean meat and only 12 percent fat. A round steak is leaner still—86 percent meat and only 11 percent fat. A rib steak, by comparison, is only 51 percent lean meat and 41 percent fat.

Be sure your steak is at least 2½ inches thick. Have the butcher cut one for you if you don't see what you want at the meat counter.

You can cook this immediately or freeze it. If you freeze it, do not thaw before cooking. Baking your steak from the frozen state assures a "charcoal-broiled" exterior and a rare interior. No turning needed.

4 pounds boneless beef round or chuck, 2½ to 3 inches thick
1 tablespoon papain (tenderizer)
   Garlic or onion powder
   Coarsely ground pepper

Trim away all border fat. Moisten the meat with water and sprinkle liberally with the tenderizer and seasonings. Puncture all over with a fork to assure penetration. Cook immediately or wrap and freeze.

To cook: Preheat the oven to 450 degrees. Place the steak on a rack in a roasting pan. Bake at 450 without turning. A thawed steak will require 20 to 30 minutes, depending on the degree of doneness desired, and a frozen steak will need 30 to 40 minutes. Slit the steak with a sharp knife to check interior pinkness; the steak should be rare for best flavor and tenderness.

Remove the steak to a platter or steak board and cut in very thin diagonal slices. *Twelve 4-ounce servings, 210 calories each.*

⊷ RED WINE SKILLET STEAK ⊷

1 beef shoulder chuck steak
½ cup dry red wine
   Garlic salt and freshly ground pepper
   Pinch of poultry seasoning

Pick out a lean steak. Trim away every bit of fringe fat. Put the steak in a plastic bag and set it in a bowl. Pour the wine into the bag and draw up the sides so that the meat is covered. Marinate at room temperature for 2 to 4 hours, or all day in the refrigerator. The wine will tenderize the meat.

Put the steak and 3 tablespoons of the marinating wine in a nonstick skillet. Cook over high heat until the wine evaporates and the steak begins to brown in its own melted fat. Season the meat and brown it well on both sides. Drain away the fat. Pour the remaining wine on and continue to cook over high heat until the wine evaporates to a sauce-y consistency and the steak is cooked to desired doneness. *Each 4-ounce serving, weighed after cooking, will be 263 calories.*

If You Can Afford the Best, Tenderloin Is Your Meat!

Tenderloin is boneless, lean, and tender. It usually forms part of much fattier steaks like porterhouse or T-bone. When the tenderloin is stripped away, it's sometimes cut into luxury steaks known as filet mignon, Château-briand, or tornedos. These extravagant steaks also happen to be the least fattening of all the luxury cuts because tenderloin beef has no fatty marbling.

The price of an entire tenderloin will seem staggering by anybody's standards—especially after you find that the meat itself is buried in a thick layer of fat that must be trimmed and discarded. However, home-broiled tenderloin, although expensive, is only a fraction of the price you'd pay in a restaurant. And simple broiling or pan frying is all they need. It is usually necessary to "special order" an entire tenderloin—about 12 pounds—and cut it into steaks yourself.

Whole tenderloins from the supermarket often come vacuum packed in a heavy plastic bag. Unwrap the meat and trim away all the exterior fat with a sharp pointed knife. There will be quite a bit of it! The remaining meat will be lean, with little inside fat, which means that there will be little shrinkage when the steaks are cooked. Before you begin cutting your tenderloin fillet into individual boneless steaks, decide on the size you wish to make them. Better too small than too large—when serving steak to guests, you can always cook extras. In our Slim Gourmet kitchen, we use a postal scale to help us slice a tenderloin into 5-ounce steaks. When broiled, each steak is about 232 calories.

Each steak should be individually wrapped in plastic and quick frozen. It's not necessary to completely defrost steaks before broiling or pan-frying.

✔ ✍ FILET MIGNON AND MUSHROOMS ✍

½ cup dry white wine
4 tenderloin steaks, 5 ounces each
½ pound fresh mushrooms
Salt and freshly ground pepper

Put two tablespoons of the wine in a nonstick skillet and add the steaks. Heat over a high flame until the wine evaporates and the steaks begin to brown in their own melted fat. When the steaks are brown on one side, turn them over and add the mushrooms. Cook an additional 3 to 4 minutes, until the steak is the desired doneness and the mushrooms are lightly browned. Remove to a heated platter.

Add the remaining wine to the skillet. Cook and stir until the wine is bubbling, then pour over the steaks, season, and serve. *Four servings, about 250 calories each.*

FOILED ROAST BEEF WITH SPANISH RICE

How can you "foil" Old Devil Fat? By using aluminum foil as an aid in browning meat or poultry under the broiler, instead of frying it in a skilletful of fat. Once browned, your main course is all wrapped up with other ingredients, then baked in the oven. As a bonus benefit, there are no messy pans to clean up.

The foil-wrap method of cookery is ideal for fat-trimmed round pot roast, one of the lowest-caloried beef choices there is.

3 pounds boneless beef round
1 teaspoon garlic salt
Dash of cayenne pepper
1½ cups tomato juice
1 small package Spanish rice mix
1 can (4 ounces) mushrooms, undrained
1 onion, chopped

Trim all fat from the meat. Lay the meat on a large sheet of heavy-duty aluminum foil and set it in a broiler pan. Brown the meat on one side only under your broiler.

Combine the remaining ingredients and spoon around the meat. Bring up the sides of the foil to seal the roast. Put the pan and the foil-wrapped roast in the oven and bake at 350 degrees until the meat is very tender, about 2 hours. Put the beef on a hot platter and serve, accompanied by the Spanish rice and mushrooms. *Ten servings, 240 calories each.*

ROAST BEEF, HAWAIIAN-STYLE

This dish is a real budget saver, because it's made with an arm roast of beef, one of the so-called "less tender" cuts. Not only does the marinade of pineapple juice and soy sauce add flavor, the acidity of the pineapple juice softens the meat fibers and provides remarkable tenderness. The longer you marinate the meat, the more tender it will be.

About 3 pounds arm roast of beef
1 can (6 ounces) unsweetened pineapple juice
¼ cup Japanese-style soy sauce
2 teaspoons arrowroot or cornstarch
¼ cup cold water

Have the roast well trimmed of fat. Put the roast in a plastic bag and set it in a shallow dish. Combine the pineapple juice and soy sauce and pour into the bag. Secure with twist closure so that all surfaces of the meat are covered with marinade. Refrigerate 8 hours or longer, up to 2 days.

Empty the meat and marinade into a small ovenproof baking dish and place in a slow (275-degree) oven. Insert a meat thermometer into the meat. Bake, uncovered, until the thermometer indicates 140 degrees for rare or 150 to 160 for medium—about 2 hours. Don't overcook!

Drain the liquid from the pan into a tall glass and spoon off all the fat that rises to the surface. Pour the liquid into a saucepan and heat to boiling, then combine the arrowroot and cold water and stir into the simmering liquid. Cook and stir until thickened.

If you wish, brown the surface of the meat briefly under the broiler (not necessary). Slice the meat thinly against the grain and serve with the gravy. *Each four-ounce serving of meat (lean only) has 218 calories; 7 calories per tablespoon of gravy.*

⊷ MAKE-AHEAD YANKEE POT ROAST ⊷

About 4 pounds lean arm pot roast
2 teaspoons salt
Freshly ground pepper
¼ tablespoon polyunsaturated oil
2 bay leaves
1 teaspoon poultry seasoning
2¾ cups water
2 beef bouillon cubes
2 stalks celery, thinly sliced
1 pound turnips, peeled and sliced
2 cups peeled, small white onions, fresh or frozen
1 tablespoon all-purpose flour
1 tablespoon cornstarch

Pick out a very lean piece of meat and trim away all removable fat (four pounds of chuck arm will yield 3 pounds of lean boneless meat), then season the meat with salt and pepper. Heat the oil in a heavy nonstick pot or Dutch oven and brown the meat slowly on all sides. Drain away any remaining fat and add the bay leaves, poultry seasoning, 2½ cups of the water and the bouillon. Cover and simmer over a very low flame for 2 to 3 hours, until the meat is nearly tender. Remove from the range and allow to cool. Put the pot in the refrigerator for several hours or overnight.

About 30 minutes before dinner, remove the pot from the refrigerator and lift off all the hardened fat. Return to the range top and heat to boiling. Add the vegetables, cover, and simmer over low heat for 25 minutes, until the vegetables are tender.

Remove meat and vegetables. Combine the flour, cornstarch, and ¼ cup water into a paste. Stir into the simmering liquid and cook and stir until thickened. Surround the meat with the vegetables and serve with the gravy. *Twelve servings, 229 calories each.*

NOTE: Package single-serving portions of leftover pot roast in small aluminum trays for quick thaw-and-serve homemade frozen dinners. Cover with foil and label with a marking pen. To cook, put, frozen, into a preheated 350-degree oven and bake for 40 minutes.

ᕯᔑ SPANISH POT ROAST WITH FRUIT ᔑᕯ

  2 pounds lean boneless arm beefsteak
1½ cups Sangría or dry red wine
  1 can (16 ounces) tomatoes
  2 onions, chopped
  1 green pepper, chopped
  5 tablespoons currants or raisins
  ¼ cup chopped dried apricots
  ¼ cup chopped black olives
  2 bay leaves
1½ teaspoons dried basil
  1 teaspoon dried thyme
  1 teaspoon dried tarragon

Trim all fat from the meat and discard. Place the meat in a shallow, nonstick ovenproof baking dish and bake in a very hot (450-degree) oven for approximately 20 minutes, until browned. Pour off all fat.

Combine all the remaining ingredients and pour over the meat. Cover the meat loosely with a tent of aluminum foil and lower the heat to 350 degrees, so that the meat just simmers. Cook, covered, about 2 hours or more, until the meat is very tender and the liquid is reduced to a thick, richly flavored sauce. *Eight servings, 226 calories each.*

ᕯᔑ SUPER-SLOW-COOKED POT ROAST ᔑᕯ

Super-slow cooking is ideal for the least-fattening cuts of meat, the ones that are also lowest in cholesterol. The ideal way to slow-cook a pot roast dinner is in your oven in a heavy, covered pot or casserole, with the temperature set low—200 degrees. This way the heat is evenly distributed on all sides of the cooking vessel. (With top-of-the-range cooking, the heat comes only from the bottom. And the uneven heat, difficult to control, can lead to scorching.) Because the temperature is below boiling, none of the moisture evaporates. The meat won't shrink and the vegetables won't turn shapeless and mushy.

6 or 7 carrots
2 potatoes
2 onions
3 pounds boneless round of beef, trimmed of all fat
   Garlic salt and freshly ground pepper
½ cup water, beef bouillon, or red wine

Scrape the carrots and cut into 3-inch lengths. Peel the potatoes and onions; cut in quarters. Put half the vegetables in the bottom of a pot. (Don't choose an oversized pot; it should be at least two-thirds full when all ingredients are added.) Season the meat with garlic salt and pepper and put on top of the vegetables. Add the liquid and the remaining vegetables and cover tightly. Set on the middle rack in the center of your oven. Set the heat at 200 degrees and forget it; dinner will be ready in 8 or 10 hours. Use a bulb-type baster to strain any fat before serving. *Eight servings, 238 calories each.*

VARIATIONS

German Style: Add 3 or 4 medium dill pickles, chopped, and 1 teaspoon dillweed—*245 calories per serving.*

Italian Style: Add 1 cup plain tomato sauce and 1 teaspoon oregano or Italian seasoning. Omit potatoes and carrots—*235 calories per serving.*

French Style: Add 1 cup mushrooms and use the red wine in place of the water. Add a pinch of thyme. Omit the potatoes—*261 calories per serving.*

Skinny Stews and Ragouts

⊷ SHINBONE STROGANOFF ⊶

This is a slim-wallet special, made with shinbone (beef shank) and skim milk soured with lemon juice. Our directions for skimming the fat save you about 400 calories! Put the fat into a measuring cup and prove it for yourself.

2 pounds beef shank, cut into serving pieces
Salt and freshly ground pepper
Water
¼ teaspoon garlic powder
2 teaspoons prepared mustard
1 onion, chopped
1 can (2 ounces) mushroom stems and pieces, undrained
1 cup skim milk
1 tablespoon arrowroot or cornstarch
1 tablespoon lemon juice

Salt and pepper the meat. Put it in a nonstick pot with a tablespoon of water. Heat over a moderate flame, until the water evaporates and the shin beef has begun to brown in its own melted fat, then brown the shin pieces on both sides. Add enough water to cover the shin pieces and stir in the garlic powder, mustard, and onion. Cover and simmer over a very low flame until nearly tender, 1 hour or more. Remove from the heat; cool, then refrigerate for several hours.

About 20 minutes before dinner, remove the pot from the refrigerator and lift off all the hardened fat. Remove and discard the shinbones and any fat. Add the mushrooms, including the liquid. Heat, uncovered, over a high flame, until nearly all the liquid in the pot has evaporated.

Combine the milk and arrowroot and stir into the pot. Cook and stir over a low flame until the sauce is thick and smooth, then stir in the lemon juice. Serve immediately. *Four servings, 247 calories each.*
NOTE: A ¾ cup serving of tender-cooked macaroni for each person will add 116 calories.

SHINNECOCK STEW

2 pounds beef shank, cut into serving pieces
4 teaspoons prepared mustard
2 tablespoons Worcestershire sauce
1 can (10½ ounces) undiluted onion soup
½ cup sherry wine or water
1 can (2 ounces) mushroom stems and pieces, undrained
1 can (16 ounces) carrots, undrained
1 can (8 ounces) small boiled potatoes, undrained

Spread the shin pieces with mustard on both sides. Put them in a nonstick pot and sprinkle liberally with Worcestershire sauce. Heat over a moderate flame, turning frequently, until each piece is nicely browned on both sides in the meat's own melting fat. Add the onion soup and sherry. Drain the liquid from the canned mushrooms, carrots, and potatoes, and add the liquid to the pot, reserving the vegetables. Cover and cook the stew until tender, about 1¼ hours, then remove from the heat. Pour all the liquid into a tall glass and place it in the freezer. Remove the bones and fat from the meat, which will be very tender and break into smaller pieces.

When the broth is sufficiently cooled, remove it from the freezer and lift off the surface fat. Return the meat to the pot with the broth and add the vegetables. Cook, uncovered, for 15 to 20 minutes, until nearly all the moisture has evaporated and the vegetables are nicely glazed with meat juices. *Four servings, 312 calories each.*

⤳ SLIM IRISH STEW ⤳

2 pounds boneless leg of lamb or beef round, trimmed of fat and
    cut in cubes
1 large onion, chopped
1 clove garlic, minced
3 beef bouillon cubes
3 cups boiling water
2 bay leaves
¼ teaspoon freshly grated nutmeg
½ teaspoon dried thyme
2 pounds small carrots, scraped and left whole
2 pounds small white potatoes, peeled

If you wish, the meat may be prebrowned under the broiler or by baking in a very hot oven for 10 to 12 minutes, but prebrowning the meat is not traditional.

Combine all the ingredients except the carrots and potatoes in an ovenproof casserole or heavy Dutch oven. Stir together, then cover and bake in a preheated 325-degree oven, or simmer on top of the range, until tender, about 2½ hours. Add water if needed.

When the meat is tender, remove the pot from the heat and skim off all the fat. Add the vegetables, cover, and continue to cook until tender, about 20 minutes. *Eight servings, 275 calories each.*

To Corn a Piece of Beef

Low-calorie corned beef? Most corned beef is pickled beef brisket. Brisket weighs in at 1,300 calories or more per pound, while lean beef round is less than 650, and tastes exactly like the corned beef brisket, except it's much leaner. Here's the basic rule for making your own:

⊷ HOME-CORNED BEEF ⊱

1 cup coarse salt
2 quarts water
½ teaspoon saltpeter
2 tablespoons sugar
2 teaspoons mixed pickling spices
5 bay leaves
3 cloves of garlic
3 to 4 pounds beef round

Combine the salt, water, saltpeter, sugar, pickling spices, and bay leaves in a saucepan. Heat to boiling, then cool and add the garlic. Place the round of beef in a ceramic crock or glass bowl and pour on the marinade; be sure the meat is completely submerged. Cover tightly and refrigerate 2 to 3 weeks, turning occasionally. Cook, of course, before serving.

⊷ NOVA SCOTIA CORNED BEEF ⊱

To corn beef, Nova Scotia style, here's a recipe from Marie Nightingale, author of the charming cookbook *Out of Old Nova Scotia Kitchens*.* Much milder than the corned beef we're accustomed to, this pickled beef has the advantage of speed.

PICKLING BRINE:
8 cups water
1 cup salt
3 tablespoons sugar
1 bay leaf
6 peppercorns
1 clove garlic
2 teaspoons pickling spices

Mix together and cover a beef round. Marinate in the refrigerator for 2 to 4 days before cooking.

* New York: Scribner's, 1971.

SKINNY ST. PATRICK'S DAY
CORNED BEEF AND CABBAGE

3 to 4 pounds corned beef round, homemade (see page 76) if
    preferred
2 to 3 cloves garlic, minced
3 bay leaves
    Water to cover
1 large head cabbage, cut in wedges

Put all the ingredients except the cabbage in a large pot and heat to
boiling. Skim the surface, then cover and simmer over low heat until nearly
tender, about 1 hour per pound. Remove the meat and skim off all the fat
from surface (this is important, for cabbage will absorb fat!). Add the cabbage and simmer until tender but firm, about 10 minutes. *One serving (4
ounces corned beef and ½ cup cabbage) is 250 calories.*

REUBEN SANDWICH

A "Reuben," as any New Yorker can tell you, is a yummy tummy-filler—
corned beef, Swiss cheese, and sauerkraut on rye. No fingers for this sandwich
—it's strictly meal-sized knife-and-fork fare.

1 slice thin rye bread, toasted
    Mustard
⅓ cup well-drained sauerkraut
2 ounces cooked corned beef round
2 thin slices (1 ounce) processed Swiss cheese

Spread the rye toast with mustard and heap with sauerkraut. Add the meat
and top with cheese. Broil 5 to 6 minutes. *One serving, about 285 calories.*

⊷§ REUBEN CHEESEBURGERS §⊷

1 **can (12 ounces) corned beef, or leftover corned beef round**
½ **slice rye bread**
1 **egg, lightly beaten**
4 **slices (2 ounces) processed Swiss cheese**

Flake the contents of the can with a fork, or put leftover cooked meat through a food mill. Moisten the bread with water, then squeeze dry. Combine the meat, bread, and egg; blend and shape into 4 patties. Quick-bake in a preheated 450-degree oven for 4 to 5 minutes, then top each with a slice of cheese and continue to heat only until the cheese is melted.

Four servings, 250 calories each.

6
HAMBURGERS, MEATBALLS, MEAT LOAVES, AND SKILLET DISHES

If you're the typical American, you eat fifty-five pounds of hamburger a year. The difference between fat hamburger and lean adds up to about 35,750 calories every twelve months. Now if you can manage to cut that number of calories from your food intake, you'd lose about ten pounds.

And you start by refusing to buy fat hamburger!

Price should be some guide, but all too often it isn't. In many cases, the only real difference between "ground beef," "ground chuck," and "ground round" is price. Premium-priced "ground round" and "ground sirloin" samples are often close to 30 percent fat, the legal federal limit for ground beef. Many, but not all, states have standards, too, but they're difficult to police and enforce.

Adding extra fat to ground meat seems to be a common practice, even in meats labeled "low-calorie" or "diet lean." In the trade journal, *Supermarketing*, meat columnist Clifford G. Bowes points out that "hardly anyone makes this product 100 percent lean . . . most retailers add five to ten percent fat. This not only lowers cost but improves palatability."

Adding fat to meat labeled "low-calorie" in the guise of "improving palatability" would be a little like putting sugar in diabetic ice cream . . . to improve smoothness. Fat adds no flavor. If meat is unpalatable, it's because it wasn't palatable to begin with. Overcooking, not leanness, makes for a dried-out hamburger.

A chuck or arm roast, if well trimmed of surface fat, will probably net you a ground hamburger with a fat content of 10 to 15 percent or less. For example:

GROUND BEEF CONTENT

Fat Content (%)	Calories Per Lb.	Grams of Protein
0	653	98
14	1,012	88
18	1,166	85
30	1,597	73
41	1,814	67
45	2,014	62

HOW TO COOK LEAN HAMBURGER

Lean burgers will be tender and moist if you:

AVOID OVERHANDLING! To make 4 quarter-pound hamburgers from a 1-pound package, simply cut it in quarters with a knife and then gently "nudge" the corners into shape. Don't pat, don't press.

MIX CAREFULLY! Combining chopped meat with other ingredients? Simply toss lightly with a fork. Caress the meat into shape. Don't squeeze!

GIVE IT THE ICE TREATMENT! Shape burgers around ice cubes. Or better yet, mix chopped meat with cracked or shaved ice, about ½ cup per pound (to crack ice, wrap cubes in a clean dishtowel and bang them against a hard surface). In a hurry? Just add ice water.

STRETCH BURGERS WITH MOIST INGREDIENTS! Chopped mushrooms, green pepper, sliced onion, minced celery, shredded carrots, snipped parsley, are all flavor (and vitamin!) adders that pad out burgers without padding your hips. Try diet applesauce, crushed juice-packed pineapple, drained beansprouts for flavor variety. Much better than bread crumbs!

STRETCH THEM WITH SOY! In the last year or so, food manufacturers have come up with a new product that has revolutionized meat loaf making. Old recipes, like old values, are due for reevaluation. What is this recipe wrecker?

"Meat extender," also known as "textured soy protein" or "texturized vegetable protein." Whatever it's called, the new product consists of dry granules of spun soy meant to be mixed with ground meat. When added to hamburger, the new meat extender looks, cooks, and tastes like ground meat, only more of it! It stretches both the quantity and the nutritional quality of meat, so that one pound of hamburger can serve six instead of four. It's a bargain, not only in cost but calories and cholesterol as well.

The new meat extenders help hamburger hold together so well that neither eggs nor bread crumbs are needed to make a meat loaf. Also, the meat juices are retained, so your meat loaf remains extra moist.

Don't forget this high-protein beef stretcher can also lend a helping hand to lamb, pork, or veal.

BASTE WITH DIET DRESSING! Try different types. Italian style adds lots of spice but little calories. Diet blue cheese turns chopped meat into a "Roquefortburger." Or try a mixture of diet Caesar dressing and sherry wine, equal parts.

BROILER-BROWN CHOPPED MEAT! Brown chopped meat under the broiler for casserole dishes—less calories than browning hamburger in a skillet.

NEVER OVERBROIL! Broiled hamburgers require the same split-second timing as perfectly cooked steak, so make sure everything else is dinner-ready before you get started. Broiled burgers are best served a shade of pink inside.

HAMBURGER "HELPERS"

⋙ Oven-brown the meatballs while you make the sauce. A 400-degree oven will brown and cook meatballs in 15 to 20 minutes with no turning.

⋙ For extra-juicy, extra-nutritious hamburgers, add ¼ cup evaporated skim milk per pound of meat before shaping.

⋙ Stock your freezer with a supply of already browned and seasoned lean hamburger, rolled in plastic wrap to keep it loose. Now you have a head start on chili, sloppy Joes, or spaghetti sauce.

⋙ Shape meat loaf into individual-serving-sized loaves. Mini-meat loaves will be done in about half the time.

⋙ Add a few drops of bottled liquid smoke for cookout flavor.

⋙ For meatballs, pat lean hamburger flat, mark and cut in squares.

⋙ For quick stew, brown lean hamburger, add canned tomatoes, sliced carrots, onions, and celery. Simmer just till vegetables are tender—less than a half an hour.

⋙ Make skinny cheeseburgers Italian style; add crushed oregano to the meat, use part-skim mozzarella cheese for toppers.

⋙ HAMBURGERS—PLAIN AND OTHERWISE ⋙

In this age of freezer living, you can always have a short-order hamburger lunch or supper at home, if you're a plan-ahead shopper. On your next supermarket trip, why not order a few extra pounds of hamburger, with lunch in mind? When you get home, unwrap the meat and divide it into quarter-pound portions. It's a simple, easy arithmetic problem. For example, 1 pound equals 4 hamburgers; 1½ pounds equals 6 hamburgers; 3 pounds equals 12 hamburgers, and so forth.

Line a cookie tin or other shallow roasting pan with foil or plastic wrap and arrange your quarter-pound patties in a single layer. Then cover and freeze. Or wrap each patty separately in plastic. Or bag each one in a small, sandwich-sized plastic bag. Now you're all set whenever the hankering for a hamburger hits you.

A still-frozen hamburger can be slow-broiled to the right shade of inner pinkness in about 12 minutes. But not too close to the heat, or it will be charcoaled on the outside and red in the middle. Or take your hamburger out of the freezer an hour before mealtime and it will be thawed out and pan ready when the noon or suppertime whistle blows. One-quarter pound of ground round, lean only, will be about 150 calories. Add a few pickles, the most aggressive onion slice you can find, a hollowed-out hamburger roll and a dash of catsup for a decalorized version of the all-American lunch, at less than 300 calories.

VARIATIONS

Inside-out Cheeseburger: Divide a defrosted hamburger patty in half. Top one half with 2 tablespoons finely chopped American or Cheddar cheese. Dot with ½ teaspoon mustard (optional). Cover with the remaining half of the patty and seal the edges. Broil 4 inches from the source of heat for 3 minutes; sprinkle with salt and pepper. Turn and broil 3 minutes longer for medium doneness. *Only 225 calories.*

Burger with Wine Sauce: Pan-fry a defrosted patty in a nonstick skillet (no fat) for about 3 minutes on each side for medium doneness. Sprinkle with salt and pepper. Remove the patty from the pan. Add 2 tablespoons dry red wine and stir to deglaze the pan. Add an undrained 3-ounce can of sliced mushrooms; simmer two minutes. Pour over the burger and devour. *Only 212 calories.*

Pronto Pizzaburger: Broil a quarter-pound burger (6 minutes each side if frozen, 3 if defrosted). Top with 1 thin slice (½ ounce) part-skim mozzarella cheese, 1 tablespoon catsup, and a pinch of oregano. Return to the broiler just until the cheese melts. *Only 210 calories.*

⊷§ DEVILED HAMBURGERS ષ્ચ

1 can (4½ ounces) deviled ham
1 pound beef round, trimmed of fat and ground
2 tablespoons chili sauce
½ teaspoon salt
   Pickle slices

In a medium mixing bowl, thoroughly combine the deviled ham, beef, chili sauce, and salt. Shape into 6 patties, then broil under moderate heat for about 5 minutes on each side. Garnish with pickle slices and serve. *Six servings, 156 calories each.*

◄§ BEEFBURGERS BOURGUIGNON §►

¼ cup cracked ice (see note below)
1 pound round, trimmed of fat and ground
1 clove garlic, finely chopped
1 teaspoon salt
¼ teaspoon coarsely ground pepper
2 teaspoons polyunsaturated oil
½ pound fresh mushrooms, sliced
½ cup Burgundy wine
⅓ cup cold water
1 tablespoon all-purpose flour
¼ teaspoon dried sage
   Chopped fresh parsley

Combine the ice, ground meat, garlic, salt, and pepper and toss lightly. Shape into 4 flat patties, then brown in 1 teaspoon of the oil in a nonstick skillet over high heat, turning once. Remove to a platter.

Add the second teaspoon of oil and 2 tablespoons of the wine to the skillet. Add the mushrooms. Cook and stir over high heat until the mushrooms are lightly browned.

Stir the remaining wine, the water, flour, and sage together and add to the skillet. Cook and stir over moderate heat until the sauce thickens and bubbles, then add the meat patties and cook until heated through. Sprinkle with chopped fresh parsley and serve. *Four servings, 206 calories each.*

NOTE: To crack ice, put 3 or 4 ice cubes in a clean dishtowel and rap the cubes against a hard surface.

◄§ FLEMISH HAMBURGERS §►

2 pounds beef round, trimmed of fat and ground
   Salt and freshly ground pepper
½ teaspoon poultry seasoning
1 cup low-calorie beer
4 onions, thinly sliced
½ teaspoon cornstarch
2 tablespoons cold water
   Sugar substitute equal to 2 teaspoons sugar

Shape the meat into 8 patties. Brown slowly in a nonstick skillet, with no fat added. Drain well, then add the seasonings, beer, and onions. Cover and cook for 6 minutes. Blend the cornstarch and water together and stir into the skillet until thickened. Remove from the heat and stir in the sugar substitute. Serve immediately. *Eight servings, 180 calories each.*

⋅§ HAMBURGER CHOP SUEY §⋅

1½   pounds bottom round, trimmed of fat and ground
 2   tablespoons soy sauce
 1   large onion, thinly sliced
 1   tablespoon vegetable oil
 1   can (16 ounces) mixed Chinese vegetables, drained
 1   can (10½ ounces) beef broth, skimmed of fat
 2   tablespoons arrowroot or cornstarch

Lightly shape the meat into 18 tiny meatballs. Combine the meatballs, soy sauce, onion, and oil in a large nonstick skillet over high heat. Gently cook and stir until the moisture evaporates and the meat and onions begin to brown in the remaining oil. Add the drained Chinese vegetables and three-quarters of the can of beef broth. Cover and cook 2 minutes, until the onion is tender crisp. Stir the remaining broth and arrowroot together and stir into the skillet, until the sauce thickens and bubbles. Serve with additional soy sauce and Parsleyed Instant Rice (see below). *Six servings, 210 calories each.*

Parsleyed Instant Rice: Combine 1 tablespoon minced fresh parsley, 1 cup instant rice, and 1 cup boiling water. Cover tightly and leave until serving time. *Six servings, 68 calories each.*

⋅§ SAVORY POTTED MEATBALLS §⋅

Str-r-retch 1 pound of hamburger to serve six by using an envelope of texturized soy protein meat extender.

 1   pound lean beef round, trimmed of fat and ground
⅔   cup water
 1   envelope textured soy protein meat extender
    Polyunsaturated oil or spray-on vegetable coating
 1   onion, chopped
1½   cups tomato juice
½   cup unsweetened applesauce
 1   tablespoon cider vinegar

Combine the beef, water, and meat extender according to package directions. Shape into 12 meatballs.

Wipe a nonstick skillet lightly with oil or spray with vegetable coating for no-fat frying. Brown the meatballs slowly over a moderate flame, turning carefully. Add the chopped onion and cook briefly, then stir the remaining ingredients together and add to the pot. Simmer, uncovered, for 15 minutes, until most of the liquid evaporates into a thick sauce. *Six servings, 155 calories each.*

◄§ SWEDISH MEATBALLS §►

1   slice protein bread
¼   cup skim milk
1   tablespoon butter or margarine
1   onion, chopped
1   pound lean beef, trimmed of fat and ground
1   egg, beaten
3   tablespoons ice water
1   teaspoon salt
¼   teaspoon freshly ground pepper
⅛   teaspoon freshly grated nutmeg
½   cup dry white wine
⅓   cup buttermilk

Soak the bread in the milk and set aside. Melt the butter in a skillet and sauté the onion for 5 minutes. Squeeze the soaked bread dry and combine with the onions, meat, egg, water, and seasoning. Shape into 12 meatballs. Brown the meatballs on all sides in the skillet, then transfer to a hot platter. Pour the wine into the skillet, stir well; then, stirring vigorously, add the buttermilk. Cook and stir, but do not boil. When well blended, pour over the meatballs. *Six servings, 275 calories each.*

◄§ GERMAN MEATBALLS §►

(Königsburger Klops)

Simmered in a sauce spiked with capers or relish, these zesty lemon-accented gems have so much flavor it's hard to imagine that they're so low in calories. But "klops" aren't prefried in fat as Swedish meatballs are, and there's no calorific heavy cream in the gravy. German meatballs blend beef with veal— and veal is the leanest meat there is.

MEATBALLS:

- 1 slice protein bread
  Water
- 2 eggs, well beaten
- ¾ pound lean veal rump, trimmed of fat and ground
- ¾ pound lean beef round, trimmed of fat and ground
- ¼ cup minced onion
- ¼ cup chopped fresh parsley
- 1½ teaspoons salt
- ½ teaspoon freshly ground pepper
  Pinch of paprika
- 1 tablespoon lemon juice
- ¼ teaspoon grated lemon rind
- 1 tablespoon Worcestershire sauce

SAUCE:

- 3 beef bouillon cubes
- 3 cups boiling water
- 3 tablespoons all-purpose flour
- ¼ cup cold water
- 3 tablespoons capers or hamburger relish

Start the meatballs by soaking the bread in a little water; wring out well. Combine the bread with the eggs, meat, onion, parsley, salt, pepper, paprika, lemon juice, lemon rind, and Worcestershire. Mix well and shape into 2-inch-round meatballs.

Dissolve the bouillon in the boiling water in a large skillet. Drop the meatballs into the simmering liquid and cook, covered, for 15 minutes. Remove the meatballs and skim off the fat, if any. Mix the flour and cold water to form a paste and stir it into the simmering liquid. When the sauce thickens, return the meatballs to the skillet and correct the seasoning, adding the capers and more Worcestershire, if desired. *Six ample dinner-sized servings, 224 calories each.*

VARIATION

Extra Low-Fat Version: Simmer the meatballs in plain water, then discard the water. Heat 3 cups beef bouillon, or 2 cups bouillon and 1 cup vegetable-tomato juice. Stir in the flour paste and capers, as in the recipe above, and add the meatballs.

NOTE: A serving of ½ cup cooked long-grain rice per person adds 84 calories.

ITALIAN SPINACH MEATBALLS

1 package (10 ounces) frozen chopped spinach
1 pound beef round, trimmed of fat and ground
1 onion, minced
1 egg
1 teaspoon salt
Pinch of freshly ground pepper
½ teaspoon oregano or Italian seasoning
1 can (11 ounces) plain tomato sauce (see note below)

Defrost the spinach and press out extra moisture. Combine with all the other ingredients except the tomato sauce and shape into 8 meatballs. Arrange in a shallow baking dish and cover with the tomato sauce. Bake in a preheated 350 degree oven for 30 minutes. Or simmer, covered, on top of the range. *Four servings, 237 calories each.*

NOTE: The sauce may be diluted with 2 or 3 tablespoons of dry wine or water and seasoned with minced onion and oregano, if you wish.

SPICY INDIAN MEATBALLS

1 pound beef round, trimmed of fat and ground
2 teaspoons salt
½ teaspoon Tabasco
½ cup plain yogurt
½ teaspoon ground ginger
¼ teaspoon instant minced onion
2 teaspoons ground coriander
½ teaspoon ground turmeric
1 teaspoon poppy seeds
⅛ teaspoon garlic powder

Combine the ground beef, 1 teaspoon of the salt, and ¼ teaspoon of the Tabasco. Shape into 1-inch meatballs. Blend the yogurt with the remaining ingredients and roll the meatballs in the mixture. Broil, 4 inches from the heat, for 5 to 6 minutes, or until done. *Four main-dish servings, 165 calories each; eight appetizer servings, 82 calories each.*

SAUERBRATEN MEATBALLS

Sauerbraten meatballs make a great "company" dinner—at 221 calories or less a serving. Or—you can make the meatballs extra small and serve them as pretty party appetizers.

MEATBALLS:

1½ **pounds extra-lean beef round, trimmed of fat and ground**
  1 **egg**
  1 **small onion, minced**
    Pinch of freshly ground pepper
    Pinch of dried thyme
    Pinch of ground cloves
1½ **teaspoons garlic salt**

GRAVY:

  2 **cups water**
  3 **tablespoons vinegar**
  3 **tablespoons catsup**
  2 **teaspoons brown gravy coloring**
 ½ **teaspoon ground cloves**
  1 **bay leaf**
  2 **tablespoons brown sugar**
 ½ **teaspoon ground ginger**
  2 **tablespoons white raisins (optional)**
    Salt and freshly ground pepper
  3 **tablespoons all-purpose flour combined with ¼ cup cold water**

Combine the meatball ingredients and toss lightly to mix. Shape into meatballs, spread on a shallow pan, and place in a preheated broiler. Broil under highest heat, turning once, until browned on both sides.

In a saucepan, combine all the gravy ingredients except the flour and water. Heat to boiling and add the meatballs, then cover and simmer over low heat for 15 minutes. Uncover and stir in the flour and water mixture. Continue to simmer over low heat until the liquid is gravy thick. Add salt and pepper to taste and skim off any fat before serving. *Six servings, 221 calories each.*

NOTE: For a German-style dinner that only *seems* fattening, serve unbuttered tiny potatoes topped with the sauerbraten sauce, green beans with diet margarine, and a glass of well-chilled low-calorie, low-carbohydrate beer—all for 400 calories!

VARIATION

Extra-Lo-Cal Sauerbraten Meatballs: If you're on a low-sugar diet or would like to save even more calories, use dietetic catsup and omit the raisins, sugar, and brown gravy coloring. Just before serving, stir in liquid or granulated sugar substitute to taste, and, for a darker gravy, add soy sauce or Worcestershire sauce. (There is now a granulated brown sugar substitute in the market that's ideal for this recipe.) *Only 189 calories per serving.*

·§ HAMBURGER PIZZA §·

If you are one of those people who could "make a meal of pizza," have we got a treat for you! Not the bready, greasy snack pizza, but a main-course dish made with protein-rich hamburger meat. The hamburger becomes the "crust" by simply being shaped to fit a pie pan—including the rim—then filled with the familiar tomato-cheese-spice topping that everybody loves.

1½ **pounds lean beef, trimmed of all fat and ground**
 1 **egg**
 1 **teaspoon garlic salt**
 ¼ **cup minced onion**
 1 **can (8 ounces) plain tomato sauce**
 1 **cup (4 ounces) part-skim shredded mozzarella or pizza cheese**
 ½ **teaspoon oregano or Italian seasoning**

Combine the beef, egg, garlic salt, minced onion, and 2 tablespoons of the tomato sauce. Toss lightly in a large, nonstick pie pan. Flatten out the meat mixture to line the bottom and sides, then bake in a preheated hot (450-degree) oven for 10 to 12 minutes, until browned.

Remove from the oven and pour on the remaining tomato sauce. Sprinkle with cheese and oregano and return to the oven for an additional 5 to 7 minutes. To serve, cut into pie-shaped wedges. *Six servings, 194 calories each.*

Mini-Calorie Meat Loaf Recipes

Sometimes a penny-wise meat loaf is "pound foolish," packed with extra calories in an effort to make the meat go further. For example, stuffing a meat loaf with bread crumbs, rice, or other starchy fillers "to keep it from shrinking." Bready fillers keep a meat loaf from shrinking, all right—they act as a blotter to sop up all the melting grease that might otherwise drain into the roasting pan out of harm's way. They also add nonprotein "junk" calories to your main course. Every tablespoon of extra fat is 100 calories you might prefer to spend on something else—dessert, for example.

The making of a memorable meat loaf really begins in the butcher shop, so take your time and pick out a lean piece of beef—round, sirloin, or even chuck if it seems lean, or at least trimmable of fat (fat around the edges, not all through it). Have the butcher whack away every last greasy glob and then grind up the lean. What you'll get back is the richest, reddest, beefiest hamburger you've ever seen, with the pieces of fat off to the side, ready to be tossed to the birds if it happens to be winter.

There are probably as many meat loaf recipes as there are cooks to make them, which is what makes meat loaf so interesting. Here are some flavorful blends, all of which are oven baked for 1 hour at 325 degrees.

❦ MEAT LOAF WITH HORSERADISH ❧

1½ pounds lean beef round, trimmed of fat and ground
2 eggs, beaten
1 onion, chopped
1 tablespoon horseradish
1 teaspoon dry mustard
1 cup catsup
2 stalks celery, minced
1 tablespoon chopped fresh parsley
2 carrots, grated
⅓ cup chopped green pepper
   Garlic salt, salt, and pepper to taste

Combine all the ingredients, shape into a loaf, place in a loaf pan and bake at 325 degrees for 1 hour. *Six servings, 290 calories each.*

❦ EASY MEAT LOAF ❧

1½ pounds ground lean beef
1 egg, beaten
4 tablespoons catsup
3 tablespoons grated onion
3 tablespoons water
   Salt, pepper, and garlic salt to taste
3 tablespoons chili sauce or catsup
1 tablespoon bread crumbs

Combine all the ingredients except the chili sauce and bread crumbs. Shape into a loaf and place in a loaf pan. Spread the top with the chili sauce and sprinkle with the bread crumbs, then bake at 325 degrees for 1 hour. *Four servings, 180 calories each.*

❦ EASY EGGLESS MEAT LOAF ❧

1½ pounds lean beef round, trimmed of fat and ground
½ cup bread crumbs
2 onions, chopped
1 can (16 ounces) tomatoes, drained
1 clove garlic, minced
   Salt and freshly ground pepper
3 tablespoons catsup

Combine all the ingredients except the catsup and shape into a loaf. Place in a loaf pan and spread the top with the catsup, then bake at 325 degrees for 1 hour. *Six servings, 270 calories each.*

✑ ITALIAN MEAT LOAF PIE ✐

Did you ever make a meat loaf in a skillet? Despite its saucy Italian flavor and middle layer of melting mozzarella cheese, this jiffy main course is calorie shy—only 223 per serving. Italian Meat Loaf Pie is made with extra lean beef round and no bread crumbs—save your starch calories for spaghetti.

¾ **pound lean beef round, trimmed of fat and ground**
1 **egg**
1½ **teaspoons garlic salt**
½ **teaspoon freshly ground pepper**
¼ **cup minced onion**
1 **teaspoon oregano**
2 **teaspoons olive oil**
¾ **cup (3 ounces) shredded part-skim mozzarella cheese**

Combined the meat with the egg, garlic salt, pepper, minced onion, and oregano. Divide the meat mixture into two equal parts.

Use an 8-inch nonstick skillet. Coat the bottom with the olive oil, then put half the meat in the skillet and pat in lightly to cover the bottom. Sprinkle on the cheese. Cover the cheese with the remaining meat, patting lightly so that the cheese is completely covered.

Cook quickly over a high flame. When the bottom is well browned, cut into 4 pie-shaped slices. Turn each wedge over carefully and continue cooking until well browned and the cheese is melted. *Four servings, 223 calories each.*

VARIATION

Meat Loaf Pie with Spaghetti: Prepare the meat loaf pie as in the recipe above. When both sides are well browned, pour on 1½ cups of plain tomato sauce diluted with ¼ cup water. Sprinkle on additional garlic salt and oregano, then cover the skillet and simmer for 8 to 10 minutes. Spoon the sauce over the meat frequently as it cooks.

Serve each wedge with ½ cupful of tender-cooked spaghetti. (Spaghetti cooked until tender, 15 to 18 minutes, is only 155 calories a cupful. Firm spaghetti, cooked only 8-10 minutes, is 210 calories a cupful.) *Four servings, 325 calories each.*

⊰ SEABURY FARMS MEAT LOAF ⊱

3 cups high-protein cereal
1 cup whole bran cereal
1 cup skim milk
2 eggs
1½ pounds beef round, trimmed of all fat and ground
2 teaspoons salt
1 clove garlic, minced (optional)
2 teaspoons Worcestershire sauce
1 cup grated raw carrot
½ cup chopped onion
¼ cup chopped fresh parsley

Combine the protein cereal, bran, and milk, then stir in the eggs. Combine with the remaining ingredients and mix lightly. Shape into a loaf and bake 1 hour at 350 degrees. *Ten servings, 171 calories each.*

Stuffed Meat Loaf

Packing a savory filling in the middle of a meat loaf is one way to add dash to this otherwise all-too-familiar dish. Despite its glamour, stuffed meat loaf is a budget sparer. And if you choose extra-nutritious, low-calorie ingredients, your surprise-in-the-middle meat loaf can be slimming as well.

Here's how to stuff a meat loaf:

Put two-thirds of the meat in a loaf pan. Form a well in the middle of the meat. Now add your filling. Make a "lid" out of the remaining meat and cover over the filling. Flatten out the meat, invert the loaf pan onto a baking tray, and lift off the loaf pan. Your meat loaf will have the loaf shape without having to be baked in a loaf pan.

⊰ MEAT LOAF WITH STROGANOFF STUFFING ⊱

MEAT LOAF:
1½ pounds beef round, trimmed of fat and ground
1 egg, beaten
½ cup buttermilk
1 teaspoon salt
Pinch of freshly ground pepper
1 tablespoon Worcestershire sauce
1 tablespoon prepared mustard

FILLING:
> 1 can (4 ounces) mushroom stems and pieces, drained
> 6 tablespoons minced onion
> ½ cup buttermilk
> ½ teaspoon salt

Combine the meat loaf ingredients and toss lightly to mix. Place part of the mixture in a loaf pan and make a well in the center. Combine the filling ingredients and spoon onto the meat loaf. Cover with the remaining meat mixture and invert as directed on page 92. Bake in a 350-degree oven for 1 hour. *Six servings, 198 calories each.*

✑ LASAGNE-STUFFED MEAT LOAF ✑

MEAT LOAF:
> 2 pounds beef round, trimmed of fat and ground
> 1 can (8 ounces) tomato sauce with onion
> 1½ teaspoons garlic salt
> 1 teaspoon oregano

FILLING:
> 1½ cups pot cheese
> 1 egg
> ½ teaspoon salt

Combine meat loaf ingredients. Place part of the mixture in a loaf pan and form a well. Combine the filling ingredients and add to the well. Cover with remaining meat and invert as directed on page 92. Bake at 350 degrees for one hour. *Eight servings, 203 calories each.*

NOTE: If you wish, heat 2 cups of plain or onion tomato sauce to serve with your meat loaf. Look for a brand that lists no oil or sugar in the ingredients. Plain tomato sauce is 64 calories a cupful, according to one of the best-selling brands. (Canned spaghetti sauce is much higher!)

✑ BLENDER-EASY MEAT LOAF ✑

Minced vegetables are the perfect meat loaf stretcher, far better than empty-caloried bread crumbs. To mince vegetables in your blender, cut them up in big chunks and then add them to the blender container, a little at a time, along with ½ cup or so of cold water. Turn the blender on and off several times, just enough to chop the contents. (If you leave the blender on too long, you'll wind up with a puree!) Drain the vegetables through a colander, pressing out the excess moisture. Save the water to use in diluting your sauce or gravy, if you make one. Adding lots of minced vegetables helps to keep a meat loaf moist.

Here's my favorite Slim Gourmet meat loaf. It makes eight generous servings at only 181 calories each. It includes a lot more vegetables than most recipes, but no eggs and no starchy fillers. The flavor's so hearty that everyone loves it, dieting or not!

    1 large onion
    1 clove garlic, peeled
    3 large stalks celery, including leaves
    1 large or 2 small green peppers
    2 pounds extra-lean round, trimmed of fat and ground
    1 can (6 ounces) tomato paste
    2 teaspoons salt
    ¼ teaspoon freshly ground pepper

Cut the vegetables in big chunks and mince in your blender, adding a little cold water. Strain the vegetables and press out the moisture.

Add ⅔ cup of the tomato paste to the chopped beef. Add the minced vegetables and seasoning and toss lightly, combining well. Shape the meat into an oval loaf and place on a rack in a baking pan. Stir a little water into the remaining tomato paste and use this as a baste.

Bake the loaf in a preheated 350-degree oven for 1 hour, basting occasionally. *Eight servings, 181 calories each.*

◄§ DUTCH MEAT LOAF ϐ►

MEAT LOAF:
    ½ cup sliced onion
    1 egg, beaten
    1½ pounds beef round, trimmed of fat and ground
    1½ teaspoons salt
    ¼ teaspoon freshly ground pepper
    1 teaspoon Worcestershire sauce
    1 teaspoon dry mustard
    ½ cup plain tomato sauce

SAUCE:
    2 tablespoons vinegar
    2 teaspoons dry mustard
    ½ cup plain tomato sauce
    2 tablespoons brown sugar or brown sugar substitute
    ½ cup water

Combine the meat loaf ingredients and mix together lightly but thoroughly with a fork. Pack lightly into a loaf pan. Mix together the sauce ingredients and pour over the meat loaf. Bake, uncovered, at 350 degrees for 1½ hours, then slice and serve. *Six servings, 189 calories each (with sugar); 173 calories (with sugar substitute).*

◄§ GREEK MEAT LOAF §►

½ cup chopped onion
1 tablespoon diet margarine
½ cup shredded carrot
1 small eggplant (about 1 pound), trimmed, peeled and shredded
2 cloves garlic, minced
2 pounds beef round, trimmed of fat and ground
2 eggs
2 medium tomatoes, peeled and finely diced (1 cup)
1 tablespoon salt
½ teaspoon ground cinnamon
¼ teaspoon freshly ground pepper
2 tablespoons lemon juice

Sauté the onion in the margarine in a nonstick skillet for 3 minutes, then stir in the carrot, eggplant, and garlic. Cook for 5 minutes, covered, or until the vegetables are wilted. Combine the cooked vegetables with the remaining ingredients in a large bowl, mixing lightly. Shape into a loaf and bake in a moderate (350-degree) oven for 1 hour. *Eight servings, 203 calories each.*

◄§ NO-EGG MEAT LOAF §►

Evaporated skim milk can serve the same function as eggs in a meat loaf mixture, helping to bind the ingredients together. Moreover, a 13-ounce can of evaporated skim milk provides about 25 grams of protein—so it's like adding another quarter pound of meat to your meat loaf, without paying the meat prices. An egg adds only seven grams of protein.

To get the most nutrition and the least amount of fat and calories, be sure to use evaporated skim milk, which has all the protein and calcium benefits for only half the calories per can.

6 slices stale diet protein bread
2 pounds beef round, trimmed of fat and ground
1 onion, minced
1 teaspoon dried thyme
¼ teaspoon freshly ground pepper
2 teaspoons salt or garlic salt
1 can (13 ounces) evaporated skim milk
1 can (8 ounces) plain tomato sauce (see note below)

If the bread isn't quite dry enough, spread it on a cookie sheet and dry it out in a warm oven. Or toast it, then put the bread into a plastic bag and roll over it with a rolling pin to make crumbs. Or put the slices in your blender, a few at a time. Cover and whir into crumbs.

Combine the bread crumbs with all the other ingredients except the tomato sauce. Mix lightly but thoroughly, then shape into a loaf in a shallow baking pan.

Bake in a preheated 350-degree oven for 1 to 1¼ hours. Drain off the fat, if any, then spoon on the canned tomato sauce and bake 10 or 15 minutes longer. Slice into thin slices and serve with the pan sauce. *Ten servings, 187 calories each.*

NOTE: Read the label on your canned tomato sauce and choose a brand that lists no fat, oil, or shortening among the ingredients.

Chill leftovers and save for sandwiches. Because this meat loaf is non-greasy, it's just as good cold. Single-size servings can be wrapped in foil and frozen for future heat-and-serve meals.

✑ ITALIAN-STYLE MEAT LOAF—PLUS ༀ

1½ pounds beef round, trimmed of fat and ground
½ cup textured soy protein meat extender
½ cup water
1 can (6 ounces) tomato paste
½ cup chopped onion
½ cup chopped pepper
¼ teaspoon minced garlic
¼ teaspoon oregano or Italian seasoning
    Dash of Tabasco
    Salt and freshly ground pepper

Combine all the ingredients and toss lightly, adding a full teaspoon of salt if the meat extender is unseasoned. Pile into a shallow 13 × 9-inch nonstick roasting pan and shape gently into an oval loaf. Bake in a 325-degree oven for 1 hour, then remove to a hot platter.

To the fat-free drippings in the pan, add a few tablespoons of boiling water and scrape well. Pour over the meat loaf and serve. *Eight servings, 151 calories each.*

To Make Cabbage Rolls

Cabbage is low in calories (only 34 a cupful) and high in appetite-appeasing bulk. The basic recipe below can be used for a wide variety of stuffings and sauces, an excellent opportunity to give your imagination—and your larder of leftovers—a workout.

◄§ CABBAGE ROLLS §►

Cook a head of cabbage in boiling water for 15 minutes or so, then drain and separate the leaves. Or core the raw head and peel off the leaves. Soften each leaf in a pot of boiling water for 3 minutes.

Fill each leaf with 2 tablespoons of stuffing. Roll up, tucking in the ends. Secure the rolls with toothpicks and place, in one layer, in an ovenproof casserole. (Or simply place the rolls open side down and they'll stay together.) Add your sauce. Then cover and bake in a preheated 350-degree oven for 1 hour, or simmer on the range for 45 minutes.

◄§ ANNE HASLINGER'S DUTCH CABBAGE ROLLS* §►

1 head cabbage

FILLING:
  1 onion, chopped
  2 teaspoons diet margarine
  2 pounds lean beef round, trimmed of fat and ground
  2 teaspoons salt
  1 teaspoon coarsely ground pepper
  1 egg
  1 teaspoon poppy seeds

SAUCE:
  1 can (10½ ounces) tomato soup
  1 soup can (1¼ cups) water
  1 tablespoon minced fresh parsley
  1 teaspoon celery seed
  2 tablespoons lemon juice
  1 teaspoon garlic salt
  ½ teaspoon freshly ground pepper

* Adapted from her *Cabbage Cookbook*, New York: Arco, 1974.

Soften the cabbage as directed on page 97. Sauté the onion in the margarine in a nonstick skillet until golden, then combine with the remaining filling ingredients and fill the cabbage rolls. Mix the sauce and pour over the cabbage. Cook as directed. *Eight servings, 210 calories each.*

◄§ CREOLE BEEF CASSEROLE §►

1½ pounds beef round, trimmed of fat and ground
¾ teaspoon Tabasco
2 teaspoons salt
¼ teaspoon dry mustard
½ teaspoon leaf thyme
1 tablespoon minced fresh parsley
½ cup chopped onion
1 clove garlic, peeled
1 tablespoon diet margarine
1 can (16 ounces) tomatoes
1 can (6 ounces) tomato paste
1 package (10 ounces) frozen lima beans, thawed

Mix the meat lightly with ½ teaspoon of the Tabasco, 1 teaspoon of the salt, the dry mustard, thyme, and minced parsley. Sauté the meat, along with the onions and garlic, in the margarine, until the meat is browned. Remove the garlic.

Turn part of the meat into a 1½-quart casserole. Combine the tomatoes, tomato paste, remaining ¼ teaspoon Tabasco, and remaining 1 teaspoon salt. Pour over the meat layer. Sprinkle with the lima beans and arrange the rest of the meat in the center. Cover and bake in a 350-degree oven for 45 minutes. *Six servings, 257 calories each.*

◄§ MEXICAN BEEF ROLL-UPS §►

To make our dish, we prepare little cornmeal pancakes from an egg-rich batter, then stuff them with a spicy mixture of browned meat and onions. And to top it all off—tomato sauce and sharp Cheddar cheese. It certainly sounds fattening, doesn't it? But our south-of-the-border dish is only 238 calories a serving.

FILLING:
1 pound lean beef, trimmed of all fat and ground
1 large Bermuda onion
1 teaspoon garlic salt
¼ teaspoon freshly ground pepper

2 teaspoons vinegar
¼ teaspoon oregano
¼ teaspoon ground cumin
1½ cups water

CORNMEAL CRÊPES:
3 eggs
6 tablespoons cornmeal
7 tablespoons water
Pinch of salt

TOPPING:
1 can (16 ounces) Spanish-style tomato sauce
6 tablespoons shredded extra-sharp Cheddar cheese

Mix together all the filling ingredients except the water in a large, nonstick saucepan with no fat added. Cook over moderate heat about 10 minutes, stirring to break up the meat, until well browned. Add the water and heat to boiling. Strain the liquid into a bowl and quick-chill in the freezer until the fat rises to the surface. Set the meat mixture aside.

Skim the hardened fat off the meat liquid. Combine with the tomato sauce and allow to simmer about 10 minutes, until thick.

Meanwhile, combine the cornmeal crêpe ingredients in a small bowl and mix well. Spray a small nonstick omelet or crêpe pan with vegetable coating for no-fat frying. Heat over moderate flame. When the pan is hot, pour on about 2 tablespoons of the batter and rotate to spread evenly. Cook, undisturbed, for about 45 seconds, until the pancake is set, then invert or lift out in one piece onto a plate. Continue making crêpes until all the batter is used up. You should have about 12.

Fill each crêpe with a little of the meat filling and roll up. Arrange the rolls in a nonstick baking pan and put them in a preheated 300-degree oven to warm through. Top with the hot tomato sauce and sprinkle with cheese. Return to the oven and heat only until the cheese begins to melt. Serve immediately. *Six servings, 238 calories each.*

◄§ SKILLET BEEF CHOW MEIN ℰ►

1 pound lean round of beef, trimmed of fat and ground
½ cup chopped onion
1 can (10½ ounces) condensed beef broth, skimmed of fat
1 can (16 ounces) Chinese vegetables, drained
1 tablespoon arrowroot or cornstarch
2 tablespoons soy sauce

Brown the beef in a nonstick skillet; leave it in chunks. Add the onion and beef broth, then cover and simmer for 3 minutes. Add the drained vegetables and heat to boiling. Combine the soy sauce and arrowroot and stir into simmering skillet. Heat through until the sauce is thickened and serve. *Four servings, 194 calories each.*

ᴇᔆ HAMBURGER SKILLET ITALIANO ᔆᴇ

1 pound lean beef round, trimmed of fat and ground
1 can (8 ounces) tomato sauce with onion (no oil)
½ cup red wine or water
¼ teaspoon oregano or Italian seasonings
2 packages (10 ounces each) frozen zucchini or green beans, or
   1 of each

Brown the beef in a nonstick skillet; leave it in chunks. Add the sauce, wine or water, oregano, and vegetables. Cover and cook for 3 minutes, then uncover and break up the vegetables with a fork. Stir well. Continue cooking until the vegetables are tender. *Four servings, 209 calories each.*

ᴇᔆ ITALIAN BEEF AND NOODLE SKILLET ᔆᴇ

Spray-on vegetable coating
1 pound lean beef, trimmed of fat and ground
4 cups water
1 teaspoon garlic salt
  Pinch of freshly ground black pepper
1 teaspoon oregano
2 onions, sliced
2 cups cubed zucchini
1 can (16 ounces) stewed tomatoes
4 ounces curly noodles
¼ cup freshly grated extra-sharp Parmesan cheese (optional)

Spray a large nonstick skillet with vegetable coating for no-fat frying. Spread the chopped meat in the skillet and cook, over a moderate flame, until the underside is brown. Break up the chunks and continue cooking until well browned.

Add 1 cup of water to the skillet and heat to boiling. Drain off the liquid into a cup and wait until the fat rises to the surface, then skim off fat with a spoon or bulb baster. Return the fat-skimmed liquid to the pan. Add the seasonings, vegetables, and remaining water and heat to boiling. Stir in the noodles, a few at a time, then cover and simmer until the noodles are tender.

Uncover and continue cooking until most of the liquid has evaporated. Sprinkle with the grated cheese, if desired, and serve. *Four servings, 318 calories each; with cheese, 346 calories.*

⋞ SKILLET-EASY CHILI ⋟

Spray-on vegetable coating or polyunsaturated oil
¾ **pound lean beef round, trimmed of fat and ground**
1 **onion, chopped**
1 **green pepper, seeded and chopped**
3 **cups canned red beans, undrained**
1 **can (6 ounces) tomato paste**
¼ **cup water**
1½ **teaspoons chili powder**
1 **teaspoon garlic salt**

Spray a large nonstick skillet with vegetable coating for no-fat frying or wipe lightly with oil. Add the meat and brown over a moderate flame, breaking it up and turning it as it cooks. Drain off any fat. Add all remaining ingredients and mix well. Simmer 30 to 40 minutes and serve hot. *Four servings, 250 calories each.*

⋞ HOT TAMALE SKILLET ⋟

Spray-on vegetable coating or polyunsaturated oil
½ **pound lean beef round, trimmed of fat and ground**
¾ **cup yellow corn meal**
3 **cups chopped canned tomatoes**
1 **green pepper, seeded and chopped**
2 **onions, chopped**
1 **package (10 ounces) frozen corn, defrosted**
1 **teaspoon garlic salt**
1½ **teaspoons chili powder**
10 **sliced stuffed olives**
½ **cup shredded extra-sharp Cheddar cheese**

Spray a nonstick skillet with vegetable coating for no-fat frying or wipe lightly with oil. Brown the meat over a moderate flame and pour off any fat.

Stir the corn meal into tomatoes and add to the skillet. Add the green pepper, onion, defrosted corn, garlic salt, and chili powder. Stir well and cook, uncovered, for about 15 to 20 minutes, then sprinkle on the olives and cheese and continue to cook until the cheese is melted. *Five servings, 272 calories each.*

BEEF AND CABBAGE SKILLET WITH OLD COUNTRY FLAVOR

To prepare this dish, you'll need a large skillet equipped with a cover, or a heavy rangetop pot or Dutch oven. This dish may also be prepared in a pressure cooker (cutting the cooking time by one-third). Whatever you use, make sure it has a nonstick finish for browning the meat without added fat.

1 **pound lean round, trimmed of fat and ground**
¼ **cup soy granules (see note below) or crushed high-protein cereal**
1 **egg**
1 **tablespoon raisins**
  Garlic salt and freshly ground pepper
½ **cup chopped onion**
1 **can (6 ounces) tomato paste**
1 **can (16 ounces) tomatoes**
1 **tablespoon granulated sugar or sugar substitute**
1 **tablespoon lemon juice**
1 **small onion, sliced**
1 **head cabbage**

In a bowl, combine the meat with the soy granules or cereal, egg, raisins, garlic salt, and pepper. Add the chopped onion and one-third of the tomato paste. Shape into 8 patties and put in a large nonstick skillet. To brown the patties without added fat, heat the skillet slowly over a moderate flame; brown on both sides.

Combine the tomatoes with the sugar, lemon juice, remaining tomato paste, and the sliced onion. Pour over the meat patties and lower the heat. Cover and simmer 35 to 40 minutes.

Slice the cabbage in 8 wedges, with the leaves still attached to the core. Add to the skillet, then cover and cook an additional 8 to 10 minutes, until just tender. Spoon the tomato sauce over the cabbage wedges and meat patties and serve. *Four servings, 338 calories each.*

NOTE: Soy granules are available in health food stores.

HAMBURGER SKILLET STROGANOFF

1 **pound lean beef round, trimmed of fat and ground**
1 **onion, sliced**
2 **cups tomato juice**

1 can (4 ounces) mushrooms
3 cups water
1 teaspoon prepared mustard
   Garlic salt and freshly ground pepper
4 ounces curly noodles
1 cup buttermilk or plain yogurt

Brown the meat in a nonstick skillet; pour off any fat. Add the onion, tomato juice, mushrooms, water, and seasonings. Cook until boiling; add the noodles. Cover and simmer until most of the liquid is evaporated. Stir in the buttermilk or yogurt; heat over a low flame but do not boil. Serve immediately. *Four servings, 330 calories each.*

◆§ SKILLET HAMBURGERS DIANE §◆

2 pounds lean beef round, trimmed of fat and ground
2 teaspoons salt
2 teaspoons freshly ground pepper
1 tablespoon polyunsaturated oil
2 tablespoons prepared mustard
2 tablespoons lemon juice
1 tablespoon Worcestershire sauce
¼ cup chopped fresh parsley
   Pimiento and parsley sprigs for garnish

Lightly mix the ground round, salt, and pepper, and shape into 8 patties. Blend the oil and mustard in a nonstick skillet and sauté the hamburgers, over medium heat, for 4 minutes on each side. Stir the lemon juice and Worcestershire sauce into the skillet, then stir in the chopped parsley; spoon over the hamburgers. Garnish with pimiento and parsley sprigs and serve. *Eight servings, 175 calories each.*

◆§ HAWAIIAN BEEF SKILLET §◆

   Spray-on vegetable coating or polyunsaturated oil
1 pound lean round, trimmed of fat and ground
1 can (6 ounces) unsweetened pineapple juice
1 package (10 ounces) broccoli
½ cup chopped onion
½ cup green pepper
2 teaspoons arrowroot or cornstarch
2 tablespoons soy sauce

Spray a nonstick skillet with vegetable coating for nonfat frying or wipe with oil. Brown the beef; leave in chunks. Add the pineapple juice, frozen broccoli, onion, and green pepper. Cover and cook for 3 minutes, then uncover, stir the vegetables well, and cook until tender but crisp. Combine the arrowroot and soy sauce and stir into the simmering skillet until the mixture thickens slightly. Serve immediately. *Four servings, 216 calories each.*

◄§ SKILLET BEEF CURRY ৵►

```
 1   medium onion, minced
 2   teaspoons polyunsaturated oil
 2   tablespoons ground coriander
 ½   teaspoon ground cinnamon
 ¼   teaspoon ground cloves
 ¼   teaspoon ground cardamom
 ½   teaspoon chili powder
 ⅛   teaspoon ground ginger
1½   teaspoons salt
 ½   teaspoon Tabasco
 1   pound beef round, trimmed of fat and ground
 ½   cup water
 ½   cup evaporated skim milk
 1   teaspoon lemon juice
```

Cook the onion in the oil until golden. Add the spices, salt, and Tabasco and mix well. Stir in the ground beef and cook until brown. Add the water; cook until the mixture thickens slightly. Blend in the evaporated milk and lemon juice; remove from the heat and serve. *Four servings, 203 calories each.*

◄§ SAVORY STUFFED PEPPERS ৵►

The stuffed vegetable recipes in most cookbooks start out with raw ground beef. Some recipes use the raw hamburger meat as is, while others direct you to brown it first in extra fat. Either way, all the fat stays trapped inside and winds up on your plate (and finally on your hips!). It's so much simpler and smarter to "recycle" yesterday's leftover broiled hamburger—most of the fat has been drained away in the cooking.

If you're fresh out of leftover hamburger simply take a pound of lean ground round and spread it out on a broiler tray, the kind with a perforated inset that lets melting grease escape through small holes to the tray underneath. Brown the meat quickly under high heat.

6 **green peppers**
1 **pound cooked lean ground round**
½ **cup cooked fluffy rice**
1 **cup chopped onion**
   Salt and freshly ground pepper
1 **clove garlic, minced**
1 **teaspoon dried basil or thyme**
1 **tablespoon lemon juice**
3 **cups (24 ounces) canned tomato sauce**

Slice off the tops of the green peppers and remove the seeds. Wash and set aside. Mash the cooked hamburger with a fork, then put it in a deep bowl and add the rice, onions, 2 teaspoons salt, ½ teaspoon pepper, the garlic, basil, and lemon juice. Add 1 cup of the tomato sauce and mix well until all the ingredients are blended (add more sauce, if needed). Pack the meat mixture into the pepper cases and arrange in a casserole or deep baking dish, the kind with nonstick coating. Pour the remaining tomato sauce over the peppers and sprinkle with salt and pepper. Bake, uncovered, in a preheated 350-degree oven until tender but not mushy (about 30 minutes). *Six servings, 158 calories each.*

7

LAMB
AND
VEAL

When it comes to lamb, the weight-wary cook is wise to stick with leg of lamb. That's the least fattening cut, for most lamb meets or exceeds the calories in beef or pork. The prized leg of lamb, lean and tender, is a happy exception. Here are the comparative calorie counts in various cuts of cooked boneless lamb, calculated from data from the National Livestock and Meat Board:

Lamb Cuts	Calories Per Pound
Loin lamb chop	1,019
Rib chop	1,330
Arm chop	1,152
Blade chop	1,280
Leg of lamb	891

◦§ BROILED LAMB STEAKS ৪~

Have the butcher cut several skinny steak-sized slices from the leg roast. What you'll have are little lamb "round steaks"—every bit as flavorful and tender as the costlier rib or loin chops! (Don't confuse leg steaks with bone-in arm chops. They look alike, but the latter are far fatter and less tender.)

Rub each steak with a cut clove of garlic and sprinkle with crushed marjoram leaves. Broil under high heat, turning once, until cooked through but not overdone.

ᴥᶾ ROAST LEG OF LAMB ᶾᴥ

Make little slits in a lamb roast and insert garlic slivers. Rub the surface with rosemary, salt, and pepper. Place on a rack in a roasting pan, insert a meat thermometer, and roast at 325 degrees for 30 to 35 minutes, or until the meat temperature reaches 180 degrees. Don't overcook.

ᴥᶾ BARBECUED LEG OF LAMB ᶾᴥ

1 leg of lamb, boned and tied
   Garlic salt and coarsely ground pepper
1 cup plain tomato sauce
½ cup catsup
¼ cup chopped onion
1 tablespoon brown sugar
1 tablespoon polyunsaturated oil

Sprinkle the lamb with garlic salt and pepper, then secure on a rotisserie. Combine the remaining ingredients and brush frequently on the lamb as it revolves on the spit. Barbecue lamb 25 minutes per pound, or until a meat thermometer registers 160 to 170 degrees internal meat temperature. *Each serving is about 250 calories.*

VARIATION

Oven "Barbecued" Lamb: Place the leg of lamb on a rack in a roasting pan and bake uncovered in a 325-degree oven, about 30 minutes, to an internal temperature of 175, basting occasionally with the sauce.

⊷ SKINNY SKEWERED LAMB ⊷

For a "cook-in" instead of a cookout, bake or broil the skewers in your oven; add a generous dash of smoke-flavored seasoning.

1½ **pounds boneless leg of lamb, trimmed of fat and cut into 1-inch cubes**
6 **tablespoons lemon juice**
1 **to 1½ teaspoons garlic salt**
¼ **teaspoon dried thyme or rosemary**
1 **tablespoon Worcestershire sauce**
2 **green peppers, cut in chunks**
4 **tomatoes, cut in wedges**
6 **small onions, cut in chunks**

Put the lamb cubes in a plastic bag and add the lemon juice, garlic salt, thyme, and Worcestershire sauce. Add just enough cold water to insure that the lamb pieces are covered and marinate in the refrigerator all day or overnight (or 2 hours at room temperature).

Drain the meat, reserving the marinade, and thread on 6 skewers, alternating the pieces of lamb with chunks of pepper, tomato, and onion. Broil the meat for 15 to 20 minutes over hot coals or in the broiler. Turn frequently and brush with the reserved marinade. *Six servings, 198 calories each.*

⊷ POLYNESIAN SKEWERED LAMB AND PINEAPPLE ⊷

1½ **pounds lean lamb, trimmed of fat and cubed**
3 **tablespoons vinegar**
   Salt and freshly ground pepper
½ **teaspoon dried marjoram**
1 **can (20 ounces) juice-packed pineapple chunks, undrained**

Put the meat cubes in a plastic bag and add the vinegar and seasonings. Add just enough pineapple juice drained from the can of chunks to insure that all the meat is covered. Marinate in the refrigerator all day or overnight.

Drain the meat and thread on skewers, alternating with pineapple chunks. Broil for 15 to 20 minutes over hot coals or in the broiler, turning frequently. *Six servings, 184 calories each.*

⌐§ LAMB-STUFFED CABBAGE §⌐

1 **head cabbage**

FILLING:
1½ **pounds boneless leg of lamb, trimmed of fat and ground**
1 **tablespoon cornstarch**
1½ **teaspoons garlic salt**
Pinch of dried basil
1 **onion, minced**
1 **tablespoon chopped fresh parsley**
1 **egg**
1 **tablespoon Worcestershire sauce**

SAUCE:
1 **can (20 ounces) tomatoes**
2 **tablespoons wine vinegar**
3 **tablespoons catsup**
1 **tablespoon cornstarch**
¼ **cup cabbage water**
Garlic salt and pepper

Cut the cabbage into quarters and remove the core. Cook in boiling water for 2 to 3 minutes, just long enough to soften the cabbage. Remove the cabbage (reserving ¼ cup of the water in which it was cooked) and separate the leaves.

Combine the filling ingredients and mix thoroughly. Spoon some filling into each cabbage leaf and roll up, tucking in the ends.

Arrange the rolls in a large skillet or heavy pot and add the tomatoes and vinegar. Cover and simmer over low heat for 1 hour, then remove the rolls to a serving dish. Combine the catsup, cornstarch, and cabbage water and stir the mixture into the simmering tomatoes until slightly thickened. Season to taste, pour over the cabbage rolls, and serve. *Six servings, 223 calories each.*

INDIAN LAMB CURRY
WITH APPLE CUBES

Fruit and spice are especially nice when combined with lamb.

1¼ pounds lamb steaks, cut from the leg
 1 cup tomato juice
 2 tablespoons lemon juice
 ¼ teaspoon garlic powder
 1 or more teaspoons curry powder
 3 tablespoons golden raisins
 1 large, firm red apple, cored and cubed

On a cutting board, slice the lamb steaks into 2-inch strips. Discard any fat, then put the strips in a nonstick skillet with no fat added; gradually raise the heat until the lamb browns lightly in its own melted inner fat. Stir to brown evenly. Drain off the fat, if any.

Stir in the tomato and lemon juices, garlic powder, curry powder, and raisins, then cook and stir over high heat until most of the liquid evaporates into a thick sauce. At the last minute, stir in the apple cubes and cook only until heated through; the apple should be raw and crunchy and the meat should still be pink in the middle. Serve immediately. *Four servings, 193 calories each.*

SHISH KEBAB

 1 leg of lamb, boned, trimmed of fat and cut into 2-inch cubes
 1 cup dry vermouth
 2 teaspoons garlic salt
 ½ teaspoon freshly ground pepper
 2 teaspoons dried oregano
 2 tablespoons Worcestershire sauce
    Water, if necessary

Put the meat into a deep nonmetallic bowl. Combine all the other ingredients except the water and pour over the meat (the meat should be just covered; add a little water to the marinade, if necessary.) Put the bowl in your refrigerator and allow the meat to marinate at least 5 hours.

Remove the meat from the marinade (reserve the marinade) and thread on skewers. Grill over hot coals for 20 minutes, turning frequently and basting occasionally with the reserved marinade. *Each 4-ounce serving is 230 calories.*

◆§ CURRIED LAMBURGER ◈◆

1 tablespoon polyunsaturated oil
1 pound lean lamb, trimmed of fat and ground
1 envelope textured soy protein meat extender
1 cup unsweetened applesauce
1 onion, chopped
1 teaspoon garlic salt
1 teaspoon curry powder

Heat the oil in a nonstick skillet. Combine the remaining ingredients and fry until brown and cooked through, then serve. *Six servings, 120 calories each.*

◆§ LAMB-STUFFED CABBAGE WITH EGG-LEMON SAUCE ◈◆

1 head cabbage
1 pound lean leg of lamb, trimmed of fat and ground
2 eggs
½ cup chopped onion
½ cup instant rice
1 teaspoon salt
1 teaspoon ground cinnamon
3 tablespoons pine nuts
1 cup water
2 tablespoons lemon juice

Parboil the cabbage for 3 minutes, then drain and cool. Separate the leaves.

Combine the meat with 1 egg, beaten, and all the other ingredients except the water and lemon juice. Reserve the remaining egg.

Put a tablespoon of the meat mixture in the center of each cabbage leaf and roll up, tucking in the ends. Place the rolls closely together in a heavy Dutch oven. Add the water, cover, and cook over low heat for 1 hour. Remove the rolls to a hot serving platter, reserving the cooking liquid.

In a small mixing bowl, beat the lemon juice with the remaining egg. Slowly beat in the hot liquid from the pan, then return egg-lemon mixture to the saucepan over very low heat. Cook and stir constantly until thickened; do not allow to boil. Serve the cabbage rolls with the sauce on the side. *Six servings, 214 calories each.*

✍ ◂§ SYRIAN MEATBALLS ৯»

Fresh eggplant, pared and chopped, is added to ground meat to make this dish, and the flavor boost is nothing short of spectacular! The eggplant is also an economical meat stretcher that makes less seem like more. Adding vegetables instead of bread crumbs is a good way to pad out the hamburger without filling out your figure—a great way to sneak something past the vegetable haters, too!

To be purely authentic, this Syrian-inspired dish is made with chopped lamb instead of beef. You can get it ground to order by your butcher. Just be sure to pick out the leanest lamb (or beef) you can find—generally the leg or "round"—and have every bit of separable fat removed before chopping. Chosen this way, either lamb or beef will be between 600 and 650 calories per pound instead of the nearly 1,800 calories a pound for hamburger with a 30 percent fat content.

This recipe makes about 18 dinner-sized meatballs (six servings), or about 3 dozen tiny appetizer snacks.

1½   **pounds lamb or beef (lean round, trimmed of fat and ground)**
 2   **cups peeled, chopped eggplant**
½   **cup sliced onion**
 2   **tablespoons bread crumbs**
 1   **egg, slightly beaten**
 2   **teaspoons minced fresh parsley**
 1   **teaspoon salt**
    Pinch of freshly ground pepper
 1   **cup plain tomato sauce**
½   **cup water**
½   **teaspoon prepared mustard**

Combine the lamb or beef with the eggplant, onion, bread crumbs, egg, parsley, salt, and pepper. Shape into meatballs and brown under the broiler, turning frequently. Combine the tomato sauce, water, and mustard in a large skillet or saucepan. Bring to a boil and add the meatballs, then cover and simmer over low heat for 15 minutes. Uncover and continue to simmer until the sauce is gravy thick (another 10 minutes). *Six servings, 206 calories each.*

◂§ GREEK LAMB SKILLET ৯»

    Spray-on vegetable coating
 1   **pound lean lamb, trimmed of fat and ground**
 4   **cups water**

1 teaspoon garlic salt
  Pinch of freshly ground pepper
½ teaspoon ground cinnamon
⅛ teaspoon freshly grated nutmeg
1 tablespoon lemon juice
2 onions, sliced
2 cups peeled, cubed eggplant
1 can (16 ounces) stewed tomatoes
4 ounces curly noodles
4 teaspoons freshly grated Romano or Parmesan cheese

Spray a large nonstick skillet with vegetable coating for no-fat frying. Spread the chopped meat in the skillet and cook, over moderate heat, until the underside is brown. Break up the chunks and continue cooking until well browned.

Add 1 cup of water to the skillet and heat to boiling. Drain off the liquid into a cup and wait until the fat rises to the surface, then skim off the fat with a spoon or bulb baster. Return the fat-skimmed liquid to the pan. Add the seasonings, lemon juice, vegetables, and remaining water and heat to boiling. Stir in the noodles, a few at a time, then cover and simmer until the noodles are tender. Uncover and continue cooking until most of the liquid has evaporated. Sprinkle with the grated cheese, if desired, and serve. *Four servings, 374 calories each with cheese; 343 without.*

◄§ EASY CURRIED LAMB §►

1 pound cubed, cooked lamb
½ cup chopped onion
1 teaspoon garlic salt
1 teaspoon curry powder (or more to taste)
½ teaspoon ground ginger
1 can (14½ ounces) diced tomatoes in puree *apple*
1 tablespoon cornstarch

Combine all the ingredients in a saucepan and stir well. Simmer, covered, over low heat for 10 minutes, then serve. *Four servings, 282 calories each.*

NOTE: A serving of ½ cup cooked instant rice will add 89 calories for each.

Veal, Ground . . .

Of all the meats in American markets, none is so low in calories as lean veal—less than 700 calories per pound, while beef can run as high as 1,800 or more.

Unfortunately, veal is also expensive and hard to find in some areas. East and West Coast dwellers take veal for granted, but in other sections it's often necessary to ask for veal, or have it ordered specially. Price is the reason: meat managers don't want to stock it in sections where veal isn't popular.

But veal needn't be an expensive dish. "Vealburgers" ground from the less-expensive cuts of meat can be a good buy—in cost as well as calories! Even though the price per pound is higher than beef hamburger, veal has so little fat that 1 pound gives four full servings—while fatty hamburger offers less than three.

⋖ BREADED SWEDISH VEAL "CUTLETS" ⋗

1 pound lean veal shoulder, trimmed of fat and ground
1 envelope textured soy protein meat extender
⅔ cup water
1 teaspoon salt or garlic salt
⅛ teaspoon freshly grated nutmeg
⅛ teaspoon ground allspice
⅛ teaspoon freshly ground pepper
1 tablespoon minced onion
¼ cup bread crumbs
1 tablespoon polyunsaturated oil
 Lemon wedges for garnish

Combine all the ingredients except the bread crumbs, oil, and garnish. Mix well, then shape into 6 flat patties. Press each patty into the bread crumbs, lightly coating each side.

Heat the oil in a nonstick skillet. Fry the patties over moderate heat, turning once. Serve with lemon wedges. *Six servings, 170 calories each.*

⋖ GENOA VEAL LOAF STUFFED WITH EGGS ⋗

Turn ground veal into a party buffet loaf that's subtly spiced with Italian flavor. Our dish slices neatly and delights the eye as it reveals its buried treasure of golden hard-cooked eggs in the middle.

This Genovese specialty is adapted from a recipe collected by Waverly Root in his magnificent Time-Life *Cooking of Italy* volume. In the native version, ground meat, eggs, and vegetables are sewn into a breast of veal, which is then braised and served cold. Our Slim Gourmet adaptation gives you fewer calories.

3 slices diet protein bread
1 cup water
½ cup frozen chopped spinach (defrosted)
2 pounds lean veal shoulder, trimmed of fat and ground
½ cup chopped onion
5 tablespoons freshly grated Parmesan cheese
¼ teaspoon dried marjoram
¼ teaspoon dried thyme
2 teaspoons salt
¼ cup shelled, chopped pistachio nuts
2 cloves garlic, minced
3 small hard-cooked eggs, peeled
½ cup chicken broth, skimmed of fat

Soak the bread in the water, then press the moisture from both the bread and the defrosted spinach. Combine all the ingredients except the eggs and chicken broth and toss lightly to mix well. Add a few tablespoons of broth, if necessary, but the mixture should not be too moist.

To shape the loaf, pile part of the meat mixture into the bottom of a loaf pan. Arrange the eggs, lengthwise in a row. Cover with the remaining meat mixture and press into the loaf pan to shape. Invert the pan into a shallow baking dish and tap gently to dislodge the veal loaf from the loaf pan. Bake in a preheated 325-degree oven for 45 minutes, basting occasionally with a little of the reserved chicken broth. Chill before serving. *Eight servings, 245 calories each.*

... Chops ...

For a gourmet main course that's delectable yet calorie-shy, try veal chops. A veal chop is a T-bone steak that never grew up. Pound for pound, the T-bone is nearly triple the calorie count of veal chops; lean chops are only 573 per pound, according to the U.S. Department of Agriculture, but by the time they turn into a T-bone, the calorie count is up to 1,595!

It's the lack of fat that accounts for the veal chop's low calorie count (and its popularity among cholesterol watchers!). The same lack of fat means that you can't toss a veal chop on the grill as you would a T-bone. Slow pan frying in a minimum of fat or gentle braising brings out veal's delicate flavor and velvety tenderness.

A touch of garlic or a squirt of lemon are all you need to complement veal. But veal as a base allows you to create these Slim Gourmet favorites that skimp on calories, yet seem so extravagant nobody would ever think of them as "diet food"!

⊷ POLYNESIAN VEAL CHOPS ҩ⊷

```
 1  tablespoon polyunsaturated oil
 8  lean loin veal chops (2½ pounds), trimmed of fat
 1  envelope or cube of chicken bouillon
1½  cups boiling water
 1  can (16 ounces) low-calorie pineapple tidbits, undrained
 ½  cup sliced onion
    Pinch of ground ginger
 1  cup sliced celery
 2  tablespoons arrowroot or cornstarch
 3  tablespoons soy sauce
 2  tablespoons vinegar
 ½  pound fresh mushrooms, sliced
    Salt and freshly ground pepper
```

Heat the oil in a large nonstick skillet and brown the chops on both sides. Remove the chops and blot with paper towel to remove excess fat. Add the bouillon and boiling water to the skillet and stir to dissolve. Add the juice from the canned pineapple, sliced onions, and ginger, then return the chops to the skillet. Cover and simmer for 30 minutes, until the chops are tender. Add the celery and simmer 10 minutes more.

Combine the arrowroot or cornstarch with the soy sauce and vinegar; mix well and stir into the skillet. Stir in the pineapple tidbits and mushrooms and simmer, uncovered, until warmed through and the liquid has thickened to sauce consistency. Taste before adding salt and pepper. *Eight servings, 240 calories each.*

NOTE: A serving of ¼ cup fluffy cooked rice per person will add 44 calories.

⊷ VEAL CHOPS ITALIANO ҩ⊷

```
 1  tablespoon olive oil
 1  teaspoon salt
 ¼  teaspoon freshly ground pepper
    Garlic powder
 8  lean loin veal chops (2½ pounds), trimmed of fat
2½  cups canned tomatoes
 ½  cup sliced onion
 ½  pound fresh mushrooms, sliced
 ½  cup dry white wine
 1  teaspoon dried basil or oregano
```

Heat the oil in a large, nonstick skillet. Season the chops and brown on both sides. Add all the other ingredients and simmer for 45 minutes or longer, until the chops are tender. *Eight servings, 225 calories each.*

... Cutlets ...

✓ ◆ VEAL PARMIGIANA ◆

Just picture it—crusty cutlets of tender veal, simmering in a savory tomato sauce, spiked with Parmesan cheese and topped with melting mozzarella. There, doesn't *that* sound better than the hamburger and cottage cheese you had in mind? (I really think that people who make up diets don't like to eat!) At only 280 calories a serving, veal *parmigiana* not only sounds better, it's probably slimmer than the tedious fare found on so many reducing menus.

1½   **pounds veal cutlet, pounded thin**
¼   **cup freshly grated Parmesan cheese**
⅓   **cup bread crumbs**
1   **tablespoon olive oil**
1   **cup plain tomato sauce**
    Garlic salt (optional)
3   **slices (3 ounces) part-skim mozzarella cheese**
1   **tablespoon crushed oregano**

After pounding the cutlets thin with the edge of a heavy plate, cut them into 6 pieces. Combine the Parmesan cheese and bread crumbs in a paper bag and shake up the cutlets until well coated.

Heat the oil in a nonstick skillet and brown the meat quickly on both sides. Arrange in a baking dish and cover with the tomato sauce; add garlic salt to taste. Cut the mozzarella slices in half and top each cutlet. Sprinkle with oregano and bake in a preheated 375-degree oven for 10 minutes or longer, until the cheese is bubbly. *Six servings, 280 calories each.*

⋅§ MARY VERNI'S ROLLETTES §⋅

1¼ pounds thinly sliced veal
  3 thin slices lean cooked ("boiled") ham
  2 hard-cooked eggs, finely chopped
  ½ cup minced onion
  ¼ cup chopped fresh parsley
  ¼ cup Italian-seasoned bread crumbs
  3 tablespoons tomato sauce or catsup
  1 tablespoon olive oil
  2 tablespoons lemon juice
    Salt and freshly ground pepper
    Fresh parsley and lemon wedges for garnish

Pound the veal thin; cut it into 6 equal slices and set aside. Mince the ham, eggs, onion, parsley, bread crumbs, and tomato sauce together. Spread the filling mixture evenly among the veal slices. Roll up and fasten with toothpicks.

Moisten each rollette with a mixture of oil and lemon and place in a baking dish with a cover. Bake in a preheated 350-degree oven for 50 to 60 minutes, or until tender. Serve with fresh parsley and lemon wedges. *Six servings, 225 calories per serving.*

. . . and Stew

⋅§ EASY SKILLET STEW §⋅

  1 pound lean veal or beef round, trimmed of fat and cut in cubes
    Garlic salt and freshly ground pepper
  1 large onion, sliced in rings
  1 cup bouillon, tomato juice, or dry wine
  ½ teaspoon dried thyme
  ½ pound mushrooms, left whole if small, quartered if large
  1 can (16 ounces) sliced carrots
  1 can (16 ounces) boiled potatoes (optional)

Season the meat with the garlic salt and pepper, then brown the meat and onions the no-fat way (see page 25), using a tablespoon of the liquid. Add the remaining liquid, thyme, and mushrooms, cover, and simmer over very low heat until the meat is tender, about 1 hour. Add the drained carrots and potatoes, uncover, and continue to simmer until nearly all the liquid evaporates. *Four servings, 289 calories each with potatoes; 234 without.*

⊶ SKILLET MARENGO ⊱

1 pound lean boneless veal shoulder or beef round
  Spray-on vegetable coating or polyunsaturated oil
  Salt and freshly ground pepper
  Garlic powder to taste
1 can (10½ ounces) French onion soup, skimmed of fat
½ cup white wine
1 can (8 ounces) tomatoes
1 cup water
1 tablespoon lemon juice
1 can (4 ounces) mushrooms

Trim all the fat off the meat and cut into 1½-inch cubes. Spray a large nonstick skillet with vegetable-oil coating for low-fat frying or wipe lightly with oil. Season the meat and brown slowly over moderate heat, without added fat. Add all the remaining ingredients except the mushrooms, cover, and simmer over very low heat for 50 to 60 minutes, until tender. Uncover and add the mushrooms. Raise the heat to moderate and cook, uncovered, until the liquid reduces to a thick sauce. *Four servings, 209 calories each.*

NOTE: Serve with ½ cup rice or noodles per person, if desired; this will add 90 calories for rice and 100 for noodles.

⊶ SKILLET RAGOUT ⊱

1 pound lean veal shoulder or beef round
  Spray-on vegetable coating or polyunsaturated oil
  Salt and pepper
1 can (10½ ounces) chicken (for veal) or beef consommé,
    skimmed of fat
1 bay leaf
1 tablespoon Worcestershire sauce (optional)
½ cup dry white wine
1 can (8 ounces) boiled whole onions, undrained
1 can (8 ounces) small Belgian carrots, undrained
1 can (8 ounces) potatoes, undrained
1 can (4 ounces) mushroom caps, undrained

Trim all the fat off the meat, then cut into 1½-inch cubes. Spray a large nonstick skillet with vegetable-oil coating or wipe with oil. Season the meat and brown slowly over moderate heat, with no added fat. Add the consommé, bay leaf, Worcestershire, and wine to the skillet. Add the liquid from all the canned vegetables, cover, and simmer over very low heat for 50 to 60 minutes or more, until tender.

Uncover the skillet and add the vegetables. Raise the heat to moderate and simmer, uncovered, until nearly all the liquid is evaporated. *Four servings, 231 calories each.*

◆§ VEAL SPARERIBS, SOUTH SEAS STYLE ❧

2½ pounds lean breast of veal
¼ cup vinegar
5 tablespoons catsup
1 cup juice-packed crushed pineapple
3 tablespoons soy sauce

Have the breast of veal trimmed of fat and cut into "riblets" (individual ribs). Place the ribs in a roasting pan in a single layer. Bake, uncovered, in a hot (425-degree) oven for 20 to 25 minutes, to brown the meat and remove the excess fat. Pour off all accumulated fat.

Combine the remaining ingredients and pour over the ribs. Cover the pan with aluminum foil and return to the oven. Bake at 350 degrees for 1½ hours, until tender. *Eight servings, 234 calories each.*

8
PORK
AND
HAM

Offer a dieter a pork chop or a beefsteak and he'll probably opt for the steak, and feel quite virtuous about it. "No pork for me, thank you—it's fattening!"

If the steak is well marbled and expensive, the way most people like it, the pork chop might be a better choice. Beef rib is about 1,800 calories per pound (more if it's "prime ribs"), while lean, fat-trimmed pork loin is only 1,216 calories per pound. Cooked weight, of course, is less, depending on how much fat is rendered out by the heat.

Why is it, then, that pork has such a black eye among calorie counters while steak is assumed to be slimming? One reason is that some parts of the pig are plenty fattening—and off limits. Spareribs weigh in at 1,637 calories per pound (the meat portion, not the bone). And bacon is a whopping 3,000 calories a pound! Pork used to be a lot more fattening. The modern porker has a trim new figure; the result is 36 percent fewer calories, 57 percent less fat, and 22 percent more protein.

And, finally, pork is fattening, as are beef and lamb, if you compare them with veal or chicken, each at about 800 calories a pound. And a whole pound of flounder is only 358.

So—there's no reason to pass up pork in favor of beef if you like it. Enjoy it the Slim Gourmet way. Here are some calorie-wise tips:

◆§ Pass up any roasts or chops that betray flecks of fat through the meat.

◆§ Ask (in fact, *insist*) that your butcher trim away every vestige of fringe fat on roasts or chops—or do it yourself.

◆§ There's still plenty of fat left to cook pork nicely. So, good grief, don't add more! Broiling or barbecuing are best for chops.

◆§ The right way to roast pork is on a rack in a roasting pan. Do not add water, do not cover, do not baste. Do not do *anything* but bake it at 325 degrees until well done. (However, garlic salt, herbs, soy sauce, and other seasonings won't add any calories to speak of.)

◆§ Make sauce-slimmed pork dishes ahead and chill in your refrigerator so you can lift off the fat before serving.

◆§ Pork-happy vegetables (sauerkraut, for example) should be cooked separately so they won't absorb fat. Add a small slice of lean pork for flavor, if you like.

◆§ Couple pork with skinny side dishes; save the starchy stuff for chicken and fish nights.

◆§ EASY-SLICING BONELESS PORK LOIN §◆

1 **loin of pork, trimmed, boned, rolled, and tied**
Garlic powder
Coarsely ground black pepper
Soy sauce
½ **cup boiling water or heated apple juice**

Sprinkle the roast liberally with garlic powder, pepper, and soy sauce. Place on a rack in a shallow roasting pan. Don't add any water and don't cover. Insert a meat thermometer, then bake in a slow (325-degree) oven approximately 40 minutes per pound, until the thermometer reads 170 degrees. Remove to a carving board and slice thin.

To serve "au jus" (with its own juices), pour all accumulated fat from the roasting pan. Pour the boiling water or heated apple juice into the pan. Stir with a spoon to dissolve cooking residue and pour over the sliced pork.

Serve with unsweetened or low-calorie applesauce (sugar-free applesauce can be sweetened to taste by stirring a small amount of liquid or granulated sugar substitute into the jar). Cooked green beans and a salad complete the meal. *Each 4-ounce serving of roast pork is 288 calories.*

Pork Steak

"Fresh ham" is just another word for pork—pork before it's been smoked, cooked, cured, processed, chemicalized, water soaked, or anything else. Its color is pale grayish-white, like an ordinary pork chop (rather than pinkish-red, the way processed or cured ham looks). And being fresh pork, it must be thoroughly cooked before serving.

In some areas, fresh ham slices are called "pork steaks," to avoid confusion with the processed ham steaks. An oval piece of meat with a single, small round bone in the middle, it looks like the pork version of a beef round steak—which it is. Both pieces of meat are cut from the leg of the animal, and both have the advantage of being the least fattening part of the anatomy.

For example: pork chop meat weighs in at about 1,400 calories per pound, but pork steak meat is only half as fattening—700 calories. Boneless rib of beef, on the other hand, is likely to run more than 2,000 calories per pound.

Broiling is the most calorie-wise method of cooking any meat, pork included. However, like most low-fat meats, pork steak should be tenderized an hour or so before broiling, using a meat tenderizer or a marinade—a liquid that contains wine, vinegar, tomato, or citrus juice. (Contrary to popular opinion, marinades need no oil; it's the acid liquid that softens the meat fibers.)

⊷ ORIENTAL PORK STEAK ⊷

This recipe, with soy sauce and a touch of catsup, works best on the barbecue, but can be enjoyed year round using the kitchen range broiler. Simply add a shake of liquid smoke or barbecue-flavored salt before broiling. To keep the pork steak edges from curling up, trim away every bit of border fat, then make little half-inch slashes in 5 or 6 places around the outside of each steak.

2 **lean pork steaks (fresh ham slices), total weight 1½ to 2 pounds**
½ **teaspoon garlic powder**
½ **cup sherry wine**
6 **tablespoons soy sauce**
¼ **cup water, approximately**
2 **tablespoons catsup**
2 **teaspoons arrowroot or cornstarch**

Trim away all fat. Sprinkle the pork steaks with garlic powder and place in a plastic bag. Pour the wine and soy sauce into the bag and place it in a bowl (to catch any leakage), then draw the sides of the bag up and twist together so that the marinade completely covers the meat. Refrigerate and marinate for 2 to 4 hours or longer. When ready to cook, drain off and reserve the marinade and add cold water to make 1 cup.

Broil the steaks over hot coals or in your broiler, turning once until browned and cooked through. Meanwhile, prepare the sauce. Combine the reserved marinade with the catsup and arrowroot in a small saucepan. Cook and stir over a moderate flame until the mixture thickens, then simmer 5 minutes over a low flame. Pour over the pork steaks on a heated platter. Cut the meat into serving-sized portions and serve. *Six servings, 215 calories each.*

⋖ PORK AND SAUERKRAUT ⋗

1 thick pork steak, cut from the leg (about 2¼ pounds before trimming)
1½ cups plus 2 tablespoons water
1 large can (27 ounces) sauerkraut
2 small apples, peeled and chopped
2 small onions, peeled and chopped
2 teaspoons caraway seeds

Have the steak cut from a very lean fresh (uncured) ham. Trim away all border fat. Put the pork steak and the 2 tablespoons water into a large nonstick pot or large skillet with a cover. Cook over moderately high heat until the water evaporates and the pork steak begins to brown in its own melted fat; brown on both sides.

Rinse the sauerkraut and drain. Combine it with all remaining ingredients and pile on top of the pork. Cover and simmer over very low heat until the pork is tender, 1½ hours or more. *Six servings, 226 calories each.*

⋖ PORK STEAK AND ZUCCHINI ⋗

1¼ pounds lean pork steak, cut from the leg
2 tablespoons soy sauce
¾ cup apple juice
1 tablespoon vinegar
1 scant teaspoon arrowroot or cornstarch
2 medium green zucchini, sliced
2 tablespoons cold water
1 tablespoon toasted sesame seeds

Trim all the fringe fat off the steak, then put in a shallow nonstick baking dish along with the soy sauce, apple juice, and vinegar. Cover with foil and bake in a 325-degree oven 1½ hours, or until tender. Combine the arrowroot and cold water and stir into the liquid in the pan.

Add the zucchini to the pan, then raise the heat to 450 degrees and bake, uncovered, stirring occasionally, until the zucchini is tender-crisp and the sauce is slightly thickened. Cut the meat into serving-sized pieces, arrange on a platter, and surround with the zucchini. Pour the sauce over the meat and vegetables and sprinkle with the toasted sesame seeds. *Four servings, 243 calories each.*

⊷§ PORK CUBES WITH SAUERKRAUT §⊱

Spray-on vegetable coating
Garlic salt and freshly ground pepper
1 pound lean pork, from shoulder or leg, trimmed of fat and cubed
1 onion, chopped
1 apple, peeled and chopped
1 teaspoon caraway seeds
4 cups canned sauerkraut

Spray a nonstick skillet with vegetable coating for no-fat frying. Season the cubed meat and add to the skillet over low heat. Raise the heat gradually and brown the cubes slowly in the skillet with no added fat.

Combine the remaining ingredients and add to the skillet, then cover closely and simmer over very low heat, 1 hour or more, until the meat is fork tender. Uncover and continue cooking until most of the liquid is evaporated. *Four servings, 258 calories each.*

Pork—Ground to Order

How about porkburgers for a change? Or a spicy meat loaf made from lean ground pork?

Have your porkburger ground from a leg of pork (fresh ham), but be sure to tell the butcher that you want all the covering fat removed first. What you get back will be lean only, about 700 calories. Never buy ready-ground pork—the calories will be double that, or more! Pork shoulder, with a 30 percent fat content, weighs in at a whopping 1,500 calories. And pork sausage meat is 2,200 calories per pound.

Ground pork, like ground beef, is extremely perishable, so plan to freeze or cook it the same day. Unlike ground beef, your porkburger must be thoroughly cooked—no rare porkburgers, please!

⊷§ SPANISH PORK AND NOODLE SKILLET §⊱

Spray-on vegetable coating
1 pound lean pork shoulder, trimmed of fat and ground
4 cups water, divided
1 teaspoon salt
Pinch of red cayenne pepper
1 teaspoon oregano
¼ teaspoon cumin
1 tablespoon vinegar
2 onions, sliced
1 green pepper, seeded and chopped
16 ounce can stewed tomatoes
4 ounces curly noodles

Spray a large nonstick skillet with vegetable coating for no-fat frying. Spread the chopped meat in the skillet and cook, over moderate heat, until the underside is brown. Break up the chunks and continue cooking until well browned.

Add 1 cup of water to the skillet and heat to boiling. Drain off the liquid into a cup and wait until the fat rises to the surface, then skim off the fat with a spoon or bulb baster. Return the fat-skimmed liquid to the pan. Add the seasonings, vinegar, vegetables, and remaining water. Heat to boiling. Stir in noodles, a few at a time, then cover and simmer until the noodles are tender. Uncover and continue cooking until most of the liquid has evaporated. *Four servings, 330 calories each.*

∻ BAKED PORK 'N' APPLEBURGERS ≻

2 pounds lean pork, from the leg, trimmed of fat and ground
2 eggs
1½ cups unsweetened applesauce
3 tablespoons grated onion
2 tablespoons minced fresh parsley
1½ teaspoons salt
¼ teaspoon freshly ground pepper
  Liquid smoke (optional)

Combine all the ingredients and toss lightly. Shape into 8 patties (the meat will be very moist) and place in a shallow nonstick baking pan. Bake in a preheated 400-degree oven for 20 minutes, until cooked through. *Eight servings, 214 calories each.*

∻ PORK 'N' APPLE MEAT LOAF ≻

2 pounds lean pork, from the leg, trimmed of fat and ground
2 cups peeled, chopped apples
2 eggs
1½ tablespoons prepared mustard
½ cup minced onion
½ cup minced celery
3 tablespoons prepared horseradish
½ cup catsup

Combine all the ingredients and toss lightly. Shape into a loaf and place in a shallow nonstick roasting pan. (Do not pack into a loaf pan.) Bake in a preheated 350-degree oven until the internal temperature reaches 185 degrees, about 1 hour and 20 minutes; the meat loaf must be cooked through. *Eight servings, 236 calories each.*

⊷ PORK PATTIES AND PINEAPPLE KRAUT ⊱

1 pound lean pork, trimmed of fat and ground
  Salt and freshly ground pepper
4 cups canned sauerkraut
1 cup juice-packed crushed pineapple

Shape the meat into 8 patties. Season the patties, then put them in a nonstick skillet over low heat. Gradually raise the heat until the patties begin to brown in their own melted inner fat; brown on both sides. Pour off any fat that accumulates in the pan.

Combine the sauerkraut and pineapple in the skillet. Top with the browned pork patties, then cover and cook over a very low flame for 20 to 30 minutes. Uncover and continue cooking until most of the liquid evaporates. *Four servings, 265 calories each.*

⊷ ITALIAN PORK "SAUSAGE" STEAKS ⊱

1 pound boneless pork shoulder, trimmed of fat and ground
1 envelope textured soy protein meat extender
⅔ cup water
1 teaspoon garlic salt
½ teaspoon Italian seasoning
½ teaspoon poultry seasoning
1 tablespoon polyunsaturated oil

Combine all the ingredients except the oil. Heat oil in a nonstick skillet; rotate so the bottom is evenly coated. Shape the mixture into 6 flat patties and cook over low heat, turning once, until cooked through. *Six servings, 148 calories each.*

Re-Run Leftover Pork

The only thing better than roast pork is *leftover* roast pork. There's no extra fat to ooze unwanted calories into a sauce or combination dish that's made with leftover pork, so don't let the sandwich vultures get to your next piece of lean loin of pork! Trim away any fat and cut the leftover meat in cubes.

SKILLET-EASY PORK ALMOND DIN

1 cup thinly sliced celery
1 red or green sweet pepper, thinly sliced
1 package (10 ounces) frozen green beans
½ cup water
2 teaspoons arrowroot or cornstarch
3 tablespoons soy sauce
¾ pound lean cooked pork, cubed
1 can (2 ounces) mushrooms, undrained
½ cup sliced canned water chestnuts
2 tablespoons whole almonds

In a nonstick skillet, combine the celery, green pepper, green beans, and water. Cover and simmer for 4 minutes. Combine the arrowroot with the soy sauce and stir into the skillet, then add the pork cubes, undrained mushrooms, water chestnuts. Cook and stir, uncovered, until the sauce simmers and thickens and the meat is heated through. Garnish with the almonds and serve immediately. *Four servings, 294 calories each.*

PORK AND CHICKEN SKILLET DINNER

1 cup cubed roast pork
1 can (5 ounces) boneless chicken or turkey, cut up
6 tablespoons soy sauce
2 large onions, cut in chunks
1 package (10½ ounces) frozen asparagus or broccoli, thawed and
    sliced diagonally
1 can (2 ounces) sliced mushrooms, drained but liquid reserved
2 teaspoons arrowroot or cornstarch
2 tablespoons water or white wine

Combine the pork, chicken, soy sauce, and onions in the skillet. Cover and cook over high heat for 1 minute, then add the asparagus or broccoli and sliced mushrooms. Cover and continue cooking.

Combine the arrowroot with the mushroom liquid and water. Stir into the skillet and continue to cook and stir, uncovered, until the liquid thickens and the meat and vegetables are glazed with sauce; don't overcook. Serve immediately. *Four servings, 268 calories each.*

◄§ OVEN-EASY HAWAIIAN PORK KEBABS §►

¾ pound lean cooked pork, cut in 1½-inch cubes
1 cup juice-packed pineapple chunks, drained but juice reserved
2 green peppers, seeded and cut in squares
3 tablespoons soy sauce

Thread skewers with alternate cubes of meat, pineapple, and green pepper. Arrange the skewers on a nonstick cookie sheet and bake in a preheated very hot (450-degree) oven, basting with a combination of reserved pineapple juice and soy sauce. Bake only until the pepper is tender-crunchy. *Four servings, 258 calories each.*

Ham Delights

✓ ◄§ QUICK-GLAZED HAM STEAK §►

2 pounds lean center-cut ham steak
4 tablespoons low-sugar jam or preserves

Trim all fat from the border of the ham steak. Place on a rack in a broiling pan and broil 4 to 5 minutes on each side, turning once. Spread the upper surface with jam or preserves (pineapple, apricot, peach, or orange marmalade) and broil under high heat for 2 more minutes. *Eight servings, 260 calories each.*

◄§ MARINATED HAM STEAK §►

2 pounds lean ham steak
½ cup sherry wine
½ cup water
2 teaspoons paprika
½ cup unsweetened pineapple juice
2 level tablespoons dry mustard
2 teaspoons ground cloves
½ teaspoon garlic powder

Trim all fat from the border of the ham steak, then place in a plastic bag. Combine the remaining ingredients and pour into the bag along with the steak. (Put the bagged steak in a shallow bowl to collect any leakage.) Marinate 2 hours or more, then remove the steak from the bag and grill over hot coals for 20 to 25 minutes, turning frequently. Baste the steak with the reserved marinade as you broil. *Eight servings, 260 calories each.*

✓ ᵉᏸ HAM PATTIES Ᏸᵉ

1 pound lean cooked ham, trimmed of fat and ground
1 cup crushed high-protein cereal
1 egg, lightly beaten
½ cup skim milk
   Pinch of freshly ground black pepper
1 tablespoon prepared mustard
1 cup crushed juice-packed pineapple
1 teaspoon arrowroot or cornstarch

Combine the ham, cereal, egg, milk, pepper, and mustard. Shape into 6 patties and place in a nonstick roasting pan. Bake in a moderate (350-degree) oven for 12 to 15 minutes.

Stir the pineapple and arrowroot together and pour over the patties. Bake an additional 10 minutes. *Six servings, 179 calories each.*

ᵉᏸ ORIENTAL HAM SKILLET Ᏸᵉ

1 can (6 ounces) unsweetened pineapple juice
1 tablespoon soy sauce
1½ tablespoons arrowroot or cornstarch
1 tablespoon prepared mustard
1 can (8 ounces) juice-packed pineapple chunks, undrained
¼ teaspoon ground ginger
   Pinch of saffron (optional)
3 tablespoons raisins
1 onion, finely chopped
2 green peppers, seeded and cut in strips
1 pound cooked lean ham, cubed

Stir the ingredients in the order given, into a large skillet. Cover and simmer over low heat for 5 minutes, until heated through. Serve with ½ cup cooked rice per person. *Six servings, 198 calories each; with rice, 284 calories.*

9
SPECIALTY
MEATS

Why Some Folks Hate Liver!

Overcooking, overpaying, and overselling by overeager parents are the three biggest mistakes most people make with liver.

Overcooking: All liver is tender when quick-cooked to that just-right inner pinkness. On the other hand, even premium-priced calves' liver is shoe leather if it's cooked until gray. Which brings us to . . .

Overpaying: Why pay a king's ransom for calves' liver when properly prepared beef liver is every bit as tender and flavorful, and even better nutritionally! Beef liver has got to be the all-time meat bargain: high in protein, beef liver is all meat, no bones, less than 4 percent fat—and only 635 calories a pound, compared with 1,600 or more for fatty hamburger. However . . .

Overselling your family on the basis of vitamins, minerals, calories, or cost is a mistake. What kid cares! The real trick is to make it delicious.

LIVER SMOTHERED IN ONIONS

4 onions, sliced
2 tablespoons water
1 pound beef liver, sliced
3 tablespoons all-purpose flour
2 tablespoons margarine or butter

Put the onion slices and water in a very large, nonstick skillet with a cover. Steam, covered, over high heat for 1 or 2 minutes, until the water evaporates and the onions can be separated into rings. Remove the onions to a plate.

Coat the liver slices lightly with flour. Heat 1 tablespoon of the fat in the skillet and add the liver. Brown quickly, then add the other tablespoon of fat and turn the liver (2 tablespoons of fat are all you need!). Add the onions to the skillet and continue to cook and turn until the onions are tender. (Total cooking time for the liver is about 5 minutes, depending on the thickness. Make a little slit in the thickest part to determine doneness. The liver should still be pink.) *Four servings, 268 calories each.*

NOTE: Sprinkle on a few tablespoons of bacon-flavored bits for extra crunch—*only 25 calories per tablespoon.*

⋞ INDIAN CURRIED LIVER ⋟

1½ **pounds beef liver**
½ **cup plain yogurt**
¼ **cup lemon juice**
2 **teaspoons curry powder**
⅛ **teaspoon pumpkin-pie spice**
2 **tablespoons butter**
1 **tablespoon water**
1 **large onion, thinly sliced**
 Salt and freshly ground pepper to taste

Cut the liver in 3-inch strips. Combine the yogurt, lemon juice, curry powder, and pumpkin-pie spice and marinate the liver strips in this mixture for 30 minutes at room temperature.

Melt the butter in a nonstick skillet. Scrape the marinade off the meat with a spoon and reserve. Fry the liver strips over high heat for 3 minutes, turning frequently. Remove to a platter.

Add the water and sliced onion to the skillet. Cook and stir over high heat until the liquid evaporates and the onion is golden and tender, but still somewhat crisp. Put the onion on top of the liver.

Put the reserved yogurt marinade in the skillet. Cook and stir, scraping the pan well, until the mixture simmers. Return the liver and onion to skillet over medium heat and stir, coating with the sauce. Serve immediately. *Six servings, 216 calories each.*

✎ CHINESE LIVER, ONIONS, ৯ AND BEANSPROUTS

1 **pound baby beef liver**
½ **teaspoon ground ginger**
3 **tablespoons sherry wine**
2 **tablespoons peanut oil**
3 **onions, thinly sliced**
1 **can (16 ounces) beansprouts, well drained**
½ **teaspoon granulated sugar (optional)**
3 **tablespoons soy sauce**

Cut the liver into bite-sized cubes. Put the cubes in a bowl and add the ginger and wine. Toss lightly and marinate for 15 to 20 minutes.

Heat the oil in a wok or large nonstick skillet. Brown the liver cubes quickly over highest heat, then remove and reserve. Add the onions to the wok and cook, stirring until just translucent. Add the well-drained beansprouts, sugar, and soy sauce and stir-fry over high heat until heated through, then stir in the liver and cook until hot. Serve immediately. *Four servings, 280 calories each.*

> *Q. What's a delicacy some cooks throw away?*
> *A. Chicken livers.*

Or, to be more precise, chicken liver—singular. That's the trouble. There's only one liver per chicken, too little of a good thing. What do you do with one chicken liver?

If you are a Slim Gourmet cook, you save it in your deep-freeze, packed away in a jar or plastic bag. And you keep adding more chicken livers, each time you buy a chicken. If you have chicken often (and what low-calorie cook doesn't?), you'll soon save enough for a meal, and that's like "found money."

✎ SAUTÉED CHICKEN LIVERS IN WINE ৯

4 **chicken livers (¼ pound)**
1 **can (2 ounces) mushrooms**
1 **tablespoon diet margarine**
½ **small onion, sliced**
2 **tablespoons sherry wine**

Cut the livers in half, then combine with the remaining ingredients in a nonstick skillet. Stir-fry, over moderate heat, for about 4 to 5 minutes, until the liquid evaporates and the contents of the skillet are lightly browned. *One serving, 226 calories.*

๒ CHICKEN LIVERS IN ๒
"SOUR CREAM" FOR TWO

½ pound chicken livers
1 small onion, thinly sliced
1 tablespoon diet margarine
½ cup plain yogurt
   Salt and freshly ground pepper
   Chopped fresh parsley
2 cups hot, cooked rice

Slice the livers in half, then combine with the onion and margarine in a nonstick skillet. Stir-fry, over moderate heat, until lightly browned, about 4 minutes. Stir in the yogurt until heated through, but do not boil. Season to taste with salt, pepper, and chopped parsley and serve over the hot rice. *Two servings, 352 calories each.*

๒ LIVER AND ONION SCRAMBLE ๒

2 chicken livers, chopped
1 tablespoon minced onion
½ teaspoon polyunsaturated oil
2 eggs, lightly beaten

Stir-fry the chopped chicken liver and minced onion in the oil for 3 to 4 minutes. Then add the lightly beaten eggs and scramble over moderate heat. Makes a tasty high-protein breakfast. *One serving, 283 calories.*

Beef Tongue

Either corned or smoked, beef tongue is always tasty and tender. And at less than 300 calories a serving, this is a real nutrition bargain. Unfortunately, tongue is out of the bargain class if you buy it already cooked and sliced in the deli department. But a few steps away, over in the butcher case, you'll probably find a do-it-yourself tongue, just waiting to be taken home and prepared.

Preparing tongue is outrageously easy. The trouble is that tongue is—well, tongue. Distressingly recognizable. Guaranteed to bring a chorus of "yuks" if you let the kids unbag the groceries. But when you come right down to it, tongue is really no less lovely to look at than lobster, and the meat is a lot easier to get at. Once it's been cooked, and the tongue-ish covering is peeled away, the sliced meat is every bit as civilized as corned beef—and a lot less fattening.

⊷§ HOME-COOKED BEEF TONGUE ৪৯

1 **tongue, corned or smoked (about 4 pounds)**
  Water to cover
1 **bay leaf**
1 **clove garlic (optional)**

Unpackage the tongue and put it in a heavy pot with enough water to cover it. (Some cookbooks recommend presoaking the tongue in cold water, but this isn't necessary with today's light cure methods.) Add the bay leaf and garlic. Heat to boiling, then lower to a gentle simmer. Cover the pot tightly and let simmer slowly for about 3 hours, until a sharp knife inserted in the center indicates it's tender. Remove from the water and peel off the skin (it will slip off easily), then trim away any bone or fat at the thick end.

Slice the meat thin and serve hot. Spicy mustard and horseradish are good accompaniments, and chilled leftovers are great for lunch. *Each 4-ounce serving, about 275 calories.*

VARIATION

Tongue with Pineapple Sauce: Arrange hot slices of tongue on a platter and top with the following sauce: Cook and stir 1 cup crushed unsweetened pineapple, 1 teaspoon arrowroot, 1 tablespoon vinegar until thickened. Remove from the heat and stir in sugar substitute equal to 1 tablespoon sugar. *Each tablespoon sauce, 16 calories.*

Homemade Sausages

Lots of sausage is more fat than meat. Pork sausage that's half fat weighs in at a whopping 2,259 calories per pound—off limits for both calorie counters and cholesterol watchers. But a Slim Gourmet cook can make tasty breakfast sausage that's only 654 calories per pound.

⊷§ PORK-BEEF SAUSAGE PATTIES ৪৯

Breakfast patties are as easy to make as hamburger. In fact, sausage patties are really nothing more than spicy little porkburgers.

To get the chopped meat you'll need for your easy homemade sausage, pick out the leanest pork roast you can find in your supermarket meat case. The lowest-calorie pork is lean fresh ham (ham before it's been smoked and cured). Next in leanness is pork loin. Look for pork with a minimum of marbling, then tell the butcher you want it trimmed of all bones and fat and ground to order. Do insist on getting everything back in the package—the chopped meat plus the bones and fat. (You can freeze the bones and use them to flavor up a spaghetti sauce later.) You want the fat just to make sure that it doesn't get chopped in with the pork!

For the beef choose a boneless bottom round or extra-lean chuck roast and have it trimmed of fat and ground to order, too. It isn't necessary to have the pork and beef ground together; you can combine them yourself in the kitchen. Simply mix the two meats and add the seasonings. Shape into patties and tuck them away in your freezer. At breakfast time simply pop a few frozen patties under the broiler while you scramble up some eggs in your fat-free nonstick skillet.

1½ **pounds lean boneless pork, trimmed of fat and ground (fresh ham or loin)**
1½ **pounds boneless beef round or chuck, trimmed of fat and ground**
 1 **level tablespoon poultry seasoning**
1½ **teaspoons freshly ground black pepper**
1½ **tablespoons salt**
    Pinch of cayenne pepper
 3 **tablespoons red wine**
 1 **tablespoon liquid smoke (optional)**

Combine all the ingredients and toss lightly to mix. Shape into small flat patties, using a heaping tablespoon of meat for each sausage. Line a cookie sheet with foil or freezer wrap and place the patties on the sheet without touching. Label and deep-freeze.

To cook, simply remove the desired number of patties from the freezer and broil under highest heat, turning once, until the patties are thoroughly cooked. *Twenty-four sausage patties, 82 calories each.*

NOTE: Don't forget these cautions. Fresh sausage is as perishable as hamburger; be sure to freeze what you can't use right away. Pork must be thoroughly cooked before eating. No tasting to check the seasonings!

✥ SKINNY FRIED SAUSAGE AND APPLES ✥

Each pound of this sausage provides 92 grams of protein, more than double the protein in packaged sausage. Ordinary sausage offers only 43 grams of protein per pound because it's more fat than meat. Our sausage serves four, while a pound of purchased sausage offers barely enough protein for two.

1 pound lean boneless pork (fresh ham), trimmed of fat and ground
2 egg whites
3 tablespoons skim milk
1 teaspoon garlic salt
¼ teaspoon coarsely ground pepper
½ teaspoon poultry seasoning
1½ tablespoons minced onion
¼ teaspoon liquid smoke
  Spray-on vegetable coating
½ cup water
3 small or 2 large unpeeled apples, each cored and cut in 6 thick slices
  Ground cinnamon

Combine the pork with all the other ingredients except the apples and cinnamon. Spray a nonstick skillet with vegetable coating for no-fat frying. Shape the pork mixture into 4 patties and fry in the skillet over moderate heat, turning once, until brown on both sides; the pork will fry in its own melted inner fat.

When the patties are brown on both sides, remove them from the skillet and keep warm. Add ¼ cup water to the skillet, then drain it off, to remove all accumulated fat. Add another ¼ cup water and the unpeeled apple slices. Sprinkle with cinnamon. Cook over moderate heat until the liquid evaporates and the apples are browned on one side. Turn the apples and brown on the other side. Cook until tender but not mushy. Serve immediately, with the sausage. *Four servings, 245 calories each.*

⊰ CHORIZO SAUSAGE PATTIES ⊱

If you're a fan of Spanish or Mexican food, you've probably enjoyed *chorizos*, the zesty native sausage. Unfortunately, like most sausages, chorizos are off limits to calorie counters and cholesterol watchers, because of their high fat content (close to 50 percent).

However, you can make your own, no sausage casing needed, by combining lean pork completely trimmed of fat with the seasonings that go into chorizos.

2 pounds lean pork shoulder or leg, trimmed of fat and ground
2 teaspoons garlic salt
1 teaspoon coarsely ground pepper
¼ teaspoon ground cumin
½ teaspoon cayenne pepper
2 teaspoons oregano
¼ cup wine vinegar

Combine all the ingredients and mix well. Shape into 16 flat patties that may be cooked immediately or frozen for later.

To FREEZE: Line a cookie tin with foil or plastic wrap. Arrange patties in a single layer, just touching. Cover with additional wrap, label, and date. Remove the patties a few at a time, as needed.

These may be broiled either frozen or defrosted, 3 to 4 inches from the source of heat, turning once. Cook 7 minutes each side if frozen, 6 minutes per side if defrosted, until cooked through.

To PAN FRY: The patties must be defrosted first. Spray a nonstick skillet with vegetable coating for no-fat frying and cook the patties with no fat added, about 5 minutes each side. *Sixteen patties, 95 calories each.*

NOTE: The recipe may be doubled or cut in half. Remember that all pork patties must be cooked until no inner pinkness remains, before tasting or serving.

COUNTRY-STYLE BEEF SAUSAGE

2 pounds lean beef chuck, trimmed of fat and finely ground
1 teaspoon dried thyme, sage, or poultry seasoning
2 teaspoons salt
1 teaspoon freshly ground black pepper
  Dash of liquid smoke (optional)

Combine the meat and seasonings by tossing lightly with a fork. Shape loosely into 16 flat sausage patties.

These sausage patties are very low fat, so they're best cooked by quick-broiling on both sides until nicely browned. To pan-fry, be sure to use a nonstick skillet. Add no extra fat. Simply place the patties in a cold skillet and warm slowly. Cook over a moderate flame, turning frequently; do not press down with a spatula. *Sixteen patties, 89 calories each.*

NOTE: Don't forget that these homemade sausage patties have no chemical preservatives, so they're hamburger-perishable! Why not double or triple the recipe and hoard them in your freezer? Spread them out on a cookie tin for quick freezing; then remove the patties and store them loose in plastic bags. (Frozen patties are best broiled.)

Barbecued Franks

The typical wienie is about 140 calories uncooked and 130 calories broiled (according to U.S. Department of Agriculture estimates, based on 10 franks to a pound). However, individual brands can vary from a low of 110 calories up to 155. In general, franks with cereal added are the least fattening, and "all meat" franks (with pork and beef) the most fattening. "All-beef" franks are in the mid-range.

You can partially "de-fat" a frank by dropping it in boiling water and letting it sit for 10 to 20 minutes, then proceed to broil it as you normally would. The more fat you get rid of the less fattening it will be.

As far as toppings for franks go, mustard is around 24 calories a level tablespoon. There's little difference between types; however, the hotter it is, the less you'll use! Relishes can vary from 15 to 36 calories a tablespoon, depending on the sweetness. Pick sour or dill relish and save. Chili sauce is 16 calories a tablespoon. Sauerkraut is your best bet. At only 2 calories a tablespoon, you can really pile it on.

Barbecued Hamburgers

The typical 3½-ounce barbecued burger can range from less than 200 calories to nearly 400, depending on the fat content. The less fat, the lower the calories, so resist the urge to buy inexpensive fatty chopped meat (up to 1,600 calories per pound, raw).

Bread crumbs and other starchy "extenders" add not only their own empty carbohydrate calories, but act as a sponge to sop up the melting fat that would otherwise drain into your barbecue. If you want to make a burger seem bigger, add lots of chopped onions.

As for burger toppings, that innocuous slice of Cheddar that turns a meat cake into a cheeseburger also adds about 100 calories to the count, so stop and ask yourself if the good beefy flavor of an un-cheeseburger wouldn't be just as satisfying. If you must cheese it, make it a half a slice of extra sharp Cheddar. A tablespoon of catsup is about 18 calories; if you're dead serious about eliminating every last calorie, switch to dietetic catsup—it's one-third the calories, only 6 per tablespoon.

↝ GERMAN HASSENPFEFFER IN A HURRY ↜

Like chicken, rabbit is low in calories. In fact, chicken and rabbit have a lot in common, including flavor and texture. Here's how they compare, calorically:

1 Pound	*Chicken*	*Rabbit*
Total calories	382	581
Waste	32%	21%
Protein	57 gm	75 gm
Fat	15 gm	29 gm
No. of servings	2	3
Calories per serving	191	193

Somewhat meatier than chicken, a 2-pound rabbit can serve six. Cut-up rabbit is sold in the frozen food case of many large supermarkets.

1 **package cut-up rabbit (about 2 pounds)**
1 **tablespoon polyunsaturated oil**
3 **tablespoons bread crumbs**
½ **cup red wine vinegar**
1 **cup water**
1 **teaspoon sugar or sugar substitute**
1 **onion, chopped**
⅛ **teaspoon ground allspice**
1 **teaspoon salt**
1 **teaspoon whole cloves**
3 **bay leaves**

Defrost the rabbit pieces and roll them first in the oil, then the bread crumbs. Place the lightly coated pieces in a shallow 13 × 9-inch nonstick baking pan. Place the pan in a preheated 450-degree oven for 30 minutes, until rabbit is well browned.

Combine the remaining ingredients and pour around the rabbit pieces, then cover the pan loosely with a tent of aluminum foil. Lower the oven heat to 350 degrees and continue baking for 1½ hours. *Six servings, 236 calories each.*

VARIATION

Chicken Hassenpfeffer: Substitute a small cut-up chicken for the rabbit pieces. Follow the recipe above, but reduce the final baking time to about 1 hour.

10
CHICKEN

Of all the edibles that swim, skitter, cackle or moo, nothing beats chicken for versatility. It can be fuss-free or fancy, friendly or formidable, foreign or familiar. The creative chicken lover could serve this dish every night for a year and never run out of innovations.

As a calorie- and cost-conscious consumer, you want to choose chicken with an eye for getting the most protein—and the least fat and calories—for your money. First consult the guide on page 142.

FOILED CHICKEN BREASTS WITH SAVORY DRESSING

2 whole chicken breasts, split
    Garlic or onion salt and freshly ground pepper
½ cup chopped celery
½ cup chopped onion
1 cup seasoned bread cubes
¼ cup water

Trim the fringe fat from the chicken breasts. Lay the breasts, skin side up on a large sheet of heavy-duty aluminum foil and set it in a shallow broiling or roasting pan. Season the chicken. Brown, on one side only, under your broiler until the skin is golden. Pour off any melted chicken fat.

141

Combine the remaining ingredients and spoon into the center of the foil, with the browned chicken breasts on top. Cover the chicken with foil. Put the roasting pan with the foil-wrapped chicken in a preheated 350-degree oven and bake for 45 minutes, until tender. *Four servings, 223 calories each.*

CHICKEN PLUCKER'S GUIDE

	1 Pound		*3½ ounces, meat and skin only, raw*		
Type	*Waste*	*Protein*	*Fat*	*Calories*
Fryers/broilers (whole)	32%	57 gm	5%	126
Cut-up parts: Back	46%	40 gm	10%	157
Breast	21%	75 gm	2%	110
Drumstick	40%	51 gm	4%	115
Neck	52%	34 gm	9%	151
Rib	49%	41 gm	5%	124
Thigh	25%	62 gm	6%	128
Wing	51%	41 gm	7%	146
Roasters	27%	60 gm	13%	197
Hens/Cocks	27%	58 gm	19%	251
Capons	27%	71 gm	22%	291

---

* Data approximate; individual chickens vary.
Adapted from U.S. Department of Agriculture data.

✍ CHICKEN JUBILEE ❧

For sheer spectacle, you just can't match the gourmet glamour of golden-brown chicken breasts lavished with rich, ripe cherries in a glistening ruby-red sauce. It's the kind of dish that simply cries for candles and crystal. Somewhere amid all that beautiful bustle, people forget it's just plain chicken —low-cholesterol, low-calorie, and low-cost!

To make this dish, you need canned, pitted red cherries—unsweetened, naturally. (They're only 196 calories per 16-ounce can, while the syrup-packed type can be as high as 500 calories or more.)

As another calorie saver, you bake the chicken independent of the sauce; the melting chicken fat that drains into the baking dish won't reach your plate!

4 **large whole chicken breasts, split**
  Salt and pepper
  Minced fresh parsley
1 **can (16 ounces) sour pitted red cherries**

1 **tablespoon cornstarch**
2 **tablespoons granulated sugar**
   A few drops red food coloring

Sprinkle the chicken pieces with salt, pepper, and parsley. Place on a rack in a baking pan, skin side up, and bake in a preheated 350-degree oven for 45 to 50 minutes, or until the chicken is tender and nicely browned. Do not baste or add any oil.

Meanwhile, prepare the sauce. Put the remaining ingredients, plus a pinch of salt, in a nonstick saucepan and stir to dissolve the cornstarch. Heat over a moderate flame, stirring constantly, until juice thickens and clears. When the chicken is done, pour the sauce over and serve. *Eight servings, 225 calories each.*

✓ ❧ CHICKEN PARISIEN ❧

Here's a low-calorie gourmet dish that can take care of itself. Don't let the lengthy list of ingredients deter you—it's just an assembly job. Toss it all together and toss it in the oven. After that it's on its own. Watching your cholesterol? This dish is heart-smart, too.

CHICKEN:
1¾ **pounds chicken breasts, split, or 2 pounds cut-up fryer parts**
   ½ **cup sliced onion**
   ¼ **cup chopped green pepper**
   1 **cup sliced fresh mushrooms**

SAUCE:
   1 **cup orange juice**
   3 **tablespoons sherry wine**
   ½ **cup water**
   1 **tablespoon brown sugar or equivalent sugar substitute**
   1 **teaspoon salt**
   ¼ **teaspoon freshly ground pepper**
   1 **teaspoon grated orange rind**
   1 **tablespoon all-purpose flour**
1½ **tablespoons chopped fresh parsley**

GARNISH:
   Paprika
   Orange slices (optional)

Place the chicken pieces, skin side up, in a shallow baking dish. Add the onions, pepper, and mushrooms.

Combine the sauce ingredients in a shallow saucepan. Cook, stirring, over moderate heat until the mixture thickens and bubbles. Pour over the chicken. Bake in a preheated 375-degree oven for 1 hour or more, basting occasionally, until tender. Sprinkle with paprika and garnish with fresh orange slices, if you wish. *Six servings, 157 calories each if made with chicken breasts; 185 if made with light and dark meat chicken.*

✓ ◄§ CHICKEN WITH APRICOTS ৪►

Here's a Slim Gourmet chicken dish that seems quite rich and fattening, thanks to dried apricots and wine. They combine to make a simply smashing sweet and sour sauce that's so sophisticated yet so simple to prepare. Don't worry about the wine calories. Most of them evaporate, along with the alcohol. All you get is the flavor!

2 large whole chicken breasts, split
½ cup dried apricots
3 tablespoons soy sauce
¼ cup white wine
2 cups water
2 teaspoons arrowroot or cornstarch
   Salt and freshly ground pepper

Put the chicken, skin side down, in a cold nonstick skillet with a cover or a large pot with a nonstick surface. Place it on the range and turn on the heat. Allow the chicken pieces to warm gradually so that the chicken fat melts and the breasts brown in their own fat. When well browned, turn the chicken pieces skin side up.

Combine the remaining ingredients, stirring to be sure the arrowroot or cornstarch is dissolved. Pour over the chicken, cover, and simmer over low heat for 30 to 40 minutes, until the chicken is tender. Simmer, uncovered, another 10 minutes or more, until the liquid evaporates to a thick sauce.

Remove the chicken to a platter, pour the sauce over, and serve. *Four servings, 225 calories each.*

✓ ◄§ CHICKEN PARADISE ৪►

4 whole chicken breasts, split
1 large McIntosh apple, peeled and diced
½ cup sherry wine (or dry vermouth)
2 tablespoons raisins, chopped
2 tablespoons chopped fresh parsley
   Salt and freshly ground pepper

Trim away the border of chicken fat attached to the edge of the skin, then place the chicken, skin side up, in a nonstick baking dish. Surround with apples and raisins and pour on the wine. Sprinkle with the parsley, salt, and pepper and bake in a preheated 350-degree oven for about 35 minutes, basting occasionally.

Raise the oven temperature to 425 degrees and bake an additional 10 to 15 minutes, until chicken is browned. If the sauce evaporates too much, add a few tablespoons of water. *Four servings, 272 calories each.*

✓ ✑ MEXICALI CHICKEN ℘

3 large whole chicken breasts, split (about 2 pounds)
1 teaspoon garlic powder
1 teaspoon oregano
  Pinch of cayenne pepper
  Pinch of freshly grated nutmeg
1 chicken bouillon cube
1 cup boiling water
2 cups plain tomato sauce
1 cup sliced onion
1 green pepper, seeds removed and chopped

Rub the chicken with the garlic, oregano, cayenne, and nutmeg, then brown with no added fat by placing the chicken pieces, skin side down, in a cold nonstick skillet. Turn the flame on your range to moderate heat, allowing the chicken to warm slowly—the fat under the skin will begin to melt and the chicken will brown in its own fat.

Add the bouillon cube and boiling water and stir to dissolve. Add the remaining ingredients, cover, and simmer for 30 minutes, or until tender. Uncover and continue to simmer until sauce is reduced to a gravy consistency, then serve. *Six servings, 160 calories each.*

✑ CHICKEN DIVAN ℘

2 large whole chicken breasts, split
¾ cup sherry wine or dry vermouth
¾ cup low-calorie Caesar dressing
2 tablespoons chopped fresh parsley
1 package (10 ounces) frozen broccoli

Place the chicken breasts, skin side up, in a nonstick shallow baking dish. Combine the wine, salad dressing, and parsley and mix vigorously together until well-blended. Pour over the chicken, then bake for 50 minutes in a preheated 350-degree oven, basting occasionally.

Near the end of the baking time, cook the broccoli. Serve the chicken with the broccoli, with the sauce poured over both. *Four servings, 235 calories per person.*

◄§ PRESSURE-COOKER "COQ AU VIN" §►

2 whole chicken breasts, split
1 tablespoon all-purpose flour
1 cup dry red wine
1 cup water
½ cup minced onion
½ teaspoon grated orange rind
½ teaspoon poultry seasoning
1 tablespoon chopped fresh parsley
  Garlic salt and pepper

Place the chicken pieces, skin side down, in a cold pressure cooker (see note below). Heat over a moderate flame until the chicken begins to brown in its own melting fat. When the skin side is brown, drain off the fat and turn the pieces over. Sprinkle with the flour, then add the remaining ingredients. Cover and simmer at 15 pounds pressure for 15 minutes. Reduce the pressure, according to manufacturer's instructions, then uncover and return to the heat. Simmer, uncovered, for a few more minutes, until the liquid evaporates into a gravylike sauce. *Four servings, 143 calories each.*

NOTE: Add a small (2-ounce) can of mushrooms, including the liquid, to the recipe. Adds only 5 calories per serving.

If you have no pressure cooker, you can make this recipe in a heavy pot or top-of-the-range Dutch oven. Increase cooking time to 45 minutes and add more water, if needed.

◄§ EASY PHILIPPINE BREAST OF CHICKEN §►

Count on the tangy-tart taste of pineapple to really "juice up" mild-mannered main courses like chicken or veal. Luckily for dieters, most pineapple products are available today with no sugar added. The calorie difference can be sizable. For example, 1 cup of crushed pineapple can be as little as 88 calories. But packed in syrup, the calorie count zooms to nearly 200—or more, if it's extra-heavy syrup.

The following recipe has a tropical flavor, just right for summer. Philippine cuisine is a curious combo of Chinese, Japanese, Spanish, and American influences. In the original recipe, chicken is simmered in pineapple juice, vinegar, soy sauce, and spices for flavor, then browned on the barbecue. We simplify things by doing it all in the oven.

3 **whole large chicken breasts, split**
1 **can (6 ounces) unsweetened pineapple juice**
1 **bay leaf, crumbled**
¼ **cup vinegar**
¼ **cup soy sauce**

Place the chicken pieces, skin side up, in a single layer in a shallow roasting pan. Combine the remaining ingredients and pour over the chicken.

Cover the pan with a sheet of aluminum foil and place it in a hot (425-degree) oven. Bake, covered, for 30 minutes.

Uncover and continue to bake for an additional 20 minutes or more, basting frequently, until nearly all the liquid is evaporated and the chicken has a rich, dark color. *Six servings, 155 calories each.*

⤟ CHICKEN MELANZANA WITH SPAGHETTI ⤞

Garlic salt and freshly ground pepper
2 **whole large chicken breasts (1½ pounds total), split**
1 **small eggplant (¾ pound), peeled and cubed**
½ **cup chopped onion**
1 **can (6 ounces) tomato paste**
1 **cup water**
½ **teaspoon Italian seasoning**
3 **cups tender-cooked spaghetti**

Season the chicken pieces and place them, skin side up, in a shallow roasting pan. Quick-bake in a very hot (450-degree) oven for 15 to 20 minutes, until well browned. Pour off all fat.

Combine all the other ingredients except the spaghetti and surround the chicken. Cover the roaster loosely with foil and bake at 350 degrees for 40 to 50 minutes, stirring occasionally, until the chicken is tender and the liquid is reduced to a thick sauce. Serve with ¾ cup tender-cooked spaghetti per person. *Four servings, 297 calories each.*

Chicken Cutlets

◄§ ORIENTAL CHICKEN ON SKEWERS §►

1¼ pounds chicken cutlets (boneless, skinless chicken breasts)
4 ounces Canadian bacon or cooked ham
1 large onion
2 green peppers
½ pound fresh mushrooms
1 tablespoon polyunsaturated oil
2 tablespoons soy sauce
  Garlic salt
  Dash of cayenne pepper

Have ready 6 skewers.

Flatten out the chicken breasts and cut them into ¾-inch lengthwise strips. Cut the Canadian bacon or ham into ½-inch cubes and the onion and green peppers into chunks. Slice the mushrooms or leave whole, depending on the size. Wrap the chicken strips around the bacon cubes and vegetable chunks, then thread on the skewers.

Combine the oil, soy sauce, and seasonings in a shallow plate. Rotate the skewers in this mixture to coat evenly, then barbecue over hot coals for 15 minutes, turning frequently. Or place the skewers in a shallow nonstick roasting pan or cookie tin. Pour on the remaining marinade and place in a preheated very hot (450-degree) oven. Bake for 15 minutes, turning once or twice during cooking. *Six servings, 174 calories each.*

For an easy dinner, under 300 calories, serve with a tossed salad, diet dressing, and ½ cup cooked rice.

◄§ PERSIAN CHICKEN ON SKEWERS* §►

1½ pounds chicken cutlets (boneless, skinless breasts)
1 teaspoon monosodium glutamate
2 teaspoons salt
1 tablespoon polyunsaturated oil
3 tablespoons tarragon wine vinegar
½ teaspoon dried mint leaves
¼ teaspoon dried rosemary
1 clove garlic, crushed
¼ teaspoon Tabasco
4 tomatoes, quartered
16 small white onions

* Adapted from Dr. Harold Hamid Tara's $4,000-winning chicken recipe.

2 green peppers
16 mushroom caps

Cut the chicken into 2 × 2-inch pieces. Sprinkle with the monosodium glutamate and 1 teaspoon of the salt, then add the oil, vinegar, mint, rosemary, garlic, and Tabasco. Cover and refrigerate for several hours or all day, turning once or twice.

Cut up the vegetables into skewer-sized pieces. Drain the chicken, reserving the marinade, and thread on skewers, alternating with vegetable chunks. Sprinkle with the remaining salt and brush with marinade. Broil or barbecue, about 6 inches from the heat, for 30 minutes. Turn and baste while cooking. *Six servings, 216 calories each.*

৽ SLICED CHICKEN ও

(*Lai Tse Chi Ding*)

1 pound chicken cutlets (boneless, skinless chicken breasts)
2 tablespoons cornstarch
2 teaspoons polyunsaturated oil
2 cloves garlic, minced
¼ cup soy sauce
1 tablespoon vinegar
1 teaspoon granulated sugar
1 small bunch scallions, green part and all, sliced
⅛ teaspoon cayenne pepper, or to taste

Cut the chicken into 2-inch cubes. Toss lightly with the cornstarch. Heat the oil in a wok or large nonstick skillet and brown the chicken pieces and the garlic. Stir in all the other ingredients except the scallions and cayenne. Cover, and cook for 3 to 4 minutes, until the chicken is cooked through and the sauce is thickened slightly. Uncover and stir in the scallions. Cook and stir over a moderate flame until the scallions are heated through but still crisp; don't overcook. Add cayenne hot pepper to taste and serve immediately. *Four servings, 155 calories each.*

৽ CHICKEN PIZZARELLA ও

2 pounds chicken cutlets (boneless, skinless breasts)
1 can (8 ounces) plain tomato sauce
1 can (4 ounces) mushrooms, undrained
2 tablespoons minced onion
½ teaspoon oregano or Italian seasoning
　 Garlic salt and freshly ground pepper
1 cup (4 ounces) shredded part-skim mozzarella cheese

Slice the boneless, skinless breasts into halves if they are connected and arrange in a shallow baking dish. Combine all the other ingredients except the cheese and pour on the chicken breasts. Bake, uncovered, in a 350-degree oven for 35 minutes or more, until the chicken is tender, then sprinkle with the cheese and return to the oven. Bake an additional 5 minutes or so, until the cheese is melted and bubbly. *Eight servings, 186 calories each.*

◄§ CHICKEN CORDON BLEU, ITALIAN STYLE ᮗ

1¼ pounds chicken cutlets (boneless, skinless breasts)
  3 slices (3 ounces) lean, cooked ("boiled") ham
  3 slices (3 ounces) part-skim mozzarella cheese
    Oregano or Italian seasoning
    Onion or garlic powder
    Salt and freshly ground pepper
  1 can (13 ounces) chicken broth, skimmed of fat
  1 can (6 ounces) tomato paste
  3 tablespoons freshly grated extra-sharp Romano cheese

Slice the breasts where they join, so you have 6 equal pieces, and flatten the pieces out. Cut each piece of ham and cheese in half and place one slice of each on top of each chicken piece. Sprinkle lightly with the seasonings and roll each piece so that the ham and cheese are in the inside. Arrange the 6 chicken roll-ups in a shallow baking dish so that the seam side is on the bottom.

Combine the chicken broth and tomato paste with ¼ teaspoon each of Italian seasoning and onion powder and stir until smooth. Pour over the chicken, sprinkle with the Romano, and bake in a preheated hot (425-degree) oven for 15 minutes. *Six servings, 173 calories each.*

◄§ DIETER'S CHICKEN CREOLE ᮗ

To make this dish extra easy, you can use frozen chopped onion and green pepper, available in plastic bags in the supermarket freezer case. If you'd like to make your own freezer-handy sliced celery, simply take the freshest celery, slice it up, wash it and spread it on an aluminum cookie tin in the coldest part of your freezer. When frozen, scoop it all up into a plastic bag. The celery will stay loosely packed so you can take out only as much as you need for a recipe.

1 **pound chicken cutlets (boneless, skinless breasts)**
1 **can (16 ounces) peeled tomatoes**
1 **cup consommé or tomato juice**
1 **onion, peeled and sliced**
1 **green pepper, seeded and chopped**
1 **cup sliced celery**
1 **bay leaf**
½ **teaspoon dried thyme**
1 **teaspoon garlic salt**
   Pinch of cayenne pepper

Cut the chicken cutlets in half, then combine, with the remaining ingredients, in a covered pot. (If you're using canned chicken consommé, spoon off the floating chicken fat before adding to the pot.) Bring to a boil and then lower the heat to just simmering. Cover and simmer over very low heat until the chicken is tender, about 25 minutes. Uncover and cook over medium heat until the liquid evaporates to a sauce consistency. *Four servings, 164 calories each.*

PENNSYLVANIA DUTCH CHICKEN 'N' NOODLES

In Ireland it's potatoes, in China it's rice, in Italy it's spaghetti, and in Pennsylvania Dutch country it's egg noodles. Not the machine-made starchy stuff in the supermarket, but homemade, egg-rich, hand-cut, golden-yellow ribbons of goodness.

We've taken the basic Pennsylvania Dutch recipe and created homemade noodles that are even more so—more protein and less starch. We put them in a chicken dish that even dieters can enjoy. It seems so rich and fattening, you'll find it hard to believe the low calorie count.

The natives call this dish "Bott Boi," which means "pot pie." Here, however, pot pie has nothing to do with pie pastry. It's a savory stew with tender chunks of chicken, vegetables, and homemade egg-rich noodles swimming in a rich chicken gravy. Traditionally it's made with a fat hen and lots of flour—far too fattening for the figure-wise.

But we've recaptured the hearty down-home flavor without the extra calories. We make our "Bott Boi" with lean broiling chicken, only 382 calories a pound instead of 987. We carefully skim the fat from the broth and thicken it with arrowroot—double the thickening power of flour. We save so many calories, there's still room for our protein-rich noodles.

CHICKEN:
  1 **broiling chicken (2¼ pounds)**
  3 **cups water**
  1 **onion, chopped**
  1 **cup chopped celery**
  1 **teaspoon salt**
     Pinch of freshly ground pepper
  1 **teaspoon monosodium glutamate**
  1 **pound carrots, scraped and sliced**
  2 **teaspoons arrowroot or cornstarch**

NOODLES:
  2 **eggs**
 ½ **teaspoon salt**
 ¾ **cup all-purpose flour**

Combine the chicken in a pot with the water, onion, celery, salt, pepper and monosodium glutamate. Cover and simmer over low heat until tender, about 45 to 50 minutes. Pour the broth into a measuring cup and refrigerate.

Meanwhile, prepare the noodles. Fork-blend the eggs and salt together, then add enough flour to make a stiff dough. Shape into a ball and pat on any remaining flour. Turn onto a well-floured board and roll very thin with a floured rolling pin. Cut into half-inch strips.

At dinner time, skim the broth of fat, put broth in a saucepan, and add enough water to make 3 cups. Add the carrots and heat to boiling, then drop in the noodles, a few at a time. Cover and simmer until tender, 15 to 20 minutes.

Remove the chicken from the bones and cut into large chunks. Add to the pot. Combine the arrowroot with a little cold water and stir into the simmering broth. Cook until the chicken is hot. *Six servings, 266 calories each.*

⊰ CHICKEN IN RED WINE ⊱

  1 **frying chicken (3½ pounds), cut up**
  6 **tablespoons all-purpose flour, seasoned with freshly ground**
      pepper and salt
  2 **cups water**
  1 **cup red wine**
 ½ **teaspoon dried sage**
  2 **bay leaves**
     Pinch of dried thyme
  1 **cup tomato juice**

Shake the chicken with the seasoned flour in a paper bag, then place, skin side up, on a baking tray and bake in a very hot (450-degree) oven for 15 minutes. Remove chicken pieces to an ovenproof casserole and add the remaining ingredients. Cover and bake for 30 minutes at 350 degrees, then uncover and continue baking until the liquid thickens to sauce consistency. *Eight servings, 200 calories each.*

✺ WINE-GLAZED CHICKEN AND CARROTS ✺

Wine-Glazed Chicken and Carrots is one of the simplest dishes there is, yet epicurean in flavor! It's ideal for both wallet and waistline watchers—only 260 calories a serving—yet the chicken and vegetables are coated with a rich, chicken-y wine sauce that tastes like a million!

The sauce is "au naturel"—no flour or starchy thickeners added. And this sauce makes itself, right in the pot. What could be better for busy-day cooks?

The dish gets its intoxicating flavor from sherry wine. But no alcohol calories—they evaporate in the cooking. The chicken itself is moist and tender, not dry the way naked broiled birds tend to be. And the carrots are so flavorful, there's no butter needed.

1 **frying chicken (2 pounds), cut up**
2 **cups water**
½ **cup sherry wine**
2 **onions, sliced**
1 **clove garlic, minced**
1 **bay leaf**
1 **teaspoon salt**
  Coarsely ground pepper
1 **pound baby carrots, scraped and left whole**
  Chopped fresh parsley

No need to remove the skin from the chicken; however, carefully trim away as much yellow fringe fat as possible. Place the chicken pieces, skin side down, in a heavy Dutch oven, chicken fryer, or pressure cooker with a nonstick surface. Add 2 tablespoons of the water. Cover and place over high heat. When the moisture evaporates, uncover and the chicken will begin to brown in its own melting fat; brown slowly on all sides. Pour off any fat that accumulates, then blot the chicken pieces and return to the pot.

Add the remaining water, the wine, onions, garlic, bay leaf, salt, and a generous grind of pepper. Cover and simmer over very low heat until the chicken is almost tender, about 35 minutes in a conventional pot, or 12 minutes in a pressure cooker.

Drain the liquid into a tall glass and place in the freezer for a few minutes, until the fat rises to surface. Skim off all the fat, then return the liquid to the pot. Add the carrots, cover, and cook until tender, about 20 minutes (7 or 8 minutes in a pressure cooker).

Uncover the pot and raise the heat. Continue to cook, uncovered, until most of the liquid has evaporated and the chicken and carrots are coated with a thick, rich glaze. Remove the bay leaf, stir in the fresh parsley, and serve. *Four servings, 260 calories each.*

◄§ IRANIAN CHICKEN ፄ►

```
  1  frying chicken (2 pounds), cut up
 ½  teaspoon garlic salt
 ¼  teaspoon ground cinnamon
 ½  teaspoon turmeric
1½  teaspoons vinegar
  1  cup water
  1  can (16 ounces) small white onions
  1  can (16 ounces) kidney beans, drained
1½  tablespoons arrowroot or cornstarch
```

Place the chicken pieces, skin side down, in a large nonstick skillet or chicken fryer over a medium flame. Add no fat; the chicken will brown in its own melted inner fat. When the chicken pieces are well browned, turn them skin side up and sprinkle with the garlic salt, cinnamon, and turmeric. Add the vinegar, ¾ cup of the water, and the liquid from the canned onions. Cover and simmer until tender, about 40 to 50 minutes.

When the chicken is tender, strain the fat from the cooking liquid with a bulb-type baster. Add the onions and kidney beans and cook for 2 minutes, until heated through. Combine the arrowroot with the remaining ¼ cup water and stir into simmering skillet until the sauce is thickened. Serve hot. *Six servings, 233 calories each.*

◄§ CHICKEN-MUSHROOM PAPRIKASH ፄ►

```
  1  frying chicken (2¼ pounds), cut up
  1  cup water
 ½  pound fresh mushrooms, sliced
  1  onion, sliced
 ¾  teaspoon garlic salt
     Pinch of freshly ground pepper
  1  container (5 ounces) plain low-fat yogurt
  1  tablespoon paprika
```

Place the chicken, skin side down, in a large, cold nonstick skillet. Add a few tablespoons of the water, then cover and heat very slowly, over a moderate flame, until the water evaporates and the chicken begins to brown in its own melting fat; brown slowly on both sides. Pour off any fat that accumulates in the pan.

Add the mushrooms, remaining water, the onion, garlic salt, and pepper. Cover and simmer for 35 to 40 minutes, until the chicken is tender. Remove the chicken to a hot serving dish.

Carefully skim off any fat from the surface of the pan liquid, then stir in the yogurt and paprika. Cook and stir over a low flame until heated through but not boiling. Pour over the chicken pieces and serve immediately. *Four servings, 265 calories each.*

◄§ CHICKEN SANGRÍA §►

Adding a Continental touch to chicken is easy. For example, red wine and herbs translate ordinary chicken into the French dish *Coq au vin.* Combine chicken with orange and you've created *poulet à l'orange.* Now put oranges and wine together and you've changed the flags from France to Spain—with chicken (or *pollo*) *sangría.* It's company fare that seems extravagant and rich, although neither is true.

Our Slim Gourmet chicken dish is inspired by the Spanish drink sangría, a fresh-made blend of dry red table wine and fresh-squeezed citrus juices, a drink that's generally served with ice and a garnish of fresh fruit. If you're a purist about such matters, you'll want to make your Chicken Sangría with one of the Spanish Rioja wines—even the best is relatively inexpensive. However, you can make this dish with a red Bordeaux, which is similar, or any dry red wine. Most such wines leave just a trace of sugar calories after the alcohol calories have evaporated in the cooking.

1 **frying chicken (3 to 3½ pounds), cut up**
   Garlic salt and freshly ground pepper
¾ **cup dry red wine**
½ **cup orange juice**
¾ **cup water**
1 **teaspoon pumpkin-pie spice**
1 **tablespoon arrowroot or cornstarch**
1 **orange, peeled and sliced**
   Snipped fresh parsley

Salt and pepper the chicken pieces and place them, skin side down, in a cold nonstick skillet. Turn the heat high and allow the chicken pieces to brown in their own melted fat; brown both sides. Drain off any fat that accumulates.

Combine the wine, orange juice, water, pumpkin spice, and arrowroot and pour over the chicken pieces, skin side up. Cover and simmer slowly for 1 hour and 15 minutes or longer, until the chicken is quite tender. Uncover and continue to simmer until the liquid evaporates to a sauce consistency. Remove to a serving casserole and garnish the chicken with fresh orange slices and snipped parsley. *Six servings, 178 calories each.*

VARIATIONS

Oven-Baked Chicken Sangría: Bake the chicken in a covered ovenproof casserole at 325 degrees for 45 minutes. Uncover and bake an additional 20 to 30 minutes, basting frequently.

Hurry-Up Chicken Sangría: You may use 1½ cups bottled sangría in place of the red wine and orange juice. Or combine one envelope low-calorie orange breakfast drink mix with 1 cup dry red wine and ½ cup of water. Garnish with unsweetened canned mandarin orange sections before serving.

⤳ CHICKEN MARENGO ⟿

  1 frying chicken (3 pounds), cut up
  2 teaspoons salt
  ½ teaspoon coarsely ground pepper
  2 cloves garlic, minced
  ½ teaspoon dried thyme
  1 cup fresh tomato pulp
  1 onion, chopped
  ½ pound fresh mushrooms, sliced
  ¾ cup dry vermouth or Sauterne wine
  ½ cup water
  2 tablespoons chopped fresh parsley

Trim away any fringe fat from the chicken. Salt and pepper the pieces and place them, skin side down, in a cold nonstick skillet or heavy pot. Heat slowly over moderate flame, allowing the skin to warm gradually; the chicken will brown in its own fat.

When browned, pour off any fat and add the remaining ingredients. Cover and cook over a low flame for 45 minutes, until the chicken is tender. Uncover and continue to simmer until the liquid is reduced to a thick sauce. Skim off any fat before serving. *Six servings, 162 calories each.*

VARIATION

Hurry-Up Marengo: Salt and pepper the chicken pieces and brown as directed in the recipe above. Then add 1 can (10 ounces) of condensed tomato soup, 1 can (8 ounces) of mushrooms, and 2 cans (8 ounces each) of boiled onions, undrained. Season with salt, pepper, garlic, and thyme and simmer, covered, for 45 minutes. *Six servings, 187 calories per serving.*

⋖ "COUNTRY CAPTAIN" ⋗

(American Chicken Curry)

1 **frying chicken (about 2¼ pounds), cut up**
3 **tablespoons all-purpose flour**
1 **teaspoon garlic salt**
1 **tablespoon paprika**
1 **can (16 ounces) tomatoes**
½ **cup minced onion**
1½ **teaspoons curry powder**
½ **cup chopped green pepper**
1 **teaspoon dried thyme**
2 **tablespoons raisins**
1 **tablespoon dry-roasted peanuts (optional)**
1 **tablespoon shredded coconut (optional)**

Trim the fringe fat from the chicken. Combine the flour, garlic salt, and paprika in a large brown paper bag. Add the cut-up chicken pieces all at once and shake up.

Put the chicken pieces, skin side down, on a nonstick cookie sheet or shallow roasting pan. Bake in a very hot (450-degree) oven until well browned, about 25 minutes. Turn the chicken pieces over after 15 minutes.

Discard the fat in pan. Blot the browned chicken with a paper towel to remove fat, then place the chicken pieces in an ovenproof casserole with a cover.

Break up the tomatoes with a fork, then combine with all the remaining ingredients except the peanuts and coconut and pour over the chicken. Cover and return the casserole to oven. Lower the heat to 350 degrees and bake an additional 30 to 45 minutes, until the chicken is tender and the sauce is reduced. Check occasionally; if the sauce becomes too dry, add a little water. Sprinkle with peanuts and coconut, if desired, before serving. *Four servings, 236 calories each (257 with the peanut-coconut garnish).*

⋖ CLASSIC CHICKEN À LA KING ⋗

(At Only Half the Calories)

Chicken à la king—an American classic! It can be horrendously fattening or cleverly calorie wise, but equally delicious either way. Our fat-trimmed recipe is only 230 calories per serving, less than half the calories of conventionally prepared recipes. And despite being rich and creamy as well as low caloried and nutrition rich, this recipe is so low in saturated fat that it's a must for all heart-smart recipe clippers.

1 fryer (2 pounds), whole or cut up
  Salt and freshly ground pepper
3 cups water
¼ cup sherry wine
1 onion, quartered
¼ teaspoon freshly grated nutmeg
1 teaspoon monosodium glutamate
½ green bell pepper, chopped
½ red bell pepper, chopped
1 can (13 ounces) evaporated skim milk
3 tablespoons arrowroot or cornstarch
  Turmeric or yellow food coloring (optional)
  Toasted protein bread triangles (optional)

Wash and rinse the whole or cut-up chicken, then season with salt and pepper. Combine with the water, wine, onion, nutmeg, and monosodium glutamate in a heavy covered pot or Dutch oven. Simmer on top of the range or bake in a 350-degree oven until tender, about 50 or 60 minutes. Pour the broth through a strainer and chill in the refrigerator or freezer so that the fat rises to the surface and hardens. When the chicken is cool enough to handle, cut the meat into bite-sized chunks. Discard the bones and skin.

Skim the fat from the surface of the broth. Combine the broth and chopped pepper in a saucepan and cook, uncovered, until the broth is reduced by half and the pepper is tender.

Stir the evaporated milk and arrowroot together in a bowl until smooth, then add to the simmering broth. Cook and stir over moderate heat until the sauce simmers and thickens. Stir in the chicken and continue cooking until heated through, adding salt and pepper if needed. Turmeric or a few drops of yellow food coloring will give the sauce a rich golden color.

Serve on triangles of toasted protein bread, if desired. *Six servings, 230 calories each.*

◄§ QUICKIE CHICKEN À LA KING ß►

1 can (13 ounces) evaporated skim milk
3 tablespoons all-purpose flour
2 chicken bouillon cubes
¾ pound (2 cups) cooked, cubed chicken meat
¼ cup chopped red or green pepper (fresh or frozen)
  Salt, pepper, nutmeg, onion powder

Combine the milk, flour, and bouillon cubes in a saucepan. Cook and stir until simmering, then stir in the chicken, red or green pepper and cook until heated through. Season to taste, and thin the sauce with a little boiling water, if needed. *Four servings, 241 calories each.*

⋅§ COUNTRY CHICKEN DINNER §⋅

For a "down-home" dinner that also happens to be very chic and citified about calories and cholesterol, try the Slim Gourmet's Country Chicken—old-fashioned flavor prepared in a newfangled, no-fuss way.

1 **frying chicken (2 pounds), cut up**
1 **tablespoon all-purpose flour**
1 **teaspoon salt**
½ **teaspoon coarsely ground pepper**
  Garlic powder (optional)
  Half a bay leaf
2 **tablespoons chopped fresh parsley**
1 **cup canned whole onions**
1 **cup canned sliced carrots**
1 **cup canned sliced mushrooms**
½ **cup sherry wine or water**

With a sharp, pointed knife, trim away every bit of fringe fat from the chicken pieces. Brown the chicken without adding any extra fat by putting the chicken pieces, skin side down, in an unheated flameproof casserole or large skillet. Let the chicken warm gradually over a moderate flame; the fat under the skin will melt slowly and the chicken will begin to brown in its own fat. When completely browned, drain every bit of melted fat from the pan and blot the chicken pieces with paper toweling. (That's how to make a slim chicken even thinner!)

Return the chicken to the pot and sprinkle with the flour, salt, pepper, and a pinch of garlic powder. Add the bay leaf and parsley and canned onions, including the liquid. Add the liquid from the carrots and mushrooms, but reserve the vegetables. Add the wine or water.

Cover and simmer slowly for 30 to 40 minutes, until the chicken is nearly tender. Add the carrots and mushrooms and simmer, uncovered, until the liquid reduces and the sauce is gravy thick. *Four servings, 235 calories each.*

⋅§ BATTER-DIPPED "FRIED" CHICKEN §⋅

If there's any chicken dish more delicious—or fattening—than fried chicken, it's batter-dipped chicken. Tender, meaty, and moist, wrapped in a crunchy, flaky crust of spiced and seasoned batter!

The Slim Gourmet method doesn't fry the chicken. It's baked in the oven, so, in addition to saving calories, we cut short the usual mess! Our recipe is also higher in protein, lower in fat and carbohydrates, and much less expensive than convenience mixes, which add 845 calories to chicken, while ours adds only 360.

To coat our chicken, we use plain pancake mix, combined with water and seasoning. (For extra protein, use soy-enriched, high-protein pancake and waffle mix, available in health food stores.) The chicken pieces are baked in a hot oven, with no fat added.

During the first half hour of cooking, the chicken pieces look dry and brittle, exceedingly unappetizing, and you'll probably fear that our method won't work. But by the end of the cooking time, your chicken will emerge crisp and flavorful outside and moist and tender in the middle—just like fried chicken, but without the grease and excess calories.

  1 **frying chicken (2 pounds), quartered**
  ¾ **cup plain pancake mix**
  1 **teaspoon celery salt**
  1 **teaspoon onion powder**
  1 **teaspoon monosodium glutamate**
  1 **teaspoon paprika**
  ⅔ **cup hot water**

No need to remove the chicken skin, but trim away as much fringe fat as possible. Rinse, pat dry, and set aside.

Combine the remaining ingredients in a shallow pie plate or soup bowl, stirring only until blended. Dip or roll the chicken pieces in the batter, until lightly coated; the remaining batter may be spread on the chicken pieces with a knife.

Place the chicken pieces, skin side up, in a nonstick roasting pan or cookie sheet. Bake in a preheated 375-degree oven for 50 to 60 minutes, until the chicken is brown and crispy and tender inside; turn twice during the cooking. Blot the chicken pieces in absorbent paper toweling and serve. *Four servings, 281 calories each.*

◄§ GREEK CHICKEN AVGOLEMONO §►

Despite its luxurious flavor, this richly sauced Greek dish is low in calories, inexpensive, and easy to make. It is simply poached chicken, served in a delightfully flavored lemon-and-egg sauce. In Greek cuisine, lemon and egg is a favorite combination, and here we combine the flavors into a protein-rich chicken dish everyone will love.

  1 **frying chicken (3 pounds), cut up**
  3¼ **cups water**

1 teaspoon garlic salt
   Pinch of cayenne pepper
   Pinch of poultry seasoning
1 onion, sliced
4 stalks celery, sliced
1 bay leaf
1 tablespoon minced fresh parsley
1½ lemons
1 tablespoon all-purpose flour
2 teaspoons cornstarch
2 egg yolks
   Lemon slices for garnish

Trim the chicken of fringe fat. In a pot combine the chicken, 3 cups of the water, the seasonings, onion, celery, bay leaf, and parsley. Add ½ lemon, sliced. Cover and simmer over a low flame until tender, about 30 to 40 minutes. Remove the chicken to serving dish and keep warm; discard the lemon and bay leaf.

Heat the broth to boiling. Combine the flour, cornstarch, and remaining ¼ cup cold water into a paste and stir into the simmering broth.

In a small bowl, beat together the 2 egg yolks and the juice of the remaining lemon. Beat in a little of the hot broth. Stir this mixture into the pot and continue to cook, stirring constantly, until heated and thickened; don't boil or the sauce will curdle. Pour over the chicken, garnish with a few fresh lemon slices, and serve. *Six servings, 225 calories each.*

NOTE: Serve broccoli spears with this main course, and pour a little of the avgolemono sauce over your vegetables. It tastes like an especially fattening hollandaise.

CHICKEN VALENCIA

   Salt and freshly ground pepper
1 frying chicken (1¾ pounds), cut up
1 can (10½ ounces) condensed tomato soup
2 tablespoons Chablis wine
1 eggplant, peeled and diced
1 cup sliced mushrooms
½ cup chopped green pepper
1 small bay leaf
   Pinch of cayenne pepper

Salt and pepper the chicken pieces lightly and place, skin side up, in a small roasting pan. Bake in a preheated 400-degree oven for about 20 minutes, until the skin is brown and crispy. Pour off all fat.

Combine the remaining ingredients and add to pan, then cover with aluminum foil and place in the oven. Lower the heat to 325 degrees and bake until the eggplant is tender, an additional 30 to 40 minutes. *Four servings, 249 calories each.*

✓ ⊷ CHICKEN THIGH GOULASH ⊱

2 pounds chicken thighs
1 tablespoon paprika
1 teaspoon garlic powder
5 cups tomato juice
3 large onions, sliced
8 ounces broad noodles

Arrange the chicken thighs in a shallow, ovenproof baking dish and brown under the broiler until the skin is crackly. Drain off and discard all melted fat. Sprinkle the thighs with paprika and garlic powder, cover with the onions, and pour on the tomato juice. Bake, uncovered, in a 350-degree oven about 40 to 50 minutes, until the chicken is tender and the liquid has evaporated into a thick sauce.

Meanwhile, cook the noodles, according to package directions, in rapidly boiling water. Drain and serve with the chicken and sauce. *Six servings, 350 calories each.*

⊷ CHICKEN THIGHS CACCIATORE ⊱

2 pounds chicken thighs
   Salt and freshly ground pepper
2 tablespoons wine or water
½ cup chopped onion
4 cups canned Italian tomatoes
2 cups water
1 cup chopped celery
1 green pepper, chopped
1 clove garlic, chopped
½ teaspoon Italian seasoning
2 tablespoons freshly grated Parmesan cheese
12 ounces spaghetti

Season the chicken pieces with salt and pepper. Place in a heavy nonstick skillet or Dutch oven over moderate heat. Add the 2 tablespoons wine and cook until the liquid evaporates and the chicken begins to brown in its own melted fat. Add the onion and continue to cook until the onion is lightly browned. Add all the other ingredients except the spaghetti. Cover and cook until the liquid evaporates to a sauce consistency.

Meanwhile, cook the spaghetti until tender. Serve the chicken and sauce over the spaghetti. *Six servings, 377 calories each.*

⊷ CHICKEN THIGHS ROMANO ↦

2 pounds chicken thighs
1 onion, chopped
1 clove garlic, minced
1 can (16 ounces) tomatoes, chopped
3 cups tomato juice
¼ teaspoon oregano or Italian seasoning
2 tablespoons freshly grated extra-sharp Romano cheese
8 ounces protein-enriched spaghetti

Arrange the chicken thighs in a shallow, nonstick ovenproof baking dish and brown under the broiler. Pour off fat, then add the onion, garlic, tomatoes, and tomato juice. Sprinkle with the oregano and Romano and bake, uncovered, in a 350-degree oven until the chicken is tender and the liquid has evaporated.

Meanwhile, cook the spaghetti until tender, and serve it with the chicken and sauce. *Six servings, 343 calories each.*

⊷ MOCK DUCK IN ORANGE SAUCE ↦

Want to do some slimming sleight-of-hand? Be a kitchen wizard and turn low-cost, low-calorie chicken into succulent duck. If you don't think you can palm off chicken as duck, give it a fanciful name in restaurant French: *canard faux à l'orange* ("mock duck in orange sauce"). If your pronunciation is good enough, they'll be into dessert before they get it translated!

For your *canard faux*, you need cut-up chicken thighs, the ideal stand-in for duck. The flavor is deceivingly duck-y and, luckily for duck lovers, the thighs are among the least expensive parts of the chicken. They're often featured on "special," but the real economy is in the calories. Duck weighs in at 1,213 calories per pound, while dark-meat chicken is only 435.

Salt and freshly ground pepper
2½ pounds chicken thighs
1½ tablespoons cornstarch or arrowroot
2 teaspoons granulated sugar
1 cup chicken broth
¾ cup orange juice
2 teaspoons cider vinegar
2 tablespoons Cognac or 2 teaspoons brandy flavoring
1 tablespoon chopped fresh parsley
1 cup low-calorie mandarin oranges (packed in water or juice, not in syrup), drained
Fresh parsley for garnish

Salt and pepper the chicken and place on a rack in a roasting pan. Bake in a preheated 375-degree oven for 45 minutes, or until brown and tender.

Meanwhile, prepare the sauce. Combine all the other ingredients except the oranges and garnish in a saucepan. Cook and stir over low heat until the mixture boils, then simmer over low heat for about 10 minutes, until reduced to sauce consistency. Stir in the drained oranges and return to the boiling point. Pour over the chicken thighs and garnish with fresh parsley. *Six servings, 220 calories per serving.*

VARIATION

Quick Orange Baste: Mix together equal parts dry white wine and low-calorie orange marmalade. Add a dash of soy sauce and brush the chicken as it bakes or broils.

⋖ OVEN-FRIED CROQUETTES FROM BARGAIN CHICKEN ⋗

Why pay a premium price for chicken in parts when whole chickens are so much cheaper? Buy several chickens at the same time and cut them up yourself. Freezer-wrap, in meal-size portions, the premium-value legs, thighs, and breasts. And turn the necks, wings, backs, and giblets into soup and stock (see below)—and a very special favorite, chicken croquettes.

Most restaurant-style croquette dishes are deep-fat fried—short on chicken and long on bready fillers and fatty gravies. Not our version!

CROQUETTES:
2 cups (1 pound) chopped, cooked chicken meat (see below)
2 eggs
½ teaspoon poultry seasoning
1 tablespoon minced onion

 1 teaspoon salt or garlic salt
    Pinch of freshly ground pepper
¼ cup minced fresh parsley
 1 teaspoon monosodium glutamate

COATING:

 1 egg
 1 teaspoon salad oil
 5 tablespoons bread crumbs

CHICKEN CREAM SAUCE:

1½ cups Fat-Skimmed Chicken Broth (see below)
 2 teaspoons arrowroot
½ cup nonfat dry milk
1½ teaspoons minced fresh parsley

Combine the croquette ingredients and toss lightly; the mixture will be very moist. Fork-whip the egg and oil for the coating in a shallow bowl. Spread the bread crumbs on a plate.

Use an ice-cream scoop to form 8 balls of chicken mixture. Coat the balls lightly with egg, then roll in crumbs. (Pat into a restaurant-style "cone" shape, if desired.) Arrange the croquettes on a nonstick cookie sheet and bake in a preheated very hot (450-degree) oven for 12 to 15 minutes, until golden brown.

Meanwhile, prepare the sauce. Combine the sauce ingredients in a nonstick saucepan, then cook and stir over moderate heat until the mixture simmers and thickens. Pour over the baked croquettes and serve. *Each croquette equals 166 calories. Four servings, including sauce, 365 calories each.*

Fat-Skimmed Chicken Broth: Put the necks, giblets, wings, and backs from 4 or 5 cut-up chickens into a big soup pot with enough water to cover, plus an onion, a few ribs of celery, salt and pepper, and a tablespoon of monosodium glutamate, which will heighten the flavor. Simmer, covered, for about 2 hours, until very tender (or 40 minutes in a pressure cooker). Pick the meat from the bones, discarding the bones and skin, and grind the meat up for the croquettes. Refrigerate the broth so you can skim all the fat from the surface. Your home-made fat-skimmed broth can be spooned into 1- or 2-cup jars and frozen for all sorts of uses.

⋈ LUNCHEON CHICKEN AND WAFFLES ⋈

1 cup skim milk, more if necessary
2 tablespoons dry white wine (optional)
1 tablespoon arrowroot or cornstarch
1 cup cubed, cooked white chicken meat
  Salt and freshly ground pepper
  Monosodium glutamate
  Onion powder
  Minced fresh parsley and paprika for garnish
  Waffles for Two (page 290), prepared without vanilla extract

Combine the skim milk with the wine and arrowroot or cornstarch in a saucepan. Cook, stirring, over moderate heat until thickened. Stir in the chicken and season to taste with salt, pepper, monosodium glutamate, and onion powder. Cook, stirring, until heated through, thinning with additional skim milk if needed. Add a sprinkle of minced parsley and paprika for color and serve over hot waffle sections. *Four servings, 189 calories each.*

NOTE: Add a tossed salad or cooked parsleyed carrots for a satisfying lunch.

⋈ CAN-OPENER PAELLA ⋈

1 can (8 ounces) carrots
1 can (8 ounces) boiled onions
1 can (4 ounces) pimientos
1 can (16 ounces) artichoke hearts
1 cup instant rice
1 can (13 ounces) boned chicken
1 can (7 ounces) shrimp, rinsed
¼ teaspoon saffron
  Garlic salt and freshly ground pepper

Drain the vegetables and reserve the liquid. Measure out 1½ cups into a large skillet, bring to a boil, and add the rice. Cover and let stand for 10 minutes, then add all the other ingredients. Cook, covered, over low flame until heated through, stirring occasionally. *Six servings, 285 calories each.*

NOTE: Paella is a Spanish dish that varies from region to region, according to what's available, so you can vary the recipe with canned vegetables you happen to have on hand. Canned mushrooms, asparagus, green beans would be good choices. For a luxury touch, use lump lobster or crabmeat or "clams in their shells" (all available in cans).

11
TURKEY

Planning a holiday dinner? Let's talk turkey!

If you have to count calories as well as pennies, the price per pound isn't the only consideration to keep in mind when turkey choosing. As a Slim Gourmet cook, you want the most turkey and the least calories for your Thanksgiving dinner dollar. That means a reexamination of some generally accepted notions.

Take the topic of size. It's axiomatic that the bigger the bird, the less it costs per pound. But not in calories. Superbirds—those unwieldy giants that need two brothers-in-law and a teen-age quarterback to heft into the oven—contain more fat and calories than younger, trimmer turkeys. Also, as the noble native bird puts on weight, the proportion of valuable body-building protein decreases.

If you think you get "more meat and less waste" with bigger, older birds, you're wrong. To see how they stack up agewise, according to data provided by the U.S. Department of Agriculture, check the table on page 168.

And what about those premium-priced birds that imply they're basted with butter? In some cases it's not butter at all, but a conglomeration of vegetable oils (including cholesterol-inducing coconut oil) plus water, salt, chemicals, and phony coloring and butter flavoring. The extra cost buys you less turkey and more fat and calories—quite a bit more, according to a study by Consumers Union. Young birds that might normally contain 6 percent fat re-

CALORIE COUNTERS' TURKEY BUYING GUIDE

	*Young**	*Medium-fat**	*Fat**
Protein	21%	20%	18%
Fat	6%	16%	29%
Bones	27%	27%	27%
Calories per pound	480	752	1136

* "Young" refers to birds under 24 weeks; "medium-fat" birds are those 26 to 32 weeks; and "fat" refers to larger, more mature birds over 32 weeks.

vealed fat contents as high as 16 percent in test samples; in some birds, the study said, "the fat was about as saturated as lard."

Here are our Slim Gourmet turkey suggestions:

◄§ Avoid oversized, overage birds. Choose a turkey no bigger than you need.

◄§ Look for an untampered-with turkey; read the label carefully. Don't pay a premium price for a turkey injected with grease.

◄§ Don't add fat. Roast your turkey according to the wrapper's directions. If you must baste, use water, fat-skimmed canned broth, or a broth you've made from the giblets.

Tips for Surviving Thanksgiving Turkey Dinner

If the Pilgrims had been on diets, there probably wouldn't be any Thanksgiving Day. A few slabs of turkey and a plateful of celery sticks aren't much to celebrate with; yet that's all most diet books tell you to eat. "You can enjoy Thanksgiving," they say. "Eat all the turkey you want. Just keep away from the dark meat, the skin, the dressing, the gravy, the cranberry sauce, the mashed potatoes, the creamed onions, the appetizers, the cider, the wine, and the pumpkin, apple, and mincemeat pie!"

Here's our Slim Gourmet guide to surviving Thanksgiving—with seams intact:

APPETIZERS: Soup, celery sticks, tomato juice, pickles, shrimp cocktail, and all the other little goodies set out before the meal are really "de-appetizers," you know. So don't dispense with these festive holiday additions. If there was ever a day to "ruin your dinner," this is it!

TURKEY: White-meat turkey is only half as fattening as most cuts of beef, pork, lamb, or ham, so eat hearty.

GRAVY: Grease is tasteless, yet grease is what makes most gravies off limits for calorie counters. Drain the meat juices from the pan and quick-chill in your freezer so you can lift the fat off before thickening your gravy. Cornstarch is a more calorie-conscious thickener than flour because you need less. Fat-free turkey gravy can be as low as 20 calories a quarter cup, while the same amount of greasy gravy is over 100.

MASHED POTATOES: Prepared with skim milk they're less than 50 calories a half cup. It's the melted butter or greasy gravy that packs on the pounds. But a candied sweet potato is close to 300 calories.

DRESSING: Yes, you can make a lower-calorie stuffing simply by leaving out the extra fat. Packaged dry-dressing mixes are easy to use, but you can also make a superb stuffing that never gets soggy from leftover protein or diet bread. Be sure to add lots of chopped celery and onions, plenty of fresh parsley and chopped-up giblets—the more you add, the less fattening it is.

VEGETABLES: Don't let the sheer size of your turkey tempt you into short-cutting on vegetables "since there's so much to eat anyway." Mashed turnips, parsleyed carrots, green beans and mushrooms, squash—these colorful additions to a holiday table can compete for plate room with a more fattening fare.

THE "ET CETERAS": Cranberry sauce is spectacularly fattening, so limit yourself to a dab, unless you live where a diet brand is available. The kind of wine that goes best with turkey, a crackly dry white wine like Chablis, is only 60 calories a 3-ounce glass. Cider is even less, if you can limit yourself to a tiny sip.

DESSERT: If you must sample everything, you're safer to have your dessert immediately after dinner when limiting yourself to a mini-portion. It won't seem like such a sacrifice.

LEFTOVERS: Freeze everything. Out of sight, out of mind. Or be a generous hostess and bundle up all the fattening extras into little "Care packages" for your guests to take home. After all, they ate at your house, so they won't have any leftovers of their own.

Turkey—in New Guises

Besides the ubiquitous holiday roasting turkey, most shoppers are familiar with turkey-in-parts and boneless roasts—but that's just the beginning of the bonanza we're likely to see in the next few years. Gaining ground are the following—and all of them spell good news for the cost-conscious, the calorie counter, and the cholesterol-careful. Because, ounce for ounce, no other meat is less expensive, higher in protein, or lower in saturated fat than turkey.

⊷§ Turkey steaks (see pages 194–195)—cut thick for barbecue or thin for dishes like scaloppine, cordon bleu and bracciole.

⊷§ Turkey cubes—for those quick-cooking, low-calorie Oriental dishes.

⊷§ Delicatessen delights—like turkey bologna, salami, and pastrami, all at a fraction of the fat and calories of the real McCoy.

⊷§ Even turkey breakfast sausage—with less than 7 percent fat. Most pork sausage is half fat or more.

⊷§ Best of all, now there's turkey hamburger (see page 173), already a supermarket staple in many West Coast cities. Low in calories (600 per pound as opposed to 1,200 for beef), cost, and cholesterol, ground turkey meat can take the place of fatty hamburger in any penny pincher's recipe repertoire. It sells at about the same price per pound as ordinary hamburger, but it's a better buy because 1 pound serves four or more, while fatty chopped meat shrinks to three servings or less.

⊷ QUARTER TURKEY ROAST ⊱

What's a quarter turkey? It's a sale-priced big bird cut into quarters. All you have to do is watch your supermarket ads for a good price on whole turkeys. Then pick one out and ask your meat man to saw it into four equal parts. Except in the busiest times, most supermarkets will willingly perform this service for you.

When you get your quartered turkey home, rewrap each section separately, label, store, and freeze until needed. You can roast each quarter separately.

To prepare a frozen turkey quarter for cooking, you need to thaw it only enough so that you can remove the paper-wrapped giblets that were packed inside. Or you can thaw it completely. A frozen or partly frozen turkey takes longer to cook, naturally, so rely on a meat thermometer for perfect results.

Whole turkeys can be roasted uncovered because they're protected by a covering of skin, but quarter turkeys should be moist roasted at a higher temperature in a covered pan.

¼ **young turkey, frozen or thawed (about 3½ pounds)**
   Onion or garlic salt, freshly ground pepper, and monosodium glutamate
   Meat tenderizer (optional)
3 **cups water**
1 **cup finely chopped onion**
1 **cup finely chopped celery**
2 **cups (4 ounces) seasoned bread cubes**
½ **cup boiling water**
2 **tablespoons flour**
2 **tablespoons arrowroot or cornstarch**

Season the turkey on all surfaces with generous amounts of onion or garlic salt, pepper, and monosodium glutamate. Sprinkle with meat tenderizer, if you wish, and puncture in several places with a fork. Place the turkey quarter, skin side down, in a roasting pan with a cover. Add the water and bake, covered, in a preheated 400-degree oven for 1 hour. (This method helps draw out the fat.)

Remove the pan from the oven. Drain the liquid into a tall glass or jar and place in the refrigerator.

Combine the chopped onion, chopped celery, bread cubes, and boiling water and heap in a mound in the center of the roasting pan. Place the partly cooked turkey quarter over the stuffing, this time with the skin side up. Lower the oven to 325 degrees, cover the pan, and bake an additional 45 minutes to one hour, until a meat thermometer placed in a meaty portion reads 185 degrees.

Skim all the fat from the chilled turkey broth. Combine the broth, cornstarch, and flour in a saucepan and cook, stirring, until the mixture simmers and thickens. Thin with water if needed, add seasoning to taste, and serve the gravy with the turkey and dressing. *Eight servings, 233 calories each.*

NOTE: Pack leftovers in individual TV dinner trays and freeze for future no-work meals.

⊷ TURKEY-DRESSING CASSEROLE ⊱

No turkey to stuff? You don't have to give up "stuffing"—even if you're watching your weight. Here's a Slim Gourmet side dish that's the perfect protein-rich partner for today's small-family boneless turkey roasts or turkey-in-parts. It's a casserole dish made from stuffing mix—lots of good nutrition added, but no fat. The texture is a cross between dressing, spoon bread, and bread pudding, so rich and moist it doesn't even need gravy.

2 **cups skim milk**
3 **medium eggs**
2 **onions, chopped**
3 **stalks celery, chopped**
1 **clove garlic, peeled**
2 **cups seasoned stuffing mix**
Salt and freshly ground pepper

Scald the milk and allow it to cool. Add the eggs and fork-whip lightly. Mince together the onion, celery, and garlic; add to the egg mixture. Stir in the stuffing mix, salt, and pepper. Combine all the ingredients thoroughly, place in an ovenproof casserole or nonstick loaf pan, and bake at 325 degrees for 50 minutes, until set. *Eight servings, 126 calories each.*

For Variety: Add ½ cup drained canned mushrooms (10 calories), or stir in the contents of a small (2½-ounce) can of deviled ham (200 calories). Cooked minced turkey giblets add more low-fat protein (less than 60 calories an ounce). For individual servings, pile the mixture into nonstick muffin pans and cut the baking time to about 30 minutes.

For Extra Protein: Use 2 cups of cubed "protein bread" instead of the packaged stuffing mix. (If the bread is fresh, toast it lightly before cutting it into cubes.) Season it with ½ teaspoon mixed poultry seasoning.

In a Hurry? Use 1 cup of evaporated skim milk and 1 cup water in place of the 2 cups scalded milk. Also, 2 tablespoons dried onion flakes and one tablespoon dried celery flakes can serve as a stand-in for the vegetables. Season with garlic salt.

✓ ⊷ LOW-COST TURKEY STEW ⊱

What to do when even stew meat is out of sight? Switch to turkey—but not a feast-sized bird. Look in your supermarket poultry case for frozen turkey thighs. Once defrosted, you can easily cut them into stew-sized cubes of meat. Use it to replace beef in any favorite stew or ragout-type recipe for a dish that's very easy and economical. And dark-meat turkey is under 700 calories a pound, while beef stew meat can be 1,500 or more. (Turkey is low in saturated fat and cholesterol, too.)

In preparing this recipe, add the turkey bone to the pot. You can fish it out later, along with the bay leaf.

1 **large turkey thigh (1¼ pounds)**
2 **cups plus 2 tablespoons water**
1 **cup beef stock**
2 **onions, chopped**
1 **clove garlic, minced**
1 **bay leaf**
1 **pound small carrots, scraped and left whole**
2 **potatoes, peeled and cut in half**
2 **tablespoons all-purpose flour combined with ¼ cup cold water**
  Salt and freshly ground pepper

Defrost the turkey. With a sharp knife, simply strip the meat from the bone and cut in 2-inch cubes. Put the turkey cubes, skin side down, in a heavy nonstick pot. Add the 2 tablespoons water, cover, and cook over high heat until the moisture evaporates and the turkey cubes begin to brown in their own melted fat. Uncover and brown evenly on all sides. Drain off the fat, if any.

Add the 2 cups water and all the other ingredients except the flour and water. Cover and simmer over low heat until the turkey is tender, about 35 to 45 minutes. Stir the flour and water into the pot until the gravy is thickened. Season to taste and serve. *Four servings, 292 calories each.*

VARIATION

Turkey Ragout: Follow the preceding recipe, but substitute 1 cup tomato juice for the beef broth and ½ cup dry red wine in place of part of the water. A pinch of thyme or poultry seasoning can be added, as well as an undrained 8-ounce can of chopped mushrooms. *Four servings, 308 calories each.*

Turkeyburger

Like most of these new turkey products, ground turkey is hard to find in some sections, unless you ask for it. It's in most supermarket display cases in the West, but elsewhere it's a special order or custom-ground item. Of course, if you have an electric food grinder, it's well worth the savings to turn an extra holiday bargain into several pounds of fresh ground turkeyburger for your freezer, wrapped in meal-sized portions.

◄§ TURKEY MEAT LOAF I ৯►

2 pounds ground raw turkey
2 eggs, beaten
¼ cup water
⅔ cup bread crumbs
½ cup finely chopped onion
2 large stalks celery, minced
½ teaspoon poultry seasoning
2 teaspoons garlic salt
   Pinch of freshly ground pepper

Combine all the ingredients and shape into a loaf. Bake for 1 hour 10 minutes in a preheated 350-degree oven. Delicious hot or cold, this makes a marvelous sandwich on protein bread, too. *Ten servings, 195 calories each.*

VARIATION

Turkey Meat Loaf II (A Reader's Recipe)

Dear Barbara,

I just love your blender-easy meat loaf. Tonight I used the same idea for a terrific improvisation. We can get ground turkey in our market. So, I used that gorgeous low-fat, low-calorie turkey meat instead of beef, and then I really went wild. We had some zucchini squash in the refrigerator and I minced it in the blender. I really fooled my husband—the way he sees it, if it's diet, it can't possibly be edible. But he loved it! Thank you so much for your recipes and hints.

Mrs. L. W. Grissom
Buena Vista, California

✎ HOT OR COLD TURKEY LOAF ❧

2 pounds ground raw turkey
3 slices diet or protein bread, moistened with water and squeezed
   dry
2 eggs or 4 egg whites
1 onion, minced
1 green pepper, chopped
2 tablespoons prepared horseradish
2 teaspoons salt or garlic salt
1 tablespoon prepared mustard
½ cup skim milk
5 tablespoons catsup

Lightly mix all the ingredients and mold into a loaf. Bake in a 375-degree oven for 1¼ hours. *Eight servings, 213 calories each.*

✎ COOKOUT PARMESAN PATTIES ❧

2 pounds ground raw turkey
2 teaspoons onion salt
1 teaspoon oregano or Italian seasoning
¼ pound grated Parmesan cheese
5 tablespoons catsup
3 tablespoons bread crumbs

Combine all the ingredients and shape into 8 patties. Brown for 5 minutes on each side under broiler or on barbecue. *Eight servings, 183 calories each.*

VARIATION

Pizza Turkeyburgers: Follow the preceding recipe, but omit the grated cheese. Arrange the patties in a shallow baking dish. Broil for 5 minutes, then turn and baste with 1 cup (8-ounce can) plain tomato sauce. Top each patty with a ½-ounce slice of part-skim mozzarella cheese. Broil until the cheese melts, then serve immediately. *Eight servings, 218 calories each.*

Culinary Magic: Turning Turkey into Costly "Veal"—The Turkey Steak

In the Middle Ages, chemists spent their time trying to turn tin into gold. Today they would be trying to turn it into veal cutlets! But if you're a clever Slim Gourmet cook, you can turn turkey into veal. White meat turkey steak can serve as a stand-in for veal in nearly any recipe—at a fraction of the cost and a calorie count even lower than veal's, only 522 per pound. And white-meat turkey is cholesterol-shy.

What are turkey steaks? Scaloppine-thin slices of raw turkey meat cut from the breast. They are sometimes called "turkey butterfly steaks," "white turkey fillet," or "turkey cutlet." Such specialties are not being featured in super-markets in many sections of the country, so ask your meat manager. How-ever, if you can't get it, it's easy to make your own, and even less expensive.

Simply buy a raw turkey breast and remove the skin. Remove the meat in 2 solid chunks from each side of the breastbone. Using a very sharp knife, cut ½-inch slices of raw turkey, against the grain.

⋖ TURKEY STEAKS SCALOPPINE ⋗

¼ cup water or beef broth, skimmed or fat
1 tablespoon butter or margarine
5 tablespoons lemon juice
8 turkey butterfly steaks or 1¼ pounds raw turkey breast, sliced
  Garlic salt and freshly ground pepper
  Fresh parsley and lemon slices for garnish

Combine the water, butter, and lemon juice in a large nonstick skillet. Heat until the butter is melted, then add the turkey steaks in a single layer. Season with salt and pepper and cook, uncovered, over high heat, turning occasion-ally. When the liquid evaporates, the turkey is cooked through and will begin to brown in the remaining fat; turn to brown both sides. Remove the turkey slices to a heated platter and garnish with parsley and lemon slices. *Four servings, 193 calories each.*

⋖ TURKEY STEAK PARMIGIANA ⋗

1 egg
2 tablespoons polyunsaturated oil
1½ pounds turkey butterfly steaks
½ cup Italian-flavored bread crumbs
8 small slices (3 ounces) part-skim mozzarella

Whip the egg and oil together in a shallow dish. Dip the turkey steaks into the egg mixture, then coat lightly with bread crumbs. Arrange in a single layer on a shallow nonstick baking tray or cookie tin. Place in a preheated very hot oven, 450 degrees or more, and bake for 10 minutes, turning once. Top with the cheese slices and return to the oven, just until the cheese begins to melt. Serve as is, or with Quick Sauce Italiano (see page 176). *Six servings, 249 calories.*

Quick Sauce Italiano: Combine 2 cups plain tomato sauce with ¼ cup dry white wine, 2 tablespoons freshly grated Romano cheese, and 1 teaspoon oregano. Season with garlic or onion powder and simmer for 5 minutes. *Adds 30 calories per serving.*

Turkey the Best, Easiest, and Least Fattening Way

With today's modern motorized rotisseries, outdoors has become *the* easiest place to cook turkey. And the most calorie-wise! No stuffing, dressing, or saucing needed, no gravy, candied yams or sugared cranberries. Without the calorific trappings of holiday meals, turkey emerges as one of the least fattening feasts there is. And the most delicious!

To cook turkey conveniently outdoors, you need a covered barbecue and a motorized spit. "Coals" can be the real thing or the permanent kind fueled by gas or electricity.

Look for a turkey without the added calories of "self-basting" fats or oils. Check the internal temperature near the end of the cooking period with a meat thermometer; it should reach 175 degrees.

ROTISSERIED WHOLE TURKEY

1 **small turkey (6 to 9 pounds)**
   Salt and freshly ground pepper
   Fruit Juice Baste (optional; see below)

Thaw, rinse, and dry the bird, if frozen. Rub the inside with salt, and season the skin with salt and pepper. Insert the spit rod through the turkey from the back and through the breastbone. Fasten each end with spit anchors. Tie the drumsticks together, and the wings over the breast. Cook on the revolving spit in a covered rotisserie over moderate coals or at a medium heat setting for 3 to 4 hours, depending on weight. Baste once an hour with the fruit baste, if desired. Wait 10 to 15 minutes before carving. *Each 4 ounce serving, meat and skin, contains about 175 calories.*

Fruit Juice Baste: Combine 2 cups diluted lemon juice or unsweetened orange, pineapple, or apple juice with 1 teaspoon dried sage, thyme, or poultry seasoning. Note that lemon juice and tarragon are a good combination.

ROTISSERIED TURKEY ROLL

1 **frozen boneless turkey roast (3 to 9 pounds)**
½ **cup soy sauce**
½ **cup dry white wine**

This works well with light, dark, or mixed meat turkey roll.

Unwrap the frozen turkey roll; place in a plastic bag and add the soy sauce, wine, and enough water to immerse the meat in liquid. Allow the turkey to defrost in this marinade.

Insert the spit through the turkey roll; secure each end. Roast on a revolving spit in a covered rotisserie over moderate coals or at a medium heat setting. Allow 2 hours for a turkey roll under 3 pounds, about 4 hours for a 6-pound roast, and as long as 4 hours for a 9-pound roll; check the internal temperature with a meat thermometer. Wait 10 to 15 minutes before slicing. *Each 4-ounce serving contains approximately 175 calories.*

Turkey Encores

Get that space-hogging bird out of your refrigerator and into something slimming. Dig out your biggest pot and add enough water to cover the bones. Cover and simmer for 20 to 30 minutes, just until the meat loosens easily from the bones.

Strain the stock into a bowl and season with onion or garlic salt, pepper, and a pinch of monosodium glutamate. Chill in your refrigerator. When cold, skim every last bit of fat from the surface. Package your homemade, low-calorie turkey broth in 1-cup containers and freeze, and when the bones are cool enough to handle, strip away the meat and freeze it, also in 1-cup containers.

Here are some quickie meals you can make:

⊷ KNIFE-AND-FORK SOUP ⊷

Combine 1 cup turkey meat and 1 cup fat-skimmed turkey broth. Add 1 can (8 ounces) of sliced carrots and 1 can (4 ounces) mushrooms, including liquid. Heat to boiling. A quick and easy meal-in-a-bowl for lunch or supper. *Two servings, 181 calories each.*

⊷ ORIENTAL OMELET ⊷

1 tablespoon diet margarine
4 eggs, beaten
1 cup chopped, cooked turkey meat
2 tablespoons minced onion
   Soy sauce

Heat the diet margarine in a 10-inch nonstick skillet over a high flame. When it begins to sizzle, add the beaten eggs. Sprinkle the eggs with the chopped turkey meat and the minced onion. When the underside of the omelet is golden brown, gently fold it over on itself and roll it out onto a heated serving plate. To serve, cut in half and sprinkle with soy sauce. *Two servings, 317 calories each.*

12
SEAFOOD

Fresh-caught fish—there's nothing better!

Unless you have to clean it.

Many homemakers forgo fish, unless they can fetch it fresh. A pity, if fresh-or-nothing means that you have fish only once a month, because all fish is low in calories, even so-called fatty fish. "Fatty" mackerel is only 800 calories per pound, compared with 1,800 or so for rib of beef! Lean fish like flounder and sole are only 358 calories for a whole pound.

Frozen fish is sometimes fresher than "fresh"—or what passes for fresh in some stores. Under ideal conditions, fresh fish is frozen right on the boat and never gets a chance to thaw until it reaches your kitchen. You can't get fresher than that, unless you're married to a fishing nut.

Here are some points for "fishing" in the supermarket:

◦§ In the frozen-food case, look for 1-pound brick-shaped boxes of filleted fish, including flounder, sole, cod, haddock, and perch—all low in calories and very inexpensive. But watch for telltale signs of careless handling or accidental defrosting and refreezing.

◦§ Defrosted fish, just like fresh fish, should have absolutely no odor if it's been properly handled. Discard it or return it if your frozen fish smells fishy. And unless you plan to use it immediately, don't buy it; ask the counterman to give you the still-frozen fish instead.

◦§ If you have to count calories, stick with pure, plain fish. "Fish sticks" and other fussed-up fish is coated with starch and grease. One pound of boneless cod is only 356 calories; one pound of fish sticks is 800. And that, too, means a lot less fish.

⤙ SPICY SOLE ⤚

Here's a quick dish with inexpensive frozen fillets of sole. It would work equally well with flounder.

2 **boxes (2 pounds) frozen sole**
5 **tablespoons steak sauce**
¼ **cup catsup**
1 **tablespoon polyunsaturated oil**
1 **tablespoon vinegar**
1 **teaspoon salt**
   Pinch of curry powder

Defrost the fish at room temperature. Separate the fillets and place on a broiling pan. Mix the remaining ingredients together and spread half on the surface of the fish. Broil, 3 inches from heat, for 3 to 4 minutes, then turn the fish carefully and brush on the remaining sauce. Broil an additional 3 to 4 minutes and serve. *Eight servings, 125 calories per serving.*

⤙ ELEGANT SOLE STUFFED WITH SLIM CRABMEAT ⤚

Crabmeat and sole are both extremely low in calories. Put them together, however, and somehow the calories escalate to dizzying heights. The average restaurant-style crabmeat-stuffed fish dish is generally a too-generous 500 calories or more—including several hundred additional calories in the form of a sauce or topping.

That's because the crabmeat filling is often more "filler" than crabmeat! And the sauce is a cholesterol watcher's nightmare of butterfat.

Our Slim Gourmet stuffed sole, on the other hand, is extra generous with crabmeat, but, despite its rich taste and elegant appearance, our dish is a calorie-shy 185 per serving, including the delicately flavored French wine and cheese sauce we use as the final fillip. You will like this simple sauce for any fish dish. Don't worry about the wine calories, they evaporate in the cooking. If you prefer not to use wine, simply leave it out and increase the milk to 2 cups.

2 pounds frozen fillets of sole

FILLING:
 1 can (4 ounces) mushroom stems and pieces
 3 tablespoons finely minced onion
 1 can (7½ ounces) crabmeat, drained
 ¼ cup cracker crumbs or bread crumbs
 3 tablespoons minced fresh parsley
 ½ teaspoon salt
 ¼ teaspoon freshly ground pepper

WINE SAUCE:
 2 tablespoons arrowroot or cornstarch
1½ cups skim milk
 5 tablespoons dry white wine
 ½ teaspoon salt
 2 ounces (½ cup) shredded Swiss cheese
  Paprika

Separate the defrosted fillets carefully and cut into 8 pieces.

Drain the mushrooms and chop fine. Combine with the onion, crabmeat, crumbs, parsley, salt, and pepper. Spread the mixture evenly over the fish fillets and roll up. Secure each roll with a toothpick, then arrange the fillets in a shallow 2-quart casserole or baking dish and set aside.

Combine all the wine sauce ingredients except the paprika in a small saucepan. Cook and stir over moderate heat until the sauce simmers and thickens. Pour the sauce over the fish fillets, sprinkle with paprika, and bake in a preheated 400-degree oven for 25 to 30 minutes, until the fish flakes easily. *Eight servings, 185 calories each.*

FILLET OF SOLE À LA BONNE FEMME

Filet of sole *à la bonne femme* is one of those provincial fish classics that's simply de rigueur in every French cookbook. *Bonne femme* means "good woman" or "good wife," so the dish translates out as "fillet of sole the way a good wife cooks it."

 1 pound frozen sole
 1 can (4 ounces) chopped mushrooms
 1 cup sherry wine
 ¼ cup minced onion
  Salt and freshly ground pepper
  Chopped fresh parsley
  Tarragon

1 **tablespoon flour**
¼ **cup skim milk**
  Paprika
  Butter-flavored salt (optional)

Defrost and separate the sole fillets. Drain the mushrooms (canned "stems and pieces" are fine for this recipe), and place them in the bottom of a round 10-inch baking dish or shallow casserole. Arrange the sole fillets on top of the mushrooms, pour over the sherry, and sprinkle with the onion and with salt, pepper, parsley, and tarragon to taste. Bake for 10 minutes in a preheated 450-degree oven.

Carefully drain the liquid from the fish into a shallow saucepan and heat over a high flame. Permit the liquid to reduce somewhat. Meanwhile, mix the flour and milk together, then add to the boiling liquid, stirring constantly. When thickened, pour onto the fish. Sprinkle with paprika and butter-flavored salt and put under the broiler for a few minutes, until hot. *Four servings, 120 calories per serving.*

✑ MARYANN'S SEAFOOD SUPREME ❧

Here's a "company dish" contributed by our friends Pete and Maryann Burns. Try it with any local fish—flounder or sole fillets—from your fish store or supermarket freezer chest. This is a company-easy, one-dish dinner that needs little more than a salad and white wine.

2 **pounds flounder or sole fillets**
½ **cup dry white wine**
1 **package (10 ounces) frozen green beans or asparagus tips, defrosted**
1 **can (8 ounces) sliced mushrooms, drained**
1 **cup cherry tomatoes, cut in half**
2 **tablespoons all-purpose flour**
½ **teaspoon salt**
  Pinch of white pepper
1¼ **cups skim milk**
1 **lightly beaten egg yolk**
2 **slices protein bread, cut in small cubes**
¼ **cup freshly grated Parmesan cheese**
  Paprika
  Lemon wedges for garnish

Arrange the fillets in a single layer in a decorative oven-to-table baking dish. Pour on the wine. Bake in a preheated 400-degree oven for 6 minutes, until the fish loses its transparent look. Remove the dish from the oven, drain off the wine (reserving it), and arrange the defrosted vegetables, mushrooms, and tomatoes on top of the fish.

Combine the flour, salt, pepper, and milk in a saucepan. Cook and stir until thickened, then remove from the heat. Combine a little of the hot sauce with the beaten egg yolk, then add the egg yolk to the saucepan. Reheat, stirring constantly, but do not boil. Stir in the reserved wine.

Pour the sauce over the fillets and vegetables. Top with the bread cubes and cheese, sprinkle with paprika, and bake, uncovered, in a 350-degree oven for 25 to 30 minutes. Serve with lemon wedges. *Eight servings, 165 calories each.*

◄§ SEAFOOD PARMESAN §►

To prepare this dish you'll need "sour half-and-half," real sour cream with a reduced fat content. It's one-third lower in calories than regular sour cream, and a better buy, figure-wise, than imitation sour cream. Here's how they compare:

Product	Calories per Tablespoon	Calories per Cup
Sour cream	32	506
Imitation sour cream	24	388
Sour half-and-half	20	320

2 pounds flounder or sole fillets
1 cup sour half-and-half or imitation sour cream
¼ cup freshly grated Parmesan cheese
1 tablespoon minced onion
1 tablespoon lemon juice
½ teaspoon garlic salt
 Cayenne pepper
 Chopped fresh parsley
 Paprika

Thaw the fish completely if frozen, then cut into serving pieces and place in a single layer in a nonstick baking dish. Combine all the other ingredients except the paprika and spread over fish. Bake in a preheated 375-degree oven for 10 to 15 minutes, until the fish flakes easily. Sprinkle liberally with paprika and serve. *Eight servings, only 143 calories each.*

⊷ EASY WINE-POACHED FISH AU GRATIN ⊷

1 pound frozen fillets of flounder or sole
2 tablespoons minced onion
½ small sweet red or green pepper, cut in strips
½ cup dry white wine
3 ounces sliced or shredded Cheddar cheese
2 tablespoons bread crumbs

Spread the fillets in a 12-inch pie pan or other shallow ovenproof dish, just large enough to hold them. Sprinkle on the minced onion and pepper strips and pour on the white wine. Cover the dish with aluminum foil and place in a hot (450-degree) oven. Bake for 15 to 20 minutes, until the fish turns opaque white and is cooked through.

Remove from the oven and pour off all the liquid. Cover the top of the fish with the cheese and sprinkle the bread crumbs evenly over the surface. Return to the oven and bake or broil, uncovered, until the cheese is just melted and browned. *Four servings, 189 calories each.*

⊷ FLOUNDER FLORENTINE ⊷

It took Popeye the Sailor Man to talk little kids into eating their spinach, but grown-up spinach unenthusiasts need stronger inducement. So we offer our Slim Gourmet Flounder Florentine, a sophisticated seafood-spinach dish accented with cheese. Maybe it won't help you be as strong—or live as long—as Popeye, but spinach is a low-calorie bargain that's rich in nutrition, particularly iron and vitamin A.

1½ pounds (two 12-ounce packages) flounder fillets
2 packages (10 ounces each) frozen spinach
1 cup water
2 tablespoons lemon juice
1 teaspoon onion salt
½ teaspoon freshly ground pepper
1½ tablespoons all-purpose flour
¼ cup skim milk
¼ cup freshly grated Parmesan cheese
Paprika

Defrost the fish if frozen. Defrost and drain the spinach.

Place the fish fillets in the bottom of a baking dish. Add the water, lemon juice, salt, and pepper. Cover the dish and bake in a preheated 350-degree oven for about 12 minutes, until the fish flakes easily.

Remove from the oven and drain the liquid into a saucepan. Heat to boiling. Mix the flour with the skim milk and stir into the liquid. Cook and stir over a moderate flame until the mixture simmers and thickens.

Spread the drained spinach over the fish fillets and pour on the sauce. Sprinkle with the cheese and paprika and return to the oven to bake or broil, until the cheese is melted and the top is browned. *Six servings, 198 calories each.*

✑ CURRIED FISH ॐ

1 **pound fresh or frozen haddock, sole, pike, or pollack fillets**
1 **small onion, sliced**
½ **cup water**
2 **tablespoons all-purpose flour**
1 **cup skim milk**
1 **teaspoon curry powder**
½ **teaspoon salt or butter-flavored salt**
1 **teaspoon granulated sugar or equivalent substitute**
⅛ **teaspoon ground ginger**
2 **cups hot, cooked rice**

Defrost the fish fillets, if frozen, then combine with the onion and water in a large saucepan. Cover and simmer for 8 minutes, until the fish flakes easily. Remove the fish from the pan and break into bite-sized pieces. Reserve the liquid in the pan.

Combine the flour with the milk and add to the liquid in the pan. Cook and stir over medium heat until the sauce thickens, then season with the curry powder, salt, sugar, and ginger and simmer for 1 minute. Stir in fish and heat through. Serve on the hot rice. *Four servings, 227 calories each (including ½ cup rice per serving).*

"Fried" Fish in the Oven

Fish! You've tried it *alla romano, en brochette, con vino,* and *aux fenouilles et groseilles,* but the only way your family will eat it is à la Truckers-Welcome Diner, right? Deep fat-fried and all bundled up in a heavy overcoat of bready batter.

Our method "deep-fries" without melting so much as a millimeter of fat and doesn't even demand a fryer, while our Skinny Shake Mix is but 50 calories a serving—and a whole lot less expensive than the commercial mixes.

◆§ SKINNY SHAKE MIX ẞ►

(For oven-fried foods)

4 cups (16 ounces) bread crumbs
½ cup salad oil
1 tablespoon salt
1 tablespoon celery salt
1 tablespoon paprika
1 teaspoon freshly ground pepper
   Additional seasonings to taste

Put the bread crumbs in a deep bowl. Stir in the salad oil with a fork or pastry blender. Add all the seasonings and others to suit yourself—herbs, garlic or onion powder, lemon pepper, etc. Keep, well covered, in a moisture-proof container with a tightly fitted lid. Use as needed. *Makes enough for about 20 cut-up chickens or 30 servings of fish; use ⅓ cupful per pound of fish.*

◆§ OVEN-FRIED FISH ẞ►

Put the Skinny Shake Mix (above) in a plastic or heavy paper bag. Add water-moistened fillets, a few at a time, and shake to coat. Place the coated fillets on a nonstick baking dish in a preheated 375-degree oven, adding absolutely no other fats or oils. The fish will be done to perfection in 10 to 12 minutes. *Only 144 calories per serving.*

◆§ CHEESE-Y OVEN-FRIED FLOUNDER FILLETS ẞ►

2 pounds flounder fillets
1 cup crushed cheese crackers
½ cup low-calorie French dressing
   Paprika
   Lemon wedges for garnish

Cut the fish into serving pieces. Pour the crushed crackers onto a plate or sheet of waxed paper. Dip each fillet in French dressing, then press the fillets into the crumb mixture, coating both sides.

Place the fillets on a nonstick cookie sheet and sprinkle with paprika. Place them in an oven preheated to the highest temperature and bake for 10 to 12 minutes, until the fish flakes easily. Serve with lots of fresh lemon wedges. *Eight servings, only 140 calories each.*

◦§ BATTER-BAKED FISH FILLETS ε»

To the calorie-conscious cook, "deep-fried" is the culinary equivalent of pornography. All that starchy coating soaking up all that fattening grease. Why, the very thought of it is practically obscene! But tempting. After all, what turns on the flavor of fish better than a golden-brown wrapping of batter? What more sensuous dress is there for slender slices of veal scaloppine or turkey cutlets?

Well, you can give in to those lascivious longings for batter-dipped foods if you're a Slim Gourmet cook. But instead of dipping food in rich batter and dropping it in a kettle of bubbling oil, this two-step method of coating eliminates the need for frying.

1 **pound flounder or other fillets**
2 **egg whites or 1 whole egg**
3 **tablespoons polyunsaturated oil**
6 **tablespoons self-rising flour**
   Paprika
   Salt and freshly ground pepper

Thaw and rinse the fish if frozen, then pat dry. Fork-whip the egg and oil together in a shallow bowl. Place the flour in another shallow bowl. Dip the fish pieces first in the flour, then the egg mixture, then again in the flour. Arrange the coated fish fillets on a nonstick cookie sheet, place in a very hot (450-degree) oven, and bake for 6 minutes. Turn with a spatula. Sprinkle liberally with paprika, salt, and pepper and bake for 3 to 4 minutes more. *Four servings, 225 calories each.*

VARIATIONS

Batter-Baked Cutlets: Follow the previous recipe, but substitute 1 pound of lean veal cutlet or cutlets of chicken or turkey. Bake 6 minutes each side. *Four servings, 292 calories each.*

Serve as is, or turn them into this Italian meal:

Quick Cutlets Romano: After the cutlets are baked, arrange them in a shallow, heatproof oven-to-table dish. Pour on an 8-ounce can of plain tomato sauce (no oil added) and sprinkle with ¼ cup freshly grated extra-sharp Romano cheese. Return to the oven for an extra 3 or 4 minutes, until the sauce is hot and the cheese is melted and bubbly. *Four servings, 331 calories each.*

❧ DOCKSIDE FOILED FISH ❧

1 fresh fish (1 to 3 pounds), cleaned, head and tail removed
1 tablespoon butter
1 onion, sliced
   Salt or garlic salt
   Freshly ground pepper
   Dried tarragon or thyme
   Lemon wedges for garnish

Dot the inside of the fish lightly with butter, then add the onion and seasonings. Place the fish, off center, on a large sheet of heavy foil (or a double layer of ordinary foil). Bring the foil up over the fish and double-fold the foil on both ends, crimping tightly so the "packet" won't leak. Place the packet on a grate over hot coals and cook—15 minutes for a 1-pound fish, 25 minutes for a 2-pounder, and 35 minutes for a 3-pounder. As the fish cooks, turn the packet two or three times by carefully gripping the ends of the foil packet and flipping it over.

Remove to a platter and open the foil. To serve, lift fish from the bones, spoon on some of the liquid, and garnish with fresh lemon wedges. *Each 4-ounce serving, 180 calories.*

VARIATION

Freezer-Foiled Fish: Prepare fresh fish as above, but substitute dried onion flakes for the fresh onion. Store in the freezer. The still-frozen foil package may be placed on a cookie tin and baked in a 325-degree oven for 45 minutes to 1 hour or more, depending on the size of the fish. Serve with lemon wedges.

❧ COD CREOLE ❧

2 pounds cod steaks
1 can (29 ounces) tomatoes
½ cup chopped pepper
½ cup chopped onion
1 teaspoon garlic salt
   Pinch of cayenne pepper
2 tablespoons chopped stuffed green olives
1 tablespoon arrowroot or cornstarch
½ cup water.

If the fish is frozen, defrost and drain before using.

Cut the fish into 2-inch cubes. Break up the tomatoes with a fork. Combine the tomatoes with all the remaining ingredients and pour over the fish cubes in an ovenproof baking dish. Bake 30 to 40 minutes in a preheated 350-degree oven, checking occasionally and adding water if needed. *Six servings, 166 calories each.*

⊷ SWEET AND SOUR COD ⊶

  2 pounds cod steaks
½ cup chopped green pepper
½ cup chopped onion
½ teaspoon ground ginger
  2 teaspoons honey
    Squirt of lemon juice
  1 tablespoon arrowroot or cornstarch
  2 tablespoons soy sauce
  1 can (20 ounces) unsweetened pineapple tidbits

Have the fish defrosted and well drained if frozen.

Cut the steaks into 2-inch chunks and put in a shallow baking dish. Combine all the remaining ingredients and stir well. Pour over the fish and bake for 30 minutes, uncovered, in a preheated 350-degree oven. Add a little water if needed. *Six servings, 185 calories each.*

⊷ FLORIDA-STYLE SNAPPER ⊶

  2 pounds red snapper or other fillets
  2 tablespoons polyunsaturated oil
  3 tablespoons orange juice
  2 teaspoons grated orange rind
⅛ teaspoon freshly grated nutmeg
    Salt and freshly ground pepper
    Thin orange slices for garnish (optional)

Thaw the fish, if frozen, and drain well. Place in a single layer, skin side down, in an ovenproof dish. Combine the oil, orange juice, orange rind, and seasonings. Pour over the fish and bake at 375 degrees for 20 minutes, or until the fish flakes easily. *Eight servings, 140 calories each.*

⊷ MARINATED KINGFISH ⊶

  2 pounds king mackerel or other steaks
  5 tablespoons fresh orange juice
  5 tablespoons soy sauce

2 tablespoons catsup
1 tablespoon lemon juice
½ teaspoon freshly ground pepper
½ clove garlic, minced
1½ tablespoons chopped fresh parsley

Marinate the fish steaks in remaining ingredients for 30 minutes at room temperature or several hours, covered, in the refrigerator. Remove the fish from the marinade and broil 4 to 5 minutes on each side, basting frequently with the reserved sauce. *Six servings, 176 calories each.*

The Miraculous Sardine

Name a food that's elegant, inexpensive, easy to prepare, needs no refrigeration, and is nutritious and nonfattening as well. The miracle food that fits this description is the canned sardine. Sardines are vitamin-rich and high in protein, but low in calories, fat, and cholesterol.

SARDINES MARINARA WITH SPAGHETTI

1 can (8 ounces) plain tomato sauce (no oil added)
¼ teaspoon oregano or Italian seasoning
¼ teaspoon onion or garlic powder
2 tablespoons dry white wine or water
1 can (8 ounces) sardines packed in tomato sauce
2 cups tender-cooked, protein-enriched spaghetti

Combine the tomato sauce, oregano, onion powder, and wine in a saucepan. Simmer for 2 minutes. Open the sardines and gently add the contents to the sauce. Cover and simmer for 1 minute, without stirring, until the sardines are thoroughly heated. To serve, gently spoon the sardines and sauce on top of well-drained hot spaghetti. *Two servings, 325 calories each.*

OVEN-SAUTÉED SARDINES

2 small cans (3¾ ounces each) sardines in oil
2 tablespoons lemon juice
5 tablespoons seasoned bread crumbs
1 teaspoon dry mustard
½ teaspoon onion salt

Drain the sardines well to eliminate the oil, then sprinkle with the lemon juice and reserve. Combine the bread crumbs, mustard, and onion salt on a plate or sheet of waxed paper. Roll the sardines in crumbs to coat lightly and arrange on a nonstick cookie sheet. Bake in a preheated very hot oven (425 degrees or more) until golden brown, about 8 minutes. *Two servings, 254 calories each.*

⤝ SARDINES WITH WINE AND MUSHROOMS ⤞

1 **tablespoon butter or margarine (optional)**
  Onion or garlic salt (optional)
¼ **pound fresh mushrooms, sliced**
½ **cup dry white wine**
2 **cans (3¾ ounces each) sardines in brine or oil**

If the sardines are canned in oil, 1 tablespoon of the oil may be used in place of the butter. Gently rinse away all remaining oil.

Combine the butter (or margarine or oil) with the mushrooms and half of the wine in a nonstick skillet. Cover and cook over high heat until the liquid evaporates and the mushrooms brown in remaining oil. When brown, add the remaining wine and the rinsed sardines. Cook only until the sardines are heated through. *Two servings, 236 calories each.*

The Slimming Scallop

Sweet, succulent scallops—but their high price-per-pound puts them in that "special occasion" category for cooks who have to count their pennies.

Which is too bad if you have to count your calories, too. Because slimming scallops are a scant 367 calories per pound, only one-fourth or one-fifth as fattening as most meats. That's because the fat content is so low it doesn't even add up to 1 percent.

In fact, when you consider their lack of fat—and lack of bone, skin, or other waste—scallops don't seem so expensive after all. They're all meat, so one pound of scallops serves up four 4-ounce portions, while an equivalently priced pound of steak may barely serve two, and with a lot more calories and fat in the bargain.

⤝ OVEN-FRIED SCALLOPS ⤞

1 **pound scallops, fresh or frozen**
½ **cup evaporated whole milk**
½ **cup seasoned bread crumbs**
  Paprika
  Fresh parsley, lemon wedges, or dill pickle relish for garnish

Defrost the scallops, if frozen; drain and pat dry with a paper towel. Dip the scallops in evaporated milk, then roll in seasoned crumbs and sprinkle with paprika. For best results, refrigerate and allow to dry.

Spread the scallops in a single layer on a nonstick baking tray or cookie sheet. Bake in a preheated very hot oven—500 degrees or more, the top setting on your range. Bake for 8 to 10 minutes, or until golden brown. Serve with fresh parsley, lemon wedges, or well-drained dill pickle relish. *Four servings, 185 calories per serving.*

✓ ⊷ PERFECT BROILED SCALLOPS ⊶

1 **pound scallops, fresh or frozen**
2 **tablespoons salad oil or melted margarine**
  Salt and freshly ground pepper
  Paprika

Be sure to defrost scallops thoroughly if they are frozen; drain and pat dry. Put the scallops in a shallow dish and sprinkle with the oil or melted margarine; rotate the scallops to be sure the oil is evenly distributed. Arrange the scallops in a single layer in a shallow nonstick baking dish or cookie tin. Sprinkle with salt, pepper, and paprika and broil for 2 minutes on highest heat. Turn, sprinkle with additional paprika, and broil for another 3 to 4 minutes, until the scallops are browned and all the moisture in the pan has evaporated. *Four servings, 124 calories each.*

⊷ CRAB NEWBURG ⊶

Differing from fake creams and ersatz coffee lighteners, evaporated skim milk is a natural product—double-rich milk, but with most of the butterfat removed. The lack of fat makes it especially appealing to cholesterol watchers, and it can sit on your shelf, while real cream is very perishable. It's also a lot less expensive, but the real saving is in the calories—only 176 a cupful, while heavy cream is 840 and even light cream is a whopping 500 calories.

Evaporated skimmed milk can serve as a stand-in for cream in nearly any recipe; even a calorie-crammed, creamy rich luncheon dish like crab Newburg can be made diet safe.

 6 **slices Melba-thin white bread**
12 **ounces crabmeat, fresh-cooked or canned**
 3 **egg yolks, beaten**
 1 **cup evaporated skim milk**
 2 **tablespoons chopped fresh parsley**
 1 **tablespoon chopped pimiento**
 1 **teaspoon butter-flavored salt**
  Pinch of freshly grated nutmeg
 2 **tablespoons sherry wine**

Toast the bread and trim the crusts. Cut into triangles and set aside. Rinse the seafood under cold running water and drain well. Mix the egg and milk in a saucepan and heat over a very low flame, or in a double boiler. Add the parsley, pimiento, seasonings, and sherry and cook, stirring, until the mixture thickens and is heated through. Do not boil. Serve over the toast points. *Six servings, 150 calories each.*

Main Course Shrimp Dishes

At only 26 calories an ounce, shrimp is so calorie skimpy that there's no reason to relegate it to appetizer-only status. Here are some main-course dishes that are amazingly low in calories.

✒ ORIENTAL SHRIMP OMELET ࢙

6 **eggs**
  Pinch of salt
4 **scallions, chopped**
1 **cup (8 ounces) cooked or canned shrimp**
1 **tablespoon polyunsaturated oil**
  Soy sauce

Beat the eggs well. Stir in a pinch of salt, the chopped scallions, and the shrimp (well-drained, if canned).

Heat the oil, over a high flame, in a large nonstick skillet. Add the eggs all at once. As the omelet cooks, lift the edges so the egg mixture can reach the bottom of the pan. Fold over and flip onto a prewarmed platter, then douse liberally with soy sauce and serve immediately. *Four servings, 214 calories each.*

✒ CANTONESE SHRIMP WITH CRUNCHY VEGETABLES ࢙

  1 **tablespoon polyunsaturated oil**
1½ **pounds raw shrimp, peeled and deveined**
  ¼ **cup chopped scallions**
  1 **clove garlic, minced**
  1 **cup chicken bouillon**
  ½ **teaspoon ground ginger**
  1 **can (16 ounces) Chinese vegetables, well drained**
  1 **tablespoon arrowroot or cornstarch**
  ¼ **cup cold water**
  Soy sauce

Heat the oil in a nonstick skillet or wok (see page 29) and cook the shrimp, scallions, and garlic for 3 minutes, stirring constantly. Pour on the chicken bouillon (fresh, canned, or reconstituted), then add the well-drained vegetables and ginger and bring to a boil. Dissolve the arrowroot in the water, then stir into the skillet and cook until the mixture thickens. Add soy sauce to taste and serve immediately. *Six servings, 120 calories per serving.*

VARIATION

Cantonese Shrimp with Beans: Use 1 package (10 ounces) of defrosted French-style green beans instead of the Chinese vegetables. Cook only until the beans are crunchy. *Six servings, 144 calories each.*

⋙ SHRIMP SHEN ⋘

1½ pounds fresh or frozen raw shrimp, cleaned and deveined
1 bunch scallions
1 pound fresh mushrooms
6 tablespoons soy sauce
6 tablespoons catsup
6 tablespoons white wine
    Dash of Worcestershire sauce
4 teaspoons cornstarch
1 tablespoon polyunsaturated oil

Defrost the shrimp, if frozen, and drain thoroughly. Don't attempt to cook the shrimp while still frozen because they contain too much moisture. (To quick-defrost shrimp, soak them in cold—never hot—water.)

Wash and slice the scallions and mushrooms.

Measure and combine the soy sauce, catsup, wine, Worcestershire sauce, and cornstarch. Line up everything on your counter, including a wok (see page 29) or a large nonstick skillet, wooden spoon, and the oil.

Heat the oil in the wok or skillet over highest heat. Add the shrimp and stir-fry for 2 minutes. Add the scallions and mushrooms; stir-fry 2 more minutes. Give the soy mixture a quick stir and pour it into the skillet. Cook, stirring, until the mixture simmers and thickens slightly. Serve immediately. *Six servings, 185 calories each.*

NOTE: A cucumber-onion salad with a dash of vinegar is a good accompaniment. At only 30 calories a cupful, eat all you want. Be sure to have big steaming bowls of rice for the "skinnies": 90 calories a ½-cup serving. (Use instant rice, it needs no watching!) Pop-in-the-oven frozen egg rolls will add 130 calories apiece for your slimmer tablemates.

ᴁ CHINESE BUTTERFLY SHRIMP ᴂ

For an easy, elegant Oriental dish that's ready in less than 10 minutes, try butterfly shrimp.

20 large raw shrimp (about 1¼ pounds)
 4 stalks celery, trimmed
 4 scallions, green part and all
 1 tablespoon oil
 1 teaspoon granulated sugar
 ½ teaspoon salt
    Pinch of monosodium glutamate (optional)
 ½ teaspoon ground ginger
 ½ cup water
 2 tablespoons soy sauce
 1 tablespoon sherry wine

Wash the shrimp and remove the shells, except for the tails. Devein the shrimp, then, with a sharp knife, slit in half up to the tail. (When the shrimp cook, they will fan out into a butterfly shape.)

Slice the stalks of celery and the scallions on the diagonal. Set aside.

Heat the oil in a heavy nonstick skillet and add the shrimp. Sprinkle on the sugar, salt, monosodium glutamate, and ginger. Stir-fry over moderate heat for about 3 minutes, until the shrimp are pink and tender. Don't overcook.

Using a slotted spoon, remove the shrimp to a plate. Put the celery in the skillet. Add the water, soy sauce and sherry and simmer, uncovered, until nearly all the liquid has evaporated and the celery is tender-crisp. Add the scallions and shrimp and stir-fry just until heated through. *Four servings, 128 calories each.*

ᴁ MARTINI-STYLE SHRIMP ᴂ

Spiked with vermouth! Serve it hot or cold, as a meal or an appetizer.

 2 pounds raw shrimp, shelled and deveined
 2 tablespoons diet margarine
 2 teaspoons salt
    Dash of cayenne pepper
 3 tablespoons dry vermouth
1½ tablespoons lemon juice

Thaw the shrimp, if frozen; drain well. Cook in a nonstick skillet in the margarine for 8 to 10 minutes, until pink. Add the remaining ingredients and cook, stirring over high heat for 1 to 2 minutes. Serve hot or cold. *Four servings, 169 calories each.*

◄§ BOUILLABAISSE AMERICAINE §►

Bouillabaisse, as it's prepared at famous French restaurants, is a career—too complicated for most busy American homemakers. Bottled clam juice, frozen seafood, and canned tomatoes simplify the task. Add some minced stuffed olives to replace the flavor of the missing olive oil calories, and you've got a quick and easy Slim Gourmet dish.

3 pounds fish fillets, fresh or frozen
4 cups canned tomatoes, chopped
1 cup sliced onion
2 cups fish stock, clam broth, or clam-tomato juice
1 cup dry white wine or water
2 bay leaves
2 teaspoons salt
¼ cup lemon juice
2 to 3 cloves garlic, minced
  Pinch of saffron threads
5 small stuffed olives, minced
1 teaspoon fennel seeds
2 dozen whole, shelled oysters or clams, fresh or canned
  Tabasco to taste

For fish fillets, choose at least three of the following (the more the merrier): halibut, perch, red snapper, bass, haddock, pollack, cod, hake, pike, trout, whitefish, or rockfish. If fresh, have the fish skinned, boned, and cut into 2-inch pieces; if frozen, thaw, drain and then cut into pieces.

Combine the tomatoes, onions, fish stock, wine, bay leaves, salt, lemon juice, garlic, saffron, olives, and fennel in a soup pot. Heat to boiling, then add the fish pieces and simmer over low heat, covered, for 20 minutes. If the oysters are fresh, add them in the last 5 minutes; if canned, add them at the end, and simply reheat to boiling. Season to taste with Tabasco and serve in shallow soup dishes. *Eight servings, 215 calories each.*

NOTE: Tossed salad, dry white wine, and crusty French bread (for non-dieters) are all you need to complete this low-calorie, high-protein gourmet treat.

CALIFORNIA'S CIOPPINO,
STREAMLINED FOR SLIMMERS

This famed seafood stew with an Italian name actually was born on American soil. Depending on the chef's whim and the day's haul, it may include clams, oysters, or other bivalves with their "valves" still attached, lobsters still in their shells, cracked crabs or unshucked shrimp, plus tender chunks of fish, tomatoes, garlic, onions, and a winy, briny broth. Armed with soup spoon, cocktail fork, forbearance, and finger towels one muddles through somehow, but this ambrosia of the sea is well worth the effort to eat.

If you've never had *cioppino* and prefer not to tackle all that flotsam on your first try, then by all means make it with shells removed beforehand. The flavor's the same, but neat *cioppino* seems to lack soul!

1   **pound halibut or bass fillets**
1   **pound jumbo shrimp**
2   **pounds small rock lobster tails**
4   **cups canned tomatoes, with their liquid**
1   **cup chopped onion**
½   **cup chopped green pepper**
2   **cups clam-tomato juice or 1 cup each clam and tomato juice**
1   **cup Chianti wine**
1   **cup water**
2   **teaspoons garlic salt**
2   **bay leaves**
½   **teaspoon dried basil, oregano, or Italian seasoning**
2   **cans clams-in-shells or 1 can (16 ounces) whole clams**

If frozen, have the fish, shrimp, and lobster tails defrosted; drain well. Cut the fish in 2-inch chunks. Remove the legs from the shrimp and peel them if you wish. Split the lobster tails as you would for broiling, following package directions.

Put the tomatoes and their liquid in a soup kettle; break up with a spoon. Add the onions, green pepper, clam-tomato juice, wine, water, and all the seasonings. Simmer, covered, for 20 minutes. Add fish and lobster tails, cover, and simmer for 10 more minutes. Add the shrimp and simmer another 10 minutes. Add the canned clams, including the liquid, and simmer until heated through. *Eight servings, 186 calories each.*

NOTE: Absent from our version is about 500 calories' worth of unneeded olive oil!

Tuna—Lo-Cal Meat Stand-in Supreme

Lately every publication seems to be drawing up lists of low-cost meat substitutes, comparing the price per ounce or gram of protein of such steak stand-ins as cheese, eggs, peanut butter, and seafood.

Such lists generally don't take calorie counts into consideration. However, if *you* have to consider calories, take special note of the one food that makes most of the top-ten lists—canned tuna fish.

The best buy of all tuna is the kind that's packed in water. It offers even more protein than the oil-packed variety for less than half the calories. Canned tuna's advantages are even more striking when compared with luxury-priced beef. Three and one-half ounces offer:

Product	Protein (in grams)	Calories
Water-pack tuna	28	127
Oil-pack tuna	24	288
Roast prime ribs	18	481

◄§ TUNA ITALIANO §►

1 tablespoon polyunsaturated oil
1 onion, sliced
2 cloves garlic, minced
2 small eggplants, peeled and cut into cubes
1 can (16 ounces) Italian peeled tomatoes
2 teaspoons dried oregano or basil
½ teaspoon salt
¼ teaspoon freshly ground pepper
2 cans (7 ounces each) water-pack tuna
5 tablespoons freshly grated Romano or Parmesan cheese

Heat the oil in a nonstick skillet and sauté the onion and garlic until soft. Add the eggplant, tomatoes, oregano, salt, and pepper, then cover and simmer over low heat for 30 minutes.

Drain the tuna and fork-flake into chunks in the bottom of a shallow 2-quart baking dish. Spoon the tomato-eggplant mixture on top of the tuna and sprinkle with the cheese. Bake in a preheated 250-degree oven for 30 minutes. *Four servings, 284 calories per serving.*

⋖§ TRIM TUNA FLORENTINE §⋗

  1 package (10 ounces) frozen spinach
  2 cans (7 ounces each) water-pack tuna
1½ tablespoons all-purpose flour
  1 cup skim milk
     Salt and freshly ground pepper
 ¼ cup grated extra-sharp Cheddar cheese

Prepare the spinach according to package directions, then drain and place in a 2-quart casserole. Flake the tuna on top of the spinach and reserve.

Combine the flour, milk, salt, and pepper in a saucepan and cook, stirring, till simmering. Pour over the tuna, top with grated cheese, and heat under the broiler until the cheese is brown and bubbly. *Four servings, 200 calories each.*

⋖§ BAKED BROCCOLI AND TUNA §⋗

2 bunches broccoli (2½ pounds)
2 cans (10½ ounces each) mushroom soup
⅔ cup skim milk
⅓ cup lemon juice
2 cans (7 ounces each) water-pack tuna
2 tablespoons seasoned bread crumbs

Rinse and cut up broccoli, slicing the stems and dividing the tops into florets. Cook, covered, in 1 inch of salted water until just barely tender, about 8 minutes. Drain and combine with the remaining ingredients in a 2-quart casserole, sprinkling the top with the bread crumbs. Bake in a 450-degree oven until bubbles appear and the top is browned. *Six servings, 238 calories each.*

⋖§ TUNA-STUFFED EGGPLANT §⋗

2 tablespoons diet margarine
1 green pepper, seeded and chopped
1 onion, chopped
2 small eggplants
1 tablespoon lemon juice
1 teaspoon garlic salt
2 tomatoes, peeled and chopped

1 teaspoon oregano or Italian seasoning
2 cans (7 ounces each) water-pack tuna, drained and flaked
6 tablespoons seasoned bread crumbs

Melt the margarine in a nonstick skillet and add the green pepper and onion. Cook and stir over moderate flame until tender.

Meanwhile, cut the eggplants in half lengthwise and scoop out most of the pulp, leaving a shell about ½ inch thick. Add the eggplant pulp to the skillet along with the lemon juice, garlic salt, tomatoes, and oregano. Cook, stirring occasionally, for 5 minutes.

Add the tuna to the skillet and toss the mixture lightly, then spoon into the eggplant shells and sprinkle with the bread crumbs. Place the shells in a shallow baking pan and surround them with about ½ inch of water. Bake at 350 degrees for 25 to 30 minutes. *Four servings, 258 calories each.*

⋖§ BAKED TUNA ROMANOFF §⋗

     8 ounces egg noodles, cooked
     4 tablespoons minced onion
  1½ cups low-fat cottage cheese
     3 cans (7 ounces each) water-pack tuna
  1½ cups plain yogurt
     ½ teaspoon dry mustard
     3 tablespoons catsup
     ½ teaspoon minced garlic
     1 teaspoon salt
        Pinch of cayenne pepper
     ¼ cup freshly grated extra-sharp Romano cheese

Spread the cooked noodles in the bottom of a shallow ovenproof baking dish. Combine the minced onion and cottage cheese and spoon over the noodles. Drain tuna and separate into flakes, then sprinkle over the cottage cheese. Stir the yogurt, mustard, catsup, garlic, salt, and pepper together and pour over the tuna. Sprinkle with the Romano cheese and bake in a preheated 325-degree oven for 30 minutes. *Eight servings, 282 calories each.*

⋖ MEDITERRANEAN TUNA CASSEROLE ⋗

2 cans (7 ounces each) water-pack tuna
1 eggplant, peeled and cut in cubes
3 small tomatoes, sliced
1 teaspoon garlic salt
1½ teaspoons oregano or Italian seasoning
1 onion, chopped
1 can (3 ounces) sliced mushrooms, drained
1 cup shredded part-skim mozzarella

Drain the tuna and break into chunks, then in a 2-quart casserole, combine with all the other ingredients except the cheese. Mix lightly and bake in a preheated 350-degree oven for 30 minutes. Sprinkle with the cheese and continue baking for 10 to 15 minutes more, until the cheese is melted. *Four servings, 268 calories each.*

13
EGGS
AND
CHEESE

Let's start this chapter on eggs with a warning about cholesterol. Cholesterol is that nasty stuff that's believed to block up our arteries and provide Americans with the highest heart disease rate in the world. The American Heart Association has urged drastic changes in the way we eat, curtailing our intake of fatty meats, butterfat-laden dairy products—and eggs.

Eggs, or more specifically egg yolks, are the highest single source of cholesterol in the American diet. But there are millions of Americans who simply don't consider it morning without eggs. With the products described below, you can have eggs and a low-cholesterol diet, too.

Depending on the brand you choose, you may even save calories. Weight watchers will want to choose these products carefully, because some have only half the calories of whole eggs, while others have considerably more.

EGGS IN A CAN: Powdered eggs you can measure out and reconstitute with water. One of the best-known brands is Cellu (Chicago Dietetic, Inc., La Grange, Illinois). Three tablespoons combined with ⅓ cup water makes the equivalent of 2 eggs. It has half the calories and protein value of real eggs.

EGGS IN AN ENVELOPE: Premeasured packets of powdered egg that equal two whole eggs when mixed with water. Eggstra (Tillie Lewis Foods, Stockton, California) is one example. Enriched with soy, the Eggstra has a protein content nearly as high as real eggs, some cholesterol, but a lot fewer calories.

EGGS FROM THE FREEZER: Best known of this new entry is made by Fleischmann, the margarine people (Standard Brands, New York, New

York). Named Eggbeaters, this is a frozen liquid you simply defrost and pour—½ cup equals 2 eggs. But Eggbeaters contains extra oil, so it's more fattening than real eggs.

Let's see how these products compare:

	Cholesterol	*Protein*	*Calories*
2 large eggs	550 mg.	14 gr.	176
Cellu brand	none	7.6 gr.	78
Eggstra	114 mg.	11 gr.	86
Eggbeaters	none	13.30 gr.	200

If convenience is more important than calories, eggbeaters might be the preferred choice, but the powdered egg substitutes are considerably lower in calories. Cellu brand contains no cholesterol, but Cellu is lower in protein than Eggstra. So, read the label and take your choice. Or make your own.

How to Make Your Own "Eggs"

It's easy to make your own low-calorie, low-cholesterol "eggs." And your homemade eggs will be fresher, better tasting, less fattening, and cheaper than substitutes because you make them with fresh eggs.

Egg whites, that is. The yolks, alas, have to go because they are the source of the cholesterol. Save your yolks, freeze them, use them in baking or making eggnogs (not for you, of course!)—even an egg shampoo.

How do you turn whites-only into eggs? Add a little dry powdered milk and a few drops of yellow food coloring. Mix it up and you've got it made— scrambled or an omelet, or a dip for French toast.

⊷ LOW CHOLESTEROL STORE 'N' POUR EGGS ෂ

1 dozen large egg whites
1 egg yolk (optional)
½ cup nonfat dry milk
½ teaspoon yellow food coloring

Stir all the ingredients together, or whir in the blender, then store in a covered jar in your refrigerator. Shake well before using. One-half cup of mix equals 2 eggs (176 calories). This makes enough for four mornings. It may be frozen, but use within the week.

ᴈ§ CHOLESTEROL-FREE "SLIM" EGGS ᵌᴥ

If you want to make your "eggs" by the individual batch, here is the recipe for you. Let's see how it compares with 2 large eggs:

	Whole Eggs	"*Slim Eggs*"
Cholesterol	550 mg.	none
Protein	14 grams	15 grams
Calories	176	99

If you eat two eggs every morning, that's a saving of 28,105 calories a year—the equivalent of an eight-pound weight loss—not to mention the cholesterol saving. The American Heart Association has recommended that Americans limit eggs to three or less a week.

3 large egg whites
2 tablespoons nonfat dry milk
4 drops yellow food coloring
   Polyunsaturated oil or spray-on vegetable coating

Fork-blend the egg whites, nonfat dry milk, and food coloring in a bowl until lump free. Wipe a nonstick skillet with a little oil, or spray it with vegetable coating for no-fat frying. Heat the skillet over the highest flame. When hot, pour in the eggs and cook as you would any other eggs. For an omelet, shake the pan gently, and lift the edges so that uncooked egg can flow to bottom; roll out of the skillet onto a plate. Or scramble lightly over a low flame.

Make the Perfect Omelet and You'll Never Go Hungry

ᴈ§ An omelet can be breakfast, lunch, dinner, or dessert.

ᴈ§ It can be gourmet fare, like an *omelette aux fines herbes* (with herbs), or just folks—like a Western omelet.

ᴈ§ It's inexpensive. Even in this age of ever-escalating food costs, eggs are still the best buy in town.

ᴈ§ It's fast!

ᴈ§ It's nutritious. Protein-powered eggs beat out empty-caloried cereals or bready sandwiches any time.

ᴈ§ It's low in calories.

Forget anything you've ever read about omelets. The added fat in most recipes is double the calories of the eggs themselves. You can make an omelet with a minimum of fat, or no fat at all. Furthermore, you don't need an extravagantly expensive French omelet pan. In fact, the best pan of all is your everyday, dime-store-variety nonstick skillet or frying pan. And you can use the egg products, commercial or homemade, described on pages 201–202, as a substitute for the eggs (adjusting the calorie count accordingly).

Here are three ways to make an omelet, then our Basic Slim Gourmet Omelet recipe:

WITH A MINIMUM OF FAT: Use a measuring spoon to measure out 2 teaspoons of butter, margarine, or solid shortening. Heat the nonstick skillet over highest heat and use the spoon to spread the melting fat evenly.

WITH DIET MARGARINE: It's half water, so it's half the calories! Measure out 1 tablespoon. The moisture content makes it easy to spread the margarine evenly over the bottom and sides. Do not add the eggs until the skillet begins to sizzle, signifying that all the water has evaporated.

WITH NO ADDED FAT: Spray inside of your nonstick skillet with one of those new spray-on vegetable coatings that come in aerosol containers. These products add no calories, but let you bake or fry with no added fat.

⤙ BASIC SLIM GOURMET OMELET ⤚

Break 2 medium eggs into a small bowl, sprinkle in salt to taste, and fork-whip lightly.

Add the fat, diet margarine, or spray-on vegetable coating to your skillet, according to the directions above, and heat over the highest flame. When the skillet is well-coated—and good and hot—add the eggs.

Count to ten. Now that the eggs have begun to set, shake the skillet lightly.

When almost cooked but still slightly liquid, take your fork and loosen one end of the omelet, rolling it over onto itself. Tip the skillet over your plate and the omelet will roll out, perfectly formed. The heat of the eggs will finish cooking the interior. Your omelet will be light and creamy on the inside, golden brown on the outside. *One serving: with 2 teaspoons fat, 210 calories; with 1 tablespoon diet margarine, 192; with no fat added, 142.*

NOTE: You can dress up your omelet by sprinkling the surface as it cooks with chopped leftover ham or chicken, herbs, onion, shredded part-skim cheese, minced green pepper, flaked water-pack tuna, drained crushed low-calorie pineapple, or canned Chinese vegetables. Or—top it with tomato sauce, soy sauce, crushed fresh berries, or diet jam or jelly. What you add to an omelet determines whether it's breakfast, lunch, dinner, or dessert!

✓ ⊷ CANADIAN BACON OMELET ⊶

Spray-on vegetable coating
1 **ounce Canadian bacon**
2 **eggs**

Spray a small nonstick skillet with vegetable coating for no-fat frying until the inside surface is slick. Dice the Canadian bacon into ¼-inch cubes and brown in the skillet over high heat. Set aside the bacon while you prepare an omelet in a second, clean skillet—or wash and dry the skillet well and reuse it.

Prepare the omelet according to the directions in the basic recipe, but omit the salt. When the omelet is nearly set, sprinkle it with browned Canadian bacon cubes. Fold over, and serve with mustard. *One serving, 205 calories.*

⊷ CORN OMELET FOR ONE ⊶

Spray-on vegetable coating or polyunsaturated oil
3 **eggs, beaten**
Salt and freshly ground pepper
5 **tablespoons corn—fresh, canned, or frozen and defrosted**

Spray a small, nonstick skillet or omelet pan with vegetable coating for no-fat frying or wipe lightly with oil. Place the skillet over a high flame. When the skillet is hot, pour in the eggs, and season with salt and pepper. Sprinkle the corn evenly over the surface. Wait about 30 seconds, then begin lifting up the edges of the omelet so that the uncooked portion runs underneath. When the omelet is set, loosen one end, then roll onto a heated plate. Serve immediately. *Serves one, 273 calories.*

NOTE: A chilled tomato salad is all you need to complete the meal.

⊷ GOLDEN GATE FRUIT OMELET ⊶

With the ever-widening availability of low-cholesterol egg substitutes, even those on low-cholesterol diets can enjoy this high-protein salute to whatever fruit is in season. Depending on the season, you may add or substitute other fruit: blueberries, strawberry slices, melon balls, watermelon cubes, unpeeled pear chunks, etc. Allow ½ cup fruit per serving. And, if using egg substitute, consult the package for directions, or see pages 201–202.

1 unpeeled red apple, cubed
1 banana, sliced
1 tangerine, sectioned and sliced
½ cup seedless green grapes
10 medium eggs
¼ cup skim milk
   Spray-on vegetable coating or polyunsaturated oil
4 ounces shredded or sliced Monterey jack or low-fat Cheddar-type
   "diet" cheese

Have the fruit at room temperature, not chilled. Combine and toss lightly. Combine the eggs and milk and fork-blend lightly.

Liberally coat a 9-inch nonstick skillet with vegetable coating for no-fat frying, or wipe lightly with oil. Pour in the eggs and heat over a moderate flame until the eggs begin to set, then lift the edges to allow the unset portion to run underneath. Sprinkle on the cheese, then top with the fruit. With a spatula, gently fold the omelet over and place on an oven-proof platter. Place in a preheated medium (350-degree) oven for 10 minutes, until the fruit is warmed through but not cooked, and the cheese is melted. *Four servings, 350 calories each (or 294 with diet cheese).*

◄§ REUBEN LUNCHEON OMELET §►

   Spray-on vegetable coating or polyunsaturated oil
2 eggs, lightly beaten
1 ounce cooked corned beef round, thinly sliced
1 ounce sliced or shredded processed Swiss cheese
   Caraway seeds

Spray a small nonstick skillet or omelet pan with vegetable coating for no-fat frying or wipe lightly with oil, then heat over a moderate flame. When hot, pour in the eggs, topping them with the corned beef, cheese, and a sprinkle of caraway seeds. Lift the omelet to let the uncooked portion reach the bottom of the pan. When set, fold over and roll out onto a plate. Serve with hot mustard and a "side" of sauerkraut, if you like. *One serving, 303 calories.*

◄§ CHEESE OMELET FLORENTINE §►

Make omelets one at a time. If preparing several, set them on a tray in your oven at a low temperature, about 200 degrees, until ready to serve. For each serving:

½ cup cooked chopped spinach
  Spray-on vegetable coating
3 eggs, lightly beaten
½ ounce shredded part-skim mozzarella cheese
  Pinch of freshly grated nutmeg
  Salt and freshly ground pepper

Make sure the spinach is well pressed of all moisture.

Spray a small frying pan or omelet pan with vegetable coating for no-fat frying. Heat over a high flame, then add the lightly beaten eggs and wait 1 minute. Gently lift the eggs with a spatula, permitting the uncooked portion to run underneath. When the eggs are almost set, sprinkle with the cheese, spinach, and nutmeg. Unroll onto a plate and place in a warm oven until serving time. Season to taste before serving. *One serving, 292 calories.*

⋖ᶴ CRABMEAT OMELET IN WHITE WINE SAUCE ᶾᵂ

 1 tablespoon butter or margarine
 6 eggs, lightly beaten
 2 tablespoons minced onion
 2 cans (7 ounces each) crabmeat
1¼ cups skim milk
 ½ cup white wine
1½ tablespoons all-purpose flour
 1 teaspoon salt
   Pinch of freshly ground pepper
   Paprika

Melt the butter or margarine in a large nonstick skillet. Pour in the eggs, then sprinkle the surface evenly with the minced onion and crabmeat. Continue cooking over moderate heat until the eggs are set. Since an omelet this large cooked in very little fat is unwieldy to turn or roll, cut into 4 quarters and turn each section over carefully. Continue cooking only long enough to assure that the crabmeat is heated through.

While omelet is heating, prepare the sauce. Combine the milk, wine, flour, and seasonings in a small saucepan and heat to boiling, stirring constantly. Simmer until thickened, pour over the omelet, and serve immediately. *Four servings, 297 calories per serving.*

⋖ᶴ PUFFY OVEN-BAKED OMELET ᶾᵂ

This low-calorie recipe is a good choice for egg lovers who have to limit their intake of egg yolks. This omelet gets its extra protein from the cheese, and the extra egg whites add volume. For variety, add drained, low-calorie crushed pineapple and a sprinkle of cinnamon to the omelet mixture before cooking, or fold in two tablespoons of bacon-flavored soy protein bits.

½ teaspoon salt
4 egg whites
2 egg yolks
½ cup low-fat cottage cheese
1 tablespoon polyunsaturated oil

Add the salt to the egg whites and beat until stiff. In another bowl, combine the egg yolks and cottage cheese and beat until smooth. Fold in the egg whites.

Oil the inside of an overproof nonstick skillet or a shallow flameproof baking dish. Add the egg mixture and cook on top of the range until the underside is lightly browned. Then place in a preheated 400-degree oven and bake until the omelet is puffy and browned. *Two servings, 140 calories each.*

◄§ EGGS AND SAUSAGE, SPANISH STYLE §►

1 Chorizo Pork Patty (page 137)
  Spray-on vegetable coating or polyunsaturated oil
2 eggs, lightly beaten
½ cup tomato juice
  Pinch of garlic powder
2 tablespoons grated onion
2 tablespoons minced green pepper
  Pinch of cayenne pepper

Cook the pork patty as directed on page 138; keep warm. Spray a separate small nonstick skillet or omelet pan with vegetable coating for no-fat frying. Place over moderate heat, and when the skillet is hot add the eggs. Wait 1 minute, then gently lift the eggs to allow the uncooked portion to run underneath. When completely set, roll the omelet onto a warm serving plate. Immediately raise the heat to high and add the tomato juice and remaining ingredients. Cook, uncovered, over high heat for 1 minute, until the pepper is cooked and the juice is thickened into a sauce. Pour the sauce over the sausage and eggs and serve at once. *One serving, 286 calories.*

⋖ PINEAPPLE SCRAMBLE DANISH ⋗

½ cup juice-packed crushed pineapple plus 1 or 2 tablespoons
  pineapple juice from can
  Pinch of salt
2 eggs
2 slices diet protein bread, toasted
  Ground cinnamon

Add the pineapple juice and salt to the eggs and scramble lightly in a nonstick skillet over a low flame, adding no fats or oil. (If your nonstick skillet needs help, try one of the spray-on vegetable coatings for frying without grease.) Turn the eggs onto the toast slices. Add the pineapple to the skillet and quick-heat until warmed through, then spoon the warmed pineapple on top of the eggs and sprinkle with cinnamon. *Two servings, 130 calories each.*

NOTE: If you're an advanced "sugar freak," add a few drops of no-calorie sweetener. And if you're egg allergic or a cholesterol counter, see the version below.

⋖ OVEN-EASY FOO YUNG FOR VEGETABLE HATERS ⋗

If you'd like to add an exotic Oriental touch to something simple like broiled fish or chicken, try serving this as a side dish. It's filling, extra easy, protein rich, and low in calories. But, best of all, it just doesn't seem like a vegetable dish, so it's another inscrutable way to put one over on your I-hate-vegetables family. You can make this dish even when your vegetable crisper is empty because the main part comes from a can—canned Chinese or chop suey vegetables.

Be sure to serve your *foo yung* dish with soy sauce; it's under 10 calories per tablespoon and really turns on the flavor of egg and vegetable dishes. Or you can make authentic Foo Yung Gravy (see below).

1 can (16 ounces) Chinese vegetables
  Garlic salt
2 tablespoons minced onion
½ cup skim milk
4 eggs

Drain the vegetables well and mix with the garlic and minced onion in an ovenproof casserole. Scald the milk and allow it to cool slightly. Fork-whip the eggs into the milk and pour the mixture over the vegetables. Bake, uncovered, in a preheated 350-degree oven for 30 minutes. *Six side-dish servings, 72 calories each.*

Oven-Easy Main-Dish Foo Yung: For an easy luncheon or supper dish, try adding a cup or so of cooked cubed chicken, turkey or fish to the recipe above. *Four main course servings, under 225 calories each.*

FOO YUNG GRAVY:

1¼ cups chicken broth or water
⅓ cup soy sauce
1 tablespoon arrowroot or cornstarch

Homemade broth (skimmed of fat) is preferred, since bouillon is quite salty. So, if you don't have broth, use plain water. Bring it to a boil. Combine the soy sauce and arrowroot and stir into the pan. Cook and stir until slightly thickened. *Four calories per tablespoon, 16 calories per quarter-cup serving.*

⊷§ BLENDER-EASY TUNA EGG FOO YUNG ৡ৯

1 onion, peeled and quartered
2 stalks celery, including leaves
½ green pepper, seeded
4 eggs
1 can (7 ounces) water-pack tuna
   Spray-on vegetable coating
   Soy sauce

In a blender, blend the onion, celery, and pepper until coarsely chopped. Add the eggs and blend 30 seconds. Flake the tuna and stir into the egg mixture with a long-handled spoon.

Spray a 7-inch nonstick skillet or omelet pan with vegetable coating for no-fat frying and heat over a high flame. When the skillet is hot, pour in half the egg mixture. Cook, undisturbed, for 30 seconds, then lift the edges of the egg mixture with a spatula to let the uncooked portion run underneath. Continue cooking and lifting until the omelet mixture is set. Roll out onto a heated plate.

Quickly prepare a second omelet with the remaining egg mixture, then serve both omelets at once, with soy sauce, or Foo Yung Gravy (see page 209). *Two servings, 279 calories each.*

The Soufflé and the Meatless Meal

With meatless meals becoming the fashion, it's time to rediscover the soufflé. Eggs are the main ingredient, which may be paired with other high-protein ingredients like fish or cheese.

Soufflés really aren't difficult to make. The main point is that soufflés wait for no man. Everyone must be ready to sit down when your oven-timer bell signifies the peak of perfection. But what other recipe creates an elegant gourmet dish with less than a dollar's worth of inexpensive dairy products? And, nutritionally speaking, the soufflé is a powerhouse of protein.

❧ SLIM GOURMET COTTAGE SOUFFLÉ ❧

4 eggs, separated
¼ cup skim milk
¼ cup all-purpose flour
1 small onion, finely chopped
1 tablespoon minced fresh parsley
1 teaspoon prepared mustard
¼ teaspoon paprika
1½ teaspoons salt
   Pinch of white pepper
2 cups low-fat creamed cottage cheese
   Pinch of cream of tartar

Beat the egg yolks until light yellow. Combine the milk and flour into a smooth paste and add to the egg yolks; beat well. Add the onion, parsley, mustard, paprika, salt, pepper, and cottage cheese. Beat until smooth.

Add the cream of tartar to the egg whites and beat until stiff, then carefully fold into the cheese mixture. Spoon into a 1½-quart casserole and bake in a preheated slow (300-degree) oven for 1 hour. Serve immediately. *Four main-dish servings at 211 calories each, or six side-dish servings at 140 calories each.*

❧ EASY SPINACH SOUFFLÉ ❧

2 packages (10 ounces each) frozen chopped spinach, defrosted
4 eggs
1 cup evaporated milk
½ teaspoon onion salt
¼ teaspoon freshly grated nutmeg
2 tablespoons freshly grated Parmesan or Romano cheese

In the blender, combine the spinach, eggs, evaporated milk, onion salt, and nutmeg. Pour into a 1-quart baking dish and sprinkle with the grated cheese. Bake in a preheated 350-degree oven for 1 hour or more, until the center is set. *Eight servings, 77 calories each.*

◄§ TUNA SOUFFLÉ §►

4 eggs, separated
1 can (10½ ounces) cream of celery soup
1 can (7 ounces) water-pack tuna, flaked
1 teaspoon dried dill weed
1 teaspoon onion salt
  Paprika

Beat the egg yolks lightly and stir into the soup until well combined. Stir in the tuna, dill, and salt. Beat the egg whites until stiff peaks form, then fold into the soup mixture. Pour into an ungreased soufflé dish, sprinkle with paprika, and bake in a preheated 350-degree oven for 45 minutes. Serve immediately. *Four servings, 185 calories each.*

Cottage Cheese and the Yogurt Myth

For the past few years, sweetened fruit-flavored yogurt has enjoyed a well-financed, carefully cultivated mystique as a "health food," with implications that it's low in calories and will somehow promote weight loss. High protein and a minimum of calories are the keys to a satisfying diet-wise meal, but yogurt makes as much protein sense as a glass of chocolate milk. In fact, chocolate milk has the same amount of protein, but it's less fattening!

The only yogurt that's low in calories is *plain* yogurt, only 120 calories a cupful. Most sugared, fruit-flavored yogurts are between 260 and 280 calories, more than double. And it's the sugared-up yogurts that people buy. In many supermarkets you can't even find plain yogurt; there's no room among the dozens of brands and flavors of sweetened yogurts.

Since sugared yogurt is so fattening, where did it get its reputation as a diet food? Well, many calorie guides simply list "yogurt, 120 calories," meaning plain yogurt, naturally. And then nearly every brand emblazons its carton with "98" and "99% fat-free."

Yogurt's captivation of the unaware dieter has overshadowed the much more satisfying lunch choice, right there in the same dairy case—fruit-flavored, low-fat creamed cottage cheese. Like yogurt, it comes in a carton. You can bring it home and eat it with a spoon. But it has triple the protein content and only one-quarter the carbohydrate content.

Here is how fruit-flavored cottage cheese and yogurt stack up. Just for comparison's sake, let's add a glass of chocolate milk, although nobody would seriously consider that an adequate diet lunch, right? The figures are approximate, since brands differ.

If cottage cheese turns you off, perhaps you haven't tried the right kind, or the right recipe. The type of cottage cheese and what it's mixed with will determine whether the flavor is mild or tart, creamy or tangy.

POT CHEESE OR UNCREAMED COTTAGE CHEESE, sometimes called "pot-

One Cup	Protein	Calories	Carbohydrates
Chocolate milk	7 grams	193	25 grams
Pineapple yogurt	7 grams	270	54 grams
Pineapple cottage cheese	30 grams	204	13 grams

style cottage cheese" or "Dutch cheese," is made from skim milk with nothing added but salt. The fat content is usually under 1 percent, and the calories range from 160 to 200 per cup, generally. Salt-free cottage cheese is sometimes called "skim-milk cottage cheese"—not very helpful, because all cottage cheese comes from skim milk.

LARGE-CURD COTTAGE CHEESE is sweet and mild because the cheese is washed to nullify any acid flavor. It may be creamed or uncreamed. It's sometimes called "popcorn cheese."

SMALL-CURD COTTAGE CHEESE has a tangier taste; it's sometimes called "Country style" or "farm style." But the tanginess depends on whether (or what type of) cream is added.

CREAMED COTTAGE CHEESE is prepared by adding cream—either sour cream (tangy style) or sweet cream (California style). This makes the fat content 4 percent or more, so the calories can range to 240 a cup and up.

LOW-FAT COTTAGE CHEESE, sometimes known as "partially creamed cottage cheese," is midway between plain and creamed cottage cheese in fat content and calories. But not always. One maker's low-fat cottage cheese is only 153 calories a cup, while another's *un*creamed cottage cheese is 200! And, of course, the cream can be sour or sweet; the curds large or small (or medium).

FRUIT-FLAVORED OR VEGETABLE COTTAGE CHEESE can be any of the above, give or take a few calories depending on the sugar content. Another variable that can make pineapple cottage cheese 204 calories or 240 per cup! Chive or vegetable salad cottage cheeses are around 220.

Then there are these cottage cheese "kissing cousins":

FARMER CHEESE: A very concentrated, low-moisture form of cottage cheese pressed into a loaf and wrapped like cream cheese. It's uncreamed and small curd and only 19 calories a tablespoon, compared with 55 calories per tablespoon for cream cheese.

RICOTTA CHEESE, sometimes called "Italian cottage" or "pot cheese," but it's really something else again! Made from cheese whey instead of curds, ricotta has a much higher fat content, about 10 percent, and a higher calorie count—from 340 to 400 per cupful.

PART-SKIM RICOTTA CHEESE, with its reduced butterfat content, is around 250 to 260 calories per cup, depending on the brand. For such Italian specialties as lasagne, part-skim ricotta, or better yet, pot-style cottage cheese is the calorie-wise choice.

Cream Cheese

To get the flavor of cream cheese without the calories, use either low-fat Neufchâtel cheese (a part-skim taste-alike) or the new low-calorie "imitation" cream cheese. Here's how they compare:

8-ounce Package	Calories
Ordinary cream cheese	840
Neufchâtel cheese	552
"Imitation" cream cheese	432

The new low-calorie cream cheese isn't available everywhere yet. Manufacturers are test-marketing it in different areas to see if consumers will be put off by that nasty word "imitation"—a federal label requirement because it doesn't meet the minimum standards for fat content. It tastes almost exactly the same, and has far more protein and far less fat than ordinary cream cheese, so this is a case where the so-called imitation is better than the real thing. (Don't be a jump-to-conclusion consumer when you see the word "imitation" on a label. In some cases the product contains less of a calorically undesirable ingredient—butterfat in ice cream, for example, or sugar in jam and jellies.)

✒ FETTUCINI ✑

You can enjoy a slimmed-down version that duplicates the taste and texture of the original fettucini Alfredo at only half the calories. The secret ingredient is low-fat, protein-rich cottage cheese, lots of it, adding its rich-tasting, creamy goodness to tender-cooked noodles.

If you prefer the sweet-cream version of fettucini, use the large-curd cottage cheese (sometimes called "California style"). For a sour-cream version, stick with the small-curd, tangy variety, the type that's creamed with sour cream. In either case, be sure to choose a low-fat brand. You can save a few more calories if you like by using diet margarine in place of butter, as it's half the calories.

8 ounces curly noodles
1 tablespoon butter or margarine
1 cup low-fat creamed cottage cheese
2 tablespoons freshly grated Romano or Parmesan cheese
¼ cup chopped fresh parsley
Salt and freshly ground pepper

Add the noodles to rapidly boiling, salted water, a little at a time so the noodles don't stick together. Cook until tender. Drain well. Add butter or margarine, cottage cheese, and parsley, and toss lightly until well mixed. Add salt and pepper to taste and sprinkle with grated cheese. *Four servings, 281 calories each.*

◄§ SWEET PINEAPPLE COTTAGE CHEESE §►

12 ounces uncreamed pot-style cottage cheese
1 can (8 ounces) juice-packed crushed pineapple, well-drained
A few drops of vanilla extract (optional)
2 teaspoons liquid sweetener (optional)

Stir all the ingredients together and refrigerate. *Four servings, 80 calories each.*

◄§ PINEAPPLE CHEESE SUNDAE §►

1 cup low-fat cottage cheese
¼ cup drained juice-packed pineapple tidbits
Sugar substitute, vanilla extract, and ground cinnamon to taste

For a really delicious low-calorie lunch, combine the cottage cheese with the pineapple tidbits. Sprinkle with sugar substitute, vanilla and cinnamon. *Two servings, 107 calories each.*

◄§ PINEAPPLE CHEESE DANISH §►

2 slices white bread
3 tablespoons pot cheese or low-fat cottage cheese
3 tablespoons drained, juice-packed crushed pineapple
Cinnamon

Toast 2 slices of white bread and top with 3 tablespoons of pot cheese or low-fat cottage cheese per slice. Spoon the crushed pineapple on top of the cheese and sprinkle with cinnamon. Brown under the broiler until the cheese is bubbly. *Two servings, about 110 calories each.*

14
PASTA
AND
GRAINS

Pasta Slimmers

When you absolutely *must* have a pasta dinner, have fun knowing it's the slimmest it can be. Check the calories you've saved for the day and splurge on a Slim Gourmet pasta dish, or have something tasty with rice and still feel diet-safe.

✑ BAKED CHEESE LASAGNE ✎

If you're a Slim Gourmet, you'll want to make your own lasagne because it's less fattening than the commercial kind. And since this homemade lasagne dough is mostly eggs and very little flour, it contains much more protein and far less carbohydrate than the commercial product.

LASAGNE DOUGH:
  4 eggs
  ½ cup sifted all-purpose flour
  1 teaspoon salt
  ¾ cup skim milk

FILLING AND TOPPING:
  1 egg
  1½ cups low-fat cottage cheese or pot cheese

¼ cup freshly grated extra-sharp Romano cheese
¼ cup minced fresh parsley
2 teaspoons oregano or Italian seasoning
2 teaspoons garlic salt
¼ cup (2 ounces) shredded part-skim mozzarella cheese
2 cups plain tomato sauce
2 tablespoons Italian-style bread crumbs

Combine all the ingredients for the dough and beat until smooth. Preheat a nonstick skillet or crêpe pan over a low-to-moderate flame. Pour the batter into the skillet and rotate to spread. Cook over low heat, without turning, until cooked through. When cooked, remove the "pancake" in one piece, or cut into 2-inch strips. Set aside on a clean towel. Continue cooking the "pancakes" until all the batter is used.

Or, if you have a large, heavy 18-inch griddle or cookie sheet that's perfectly flat and not warped, you can bake the batter in a very hot oven. Cover the entire surface of the sheet with a thin coating of batter and place in a preheated 475-degree oven for 6 to 8 minutes. Cut into 2-inch strips to remove.

Combine the egg, cottage cheese, Romano, parsley, oregano, and garlic salt. Assemble all the components in a baking dish, in 3 layers: one-third each of the lasagne strips, cottage cheese mixture, and mozzarella, with tomato sauce between each layer. Top with the remaining tomato sauce and the bread crumbs and bake in a preheated 350-degree oven for 50 to 60 minutes. *Four main-course servings, 332 calories each; eight side-dish servings, 166 each.*

◆§ QUICK SKILLET LASAGNE §◆

Be sure to use pot cheese (uncreamed skim milk cottage cheese) instead of the costlier and far more fattening ricotta cheese. And in buying tomato sauce, be sure to pick a brand that contains no fat or oil (read the label). Make this dish with curly-type egg noodles; they won't stick together the way flat ones do.

1 pound lean beef round, trimmed of fat and ground
  Garlic salt and pepper
1 onion, sliced
2 cups plain tomato sauce
2 teaspoons oregano or Italian seasoning
3 cups water
4 ounces curly noodles
½ cup pot cheese (skim milk cottage cheese)

Put the chopped meat in a cold nonstick skillet and heat over a moderate flame, breaking the meat into chunks as you stir. Season with garlic salt and pepper and continue to cook, uncovered, until nicely browned. Pour off any fat that accumulates. Add the onion, tomato sauce, oregano, and water; heat to boiling. Stir in the noodles, cover, and simmer over a low flame until the noodles are tender. Remove from the heat and add the pot cheese. Stir and serve. *Four generous servings, 359 calories each.*

ᴥ§ LINGUINI WITH WHITE ᵇ⃟ TUNA-MUSHROOM SAUCE

> 1 tablespoon butter or olive oil
> ½ pound fresh mushrooms, sliced
> 1 onion, chopped
> 1 clove garlic, chopped
> ¼ teaspoon dried basil
> 1 cup water
> 2 cans (7 ounces each) water-pack tuna, undrained
> ½ teaspoon arrowroot
> ¼ cup minced fresh parsley
> 4 cups tender-cooked protein-enriched linguini or spaghetti
> Salt and freshly ground pepper

Heat the butter or oil in a large nonstick skillet and add the mushrooms, onion, and garlic. Cook and stir over moderate heat until the mushrooms are lightly browned. Add the basil and ½ cup of the water, cover, and cook for 5 minutes. Break up the tuna and stir in, along with the liquid in the cans. Combine the remaining water and arrowroot and stir into the skillet until slightly thickened, then stir in the minced parsley and heat through. Season to taste and serve over the cooked linguini or spaghetti. *Four servings, 317 calories each.*

ᴥ§ BAKED MACARONI AND CHEESE ᵇ⃟

Standard recipes for macaroni and cheese add up to 473 calories a cupful, according to the U.S. Department of Agriculture, so toss away your cookbooks and use this recipe—it's so cheesy and rich tasting you'll never want to make it any other way. And it's only 88 calories a cup instead of 473! Even more important than that, it's 88 calories worth of good protein-powered nutrition instead of the usual starchy, fatty fare that makes baked macaroni and cheese off limits for calorie counters.

2 **eggs**
1 **cup skim milk**
1 **cup pot cheese or low-fat cottage cheese**
¼ **cup freshly grated extra-sharp Romano or Cheddar cheese**
1 **teaspoon salt**
½ **teaspoon freshly ground pepper**
2 **cups tender-cooked macaroni**
1 **tablespoon bread crumbs**

Fork-blend the eggs and milk together in a 1-quart nonstick baking dish, then add all the other ingredients except bread crumbs. Stir to distribute evenly. Sprinkle the breadcrumbs on top, then bake for one hour in a pre-heated 350-degree oven. *Eight ½-cup servings, about 100 calories each.*

NOTE: The actual calorie count is 95 calories per serving with Romano cheese and 104 calories per cup with Cheddar (American) cheese.

BAKED MACARONI WITH CHEDDAR CHEESE AND TOMATO SAUCE

Here's a new idea: stretching one cup of cooked macaroni to make four servings! Usually it's the other way around. Most "ordinary" recipes use starchy pasta products to pad the food budget and fill out the main course. The only problem is that a little bit of meat and a whole lot of macaroni will "fill out" your figure as well. As a Slim Gourmet cook, you want to avoid too many starchy carbohydrate foods and put the emphasis on protein foods instead. Protein, of course, means lean meat, cheese, and eggs.

To make this dish, you need 1 measuring cupful of tender-cooked elbow macaroni. Look for a brand that's protein-enriched. If you cook your pasta products to the tender stage (15 minutes) instead of firm to the teeth, you'll be cutting calories even more. One cupful of tender macaroni is only 155 calories, compared with firm "al dente" macaroni at 192 per cup.

Be sure to use plain tomato sauce, only 65 calories a cupful, instead of spaghetti sauce, which can add up to 200 or more, thanks to the extra unwanted vegetable oil. Use the meanest, most aggressively sharp cheese you can find. Extra-sharp cheese and mousy-meek cheese have the same calorie count, but you need twice as much of the meek stuff to get a decent amount of flavor. If you're lucky enough to live where you can buy the new low-calorie, low-fat processed American cheese slices, use that instead. It's only half the calories.

1 cup tender-cooked macaroni
1 can (8 ounces) plain tomato sauce
1 egg
2 tablespoons minced onion
  Pinch of cayenne pepper
½ teaspoon salt
1 teaspoon garlic salt
2 tablespoons grated extra-sharp Cheddar (American) cheese
2 tablespoons minced fresh parsley

Combine all the ingredients in an ovenproof casserole and bake in a pre-heated 350-degree oven for 45 to 50 minutes, until a knife inserted in the center comes out clean. *Four servings, 105 calories each; if made with low-calorie, low-fat processed American cheese slices, only 92 calories each.*

⋖ TUNA TETRAZZINI ⋗

8 ounces protein-enriched macaroni
  Salt
1 can (10½ ounces) condensed mushroom soup
2 tablespoons dry white wine
3 cans (7 ounces each) water-pack tuna
2 teaspoons chopped fresh parsley
1 jar (2 ounces) pimiento, drained (optional)
2 slices American, Cheddar, or Swiss Cheese, shredded

Cook the macaroni in salted boiling water until tender. Drain off most of the water and stir in all the other ingredients except the cheese. Cook and stir until the sauce is thick and bubbling; add water if needed. Stir in the shredded cheese until melted. *Six servings, 336 calories each.*

⋖ CAMPERS' CACCIATORE ⋗

A tossed salad and some fruit for dessert are all you need to complete this meal.

2 cans (5 ounces) boned chicken
2 cans (8 ounces) tomato sauce
½ teaspoon oregano or Italian seasoning
2 cups water
6 ounces curly noodles

Simmer all the ingredients in a covered skillet or Dutch oven until the noodles are nearly tender. Uncover and continue cooking, stirring occasionally, until the liquid evaporates and the sauce is thick. *Four servings, 306 calories each.*

NOTE: You can add canned mushrooms or onions, freshly chopped onions or green pepper, a pinch of garlic powder or a dash of cayenne pepper.

SPAGHETTI WITH WHITE CLAM SAUCE

2 cans (16 ounces each) minced clams, undrained
2 cloves or more garlic, minced
1 tablespoon arrowroot or cornstarch
¼ cup chopped fresh parsley
1½ teaspoons dried thyme
Salt (butter-flavored, if desired) and freshly ground pepper
1 pound spaghetti or linguini

Drain the clam liquid into a saucepan. Add all the other ingredients except the clam meat and spaghetti and stir. Simmer gently until reduced, about 10 minutes.

Meanwhile, cook the spaghetti or linguini in boiling, salted water until tender.

Stir the clams into the sauce and heat to boiling. Serve over the hot, drained pasta. *Four servings, 284 calories each, including 1 cup tender-cooked spaghetti.*

SPAGHETTI WITH WHITE CLAM AND MUSHROOM SAUCE

1 pound spaghetti
Salt
1 tablespoon butter or olive oil
½ pound fresh mushrooms, chopped
1 tablespoon arrowroot or cornstarch
4 cans minced clams (16 ounces each), undrained
2 teaspoons dried parsley flakes
1 teaspoon oregano
Garlic salt and pepper to taste

Cook the spaghetti in boiling, salted water until tender.

Meanwhile, prepare the sauce. Lightly sauté the mushrooms in butter or oil. Drain the clam liquid into the skillet, then add all the other ingredients except the clam meat. Simmer briskly until reduced, stirring frequently. Stir in the clams, reheat to boiling, and serve over the hot, drained spaghetti. *Six servings, 267 calories each, including 1 cup tender-cooked spaghetti.*

ᡃᢢ SPAGHETTI WITH QUICK ᢝᢀ RED CLAM SAUCE

1½ pounds spaghetti
    Salt
  2 cans (16 ounces each) minced clams, undrained
  1 can (16 ounces) tomato puree
    Garlic salt and pepper
  2 teaspoons oregano or Italian seasoning
  3 olives, minced (optional)

Cook the spaghetti in boiling, salted water until tender.

Meanwhile, make the sauce. Combine the clam liquid in a saucepan with all the other ingredients except the clam meat. Simmer until reduced to gravy consistency, about 8 minutes, then stir in the clam meat and reheat. Serve over the hot, drained spaghetti. *Six servings, 262 calories each, including 1 cup tender-cooked spaghetti.*

ᡃᢢ CLAMS AND SPAGHETTI ᢝᢀ

  6 ounces protein-enriched thin spaghetti
  1 can (16 ounces) whole clams, undrained
  1 can (16 ounces) tomato sauce with onions
½ teaspoon garlic powder
½ teaspoon Italian seasoning

Cook the spaghetti in boiling salted water until tender. Drain off the water and stir in the remaining ingredients, including the clam liquid. Cook and stir, uncovered, until the liquid is reduced and the sauce is thick and bubbling. *Four servings, 259 calories each.*

ᡃᢢ QUICK PORK AND ᢝᢀ SPAGHETTI ITALIANO

  8 ounces protein-enriched spaghetti
  1 can (8 ounces) Italian peeled tomatoes, coarsely chopped
  1 can (6 ounces) tomato paste
½ teaspoon poultry seasoning

1 teaspoon oregano
½ teaspoon fennel seeds
  Garlic salt and freshly ground pepper
1½ cups cold water
½ pound lean cooked pork, cut into ½-inch cubes

Cook the spaghetti in boiling salted water until tender.

Meanwhile, prepare the sauce. Combine the peeled tomatoes with all the other ingredients in a saucepan, cover, and cook over moderate heat for 15 minutes. Serve over the spaghetti. *Four servings, 391 calories each.*

SPEEDY SPAGHETTI WITH TUNA-MUSHROOM SAUCE

2 cans (7 ounces each) water-pack tuna
1 can (6 ounces) tomato paste
1 can (10½ ounces) condensed chicken broth, skimmed of fat
1 can (4 ounces) chopped mushrooms, undrained
¼ teaspoon Italian seasoning
  Garlic salt and freshly ground pepper
4 cups tender-cooked protein-enriched spaghetti

Drain the tuna into a saucepan, breaking the meat into chunks. Add all the other ingredients except the spaghetti and stir well. Simmer for 5 minutes over low heat, then season to taste and serve over the spaghetti. *Four servings, 327 calories each.*

15-MINUTE CHICKEN AND SPAGHETTI

Boneless, skinless breast of chicken is a marvelous convenience both for the calorie-conscious cook and the cook in a hurry. Virtually free of fat and low in cholesterol, these tender cutlets of pure white meat chicken are all meat, mainly protein, and only 458 calories per pound.

And while a whole chicken might take close to an hour to cook, chicken cutlets can be dinner-ready in only 15 minutes or less. They adapt themselves beautifully to many elegant "gourmet" dishes.

1 pound chicken cutlets (boneless, skinless breasts)
1 can (13 ounces) chicken broth, skimmed of fat
1 can (6 ounces) tomato paste
½ teaspoon oregano or Italian seasoning
½ teaspoon onion or garlic powder
1 pound spaghetti

Cut the chicken into 2-inch cubes. Combine the broth, tomato paste, oregano, and onion powder in a saucepan and stir until smooth. Heat to boiling, then add the chicken pieces and simmer over a moderate flame for 10 minutes while you cook the spaghetti (in boiling water until tender). To serve, pour the chicken and sauce over the hot, drained spaghetti. *Four servings, 317 calories each.*

⋖§ TURKEY CACCIATORE §⋗

1 pound cooked white-meat turkey
1 cup sliced onion
2 green peppers, chopped
1 clove garlic, minced
1 large can (35 ounces) Italian peeled tomatoes
½ cup dry white wine
1 cup turkey broth or 1 cup water plus 1 chicken bouillon cube
1 teaspoon salt
¼ teaspoon freshly ground pepper
1 tablespoon crushed oregano
1 pound spaghetti

Cut the turkey into chunks or bite-sized cubes; you should have about 2 cups. Set it aside.

Put all the remaining ingredients in a big saucepan. (If you're using left-over turkey broth, be sure to skim off all the fat; if you're using the water and chicken bouillon cube, omit the salt.) Cover and simmer slowly over low heat for about 45 minutes, then add the turkey pieces and simmer over low heat for another 25 minutes. Uncover to permit the sauce to reduce.

Meanwhile, cook the spaghetti until tender. Drain well, then place in the center of a platter, pour over the turkey and sauce, and serve. *Four servings, 330 calories each, including 1 cup of tender-cooked spaghetti.*

⋖§ BARLEY ITALIANO WITH CHEESE §⋗

Barley is one of those "forgotten" foods. Americans don't pay it much mind, except for an occasional homemade soup fan who tosses a handful into the bubbling pot.

Barley is a grain, and when cooked it looks like giant rice and tastes a little like spaghetti. Since barley contains 43 fewer calories per cupful than spaghetti, we thought it might make an interesting "Italian" side dish for dieters.

1 can (16 ounces) Italian peeled tomatoes, undrained
2 cups water

½ cup pearl barley
1 onion, chopped
¼ teaspoon oregano
½ teaspoon garlic salt
  Dash of cayenne pepper
3 tablespoons freshly grated extra-sharp Romano cheese

Combine all the ingredients except the cheese in a 2-quart nonstick saucepan. Cover and simmer over low heat, stirring occasionally, for 1 hour or more, until the liquid is evaporated and the barley is tender. Add water if needed. Sprinkle with the cheese and serve. *Six servings, 94 calories each.*

VARIATION

Spanish Barley: Follow the recipe above but omit the cheese and add 1 chopped green pepper, 1 teaspoon prepared mustard, and ¼ teaspoon ground cumin. *Six servings, 83 calories each.*

~§ EASY ONION RICE ৪~

1 cup undiluted onion soup
1 cup instant rice

Skim the fat globules from the top of the soup. Heat to boiling and stir in the rice, then remove from the heat and cover tightly. The rice will be ready in 5 minutes. *Four servings, 133 calories each.*

~§ PINEAPPLE RICE ৪~

1 cup instant rice
1 cup boiling unsweetened pineapple juice
  Salt and freshly ground pepper
1 tablespoon minced fresh parsley

Ten minutes before dinnertime, combine the rice with the boiling unsweetened pineapple juice. Season with salt, pepper, and the parsley, then cover and keep warm until serving time. *Six servings, 80 calories each.*

⋖§ RICE WITH CURRANTS §⋗

1 cup instant rice
5 tablespoons dried currants
  Pinch ground cinnamon
1 cup boiling water

Ten minutes before dinner, combine the instant rice, the currants, cinnamon, and boiling water. Cover tightly and keep warm until serving time, then add salt and pepper to taste. *Six servings, 89 calories each.*

15
VEGETABLES

Have you ever cooked a fresh vegetable?

That may seem like a startling question to culinary purists and old kitchen hands who still buy all their produce at the greengrocer's. But the fact is, many of today's "liberated" cooks have never prepared anything other than vegetables from a can or box. After all, frozen foods have been around for more than a generation. Maybe even your mother wouldn't know what to do with fresh Brussels sprouts or zucchini.

Too bad. Convenient and tasty as they are, many frozen vegetables are still not quite the same as fresh, yet "fresh" often isn't any more work. So why not give fresh vegetables a try? The only thing you really need to know about cooking vegetables is *not* to overcook them. The amount of tenderness you desire is strictly a matter of personal preference. Nutritionally, there's no such thing as an "undercooked" vegetable. Cook your favorite vegetables in as little time—and liquid—as possible.

ASPARAGUS: Break off the ends. Simply steam or simmer for 5 or 6 minutes, then serve as a finger food, dipped in Worcestershire.

BRUSSELS SPROUTS: Cook, uncovered, in a minimum of salted water. Sprinkle with lemon juice to serve.

CABBAGE: Slice into 4 or 6 wedges, still attached to the core. Cook only till slightly tender, about 8 minutes. Or cook with simmering meat, such as tongue, ham, or corned beef round (see page 76). Or cook with tomato sauce, laced with lemon juice.

CELERY: Slice and stir-fry with 1 teaspoon oil and 2 tablespoons soy sauce, Oriental style. Add sliced onions and cook only until crisp.

EGGPLANT: Cut unpeeled eggplant in cubes and bake in tomato sauce, sprinkled with Italian seasoning. Or slice and broil for 6 to 7 minutes. Baste lightly with diet dressing.

MUSHROOMS: Sauté in a nonstick skillet with 1 teaspoon oil and 2 tablespoons wine. Season with garlic or onion salt.

PEPPERS: Red or green. Prepare your favorite meat loaf recipe and use the meat as stuffing. Bake 45 to 60 minutes.

SPINACH: Rinse well and shake off the water. Season with salt (or butter-flavored salt), pepper, and nutmeg. Cook in a covered pot, no water added, only long enough to wilt slightly. Should still be bright green.

SQUASH (*Winter*): Slice in half and scoop out the seeds. Brush the squash lightly with oil or fill the cavity with orange juice. Bake until just tender, not mushy, less than 1 hour. *Summer:* slice and sauté in 1 teaspoon oil and 1 tablespoon water until the water has evaporated and the squash is lightly browned. Cook with onions, if desired. Or simmer sliced squash in tomato, orange, pineapple, or apple juice.

Fabulous Fruit-sauced Vegetables

Pineapple-glazed zucchini, carrots in orange sauce, apple-simmered summer squash—what could be easier than a vegetable that makes its own sauce, or healthier? Vitamins go down the drain when you cook vegetables in water. Why throw away nutrition (and then add butter calories) when it's so easy to simmer fresh vegetables in a self-making sauce based on canned fruit juice. Unsweetened juice has just the right amount of natural fruit sugar to simmer down to a delightful, slightly sweet glaze. Be sure the juice you buy is "no sugar added," or your dish will be a sticky-sweet disaster.

To help thicken the glaze, we'll add a little bit of arrowroot flour (or "arrowroot powder"). Arrowroot has the same calories as flour, but three times the thickening power. Arrowroot-thickened sauces are clear and transparent, never opaque or cloudy. Look for arrowroot in small jars on your supermarket spice shelf or in larger jars or bags in the health food store. If you can't find arrowroot, use cornstarch, the next best thing.

❧ PINEAPPLE-GLAZED ZUCCHINI ❧

2 zucchini, sliced (¾ pound)
1 can (6 ounces) unsweetened pineapple juice
½ teaspoon arrowroot or cornstarch
1 tablespoon minced onion
1½ teaspoons minced fresh parsley
Salt and freshly ground pepper

Combine all the ingredients in a shallow, open saucepan. Simmer, uncovered, over moderate heat, stirring occasionally, until nearly all the liquid has evaporated into a sauce. *Four servings, 45 calories each.*

✓ ⋖ CARROTS IN ORANGE SAUCE ⋗

3 cups sliced carrots
1 can (6 ounces) unsweetened orange juice
½ teaspoon arrowroot or corn starch
½ cup water
¼ teaspoon ground cinnamon
   Salt and freshly ground pepper

Combine all the ingredients in a saucepan. Cover closely and simmer until nearly tender, then uncover and continue to simmer, stirring occasionally, until nearly all the liquid has evaporated. *Four servings, 44 calories each.*

⋖ APPLE-SIMMERED SQUASH ⋗

¾ pound sliced yellow summer squash
1 can (6 ounces) unsweetened apple juice
½ teaspoon arrowroot
2 scallions, sliced
   Salt and freshly ground pepper

Combine all the ingredients in a shallow saucepan and simmer, uncovered, stirring occasionally, until most of the liquid has evaporated. *Four servings, 43 calories each.*

⋖ CRUNCHY ASPARAGUS WITH ⋗ DIPPING SAUCE

Asparagus should be quick-cooked, steamed only long enough to heat it through, in a vegetable steamer or heads up in a tall coffee pot, with just an inch or two of water at the bottom. It's misleading to give specific times, because the time depends on the skinnyness of the stalks. Naturally, thin asparagus cooks quicker than fat spears. A point to remember when shopping! Try to hand-select asparagus spears of similar thickness—all fat or all thin. They'll take anywhere from 2 to 5 minutes of cooking, rarely more.

1½ pounds fresh asparagus
¼ cup Worcestershire sauce
1½ cups water
1 tablespoon cornstarch
1 tablespoon butter or margarine

Wash the asparagus under cold running water. Snap off the tough, reedy bottoms (it is not necessary to peel the stalks). Stand the asparagus, heads up, in a tall coffee pot and add 2 inches of water. Or lay the asparagus on a cake rack in a large skillet that's equipped with a cover. Add water to the bottom of the skillet, but not touching the asparagus. Steam, covered, for 2 to 5 minutes, depending on thickness of stalk. Don't overcook.

Meanwhile, prepare the sauce. Combine the Worcestershire, water, and cornstarch in a small saucepan over a moderate flame. Cook, stirring, until the mixture simmers and thickens slightly. Add the butter and stir until melted. Pour the sauce into individual dipping bowls and serve with the hot asparagus. *Four side-dish servings, 69 calories each.*

✓ ↝ GREEN BEANS AND MUSHROOMS ↜

1 package (10 ounces) frozen green beans
1 can (2 ounces) mushrooms, undrained
2 tablespoons water
1 tablespoon mushroom soup powder (from a 1-cup packet of instant, single-serving cream of mushroom soup)

Cover and simmer the beans, mushrooms, and water until the beans are tender. Stir in the soup powder over low heat and cook until the sauce is thickened. Serve immediately. *Three side-dish servings, 37 calories each.*

✓ ↝ SAUCY BROCCOLI ↜

1 package (10 ounces) frozen broccoli
¼ cup water
1 tablespoon mushroom soup powder (from a 1-cup packet of instant, single-serving cream of mushroom soup)

Combine the broccoli and water. Cover and cook until tender, then stir the soup powder into the liquid remaining in the saucepan. Cook, stirring, over low heat until the sauce is thickened. Serve immediately. *Two side-dish servings, 51 calories each.*

৵§ BROCCOLI QUICHE ৯৵

Today's "hottest" way to treat broccoli is not to cook it at all. Serve it raw in salads, or broken into buds around a bowl of dip. But if you do cook it, remember that leftover cooked broccoli can be both time-saver and budget-stretcher when combined with low-cost meat substitutes and protein-rich dairy foods.

> **Pastry of your choice for a 1-crust pie**
> 1½ **cups chopped, cooked broccoli**
> 1 **cup evaporated skim milk**
> 1 **cup minced onion**
> 1 **can (2 ounces) mushroom stems and pieces, drained**
> 1 **teaspoon butter-flavored salt**
> ¼ **teaspoon freshly grated nutmeg or ground mace**
>   **Pinch of cayenne pepper**
> 3 **eggs, lightly beaten**

Fork-blend the pastry ingredients and chill. Roll the pastry as thin as possible, then line a nonstick pie pan.

Combine the milk, onion, mushrooms, and seasonings in a saucepan and simmer for 1 minute. Beat the eggs in a bowl and stir in the hot milk mixture. Add the chopped broccoli, then pour the mixture into the unbaked crust and place in a preheated 400-degree oven for 15 minutes. Reduce the heat to 375 and bake for 25 minutes longer, until set. *Six main-course servings, 165 calories each.*

New Ways with Cabbage for People Who "Hate" It

Cabbage is a delicious, nutritious vegetable that most people prefer raw, as coleslaw. Most cooks—and cookbooks—overcook it. Cabbage should be cooked just enough to heat it through, so it's tender but still crisp, its crunch and color still intact. The secret is to cut the cabbage into wedges still attached to the base, and to cook it as quickly as possible. We like to combine cabbage with tomato-based dishes for hearty flavor and eye-appealing color contrast.

৵§ CABBAGE WEDGES IN
TOMATO-PINEAPPLE SAUCE ৯৵

> ½ **cup crushed pineapple, packed in juice**
> 2 **cans (8 ounces each) plain tomato sauce**
> ¼ **cup water**
> 1 **head of cabbage (about 1 pound)**

Combine the pineapple, tomato sauce, and water in a covered skillet. Cut the cabbage in quarters, then into eighths. Lay the wedges in the skillet, cover and simmer about 8 minutes, only until the cabbage is tender-crisp and still green; don't overcook or the cabbage will lose its shape and become mushy and unappetizing. Remove to a serving dish, pour the sauce over, and serve immediately. *Four servings, 70 calories each.*

◆§ SWEET AND SOUR RED CABBAGE §◆

1 large head red cabbage (about 3 pounds)
1 tablespoon all-purpose flour
3 tablespoons lemon juice
2 tablespoons brown sugar
1 teaspoon salt
½ cup unsweetened applesauce

Wash the cabbage and shred it fine, then put it in a heavy pot equipped with a cover. Sprinkle with the flour, lemon juice, brown sugar, and salt. Add the applesauce and stir well, then cover and cook over low heat for 30 minutes, stirring occasionally. Remove from the heat and serve immediately. *Eight side-dish servings, 57 calories each.*

◆§ SOUPER CARROTS §◆

3 cups sliced carrots
1½ tablespoons minced fresh parsley
1 can (10½ ounces) undiluted chicken broth, skimmed of fat

Put all the ingredients in a nonstick saucepan and cook, uncovered, over moderate heat until carrots are tender and most of the liquid is evaporated. Add no salt, unless the broth is salt-free or homemade. *Six side-dish servings, 39 calories each.*

◆§ BAKED CAULIFLOWER AND CHEESE §◆

1 package (10 ounces) cauliflower, thawed
3 eggs
½ cup skim milk
1 teaspoon prepared mustard
1 teaspoon salt
  Pinch of cayenne pepper
¼ cup freshly grated extra-sharp Romano or Cheddar cheese, or
    2 tablespoons of each

Arrange the cauliflower in an ovenproof baking dish or casserole and reserve.

Scald the milk, then combine the milk with the remaining ingredients. Mix well, pour over the cauliflower, and bake in a preheated 350-degree oven for 35 minutes. *Six side-dish servings, 75 calories each.*

◄§ CREOLE CAULIFLOWER §►

2 packages (10 ounces each) frozen cauliflower, thawed
1 can (11 ounces) stewed tomatoes
1 teaspoon garlic salt
  Pinch of cayenne pepper
2 tablespoons minced onion
2 tablespoons chopped green pepper
2 tablespoons grated extra-sharp Cheddar cheese
1 tablespoon bread crumbs

In an ovenproof casserole, combine all the ingredients except the cheese and bread crumbs. Combine the cheese and bread crumbs and sprinkle on top. Bake at 350 degrees for 35 minutes, until the top is brown. *Eight side-dish servings, 45 calories each.*

Corn—Unexpectedly Slim

Corn is fattening only when you compare it with foods like spinach or kale or kohlrabi (although spinach is only one-third the calories). But compared with French fries or potato salad or even most cold slaws, corn on the cob is a barbecue bargain.

◄§ "BUTTER-BAKED" CORN §►

6 ears of corn, in the husk
  Butter-flavored salt

On each ear of corn, pull back the husk and remove the corn silk, but don't detach the husk. Soak the ears for twenty minutes in cold water, then salt liberally with the butter-flavored salt. Rewrap the corn in their husks and roast on a barbecue grill for 20 minutes, turning several times to promote even cooking. *Each five-inch ear is 70 calories.*

NOTE: If you prefer, you can remove the husks and wrap the ears in double layers of heavy aluminum foil. Oven-bake for 25 minutes at 350 degrees.

⋅§ MEXICALI CORN CUSTARD §⋅

    2 cups skim milk
    1 onion, minced
    2 small red or green sweet peppers, or one of each, diced
 1½ cups corn kernels, fresh, canned, or frozen and defrosted
    2 eggs
    2 teaspoons salt
      Pinch of freshly ground pepper

Scald the milk, then stir in the remaining ingredients and turn into an ovenproof casserole. Bake in a preheated 325-degree oven for 1 hour or more, until a knife inserted in the center comes out clean. *Eight side-dish servings, 77 calories each.*

⋅§ CORN PUDDING §⋅

 1½ cups corn kernels, fresh, canned, or frozen and defrosted
    3 eggs
 1½ cups skim milk
    1 teaspoon salt
      Pinch of freshly ground pepper
      Dash of Tabasco or cayenne pepper
    3 tablespoons bacon bits

Combine all the ingredients in an ovenproof baking dish, sprinkling the bacon bits on the surface. Bake at 350 degrees for 60 minutes, until set. *Eight side-dish servings, 81 calories each.*

⋅§ MEXICALI CORN §⋅

    2 packages (10 ounces each) frozen corn kernels
   ¼ cup water
    1 green pepper, seeded and chopped
    1 sweet red pepper, seeded and chopped
      Salt and freshly ground pepper
 2½ tablespoons diet margarine

Combine the water, frozen corn, and chopped peppers in a saucepan. Cover and cook for 2 minutes, just until tender. Season, stir in the margarine, and serve. *Eight side-dish servings, 73 calories each.*

◄§ COOKED CUCUMBERS CREOLE §►

3 large cucumbers
1 small onion, chopped
2 cups canned tomatoes
1 teaspoon salt
　Pinch of freshly ground pepper
2 tablespoons minced green pepper

Pare the cucumbers *only* if they have been waxed (summer cucumbers usually aren't). Cut lengthwise into quarters, then crosswise into 1-inch chunks. Combine the cucumbers with all the other ingredients in a covered saucepan and simmer, over moderate heat, until the cucumbers are just tender, about 10 to 12 minutes. *Eight side-dish servings, 31 calories each.*

◄§ SESAME LETTUCE §►

1 medium head lettuce
½ chicken bouillon cube
½ cup boiling water
1 small onion, minced
2 tablespoons chopped raw carrot
1 teaspoon granulated sugar
1½ tablespoons minced fresh parsley
1 tablespoon toasted sesame seeds (see note below)

Prepare the lettuce as you would for salad. Dissolve the bouillon cube in the boiling water. Add the onion and carrot and simmer for 5 minutes, covered, then add the sugar, lettuce, and minced parsley. Cover and simmer over low heat for 5 to 8 minutes, then drain and serve, topped with the toasted sesame seeds. *Six side-dish servings, 27 calories each.*

NOTE: To toast plain sesame seeds, spread them on a cookie tin and quick-broil under highest heat for 1 to 2 minutes.

◄§ ORIENTAL STIR-FRIED LETTUCE §►

1 tablespoon polyunsaturated oil
1 clove garlic, minced
2 small heads lettuce, shredded
2 tablespoons soy sauce

Heat the oil in a nonstick skillet and sauté the garlic until browned. Add the lettuce, sprinkle with soy sauce, and cook, stirring, over highest heat for 60 seconds, no longer! Serve immediately. *Eight side-dish servings, 29 calories each.*

⋘ MUSHROOMS MONICA ⋙

1 **dozen large fresh mushrooms**
2 **tablespoons minced onion**
1 **package (10 ounces) frozen cauliflower, cooked and mashed**
2 **tablespoons grated extra-sharp Cheddar cheese**
½ **teaspoon salt**
   Pinch of freshly ground pepper
   Paprika

Wash and dry the mushrooms. Remove the stems and chop fine; reserve the caps. Combine the stems, onion, and cauliflower. Stuff mushroom caps; sprinkle with the cheese and seasonings. Bake in a 350-degree oven for 15 minutes, until the cheese browns. *Each mushroom, 22 calories.*

The Potato—Deceptively Diet-Wise

Do you have a "potato famine" going in your house? If everyone in your family is a waistline watcher, chances are the potato has been banished on caloric grounds, which really isn't fair, because the average potato is about 90 calories and not without redeeming nutritional value. A healthy helping of vitamins B_1 and C inhabit the spud.

You can indulge your taste for potatoes without acquiring a potato-sack figure by avoiding the naked potato: mashed mounds that demand pools of melting butter. Don't forget that a skimpy tablespoon of butter is 100 calories —more than the potato!

One calorie-wise trick with potatoes is to make four serve eight. You can do it very nicely with this Slim Gourmet trick. And if you've only four potato-lovers to serve, simply cut the recipe in half or freeze the extras.

⋘ BAKED STUFFED POTATOES ⋙

4 **well-shaped baking potatoes**
2 **egg whites**
1 **teaspoon salt**
   Pinch of freshly ground pepper
1 **tablespoon minced onion or chives**
½ **to ¾ cup skim milk**
3 **tablespoons grated extra-sharp Cheddar cheese**
   Paprika

Choose rather flat potatoes, all the same size. Scrub them well and pierce with a fork. Place them in a preheated 400-degree oven and bake them for 50 to 60 minutes, until tender. Remove the potatoes from the oven, carefully slice them in half, lengthwise, and let cool.

Combine the salt and egg whites in a nonplastic bowl and whip with your electric mixer until stiff peaks form. Set aside.

Carefully scoop out the potato innards, being careful not to rip the skin. Place the potato scooping in another small mixing bowl and add the pepper and onion or chives. Whip with your electric mixer, adding the milk a little at a time, until the potatoes are fluffy.

Fold the egg white mixture into the whipped potatoes, then pile the mixture back into the potato skins and sprinkle each with about a teaspoon of grated cheese. Dash on a bit of paprika.

Place the potatoes in a flat pan and return to the oven. Bake at 425 degrees until the cheese is melted and potatoes are hot. Serve immediately. *Eight side-dish servings, 71 calories each.*

Every dieter knows that plain yogurt is the perfect topping for baked potatoes. Mixed with chives, parsley, or minced onion, yogurt is the perfect stand-in for fattening sour cream, and only 130 calories a cupful instead of nearly 500. Yogurt can also rescue leftover potatoes.

ᴇᴄ§ POTATOES PIQUANT ᴈᴇ»

4 **cooked potatoes**
1 **sweet green or red bell pepper**
1 **onion**
1 **stalk celery**
1 **clove garlic (optional)**
1 **cup plain yogurt**
1 **teaspoon salt or butter-flavored salt**
  Pinch of cayenne pepper
3 **tablespoons seasoned bread crumbs**

Peel and dice the potatoes; mince the green or red pepper, onion, celery, and garlic. Combine all the ingredients in a baking dish, sprinkling the top with the bread crumbs. Bake in a preheated 350-degree oven for 15 to 18 minutes. *Six side-dish servings, 95 calories each.*

By Any Other Name . . . The Versatile Rutabaga

Lots of vegetables are stuck with unappealing names, but only the rutabaga or turnip has two of them. I'm sure it would do a lot better with a name like "Canadian love squash." But if you're a high-vitamin-C Slim Gourmet cook, you'll be happy to hear that the rutabaga has only 40 calories in a ½-cup serving and is really packed with Vitamin C. It makes a tasty teammate with other vegetables, too.

◄§ BASIC RUTABAGA §►

Simply slice off the bottom so you'll have a flat surface to stand it on. Then slice downward into inch-thick slabs. Use a sharp knife to peel off the purple skin, then cut the inside pieces into cubes. Simmer the rutabaga, in just enough salted water to cover, for 15 to 20 minutes, until tender.

◄§ RUTABAGA, ET AL. §►

◄§ Mash potatoes and rutabagas together to cut down potato calories. Add some minced onion, powdered beef bouillon, or a sprinkle of grated Cheddar.

◄§ Simmer rutabagas in orange juice before mashing. Or, sprinkle on some powdered orange juice breakfast concentrate for extra flavor and Vitamin C. (There's now a sugar-free version of the concentrate on the market for half the calories.)

◄§ Granulated brown sugar substitute, available in some areas, plus a sprinkle of nutmeg make good rutabaga dress-ups.

◄§ Carrots and rutabagas can be simmered together, then mashed into a yummy mélange, flavored with a little lemon juice and fresh parsley.

◄§ Frozen cubes of rutabaga can be added to stews and soups during the last half hour of cooking. And chunks of rutabaga are a natural with game dishes, particularly venison.

◄§ "BUTTERED" SPINACH §►

1 **package (10 ounces) frozen spinach**
3 **tablespoons water**
½ **teaspoon butter-flavored salt or 3 drops of butter extract**
   Pinch of freshly grated nutmeg

Put the frozen spinach in a saucepan and sprinkle on the water, butter salt, and nutmeg. Cook, covered, for 3 minutes. *Two servings, 36 calories each.*

Lo-Cal Squash

At less than 15 calories a ½-cup serving, squash is one of the calorie bargains of all times—except for its frightful affinity for melted butter. Tablespoon after tablespoon, at 100 calories each, seem to sink into squash without a trace. Here are some tasty dishes that bring out all the flavor of squash without using one iota of butter.

·§ SQUASH ROMANO ε·

1½ to 2 pounds fresh yellow squash or 2 packages (10 ounces
    each) frozen
  2 cups plain tomato sauce
  ¼ cup water
  1 teaspoon oregano
  1 teaspoon garlic salt
  2 tablespoons freshly grated sharp Romano cheese

Cut the fresh squash, if used, into ½-inch slices; reserve. Combine the
remaining ingredients in a saucepan and bring to a boil. Add the squash,
cover, and simmer over a low flame until just tender, about 12 minutes for
fresh squash, 8 for frozen. *Six side-dish servings, 50 calories each.*

·§ SQUASH ESPAGNOL ε·

1½ to 2 pounds fresh yellow squash or 2 packages (10 ounces
    each) frozen
  1 can (16 ounces) tomatoes
  1 teaspoon prepared mustard
  1 teaspoon oregano
  1 teaspoon garlic salt
  ¼ cup minced green pepper
    Pinch of cayenne pepper

Slice the fresh squash, if used, into ½-inch slices; reserve. Heat the tomatoes in a saucepan. When boiling, add all the other ingredients, including the
squash. Cover and simmer over low flame until the squash is nearly tender,
then uncover and continue to simmer until the liquid has evaporated to sauce
consistency. *Six side-dish servings, 41 calories each.*

·§ SQUASH AND CARROTS IN ORANGE SAUCE ε·

  1 cup orange juice
  2 cups sliced carrots
  1 package (10 ounces) frozen yellow squash
    Salt and freshly ground pepper
  2 teaspoons arrowroot or cornstarch
  ¼ cup cold water

Bring the orange juice to a boil and add the carrots. Cover and simmer for 5 minutes, then add the squash, salt, and pepper. Cover and simmer until the vegetables are just tender, about 8 to 10 minutes.

Combine the cornstarch and cold water and add to the sauce. Cook, stirring, until the mixture thickens. *Six side-dish servings, 62 calories each.*

⊰ ZUCCHINI, PLAIN AND SIMPLE ⊱

Cook zucchini as you would yellow squash (see page 239), or simmer briefly in plain tomato sauce (no oil added) seasoned with oregano. Or cut in chunks and stir-fry with onions in 1 teaspoon oil and a little soy sauce.

⊰ SAUTÉED ZUCCHINI, ITALIAN STYLE ⊱

3 zucchini (about 1 pound)
1 tablespoon minced onion
2 tablespoons olive oil
   Oregano or Italian seasoning

Wash the zucchini and cut into quarters lengthwise, then slice into 1-inch cubes. Combine all the ingredients in a skillet and cook, covered, over a medium flame for 2 minutes. Uncover and cook, stirring, for an additional 2 minutes, until the zucchini begins to brown lightly. Turn onto a paper towel and toss so the fat drains off in the towel. Pour into a serving dish and serve immediately. *Six side-dish servings, 30 calories each.*

⊰ BAKED ZUCCHINI PROVOLONE ⊱

This zucchini dish is one of those time- and effort-saving vegetable dishes that can be made in extra quantity. The leftovers can be frozen and reheated for yet another meal.

3   cups sliced or diced zucchini
1   onion, chopped
1   can (16 ounces) Italian peeled tomatoes in tomato puree
1   cup water
2   ounces sharp imported provolone cheese, sliced or chopped
2   teaspoons oregano
1   teaspoon garlic salt
¼   teaspoon freshly ground pepper
2   tablespoons bread crumbs

Spread half the zucchini on the bottom of a baking dish or ovenproof casserole. Combine the onion, tomatoes, and water and pour half the mixture over the zucchini. Sprinkle with half of the provolone and seasonings.

Make a second layer of zucchini and tomatoes. Sprinkle with the remaining provolone and seasonings and the bread crumbs, then bake in a preheated 350-degree oven for 25 to 35 minutes, until the zucchini is tender and the top is well browned. *Ten side-dish servings, 52 calories each.*

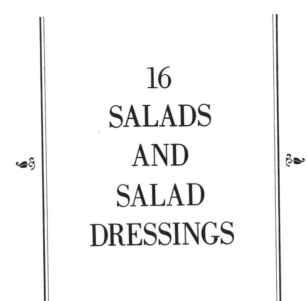

16
SALADS
AND
SALAD
DRESSINGS

The Salad Bar

Borrow an idea from the restaurant field and feast your friends with a "salad bar"!

If you're a restaurant regular, you know that the salad bar is the most popular idea in the trade since tipping. A salad bar is a help-yourself table where a variety of greenery is displayed, along with dressings and toppings. While waiting for their entrees, patrons amuse themselves assembling salads instead of buttering bread and ordering extra martinis.

So why not set up your own the next time you have dinner guests for a buffet or a barbecue? The idea will have special appeal to weight-watching guests who'd prefer a do-it-yourself salad over an already-tossed concoction drenched in somebody else's favorite fattening salad dressing. Every salad bar should include a variety of popular dressings, including some low-calorie versions.

As a hostess, you'll find that a do-it-yourself salad table is less wasteful than providing one big bowl of already-dressed greenery. Leftover salad with dressing turns limp and must be discarded. But unused salad vegetables can be bagged in plastic and returned to the refrigerator.

Your salad table's "centerpiece" is a big bowl of crisp lettuce, shredded; choose a hardy type like iceberg. Out-of-doors in warm weather, the bowl might be set in a larger bowl of crushed ice. Surround it with smaller bowls of sliced unpeeled cucumber, tomato wedges or cherry tomatoes, sliced red onions, and crisp radishes. For a more extensive table, add bowls of red or green sweet pepper, sliced raw mushrooms, drained canned artichoke hearts, carrot curls, and whatever other greenery looks good on market day.

For extra protein and appetite appeal, you might add wedges of hard-cooked egg, lean cooked ham cubes, julienne strips of white meat turkey or chicken, shredded Swiss or Cheddar cheese, and bacon-flavored bits. Or cold shrimp, crabmeat, or flaked white tuna might be provided at a luncheon where salad is the main course.

Bowls of favorite homemade dressings could be offered, but bottled dressings are quicker. For an informal meal, there's no reason to "decant" commercial dressings into serving bowls. Simply assemble a variety of bottled dressings on a decorative tray.

Arrange your salad bar ingredients in the order they'll be used. Begin with big bowls, not the usual too-scanty salad bowls. Then the lettuce, onions, and other basics, followed by the more optional choices. Finally the tray of dressings, plus such toppings as bacon bits and toasted croutons.

For a lunchtime gathering, your salad bar could be the main course, augmented with crusty loaves of French bread or crisp bread sticks, plus iced tea, lemonade, or tall drinks. If you're having a hot dog or hamburger cookout, a salad bar can provide extra appeal, and help keep everybody from congregating around the grill. A crisp do-it-yourself salad is a much more appealing accompaniment to hamburgers than the usual, heavy, starchy, mayonnaise-laden fare.

⋖ᔅ CAESAR SALAD ᔆᵇ

Be your own expert and tailor a Caesar salad to suit your taste—and figure.

Most Caesar recipes rely on the dark green romaine lettuce for their base (shredded or torn), with nothing else from the produce bin except lots of garlic. But there are those who prefer Bibb or even iceberg lettuce, and sometimes onions, endive, or tomatoes. These variations won't affect the calories much one way or the other. Nor will an egg—80 calories—or lemon juice.

But the other Caesar components really add up: olive oil (928 calories for ½ cup), grated Parmesan cheese (111 calories an ounce), and those mischievous little cubes of fried bread known as croutons (whose calorie count depends on how much oil they absorb in the frying).

Here is our calorie-reduced version of this salad classic, with a few variations on the theme for good measure.

2 tablespoons lemon juice
2 tablespoons water
1 teaspoon Worcestershire sauce
1 raw egg
2 slices low-calorie protein bread
2 teaspoons polyunsaturated oil
  Garlic salt
4 cups shredded romaine lettuce
1 clove garlic, minced
  Salt and pepper
2 tablespoons grated Parmesan cheese

Combine the lemon juice, water, Worcestershire, and egg in a small bowl and beat well; reserve.

Toast the bread and cut into cubes while still warm. Put in a bowl and toss with the oil and a sprinkling of garlic salt; reserve.

Put the lettuce, garlic, salt, and pepper in a salad bowl and pour on the dressing. Sprinkle with the cheese and croutons, toss lightly, and serve. *Six servings, 55 calories each.*

VARIATIONS

Low Cholesterol Caesar: Use ¼ cup defrosted cholesterol-free egg substitute in place of the egg. (Extra-easy: combine equal parts bottled diet Italian dressing and defrosted egg substitute.)

Eggless Caesar: Simply omit the egg and water from the recipe above. Good *—and only 42 calories per serving.*

Easy Caesar: Substitute this combination for the dressing: 3 tablespoons low-calorie mayonnaise, 3 tablespoons lemon juice, 1 tablespoon water, 1 teaspoon Worcestershire. Blend well before adding to the salad. *Only 46 calories per serving.*

Extra-Easy Caesar: Use 6 tablespoons of low-calorie bottled Caesar dressing. *Only 50 calories per serving.*

Apple-a-Day Salads

S.O.S. for boring lunches: Skip the bread and add an apple.

Instead of the same old sandwich, why not combine the filling—meat, poultry, seafood, or cheese—with a crunchy cup of juicy diced apple, plus some sliced celery or other greenery for extra dash? Mix it all up with a creamy low-calorie dressing and you've got a delicious meal-sized salad with staying power. It's every bit as easy to make as a sandwich, and much more satisfying. That's because crisp fresh fruits and vegetables provide more bulk for fewer calories. Apples are rich in natural fruit sugar. Differing from refined table sugar, natural fruit sugar provides more sweetness for fewer calories.

Mix the ingredients in the order given, and your apples will stay fresh and white for hours, even in an insulated jar for desk-top lunching. Double, triple or quadruple the recipes for family-sized lunches.

⋲§ HAM AND CHEESE APPLE SALAD §⋟

1 **cup diced unpeeled apple**
2 **teaspoons lemon juice**
1 **tablespoon low-calorie mayonnaise**
1 **cup thinly sliced celery**
2 **thick slices (2 ounces) lean boiled ham**
1 **tablespoon shredded extra-sharp Cheddar cheese**

Combine all the ingredients, in the order given, in a small salad bowl and toss. *One serving, 235 calories.*

⋲§ APPLE-REUBEN SALAD §⋟

1 **tablespoon low-calorie mayonnaise**
1 **tablespoon plain or lemon yogurt**
½ **teaspoon dry mustard**
1 **cup chopped unpeeled apple**
1 **cup shredded cabbage**
2 **slices (2 ounces) lean corned beef round, shredded**
1 **tablespoon shredded Swiss cheese**

Toss all the ingredients together in a small salad bowl. *One serving, 260 calories.*

⋲§ APPLE-SEAFOOD SALAD §⋟

1 **tablespoon lemon yogurt**
1 **tablespoon low-calorie mayonnaise**
¼ **teaspoon curry powder**
1 **cup cubed unpeeled raw zucchini or cucumber**
3 **ounces canned crabmeat or tiny shrimp, rinsed and drained**
1 **cup cubed unpeeled apple**
 A few drops of sugar substitute (optional)

Toss all the ingredients together in a small salad bowl. *One serving, 183 calories.*

◄§ ORIENTAL SALAD §►

1 cup diced unpeeled apples
1 seedless orange, peeled and cut in chunks
1 tablespoon low-calorie mayonnaise
1 cup diagonally sliced celery
1 scallion, sliced
½ cup (3½ ounces) water-packed tuna or cooked, cubed chicken
    or turkey marinated in one tablespoon soy sauce

Toss all the ingredients together in a small salad bowl. *One serving, 277 calories.*

◄§ CURRIED LAMB LUNCHEON SALAD §►

2 cups cooked, cubed lean leftover roast lamb
2 cubed unpeeled apples
3 tablespoons golden raisins
1 tablespoon minced onion
2 cups diagonally sliced celery
½ cup plain low-fat yogurt
¼ cup low-calorie mayonnaise or diet dressing
    Pinch of ground ginger
2 teaspoons or more curry powder

Combine all the ingredients and serve on lettuce leaves. *Four servings, 298 calories each.*

◄§ BEANSPROUT SALAD §►

2 cups fresh or canned beansprouts
1 cup diagonally sliced celery
1 cup thinly sliced radishes
1 cup peeled, cubed cucumbers
1 green pepper, diced
4 scallions, sliced
¾ cup commercial diet French dressing
¼ cup soy sauce

Soak the beansprouts briefly in ice water and drain well. Toss with the remaining ingredients and serve. *Six servings, 49 calories each.*

Salad Beets

The bright and beautiful beet is one of our most-forgotten vegetables. Which is a pity, as it's so high in eye appeal. The winy-rich color and crisp texture of chilled beets can add a festive note to any diet dinner. And the beet has a natural sweetness that marries well with the tartness of such low-calorie "dressings" as vinegar or yogurt, as these recipes will attest.

ᛈ PICKLED BEETS ᛒ

1 can (16 ounces) sliced beets
½ cup red wine vinegar
½ cup sliced onion
3 tablespoons granulated sugar or equivalent sugar substitute
½ teaspoon salt
¼ teaspoon freshly ground pepper
1 bay leaf, crushed

Combine all the ingredients except the sugar substitute, if used, and heat to boiling. Remove from the heat, stir in the sweetener, and chill for several hours before serving. *Four servings, 83 calories each with sugar; only 48 without.*

ᛈ CREAMY BEET SALAD ᛒ

1 can (16 ounces) sliced beets
2 tablespoons wine vinegar
2 tablespoons prepared horseradish
1 teaspoon granulated sugar or equivalent sugar substitute
½ cup plain yogurt
½ teaspoon salt

Drain the beets and discard the liquid. Combine the beets with all the other ingredients and chill. *Four servings, 61 calories each with sugar; 57 without.*

⋖§ CONFETTI SALAD ⁊⋗

½ cup shredded raw beets
½ cup shredded firm cucumber
½ cup shredded carrot
½ cup chopped apple
½ cup plain yogurt
2 tablespoons lemon juice
½ teaspoon prepared mustard
    Pinch of granulated sugar
    Salt and freshly ground pepper

Combine all the ingredients and serve immediately. *Four servings, 42 calories each.*

Raw Spinach for Salad

Offer a whole new salad green—raw spinach, tossed in a savory dressing. The taste and texture have nothing whatsoever in common with cooked spinach. We might best describe it as a brand new kind of lettuce—deep and dark, supercrisp. And noncooking has the added advantage of leaving all those vitamins and minerals intact.

⋖§ FRENCH SPINACH SALAD ⁊⋗

1 package (10 ounces) fresh spinach, washed and chopped
1 small red onion, sliced
1 cup sliced fresh mushrooms
1 cup bacon-flavored bits
1 cup low-calorie French dressing

Toss all the ingredients together and serve. *Eight servings, 67 calories each.*

⋖§ SPINACH À LA CAESAR ⁊⋗

1 package (10 ounces) fresh spinach, washed and coarsely
    chopped
1 clove garlic, minced
¼ cup minced onion
1 raw egg or ¼ cup defrosted egg substitute
¾ cup low-calorie Italian dressing
3 tablespoons freshly grated Parmesan cheese
3 slices protein bread, toasted and cubed

Combine the spinach, garlic, and onion in a salad bowl. Beat the egg, salad dressing, and Parmesan cheese together and pour over the salad. Sprinkle with bread croutons, toss, and serve immediately. *Eight servings, 62 calories each.*

⋖§ MANDARIN SPINACH SALAD §⋗

1 package (10 ounces) fresh spinach, washed and coarsely chopped
½ cucumber, peeled and diced
¼ cup chopped onion
¼ cup chopped green pepper
3 tangerines, peeled, seeded, and chopped
½ cup diet mayonnaise
½ cup plain yogurt
1 tablespoon lemon juice

Combine the spinach, cucumber, onion, green pepper, and tangerine in a salad bowl. Stir the mayonnaise, yogurt, and lemon juice together and serve with the salad. *Ten servings, 48 calories each.*

⋖§ ITALIAN SPINACH SALAD §⋗

1 package (10 ounces) fresh spinach, washed and coarsely chopped
1 onion, sliced
2 cups sliced fresh tomatoes, preferably plum tomatoes
1 cup diet Italian salad dressing

Toss all the ingredients together and serve. *Eight servings, 34 calories each.*

⋖§ QUICK ITALIAN TOMATO SALAD §⋗

3 large tomatoes
¼ cup minced onion
Garlic salt and pepper
Oregano or Italian seasoning
2 tablespoons wine vinegar
1 tablespoon olive oil (optional)
2 tablespoons bacon-flavored bits

Combine all the ingredients except the bacon bits and refrigerate at least 15 minutes before serving. Sprinkle on the bacon bits at the last minute. *Six servings, 38 calories without oil; 57 with.*

✓ ✑ MAYONNAISE-FREE MACARONI SALAD ಶ

This macaroni salad can even be diet safe for those who can't have mayonnaise. The procedure is different from any other macaroni salad you've ever made, so read the directions carefully.

1 cup skim milk, more if necessary
1 cup water, more if necessary
1 teaspoon mustard
2 tablespoons lemon juice
2 teaspoons polyunsaturated oil
½ teaspoon celery salt
1 teaspoon granulated sugar
1 cup elbow macaroni
1 small onion, minced
1 cup finely chopped celery
½ cup chopped fresh parsley
3 tablespoons chopped pimiento
  Salt and freshly ground pepper
  Paprika

Put the 1 cup each of milk and water in a nonstick saucepan. Stir in the mustard, lemon juice, oil, celery salt, sugar, and macaroni. Cook, stirring, over a moderate flame until the liquid begins to simmer.

Turn the burner flame very low. Cover the saucepan and simmer for 25 minutes, uncovering frequently and stirring with a rubber spatula to prevent sticking. (The starch from the macaroni will thicken the liquid into a mayonnaise-flavored sauce. If it threatens to get too thick, add a few tablespoons of water.) Salt and pepper to taste. Cover and refrigerate until cool.

Remove the chilled salad from refrigerator. Stir slightly with a spoon to restore creaminess. If a creamier "dressing" is desired, stir in a few tablespoons of milk. Add the onion, celery, parsley, and pimiento and toss lightly. Chill thoroughly and sprinkle with paprika before serving. *Eight servings, 96 calories each.*

✑ DIETER'S BLUEFISH SALAD ಶ

Here's a great way to use leftover baked bluefish. If you like tuna salad, you'll like this even more. Simply flake the chilled cooked fish into a bowl.

For each cup of fish, add 1 tablespoon each of chopped onion and celery. Blend with 2 tablespoons diet mayonnaise or 1 tablespoon regular mayonnaise and 2 tablespoons plain yogurt. Add salt and pepper to taste. *About 200 calories per ½-cup serving.*

⋖ ZINGY HAM SALAD ⋗

1 cup cooked lean ham, trimmed of fat and chopped
1 teaspoon dry mustard
2 tablespoons dill pickle relish
3 tablespoons crushed unsweetened pineapple
3 tablespoons low-calorie mayonnaise or French dressing

Stir all the ingredients together. Serve on lettuce leaves or as a sandwich spread. *Four servings, 108 calories per serving.*

Rice in Salads—Refreshingly Different

Salad side dishes with rice as their base can be just as delightful and calorie-wise as macaroni or potato. Like pasta and potatoes, rice in itself is not a fattening food, merely the victim of high-calorie sauces, dressings, and toppings. At less than 90 calories a ½-cup serving, there's room for rice in any dieter's menu.

⋖ RICE SALAD MOLD ⋗

2 cups water
2 tablespoons herb vinegar
2 chicken bouillon cubes
1 teaspoon celery salt
1 cup raw rice
½ cup diced cucumber
½ cup chopped green pepper
2 tablespoons sliced scallions
    Pinch of freshly ground black pepper
    Crisp lettuce and raw vegetables for garnish
¼ cup diet mayonnaise
¼ cup plain yogurt

Combine the water, vinegar, bouillon cubes, and celery salt in a saucepan. Heat to boiling, then stir in the rice, cover, and simmer for 15 minutes, until tender. Remove from the heat and stir in the cucumber, green pepper, scallions, and black pepper. Spoon into a 1-quart mold and chill for several hours. To serve, unmold on lettuce and garnish with additional vegetables.

Serve with a dressing made by combining the diet mayonnaise and yogurt. *Six servings, 130 calories each without dressing; 154 with.*

◄§ SPANISH RICE SALAD ৪►

3 cups cold cooked rice (cooked in fat-skimmed chicken broth)
1 cup chopped green pepper
1 cup chopped celery
¼ cup chopped onion
½ cup chopped pimiento
  Pinch of ground cumin
4 tomatoes, quartered
½ cup low-calorie Italian salad dressing

Toss all the ingredients together and serve. *Eight servings, 101 calories each.*

Slim Gourmet Fruit Salads

Fruit salads needn't be fattening if you're a calorie-wise cook. Add a different fruit for each person who will be eating the salad, the more the merrier! A salad to serve six might be made up of six different fruits: apple, pear, orange, banana, and ½ cup each sliced strawberries and juice-packed pineapple chunks. Other choices might be tangerines, fresh grapefuit sections, sliced pitted prunes, golden apple chunks, seedless grapes, even drained canned fruit cocktail—unsugared, of course.

Citrus fruits are the most calorie-cheap choices, so include them liberally in diet-wise salads. Grapefruit sections, orange chunks, and tangerine pieces have the advantage of keeping other fruits from turning brown.

The most fattening part of any salad is likely to be the dressing. Many commercial dressings are 60 to 100 calories a tablespoon, but the do-it-yourself blends for fruit salad on pages 263–264 will keep calories low.

Try these fruit salads on for size:

√ ◄§ WALDORF SALAD ৪►

1 cup celery, diced
1 cup apples, diced
1 tablespoon raisins (see note below)
2 tablespoons low-calorie mayonnaise or plain yogurt

Combine all the ingredients and serve on a lettuce leaf. *Four servings, 31 calories each.*

NOTE: Raisins are fattening, but one tablespoon at 28 calories is a better choice than walnut meats, about 50 calories. An even smarter idea is to chop up a prune into "raisin-sized" bits and use it as "mock raisins" in any recipe that calls for raisins. Chopped prunes taste and look like raisins, but they're 59 calories an ounce, compared with 82 calories an ounce for raisins.

◄§ MEAL-SIZED FRUIT SALAD §►

¾ cup 99% fat-free cottage cheese
1 tangerine, peeled, seeded, and cut in chunks
½ cup sliced fresh strawberries
¼ cup plain yogurt
  Dash of vanilla extract
1 tablespoon low-calorie mayonnaise

Mound cottage cheese in an individual salad bowl and cover with the fruit. Combine the yogurt, vanilla extract, and mayonnaise and pour over the fruit. *One serving, 228 calories.*

Molded Salad: Diet Gelatin Mixes Can Cut Calories

Some packages of gelatin dessert mix and a few inexpensive fancy molds are all you need to turn summer's bounty of fresh fruits and vegetables into super spectacular salads and desserts.

There are a number of low-calorie dietetic gelatin mixes on the market that can serve as the perfect stand-in for any favorite gelatin recipe. They're available in almost as many flavors as the sugary mixes, and the directions for preparation are precisely the same. In fact, you can substitute the diet mix for regular mix in just about every salad and dessert mold recipe in any cookbook. And every time you do, you'll be saving calories. One four-serving envelope of diet gelatin mix is only 40 calories; the regular mix is 324. The addition of sugar makes it eight times as fattening.

Here's a flavor "hint": most dietetic gelatin mixes are salt free as well as sugar free. If you're not on a low-salt diet, brighten the flavor by adding that missing pinch of salt.

◄§ MOLDED GARDEN SALAD §►

1 envelope (4 servings) low-calorie lemon or lime gelatin dessert
    mix
1 cup boiling water
1 teaspoon salt
2 teaspoons vinegar
1 cup ice cubes and water
1 cup finely diced cucumber
1 cup chopped raisins
1 cup thinly sliced scallions

Dissolve the gelatin in the boiling water. Stir in the salt and vinegar. Fill a cup with ice cubes, then add water to fill to the top. Pour the water and ice into the gelatin mixture and stir until all the ice melts. Refrigerate for 10 to 15 minutes, until slightly thickened. Fold in the remaining ingredients.

Pour the gelatin mixture into a decorative 1-quart mold, or into a loaf pan or individual serving dishes. Unmold or cut in cubes to serve. *Six servings, 24 calories each.*

NOTE: This salad may be garnished with plain yogurt or bottled low-calorie mayonnaise-type dressing.

◄§ LAYERED GELATIN FRUIT SALAD §►

1 envelope (4 servings) low-calorie lemon gelatin dessert mix
2¼ cups boiling water
⅔ cup plain yogurt
5 tablespoons diet mayonnaise or mayonnaise-type salad dressing
2 cups diced green or yellow apples, unpeeled
1 cup halved green seedless grapes
1 envelope (4 servings) low-calorie orange gelatin dessert mix
1 cup ice cubes and water
Green seedless grapes for garnish

Dissolve the lemon gelatin in 1¼ cups of the boiling water. Allow to cool. Stir in the yogurt and salad dressing, then stir in the diced apples and halved grapes. Refrigerate until slightly thickened.

Meanwhile, dissolve the orange gelatin in the remaining 1 cup boiling water. Stir in the 1 cup ice cubes and water until melted, then refrigerate for 10 to 15 minutes, until slightly thickened.

Pour half the orange gelatin mixture into a 6-cup mold. Spoon the chilled lemon-fruit mixture over it and top with the remaining orange gelatin. Chill for several hours or all day, then unmold and garnish with grapes, if desired. (The salad can also be prepared in a pan and cut into squares for serving.) *Twelve servings, 43 calories each.*

Coleslaw

Right near that premium-priced lettuce you'll find another head of greenery that's perfect for midwinter salads. Cabbage to the rescue! A sharp knife and some low-calorie dressing is all you need to turn a head of cabbage into crisp coleslaw, or buy it by the bag. The secret with bagged coleslaw is to rinse well in chilled water. A few minutes later, it's fresh as a daisy. Drain in a colander and then add your favorite low-calorie dressing.

Before you add your dressing, remember that coleslaw is like excelsior—it takes up a lot of room. If you don't have a bowl big enough to toss your coleslaw, put the drained cabbage in a plastic bag. Then add your dressing.

Tie the top with one of those twists that come with the bags. Give the bag a good shake and you've got it made. Instant coleslaw!

The nice feature about coleslaw is that it doesn't require last minute table-tossing. In fact, coleslaw needs to be made ahead of time.

⊷ EASY COLESLAW ϨⱩ

1 small bag (8 ounces) shredded cabbage
2 tablespoons polyunsaturated oil
2 tablespoons white vinegar
2 tablespoons granulated sugar or equivalent sugar substitute
¼ cup minced onion
½ teaspoon salt
¼ teaspoon freshly ground pepper

Soak the cabbage in cold water for 5 minutes; drain. Put in a plastic bag and add all the other ingredients. Shake to mix well. *Six servings, 68 calories each with sugar; 53 without.*

⊷ PRUNE YOGURT SLAW ϨⱩ

8 medium prunes, pitted
1 cup plain yogurt
2 tablespoons granulated sugar or equivalent sugar substitute
¼ cup vinegar
½ teaspoon celery salt
¼ teaspoon salt
  Pinch of freshly ground pepper
6 cups shredded cabbage

Cut the prunes into narrow strips. Combine the yogurt, sugar, vinegar, celery salt, salt, and pepper. Add the cut-up prunes and let sit for 30 minutes. Toss the prune dressing with the cabbage and refrigerate until serving time. *Eight servings, 65 calories each with sugar; 53 without.*

⊷ QUICKSLAW ϨⱩ

"Quickslaw" is coleslaw you chop in your blender. But there's a trick to it; otherwise you'll end up with puree of raw cabbage.

Cut a head of cabbage into quarters, then cut out the core. Cut each chunk in half, so you have 8 cabbage chunks.

Now, half-fill your blender container with cold water. Drop in a cabbage chunk and turn your blender on and then off—just long enough to chop the leaves coarsely. Empty the blender into a colander. Add more water and another wedge of cabbage and repeat the process until you've chopped it all.

Then proceed with the slaw recipe of your choice.

⋅§ CREAMY COLESLAW ও⋅

     1 head cabbage (1 pound), chopped or shredded
    ¾ cup evaporated skim milk
   1½ teaspoons cider vinegar
    ½ teaspoon celery seed
    ¾ teaspoon salt
    ½ teaspoon granulated sugar
    ¼ teaspoon freshly ground pepper

Combine all the ingredients and refrigerate until serving time. *Eight servings, 29 calories per serving.*

⋅§ PINEAPPLE COLESLAW ও⋅

   1 head cabbage
   1 carrot
   1 can (8 ounces) low-calorie crushed pineapple
   1 cup plain yogurt
   2 tablespoons vinegar
      Salt and freshly ground pepper

Chop the cabbage and carrot. Press as much liquid as possible from the crushed pineapple, then add the pineapple and all the other ingredients to the chopped vegetables. Refrigerate until serving time. *Ten servings, 35 calories each.*

⋅§ BUTTERMILK COLESLAW ও⋅

    1 head cabbage, chopped
   ¾ cup buttermilk
    3 to 4 drops liquid sweetener
    1 tablespoon lemon juice
    1 teaspoon salt
   ¼ teaspoon coarsely ground pepper
   ½ teaspoon celery salt
      Pinch of garlic powder

Combine all the ingredients and refrigerate until serving time. *Eight servings, 18 calories each.*

NOTE: This recipe was contributed by Mrs. Paul Witkin of Edison, New Jersey.

◆§ RED CABBAGE SLAW §◆

    3 **pounds red cabbage, shredded**
    1 **can (6 ounces) apple juice**
    6 **tablespoons cider vinegar**
    ¾ **teaspoon onion salt**
    ¼ **teaspoon freshly ground pepper**
    3 **tablespoons currants or raisins**

Combine all the ingredients and refrigerate for several hours before serving. *Makes eight servings, 55 calories each.*

◆§ RED CABBAGE YOGURT COLESLAW §◆

    3 **pounds red cabbage, shredded**
    ½ **cup chopped onion**
    ½ **cup minced red or green sweet pepper**
 1 ½ **teaspoons garlic powder**
    1 **container (5 ounces) plain yogurt**
    3 **tablespoons lemon juice**

Combine all the ingredients and refrigerate several hours before serving. *Eight servings, 50 calories each.*

Meal-sized Salads

Why suffer through a skimpy sandwich when you can have a supersalad for lunch? A Slim Gourmet supersalad is a whole meal in a bowl—all the meat, cheese, or other protein source you might normally pile on bread, plus lots and lots of crisp salad fixings.

Without the starchy bread your supersalad is lower in calories than a sandwich, and a lot more satisfying. A sandwich is *too* easy to eat: five minutes and it's all gone. You spend the rest of your "lunch hour" foraging in the refrigerator for something to fill that imaginary empty spot.

Supersalad, on the other hand, takes no longer to make but a lot longer to eat, so it's far more satisfying. And served up in a brimming bowl, it even looks like a lot.

⌇ CHEF'S SALAD ⌇

2 ounces lean cooked (boiled) ham
2 slices (2 ounces) processed Swiss or American cheese
2 ounces sliced white-meat turkey roll
1 small head lettuce (about 12 ounces)
½ cup sliced onion
  Pinch of dried rosemary, crushed
½ teaspoon garlic salt
  Pinch of freshly ground pepper
¼ cup diet French dressing or any preferred low-calorie salad
    dressing

Slice the ham (trimmed of fat, if any), cheese, and turkey into strips, then into squares. Toss with all the remaining ingredients and serve immediately. *Two servings, 221 calories each.*

⌇ REUBEN CHEF'S SALAD ⌇

1½ cups shredded lettuce
  2 tablespoons minced onion
    Garlic salt and pepper
  2 ounces corned beef round, cubed
  1 ounce processed Swiss cheese, cubed
  1 teaspoon polyunsaturated oil
  1 teaspoon vinegar
  1 tablespoon red wine
  1 teaspoon caraway seeds

Combine all the ingredients in a small salad bowl and toss lightly. *One serving, 272 calories.*

⌇ HERO SALAD ⌇

To save calories, use domestic ham rather than Italian cold cuts; some of the latter are double the calories. For added flavor, sprinkle on a tablespoon of bacon-flavored soy bits. They add a lot of flavor for only 30 calories.

  2 thick slices (2 ounces) imported provolone cheese, shredded
  4 ounces lean cooked domestic ham, trimmed of fat and shredded
½ head lettuce, shredded
½ cup (3 ounces) sliced fresh tomatoes, preferably plum tomatoes

½ cup sliced onion
1 clove garlic, minced
4 medium green olives, finely chopped, plus 1 tablespoon liquid
   from the jar
1 tablespoon red wine vinegar
1 tablespoon olive oil
1 teaspoon oregano
1 teaspoon salt
  Pinch of cayenne pepper

Combine all the ingredients, toss lightly, and serve. *Two servings, 290 calories each.*

⤝ SUPPER SALAD STROGANOFF ⤞

¾ pound leftover cold roast beef round
2 tablespoons dry white wine
2 tablespoons white vinegar
1 teaspoon prepared mustard
1 tablespoon catsup
½ cup plain yogurt
1 cup fresh sliced mushrooms
1 small onion, minced
3 potatoes, cooked, peeled, and diced
2 tablespoons minced fresh parsley (optional)

Trim all the fat from the beef. Slice the meat thinly against the grain, then into bite-sized chunks. Marinate the meat for 1 hour in the wine, vinegar, mustard, and catsup. Stir in the yogurt, mushrooms, onions, and cubed potatoes. Chill. Serve well chilled, sprinkled with parsley, if desired. *Four servings, 273 calories each.*

⤝ SLIM SALADE NIÇOISE ⤞

The French Riviera is a balmy Gallic paradise that offers something for everyone, and to dine in Nice without enjoying its famous salad would be like passing up pineapple in Hawaii. Named for the area, salade niçoise is a hearty main-course mélange of tuna, tomatoes, potatoes, and eggs, lavished with olives and garlic—a complete meal-in-one that needs little else but a glass of crisp wine.

Differing from the directions in many American cookbooks, our *salade niçoise* is not served drowning in olive oil. We avoid those unneeded extra calories, but boost the olive flavor with a little liquid from the olive jar.

DRESSING:
- 1 raw egg or egg yolk
- 2 tablespoons vinegar
- 1 tablespoon polyunsaturated oil
- ¼ cup liquid from the olive jar
- 1 teaspoon garlic salt
- ¼ teaspoon freshly ground pepper
  Pinch of granulated sugar
- ½ teaspoon dry mustard
- ¼ teaspoon dried tarragon

SALAD:
- 2 cans (7 ounces each) water-pack tuna, in chunks
- 1 cup diced, cooked potatoes
- 2 cups cooked or canned green beans, drained
- 2 anchovy fillets, minced (optional)
- 1 head Boston or Bibb lettuce
- 3 tomatoes, in wedges
- 3 hard-cooked eggs, in wedges
- ¼ cup sliced pitted black olives
- ¼ cup minced fresh parsley

Shake the dressing ingredients together in a closed jar. Put the tuna chunks, potatoes, beans, and anchovy fillets in a bowl and pour the dressing over. Marinate for 1 hour.

Line a bowl with lettuce and put marinated mixture in the middle. Surround with alternating wedges of tomato and egg and sprinkle on the olives and parsley. Toss to serve. *Four servings, 300 calories each.*

Hurry-Up Niçoise: Combine shredded lettuce, diced leftover potatoes, canned beans, drained tuna, fresh tomato and hard-cooked egg wedges with diet Italian-style dressing and a dash of Worcestershire sauce.

⋆§ CHICKEN SALAD §⋆

Whole young chickens are often featured as a supermarket special, making them especially appealing for a salad. And today's chicken is a dieter's dream: just 154 calories a 4-ounce boneless serving, as compared with 300 to 400 calories for most meats.

- 3 cups cooked chicken meat (see note below), cut in bite-sized pieces
- 1 cup finely minced celery
- 1 medium onion finely minced
- ¼ cup chopped dill pickle

1 tablespoon mayonnaise
¼ cup sour half-and-half or imitation sour cream
1 tablespoon lemon juice
   Salt and freshly ground pepper
   Paprika
   Crisp lettuce

Put the chicken in a medium-sized bowl and add the minced celery, onion, and pickle. Combine the mayonnaise, sour cream, and lemon juice and add to the salad. Toss lightly, then add salt and pepper to taste and sprinkle lightly with paprika. Chill thoroughly before serving, on a bed of crisp lettuce. *Six servings, 209 calories each.*

NOTE: To simmer chicken for salad, simply rinse it well and put it in a kettle or big-enough pot along with a quart or so of water. Season it with some salt, a bay leaf, a chopped onion and a few celery tops. Cover and simmer over very low heat for about 1 hour, until the chicken is tender.

Remove the chicken from the broth. When it's cool enough to handle, simply strip the meat from the bones. Save the broth in your refrigerator or freezer to make chicken soup, and discard the bones and skin.

Cut the meat into cubes and use it in salad.

✎§ MAIN-COURSE POTATO SALAD ℥

6 potatoes, cooked, peeled, and diced
6 hard-cooked eggs, shelled and chopped
1 sweet red or green pepper, seeded and diced
1 jar (2 ounces) pimiento, drained and chopped
2 onions, chopped
1 cup plain yogurt
1 tablespoon lemon juice
1 teaspoon prepared mustard
1 teaspoon salt
1 teaspoon celery salt
½ teaspoon granulated sugar or sugar substitute
   Fresh chopped parsley
   Paprika

Combine the potatoes, eggs, red or green pepper, pimiento, and onions. Stir the yogurt with the lemon juice and all the other seasonings except the parsley and paprika seasonings and gently toss with the salad ingredients. Chill well, then sprinkle with parsley and paprika before serving. *Six servings, 194 calories each.*

Top Your Skinny Salads with Gourmet Dressings

A whole cupful of greenery is less than 10 calories by itself. But along with salads go salad dressings at anywhere from 65 to 100 calories per level tablespoon—and who uses a level tablespoon?

What gives most salad dressings their scandalous calorie count is the high percentage of who-needs-it oil, at a blubbery 1,000 calories a cupful! What really hurts is that most salad oils don't have any flavor anyway, and their only function is to provide "pourability." Otherwise, how would you get the real flavor makers out of the bottle and into your salad bowl?

If you'd like to beat the high-calorie cost of salad oils, discover yogurt. Not the fattening sugared-up stuff that tries to palm itself off as diet food. (By now, let's hope all Slim Gourmet cooks know that sweetened fruit-flavored yogurt is between 260 and 280 calories a cupful, about the same as a chocolate doughnut!) The yogurt we are speaking of is *plain, unflavored* yogurt, which can add a special tang to diet-wise dressings. It gives all the good dairy nutrition of the fattening stuff at less than half the calories.

✑ CREAMY CASINO FRENCH DRESSING ☙

½ cup bottled chili sauce or catsup
3 tablespoons vinegar
1 teaspoon yellow food coloring (optional)
½ cup plain yogurt
1 teaspoon salt or garlic salt

Combine all the ingredients and stir well. *Only 10 calories per tablespoon.*

✑ CREAMY ROQUEFORT DRESSING ☙

1 cup plain yogurt
2 tablespoons vinegar
¼ teaspoon coarsely ground pepper
2 ounces Roquefort cheese
1 teaspoon salt
1 clove garlic (optional)

Whip all the ingredients in the blender, on high speed, until smooth. *Only 15 calories per tablespoon.*

⊷ TANGY YOGURT COLESLAW DRESSING ᠅

1 cup plain yogurt
2 hard-cooked eggs, peeled and roughly chopped
1 teaspoon celery salt
2 tablespoons lemon juice
1 teaspoon prepared mustard
½ teaspoon sugar (optional)

Combine all the ingredients in the blender and whip until smooth. *Only 13 calories per tablespoon.*

⊷ FRUIT SALAD DRESSING I ᠅

2 soft bananas, peeled
  Juice of 1 lemon
½ cup skim milk
½ teaspoon salt
½ teaspoon prepared mustard
1 tablespoon polyunsaturated oil
  Sugar substitute to equal 2 teaspoons

In a blender or electric mixing bowl, beat the banana smooth. Add remaining ingredients and beat until blended. *One cup, 23 calories per tablespoon.*

⊷ FRUIT SALAD DRESSING II ᠅

½ cup diet mayonnaise
½ cup plain yogurt
  Few drops liquid sugar substitute
  Water

Blend the ingredients smooth, adding only enough water to achieve the desired consistency. *About one cup, 15 calories per tablespoon.*

⊷ FLUFFY FRUIT DRESSING ᠅

½ cup plain yogurt
½ cup diet mayonnaise
½ cup aerosol whipped cream

Combine the yogurt and mayonnaise and fold in the whipped cream. *One and one-half cups, 13 calories per tablespoon.*

⋖⋧ OIL AND VINEGAR DRESSING ⋦⋗

This is "basic French" at 21 calories per tablespoon instead of 80 to 100, depending on whether you favor a 3-to-1 or 4-to-1 ratio of oil and vinegar. (If you like to premix your dressing, the ratio is usually even richer in oil than that, as vinegar has a way of refusing to leave the bottle, leaving your salad soaked almost solely in oil. This recipe won't separate.)

The calorie saver is the arrowroot, the cornstarchlike thickener much favored by professional chefs and bakers when a transparent glaze or sauce is sought. Virtually tasteless, arrowroot thickens without clouding while it takes on the flavor of the other ingredients in a recipe. Combine it with oil, vinegar, and a few green olives and the arrowroot base takes on a delightfully distinctive flavor.

At 29 calories per tablespoon, arrowroot has almost triple the thickening power of flour. Follow the same precautions you use with other thickeners: always stir it into cold liquid and then heat it slowly so it won't lump. Arrowroot is found in small jars in the spice section of your supermarket, or in one- or two-pound bags in health food stores.

⅓ cup finest-quality olive oil
½ cup finest-quality red wine vinegar (or see page 265)
1 teaspoon salt
  Pinch of freshly ground pepper
6 or 8 green olives
1 or 2 cloves garlic
1 tablespoon arrowroot
1 cup cold water

Put the oil and vinegar in your nicest decorative jar or a good-sized cruet. Add the salt and pepper and olives. Peel the garlic and drop it in, along with the olives. Stir the arrowroot into the cold water in a saucepan and heat, stirring constantly, over a low flame until the mixture thickens and becomes transparent. When cool, add this mixture to the dressing and shake vigorously. Usable immediately, but really much better if the flavors have at least a day to blend. *Almost two cups at 21 calories per tablespoon.*

NOTE: If you're on a crash reducing program or a low-fat diet, you can create a super-slim salad dressing by simply omitting the olive oil from this recipe. Less than 2 calories per tablespoon, yet surprisingly rich-tasting.

SPICED-UP VINEGAR
FOR SLIM GOURMET SALADS

Because the usual ratio of oil to vinegar of 4 to 1 or 3 to 1 is reversed by Slim Gourmets, ordinary vinegar won't do for your salads. Your vinegar will have to be a lot more flavorful and less acid than the commercial kind. (And 2 tablespoons of salad dressing is ample for a ½-cup serving of salad.)

Homemade Herb Vinegar: Chop together fresh marjoram, tarragon, and parsley. For each ½ cup of herbs add 2 cups commercial cider or white vinegar. Cover and let stand for 2 weeks or more. Strain and pour in bottles, then label.

French Tarragon Vinegar: Crush fresh tarragon leaves. For each loosely packed cupful of leaves, add 1½ cups commercial vinegar. Cover and wait 2 or 3 weeks, then strain the vinegar into bottles and label.

Mint Vinegar: Follow the directions for tarragon vinegar, substituting fresh crushed mint leaves. (This is a good marinade for lamb.)

Garlic Vinegar: Peel a whole head of garlic and crush the cloves. Heat 2 cups wine vinegar to boiling. Add the garlic, cover, and wait 2 weeks. Strain and bottle.

Quick Garlic Vinegar: Cut a garlic clove in half and drop it in your vinegar cruet.

Quick Herb Vinegar: Add 1 tablespoon of dried mixed tarragon or dried mixed herbs to 2 cups wine or cider vinegar.

Quick Spiced Vinegar: Add 2 tablespoons packaged "crab boil" spices or mixed pickling spices to 2 or more cups good wine or cider vinegar. Add garlic powder if you wish.

Onion Vinegar: Puncture a small onion with a fork and add it to wine, cider, or herb vinegar. Remove it after 5 days.

Homemade Cider Vinegar: Allow a glass jug of sweet cider to stand in the sunlight in your kitchen for a few weeks.

Mild Cider Vinegar: Combine equal parts of fresh apple cider and cider vinegar. Pour into bottles, label, and cork.

Mild Red Wine Vinegar: Combine equal parts of commercial wine vinegar with leftover Chianti, claret, Burgundy or other red table wine.

Mild White Wine Vinegar: Combine equal parts commercial white vinegar with leftover white table wine.

Champagne Vinegar: Pour leftover flat champagne into a bottle and add an equal amount of white vinegar. You can create "sherry vinegar," "vermouth vinegar," or any other kind of vinegar the same way.

Red Wine Dressing—The Spirited Salad Dressing

Some red wine dressings are as high as 80 calories a tablespoon, thanks to the high proportion of oil. We've cut back on the oil, without increasing the sharp vinegar taste by diluting with dry red wine. Any dry wine will do—Chianti, claret, or dry burgundy probably being the best.

◆§ RED WINE DIET DRESSING ৡৢ

3 tablespoons olive oil
3 tablespoons red or white wine vinegar
¼ cup water
½ cup dry red wine
½ teaspoon garlic salt
   Pinch of cayenne pepper
   Dash of liquid sugar substitute (optional)

Combine all the ingredients in a covered jar and shake well. *Only 25 calories per tablespoon.*

VARIATIONS

White Wine: Use dry white wine and white vinegar.

Roquefort: Add 5 tablespoons crumbled Roquefort cheese.

Quick Blue Cheese: Add the contents of 1 envelope blue cheese dressing mix.

Dressing Diable: Add 2 teaspoons dry mustard.

Caesar Dressing: Add raw or coddled egg, and 2 tablespoons freshly grated Parmesan cheese.

Low Cholesterol Caesar: Add ¼ cup defrosted low-cholesterol egg substitute and 2 tablespoons freshly grated Parmesan cheese.

Curry Dressing: Add 1 teaspoon curry powder.

Anchovy Dressing: Add 1 tablespoon anchovy paste and 1 tablespoon minced fresh parsley.

Vinaigrette: Add 2 teaspoons chopped chives, 1 tablespoon chopped dill pickle, 1 teaspoon capers, and 2 chopped hard-cooked eggs.

Tarragon Dressing: Add 1 teaspoon dried tarragon.

Chili-Hot Dressing: Add 1 teaspoon chili powder and 2 teaspoons prepared mustard.

◌§ THICK RED WINE DRESSING ◌➳

2 teaspoons arrowroot
1 teaspoon garlic or onion salt
Dash of Tabasco
½ cup water
½ cup dry red wine
¼ cup vinegar (see page 265)
2 tablespoons olive oil

Cook and stir all the ingredients until the mixture simmers and thickens. Cool, then refrigerate in a covered container. *Only 18 calories per tablespoon.*
NOTE: This dressing will not separate.

Mayonnaise—Mock and Just Plain "Skinny"

Nothing is more impressive—and tedious—than making your own home-made mayonnaise. If you've ever done it, you know that oil is beaten into eggs, drop by drop—thousands of drops, one at a time. And at 10 calories or so per drop, it adds up to thousands of calories! That's why mayonnaise is so supremely fattening.

Now for the lady who likes to make her own, these Slim Gourmet home-made dressings have a distinctive flair. They're less than one-fifth the calories of conventional mayonnaise and a lot easier to prepare.

◌§ EPICUREAN AVOCADO "MAYONNAISE" ◌➳

Use this mayonnaise as the base for any other dressing—an avocado "green goddess" blend, for example.

1 large ripe avocado
1 large egg
3 tablespoons lemon juice
1 teaspoon prepared mustard
½ teaspoon salt

Peel the avocado and cut into chunks. Put the avocado chunks, along with all the other ingredients, in your blender. Turn the blender on and off quickly, just long enough to whip into a mayonnaise-y texture. *One and one-half cups, 18 calories per tablespoon.*

◆§ LOW-CALORIE COOKED "MAYONNAISE" §◆

This one takes potato salad off the "forbidden" list.

2 eggs
1 teaspoon celery salt
½ teaspoon paprika
  Pinch of dry mustard
¼ cup skim milk
  Juice of 1 lemon
1 tablespoon polyunsaturated oil

Beat the eggs, salt, paprika, and mustard together. Gradually beat in the milk and lemon juice. Cook and stir over a very low flame (or in the top of a double-boiler) until thick, then beat in the oil. Refrigerate for several hours before using. *One cup, 18 calories per tablespoon.*

◆§ "MAYONNAISE," ITALIAN STYLE §◆

If you can't find ricotta, try this dressing made with low-fat, uncreamed cottage cheese.

1 cup part-skim ricotta cheese
1 hard-cooked egg, roughly chopped
  Juice of ½ lemon
½ teaspoon dry mustard
½ teaspoon salt
½ teaspoon celery salt
½ teaspoon granulated sugar (optional)

Put all the ingredients in the blender and whirl on high speed until smooth. *One and one-quarter cups, 16 calories per tablespoon.*

◆§ LANCASTER COUNTY DAIRY MAYONNAISE* §◆

2 whole eggs
1 teaspoon salt
  Pinch of freshly ground pepper
1 tablespoon granulated sugar (or sugar substitute)
1 teaspoon dry mustard

* Adapted from the *Lancaster General Hospital Benefit Cookbook* (1912).

2 **teaspoons cornstarch**
1 **cup skim milk**
½ **cup white or cider vinegar**
1 **tablespoon safflower oil**

Beat all the ingredients together in your blender or with an electric mixer. Pour into a nonstick saucepan and cook, uncovered, over a moderate flame, stirring constantly with a rubber scraper, until the mixture thickens; do not allow to boil. Pour into a jar and store in the refrigerator. Stir before using.

Two and one-quarter cups—and only 12 calories per tablespoon instead of 100!

⤚§ SKINNY MAYONNAISE §⤜

Once upon a time, a dieter had to do without mayonnaise, but now there's skinny mayonnaise. Some brands are such sensational stand-ins for the fattening stuff that most people would be hard pressed to tell the difference, yet a pint jar of ordinary mayonnaise contains more than 3,000 calories, while a jar of the "imitation" contains 600 or 700; 16 to 24 calories a tablespoon instead of 100.

The word "imitation" used to be required on the label because mock mayo doesn't contain anywhere near the fat of the real thing. Most of the other ingredients, including eggs, are generally similar. Some have a milk base and are higher in protein than ordinary mayonnaise. So don't be put off by the word "imitation."

Do choose a brand that's truly low calorie, not a "dietetic" mayonnaise that's simply sugar free, salt free, egg free or made with a special oil (and lots of it) at the same calorie count of ordinary mayonnaise. Look for the calorie count on the label.

The variations that follow are added to 1 cup of diet mayonnaise. The calorie count refers to 1 tablespoon of prepared sauce or dressing.

Horseradish Dressing: Stir in ½ cup prepared horseradish. Serve with cold meats. *15 calories.*

Mustard Mayo: Stir in 5 tablespoons mild or hot Dijon-style mustard. Serve with shellfish, ham. *20 calories.*

Tartar Sauce: Stir in ½ cup well-drained chopped dill pickle or sour relish and 1 tablespoon mustard. *15 calories.*

Roquefort: Stir in 2 tablespoons crumbled Roquefort cheese, 1 tablespoon minced chives, and a splash of Worcestershire. *23 calories.*

Russian: Add ¼ cup chili sauce and 3 tablespoons finely minced green pepper. *19 calories.*

Thousand Island: Add 3 tablespoons chili sauce, 3 tablespoons minced red or green sweet pepper, and 2 tablespoons drained pickle relish. *20 calories.*

Yogurt Fruit Dressing: Combine the diet mayonnaise with an equal part plain yogurt; add lemon juice or vanilla extract, if desired. Serve with fruit. *16 calories.*

"Whipped Cream" Dressing: Spray aerosol whipped cream into a cup measure. Fold into diet mayonnaise. Serve with fruit. *30 calories.*

Greek Vegetable Sauce: Stir in ½ cup hot skim milk and 2 tablespoons chopped fresh parsley. Serve on hot vegetables. *15 calories.*

Louis Dressing: Stir in 1 cup chili sauce and 1 tablespoon Worcestershire sauce. Serve with shellfish. *17 calories.*

Creamy Caesar: Beat the diet mayonnaise with ¼ cup freshly grated Parmesan cheese and a large pinch of garlic powder. Serve with romaine salad and toasted croutons. *16 calories.*

Goof-Proof Hollandaise: Thin the diet mayonnaise with ½ cup boiling water vegetables were simmered in. Serve over hot, drained vegetables. *13 calories.*

Béarnaise Sauce: Thin the diet mayonnaise with ½ cup hot water or liquid in which fish was poached. Stir in ¼ teaspoon onion powder, ¼ teaspoon dried tarragon and 1 teaspoon chopped fresh parsley. Serve with broiled or poached fish. *13 calories.*

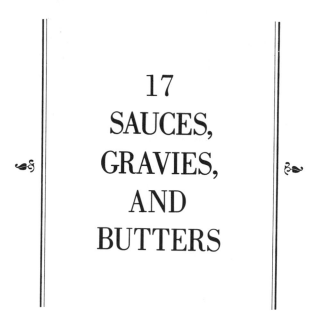

17
SAUCES,
GRAVIES,
AND
BUTTERS

LOW-FAT GRAVY FROM
ROAST MEAT OR POULTRY

Most diets warn you to eat your meat unsauced. That's because most gravy *is* fattening. Here is a recipe for gravy that is calorie-wise:

About 1½ cups pan juices and other liquid, skimmed of fat
½ cup cold water
3 tablespoons flour
Seasonings as desired

Use a teflon-coated pan to roast your meat or poultry. While the roast cooks, baste it occasionally with a little water, or water diluted with other liquids (wine, tomato juice, canned fat-skimmed broth, etc.). When roast is cooked, remove it from the pan and pour the pan juices into a 2-cup measuring cup, scraping up all the residue.

Add enough ice cubes to the measuring cup to make 2 cups. When ice melts and the fat has risen to the top, remove the fat with a spoon or bulb-type baster. (As an alternative, the measuring cup can be placed in the refrigerator or freezer and the fat will harden on the top.)

Heat the skimmed gravy stock in a saucepan until it simmers. Meanwhile, combine the cold water and flour and blend well (mix in a small bowl or shake in a covered jar). Stir into the simmering stock over low heat until the mixture simmers and thickens. Simmer 6 to 8 minutes, then season to taste with salt, pepper, garlic or onion powder, butter-flavored salt, freshly chopped parsley, and/or other herbs. *About 5 calories per tablespoon; 20 calories per quarter-cup serving.*

VARIATIONS

Thicker Gravy: Use less water. Or allow the gravy to simmer down to the desired thickness.

Thinner Gravy: Use more liquid.

Stronger Gravy: Augment the pan drippings with fat-skimmed canned broth. Or add bouillon cubes. Or intensify the existing meat flavor with a generous sprinkle of monosodium glutamate.

Darker Gravy: Stir in a little bottled brown gravy seasoning. Soy sauce or Worcestershire sauce will also darken the color.

Clear Gravy: Substitute 2 tablespoons of arrowroot or cornstarch for the 3 tablespoons of flour called for.

Chinese Gravy: Add 2 tablespoons of dry sherry wine and 2 or 3 tablespoons soy sauce. For a clear Chinese gravy, substitute cornstarch or arrowroot for flour, as directed above.

Oriental Turkey Gravy: Combine ¾ cup fat-skimmed turkey broth with ¼ cup soy sauce and 2 teaspoons arrowroot or cornstarch. Cook and stir over low heat until the mixture simmers and thickens. *Only 32 calories per ½ cup.*

Barbecue Sauces

Did you know that some brush-and-baste barbecue mixtures can be 25 calories a tablespoon or more? That's 400 calories a cupful. That's because most are well laced with sugar and oil, neither of which is really necessary to do the job. The tenderizing effect is provided by the tomato, lemon juice, vinegar, wine, pineapple or whatever other acid liquid makes up the marinade, and which also adds to the flavor!

Extra-lean meats like flank steak or beef round will be flavorful and fork tender if marinated several hours (overnight if possible) in a well-seasoned barbecue baste. Poultry or seafood should enjoy several hours of basking in baste to get well-slathered with seasonings.

◄§ SUGARLESS BARBECUE SAUCE §►

1 cup tomato puree
1 cup water
¼ cup lemon juice

 1 tablespoon prepared mustard
 1 teaspoon celery salt
   Sugar substitute equal to 3 tablespoons sugar

Combine all the ingredients except the sweetener. Simmer, covered, for 10 minutes, then remove from the heat and stir in the sweetener. *Only 3 calories per tablespoon.*

◦§ APPLESAUCE BARBECUE BASTE ჰ◦

½ cup soy sauce
¼ cup white wine
 3 tablespoons water
½ cup unsweetened applesauce
 2 teaspoons garlic salt
   Sugar substitute equal to 3 tablespoons sugar (optional)

Combine all the ingredients and pour over lean, fresh ham steak (well trimmed of fringe fat before broiling), lamb, or chicken. *Only 6 calories per tablespoon.*

◦§ JAPANESE BARBECUE SAUCE ჰ◦

 5 tablespoons soy sauce
½ cup sake or sherry wine
½ cup water
 1 teaspoon freshly grated ginger
 1 clove garlic, crushed
 1 teaspoon cornstarch

Combine all the ingredients and mix thoroughly. Bring to a boil. Use, warm, as a marinade for meat or poultry; use also as a baste while broiling. *Only 10 calories per tablespoon.*

◦§ POLYNESIAN PINEAPPLE BASTE ჰ◦

 1 can (8 ounces) juice-packed crushed pineapple, undrained
 1 cup chicken broth or bouillon
 3 tablespoons vinegar
 1 tablespoon soy sauce
 2 tablespoons minced onion
 1 tablespoon brown sugar
 1 clove garlic, finely minced

Bring all the ingredients to a boil in a saucepan and simmer for 10 minutes, covered. Good marinade for poultry and seafood. *Only 5 calories per tablespoon.*

Weight-Wary White Sauce

White sauce is a culinary basis, the foundation of hundreds of recipes. A white sauce can top vegetables smartly, dress up seafood, hold croquettes together, or recycle yesterday's chicken into a creamy noodle dish. And, depending on what you add to it—wine, cheese, curry, herbs, onions, chives, horseradish, mushrooms—it can easily be transformed.

But ordinary white sauce is not for the weight-wary. Most conventional recipes call for too much fat and flour, and generally add up to nearly 500 calories per cup.

The following white sauces contain little or no fat and a minimum of starch. The butter is missing, but not the buttery flavor. The list of variations that follows Basic White Sauce IV applies to all these white sauces.

◄§ BASIC WHITE SAUCE I §►

1 cup skim milk
1½ tablespoons all-purpose flour
½ teaspoon butter-flavored salt
    Pinch of white pepper

Combine all the ingredients in a nonstick saucepan. Beat with a wire whip until smooth, then cook, stirring, over low to moderate heat until thickened. Simmer for 1 minute. *One cup, 132 calories.*

NOTE: To this basic sauce you can add nutmeg or herbs; garlic, onion, or celery powder; 1 or 2 teaspoons lemon juice, Worcestershire sauce, or white wine; a pinch of paprika or cayenne; curry or chili powder; chopped parsley or chives.

◄§ BASIC WHITE SAUCE II §►

1 cup evaporated skim milk
2 teaspoons cornstarch
1 capful liquid butter flavoring
¼ teaspoon salt
    Pinch of white pepper

Beat all the ingredients together in a nonstick saucepan. Cook, stirring, over low to moderate heat until thickened. Simmer for 1 minute. *One cup, 196 calories.*

◄§ BASIC WHITE SAUCE III ℥►

⅔ cup instant nonfat dry milk
1½ teaspoons arrowroot
¾ cup cold water
½ teaspoon butter-flavored salt
　　Pinch of white pepper

Beat all the ingredients together in a nonstick saucepan. Cook, stirring, over low to moderate heat until simmering. *One cup, 103 calories.*

◄§ BASIC WHITE SAUCE IV ℥►

1 cup skim milk
1½ teaspoons arrowroot
¼ teaspoon salt
　　Pinch of white pepper
1 tablespoon diet margarine

Beat together all the ingredients except the diet margarine. When smooth, put in a nonstick saucepan and cook, stirring, over moderate heat until the mixture thickens and bubbles. Stir in the diet margarine until melted. *One cup, 153 calories.*

VARIATIONS

Cheese: Stir in ¼ cup grated cheese until melted. Don't overcook.

Egg: Mix in 1 grated hard-cooked egg before serving.

White Mushroom: Add a dash of Worcestershire sauce and the contents of a 4-ounce can of mushroom stems and pieces, finely chopped.

Herb: Add 2 teaspoons chopped chives, 2 teaspoons minced fresh parsley, and a pinch of dried thyme.

Hot Horseradish: Add 3 tablespoons drained prepared horseradish.

Quick Béchamel: Omit the salt and add 1 chicken bouillon cube, 1 finely minced hard-cooked egg, and a generous shake of paprika. Whir in the blender for maximum smoothness.

Pickle: Add 3 tablespoons chopped dill pickle.

Pimiento: Add 2 tablespoons chopped pimiento.

Curry: Add ½ teaspoon curry powder.

⊷ FRENCH WINE AND CHEESE SAUCE ⊱

There's nothing that turns on flavor like a fancy French sauce. The trouble with sauces, fancy French or otherwise, is that they're fattening. The most glamorous Gallic sauces are packed with unchic calories. Cheese and wine give them flavor, but fat and flour pack on the poundage—around 600 calories a cupful.

You can duplicate the same velvety texture and exquisite flavor in this fabulous French translation, which is a lot less trouble—and only one-third the calories.

This sauce is made without butter or margarine, but you may add buttery flavor by using butter-flavored salt, or a few drops of butter flavoring, sold in small bottles on your supermarket shelf. If neither of these no-calorie products is available in your store, simply omit it—the cheese and wine flavor predominate. Incidentally, the alcohol calories evaporate, leaving only the wine flavor.

Try this sauce on broiled chicken breasts or baked flounder or sole. It's a simply smashing topper for broccoli, green beans, and asparagus, too.

    2 cups skim milk
    ½ teaspoon salt or 1 teaspoon butter-flavored salt
       Pinch of freshly grated nutmeg
    ½ teaspoon dry mustard
       Pinch of cayenne pepper
    4 teaspoons arrowroot or 2 tablespoons cornstarch
    ¼ cup sherry wine or dry vermouth
    ⅓ cup (3 ounces) grated Swiss or Gruyère cheese

Put the milk, salt, nutmeg, mustard, and cayenne in a nonstick saucepan and bring rapidly to a boil over high heat. Combine the arrowroot and wine and add to the sauce; stir over a low flame until slightly thickened.

Remove from the flame and add the cheese; the heat of the sauce will melt it. Stir before serving. *Two and one-half cups, 12 calories per tablespoon.*

BLENDER-SLENDER
⊷ TARTAR SAUCE FOR SEAFOOD ⊱

    1 cup commercial low-calorie mayonnaise
    1 dill pickle, quartered
    1 tablespoon lemon juice
    1 small onion, peeled and quartered
    1 tablespoon prepared mustard
   1½ tablespoons chopped fresh parsley

Blend, covered, until the pickle and onion are finely chopped. *One and two-thirds cups, 17 calories per tablespoon.*

⊷ MAPLE-HONEY SYRUP ⊶

What to put on your no-butter pancakes or French toast? Try our maple-honey syrup, only 19 calories a tablespoon instead of the 60 calories or more you'd spend for honey or sugar-packed pancake syrup.

2 ounces dark honey
2 ounces pure maple syrup (*not* "pancake" syrup)
2 teaspoons arrowroot
1 cup cold water

Combine all the ingredients in a saucepan and stir until blended. Heat until the mixture simmers and thickens. *One and one-half cups, 19 calories per tablespoon.*

VARIATION

Really Lo-Cal Maple-Honey Syrup: Reduce the maple syrup in the recipe above to 1 teaspoon, and add sugar substitute equal to 7 tablespoons. Combine all the ingredients in a saucepan and stir to blend. Cook, stirring, over a moderate flame until thickened and clear. *Only 7 calories per tablespoon.*

⊷ BLUEBERRY SAUCE ⊶

1 cup fresh or frozen blueberries, defrosted if frozen
¾ cup unsweetened grape juice
1 teaspoon arrowroot or cornstarch
Sugar substitute to taste (optional)

Combine all the ingredients in a saucepan. Cook, stirring, over a moderate flame until the mixture bubbles and thickens. Stir in sugar substitute, if desired, and serve on waffles, pancakes, or French toast. *One and one-half cups, 10 calories per tablespoon.*

⊷ MOCK "SOUR CREAM" ⊶

If you're a Slim Gourmet cook, you can recreate rich sour cream, a dieter's devastation at 485 calories a cupful, in your blender at barely 180. And this great pretender is so dairy rich and tangy tart, so sour cream-y, it simply defies detection.

Our mock sour cream is cholesterol-wise as well as calorie-safe because it's virtually free of saturated fat. Differing from what you may think, most of the commercial "sour dressings" on the market today are packed with cholesterol-rich coconut oil, making them even higher in saturated fats than the real thing. They have crowded out the once-popular "sour half-and-half" (real sour cream with a reduced butterfat content).

Here's how they compare:

One Cup	Calories	Saturated Fat
Real sour cream	485	26 grams
Sour "half and half"	325	15 grams
Imitation sour dressing	320	32 grams
Slim Gourmet Mock "Sour Cream"	170	1 gram

1 **pint uncreamed or low-fat cottage cheese**
½ **cup buttermilk**
Pinch of salt

Put all ingredients in your blender and whir on high speed until smooth and creamy. (Add a few tablespoons more buttermilk, if necessary; the moisture can vary.) *Two and one-half cups at 154 calories per cupful; 9 per tablespoon.*

NOTE: If you don't care to buy buttermilk, you can make a sort of "sour cream" that's more creamy than sour by using ordinary skimmed milk in place of the buttermilk. Or try blending skimmed milk with "tangy-style" cottage cheese, the type that's creamed with sour cream.

◆§ DIET BUTTER ҩ҉

Are you ready for this? "Diet butter!" And, just like "diet margarine," it's only half the calories. Of course, diet margarine is available in the stores, but diet butter is something you'll have to make yourself.

But it's really very easy, because your low-calorie butter is made the same way the margarine makers prepare their diet product, by whipping it with water. That's why the calories are only 50 per tablespoon, half the calories and half the cholesterol.

Soft, light and magnificently spreadable—diet butter looks, tastes and spreads like butter—it *is* butter. It's unlikely that anyone could tell that you've been conniving with the calorie count. Put it in the refrigerator and it will harden to the consistency of regular butter. Your diet butter won't separate, even at room temperature, unless you accidentally leave it near the heat of your range or have some similar mishap that makes it melt.

Because your diet butter spreads twice as far, it's only half as salty, so you'll want to add a pinch of salt to make up the difference.

1 stick (4 ounces) butter
Pinch of salt
½ cup cold water

Put the butter in a mixing bowl and allow to soften to room temperature. Whip with an electric mixer until fluffy. Add the salt and continue to whip on high speed, adding the water gradually. Allow to harden in the refrigerator. *50 calories per tablespoon.*

◄§ "ALMOST BUTTER" §►

Here's an idea for those butter lovers who think they should be using margarine, but can't quite make the transition. Why not compromise?

1 stick (4 ounces) butter
1 stick (4 ounces) polyunsaturated margarine
¼ teaspoon salt
1 cup cold water

Put the butter and margarine in a mixing bowl and allow to soften to room temperature. Whip with an electric mixer until fluffy, then add the salt and continue to whip on high speed, adding the water gradually. Allow to harden in the refrigerator. *50 calories per tablespoon.*

NOTE: For the cholesterol-conscious, here are some facts and figures: Butter has 9,000 milligrams of cholesterol per pound; polyunsaturated margarine has none. Diet butter (above) has 50 percent of the cholesterol, and "Almost Butter" has 25 percent the cholesterol.

◄§ PEANUT BUTTER §►

Commercial peanut butter, even the low-calorie dietetic brands, is one of the most fattening foods there is. But our decalorized version contains less than half the calories, far less fat, and also much more protein. Two tablespoons of our Slim Gourmet Peanut Butter has 8 grams of protein, and that's more than an egg.

Calorie-wise, here's how it compares:

1 Tablespoon	Calories
Slim Gourmet	43
Commercial brands	100
Dietetic brands	100

2 cups dry roasted peanuts
1¼ cup cold water, approximately
2 teaspoons sugar or sugar substitute (optional)

Put the peanuts in the blender, cover, and blend on high speed until the peanuts are reduced to a powder. Uncover and add the water, a little at a time, blending after each addition, until the proper peanut-butter consistency is reached. Scrape down frequently with a rubber spatula. Blend in the sugar, if desired. Spoon into a jar and store in the refrigerator. (Homemade peanut butter without preservatives should be refrigerated.) *Two and one-quarter cups, 43 calories per tablespoon.*

18
JAMS
AND
JELLIES

Many old-time jam recipes contain as much as 4 cups of sugar—more than 3,000 calories' worth. Ordinary jams and jellies are 50 to 60 calories a *level* tablespoon because they're almost all sugar. Our Slim Gourmet versions are only a fraction of that, and mostly fruit.

Our super-slim spreads are made a whole new way—no pectin, no sterilized jars, no canning equipment needed! You make these jams in small quantities and keep them in your refrigerator or freezer.

For diabetics, hypoglycemia sufferers, and others on low-carbohydrate or low-sugar diets there are substitute-sweetened dietetic jams and jellies. All nonnutritive sweeteners on the market today are simply various forms of the old standby saccharin, which has been used by countless diabetics here and abroad for more than sixty years with apparent safety.

Saccharin, however, doesn't stand up very well to high or sustained heat, which accounts for the disappointing flavor of most commercially processed sugar-free jams and jellies. If the jelly makers could figure out a way to inject the sweetener into the sterilized jars of jelly after processing, they'd have the problem whipped.

But the home jam maker doesn't have that problem—if she makes small quantities to keep in her refrigerator or freezer.

⋖§ QUICKIE STRAWBERRY JAM ?֍

1 pint strawberries
1 cup water
1 envelope (4 servings) strawberry gelatin dessert mix

Wash and hull the strawberries and slice or crush them into a saucepan.
Add the water and gelatin dessert mix, then cook, stirring, over a moderate
flame until the mixture boils. Simmer for 2 minutes. Allow to cool, then pour
into three small jars—one for the refrigerator and two for the freezer. *Only
10 calories per tablespoon.*

VARIATION

Sugar-Free Strawberry Jam: Crush 1 pint of strawberries and cook them
for two minutes in 1 cup of water. Now, mix in one of the four-serving-size
envelopes of *dietetic* strawberry gelatin dessert and stil until completely dissolved. When cool, pour into small jars and freeze or refrigerate. *Only 3 calories per tablespoon.*

⋖§ PEACH JAM ?֍

1 can (16 ounces) juice-packed peaches
1 teaspoon unflavored gelatin
2 tablespoons granulated sugar
   Sugar substitute equal to 2 tablespoons sugar (optional)

Drain the fruit, reserving the juice, and puree in the electric blender. Add
enough reserved juice from the can to make one cup.
   Combine the puree, gelatin, and sugar in a saucepan. Wait for 1 minute,
until the gelatin is softened, then cook, stirring, over low heat until the gelatin
is melted. Remove from the heat and stir in sugar substitute, if desired. Store
in the refrigerator. *One cup, 17 calories per tablespoon.*

Sugar-Free Peach Jam: Omit sugar and add equivalent extra substitute
sweetener. *Only 9 calories per tablespoon.*

⋖§ FRESH BLUEBERRY JAM ?֍

2   tablespoons lemon juice
2   tablespoons water
1   envelope unflavored gelatin
1½ teaspoons arrowroot or 2 teaspoons cornstarch

1 **pint fresh blueberries or 2½ cups frozen**
9 **tablespoons granulated sugar**
   Sugar substitute equal to ¾ cup sugar (optional)

Combine the lemon juice, water, gelatin, and arrowroot in a saucepan. Heat until dissolved, then add the blueberries and sugar. Cook, stirring, until thickened, then boil for 2 to 3 minutes. Remove from heat and stir in sweetener, if desired. *One and three-quarter cups, 24 calories per tablespoon.*

Sugar-Free Blueberry Jam: Omit the sugar and add equivalent extra sweetener. *Only 9 calories per tablespoon.*

◄§ BLENDER-EASY PINEAPPLE "PRESERVE" §►

1 **envelope unflavored gelatin**
2 **tablespoons cold water**
½ **cup boiling water**
1 **can (20 ounces) juice-packed crushed pineapple, undrained**
5 **tablespoons granulated sugar or equivalent sugar substitute**

Sprinkle the gelatin in the bottom of your blender container. Add the cold water and allow to soften. Add the boiling water, then cover the container and whir on high speed until all the gelatin granules are dissolved.

Add the canned pineapple (including the juice) and sugar (or substitute) and blend on low speed just long enough to combine; don't overblend. Pour into three small jars, one for the refrigerator and two for the freezer. Keep refrigerated. *Only 13 calories per tablespoon with sugar; without sugar, 7 calories.*

◄§ PINEAPPLE-ORANGE "MARMALADE" §►

1 **envelope unflavored gelatin**
1 **can (6 ounces) frozen orange juice concentrate, defrosted**
1 **can (20 ounces) juice-packed crushed pineapple, undrained**
2 **teaspoons grated orange or lemon rind**
   Sugar substitute equal to ¼ cup sugar (optional)

Combine the gelatin with the defrosted orange juice in a saucepan. Wait until the gelatin is softened, then add all the other ingredients except the sugar substitute. Cook and stir for 2 minutes, then stir in the sweetener. Store in jars in the refrigerator. *Three cups, 15 calories per tablespoon.*

⋖§ VERY-ORANGE MARMALADE ৯▹

1 envelope (4 servings) regular or low-calorie orange gelatin dessert
   mix
1 cup boiling water
1 orange
1 cup cold water
5 tablespoons granulated sugar or equivalent sugar substitute

Empty the gelatin mix into your blender container and pour in the boiling water. Cover and blend on low speed until dissolved.

Remove about half of the peel from the orange (too much peel makes it bitter), then slice the orange and pick out the seeds. Put the orange slices, cold water, and sugar or sugar substitute into the blender. Cover and blend on low speed until the orange and peel are coarsely chopped. Pour into three jars, one for the refrigerator and two for the freezer. Keep refrigerated. *Calories per tablespoon: 11, with regular gelatin and sugar; 8 with sugar substitute; 3 with dietetic gelatin and sugar substitute.*

⋖§ REFRIGERATOR JELLY ৯▹

These recipes were developed by the maker of Sugar Twin, the substitute you use spoon-for-spoon in place of sugar. For best results, when making jellies and jams with a granulated sugar substitute, use both unflavored gelatin and pectin as thickening agents. These sugar-free jellies should be stored in the refrigerator or freezer in covered containers.

1 envelope unflavored gelatin
2 cups unsweetened apple, grape, or pineapple juice, or low-calorie
   cranberry juice cocktail
1 cup granulated sugar substitute
½ bottle (3 ounces) liquid pectin

Sprinkle the gelatin over ½ cup of the juice to soften. Bring the remaining juice to a boil. Stir in the softened gelatin and granulated sugar substitute until dissolved. Again, bring to a boil, stirring constantly. Stir in the pectin. Bring to a full rolling boil and boil hard for 1 minute, stirring constantly. Remove from the heat. Skim off any foam with a metal spoon. Ladle into clean jelly glasses; cool and cover with plastic wrap or foil. Store in refrigerator. *Two cups; calorie count depends on juice used.*

VARIATION

Refrigerator Pineapple Jam: Use 1 can (20 ounces) crushed pineapple packed in unsweetened pineapple juice. Drain the pineapple, reserving the juice, and add canned unsweetened pineapple juice to measure 2 cups. Proceed as above, heating the drained pineapple with the juice. *Only 11 calories per tablespoon.*

◦§ CRANBERRY SAUCE §◦

Fresh cranberries are so tart that lemons and rhubarb seem like candy kisses by comparison. Hence, commercial cranberry sauce is so sugar packed that it's nearly 400 calories per cupful. There is a commercial low-calorie cranberry sauce, but it's as hard to find as a turkey with teeth. For that reason, turkey lovers are well advised to make lots of homemade low-calorie cranberry sauce while the fresh berries are in season. (You can freeze the extra.)

Homemade cranberry sauce is easy to make. Either jellied or whole-berry, the ingredients and calories are the same. Here's a recipe you can use three ways: by cutting back on the sugar, you can make a tart sauce that's a change from the commercial variety; if you prefer a sweet cranberry sauce, you can combine sugar and sugar substitute to reach the usual level of sweetness without the usual calories; and if you're on a sugar-free diet, you can make your cranberry sauce with no sugar whatsoever.

2 cups (½ pound) fresh cranberries
1 cup water
1 envelope unflavored gelatin
¼ cup cold water
7 tablespoons granulated sugar
Sugar substitute equal to ½ cup sugar (optional)

Combine the cranberries and water in a saucepan and cook until the skins pop. Put the berries and liquid through a sieve, if desired, then put back into the saucepan.

Dissolve the gelatin in the cold water, then add to the saucepan, along with the sugar. Cook, stirring, for 2 minutes, then add the optional sugar substitute. Pour into jars and allow to cool. Store in the refrigerator or freeze. *About 3 calories per tablespoon.*

NOTE: You can also make the sauce without sugar. After the sauce is cooked, stir in no-calorie sugar substitute to taste, up to the equivalent of 2 cups sugar. Check the label for how much to use.

❦ FRESH CRANBERRY-ORANGE RELISH ❧

Here's an uncooked relish that's a snap to make with your blender or grinder.

1 quart fresh cranberries
1 orange
½ cup sugar
Sugar substitute to equal 1½ cups sugar

Chop up the cranberries. Cut up the orange and remove the seeds, then chop it up, skin and all. Mix the fruit together and stir in the sugar and sugar substitute to equal 1½ cups of sugar. *About 9 calories per tablespoon.*

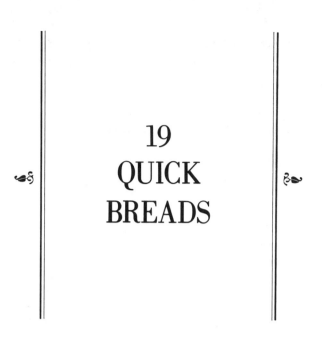

19
QUICK
BREADS

☙ COTTAGE PANCAKES ❧

Even if you're *not* a cottage cheese fan, you'll be amazed at what this low-fat dairy-rich food can do to cut the calories and boost the nutrition of a breakfast favorite like pancakes.

To prepare pancakes without adding extra fat, use a nonstick griddle that's whistle clean. Try one of the spray-on vegetable coatings that let you fry without adding any extra calories. One caution, however—don't have the griddle overhot. Use a temperature slightly lower than you would use for standard pancake recipes.

Pinch of salt
3 eggs, separated
¼ cup all-purpose flour
¾ cup low-fat cottage cheese or pot cheese

Add the salt to the egg whites and beat until stiff. In another bowl, beat the egg yolks and cottage cheese until smooth and creamy, then beat in the flour. Fold in the beaten egg whites. Spoon the batter by tablespoonfuls into a preheated nonstick skillet. Bake, turning once, until lightly browned on both sides. Top with sugar-free jam or low-calorie maple syrup, if desired, and serve. *Sixteen pancakes, 31 calories each, without topping.*

SUZANNE TOPPER'S PROTEIN BLUEBERRY PANCAKES*

1½ cups buttermilk
1 egg
¾ cup fresh blueberries, washed and picked over
1 cup low-fat soy flour
½ teaspoon baking soda
¾ teaspoon baking powder
  Pinch of salt
  Polyunsaturated oil or spray-on vegetable coating

Combine the buttermilk, egg, and blueberries. Sift in the flour, baking soda, baking powder, and salt and blend well.

Use a nonstick skillet in good condition. Wipe lightly with oil or spray with vegetable coating for no-fat frying, then heat over a moderate flame. Drop scant tablespoons of batter onto the skillet; brown on both sides. Serve with sugar-free diet syrup. Or, if you prefer, try our adaptation of Suzanne's Orange-Honey Syrup (see below). *Four servings, 143 calories each.*

ORANGE-HONEY SYRUP:
1 cup orange juice
5 tablespoons honey
2 teaspoons grated orange rind
  Pinch of salt

Blend all the ingredients well. Serve warm if desired. *Only 20 calories per tablespoon.*

COTTAGE CORN MEAL GRIDDLE CAKES

½ cup all-purpose flour
½ cup corn meal
1 teaspoon baking powder
1 teaspoon salt
½ teaspoon baking soda
1 egg
½ cup low-fat cottage cheese
¾ cup water, more if necessary

Stir all the ingredients together; add more water if needed. Spray a nonstick frying pan or griddle with vegetable coating for no-fat frying. Preheat

---

* From *The Fruit Cookbook*, New York: Avon, 1973.

until hot (until water dropped on the surface "dances"), then pour in batter to make pancakes 4-inches in diameter. Turn with a spatula when the tops are bubbly and brown the other side. *Ten pancakes, 60 calories each.*

NOTE: Serve with sugar-free diet syrup or low-sugar jam.

⊷§ FRENCH TOAST §⊷

French toast doesn't have to be fattening, though most of the time it is. The frozen toast-and-serve brands are about 160 calories a slice, and home-made French toast can be a lot more. Two or three slices, plus butter and syrup and a side order of fatty pork sausage, can easily add up to 1,200 calories or more, almost as much as some calorie-counters allot for a whole day's eating.

If you're a Slim Gourmet cook, you can make French toast at only half the calories, 80 per slice. And with some creative calorie-cutting on the rest of the menu, you can enjoy a special breakfast for 400 calories or less. Try half a grapefruit, French toast (2 slices) with diet maple syrup (2 tablespoons), broiled beef sausage (2 ounces), and coffee or tea—for a total calorie count of 380!

To make your Slim Gourmet French toast, start with a slim slice of high-protein bread that's under 50 calories a slice. White protein bread made with part soy flour has the perfect flavor and texture for delightful French toast, far better than toast made with soggy, doughy ordinary bread, and it's lower in calories and more filling, too.

Be sure you have a non-stick skillet so you can prepare your toast with a minimum of greasing. One teaspoon of oil is all you need.

1   **teaspoon polyunsaturated oil**
2   **large eggs**
⅔   **cup skim milk**
½   **teaspoon vanilla extract**
8   **slices diet protein bread (any brand)**

Wipe a large nonstick skillet with the oil. Beat the eggs, milk, and vanilla together and pour into a shallow bowl. Dip the bread in the egg mixture, a slice at a time, then brown in the skillet over a moderate flame, turning once. *Only 80 calories per slice.*

FRENCH TOAST TOPPERS: Instead of syrup, try sugarless or sugar-reduced orange marmalade. The calorie count is anywhere from 6 to 26 calories a tablespoon, depending on the brand; ordinary marmalade is 60 calories a tablespoon. Or try a tablespoon of warmed, crushed pineapple, only 7 calories per tablespoon for the juice-packed type. Or heated diet applesauce spiked with clove (7 calories a tablespoon).

VARIATION

Low-Cholesterol French Toast: Substitute two egg whites for each egg. Add a drop of yellow food coloring, if you wish.

⊷ WAFFLES FOR TWO ⊷

What makes waffles so fattening is all the extra oil in the batter, at least ¼ cup in most recipes. That's 460 calories. You can deduct that much from your favorite waffle batter. However, there's two things you'll need—a waffle maker with a non-stick surface *and* a can of spray-on vegetable coating for no-fat frying. Without both, fat-free batter will glue the grids shut like contact cement.

High-protein waffles are made with an extra egg and a packaged soy pancake mix (available in health food stores or on the health food shelf of your supermarket). You can make your own mix by putting 2 tablespoons of low-fat soy flour (soy powder) in a ½-cup measure, then fill it with regular or buckwheat pancake mix, or ¾ cup plain flour plus 1 teaspoon baking powder and a pinch of salt. Don't use biscuit mix for waffles; it contains extra fat (and calories).

The following makes just enough batter to fill a modern rectangular four-section waffle maker once. Double or triple the recipe for extra fillings.

1   **whole egg or two egg whites**
½   **cup buckwheat or soy pancake mix**
½   **teaspoon vanilla extract (optional)**
    Scant ½ cup skim milk
    Spray-on vegetable coating

Combine the egg and pancake mix; add vanilla, if desired, and just enough milk to make a pourable batter. Spray the surface of your nonstick waffle maker with a vegetable coating for no-fat frying until all surfaces are wet and shiny, doing this in a vertical position if the grids are removable. Return the grids and plug in to preheat.

Wait until the surface is very hot (when a drop of water bounces and sizzles), then pour in the batter and close the waffle maker. Don't attempt to open until the waffles stop steaming or the indicator light goes off. Unplug and gently loosen waffles with a fork or knife, being careful not to mar the nonstick surface. *Four sections (two servings), 84 calories each section.*

NOTE: Serve your waffles with diet maple syrup, warm applesauce, crushed fruit, or low-sugar jams, no butter needed. Breakfasting alone? Freeze the extra two waffles for tomorrow's breakfast. Pop them in the toaster to reheat. Or save them for lunch.

⋈ BLUEBERRY–COTTAGE CHEESE MUFFINS ⋈

Extra eggs or cottage cheese make our muffins protein rich, but much lower in fat and carbohydrates, because we use a minimum of flour and no added fat whatsoever. Our muffins are a skimpy 55 or 58 calories each, while ordinary muffins are about 135.

¼ cup low-fat cottage cheese
1 egg
¾ cup all-purpose flour
½ teaspoon salt
1¼ teaspoons baking powder
2 tablespoons granulated sugar or equivalent sugar substitute
  (optional)
⅓ cup skim milk
1 cup fresh blueberries, washed and picked over

Fork-blend the cottage cheese and egg together. Add the flour, salt, baking powder, and sugar and stir to combine. Add milk and stir lightly, then gently stir in the blueberries. Spoon into 10 muffin cups and bake in a preheated 425-degree oven for 15 to 18 minutes. *Ten muffins, 68 calories each with sugar; 58 without.*

⋈ BLUEBERRY TEA MUFFINS ⋈

2 eggs, separated
½ cup skim milk
2 tablespoons granulated sugar or equivalent sugar substitute
  (optional)
¾ cup all-purpose flour
1 teaspoon baking powder
½ teaspoon salt
1 cup fresh blueberries, washed and picked over

Beat the egg yolks, milk, sugar, flour, and baking powder together until smooth. Combine the salt and egg whites and whip until stiff. Fold the batter in carefully. Add the blueberries last, stirring in gently. Spoon into a nonstick 12-cup muffin pan and bake in a preheated 375-degree oven for 15 to 20 minutes, until lightly browned. *Twelve muffins, 60 calories each with sugar; 52 without.*

❦ BRAN MUFFINS ❧

A new-old "health" food is receiving renewed attention among nutrition-wise cooks these days—bran, the delicious, nutty-tasting outer husk of wheat, the part that's taken out in the process of refining white flour.

Bran has special interest to calorie counters. It's one of the best sources of appetite-appeasing, nonnutritive (no-calorie) fiber. The absence of fiber in the American diet has been tied to our epidemic of overweight, plus a host of other ills.

  1 **cup bran or bran-type cereal**
  1 **cup skim milk**
  1 **egg**
    Sugar substitute equal to ¼ cup sugar
  ½ **teaspoon salt**
1¼ **cups all-purpose flour**
  1 **tablespoon baking powder**

Combine the bran, milk, and egg in a bowl. Stir and wait for 1 minute, then stir in the sugar substitute and salt. Combine the flour and baking powder and stir into the bran mixture. Spoon into 12 nonstick muffin cups and bake in a preheated 400-degree oven for 20 to 25 minutes. *Twelve muffins, 78 calories each.*

❦ CORNBREAD ❧

Our cornbread is only 49 calories a slice, less than half the calories of cornbread made according to the conventional recipe, and 50 percent more body-building protein than either conventional cornbread or so-called "diet" breads.

The secret ingredient is low-fat soy powder (or "soy flour"), a product you'll find in health food stores or on the health food shelf of your super-market. This soy flour contains 65 grams of prime protein per cup, compared with only 11 or 12 grams for either wheat flour or corn meal. And it's only 320 calories a cupful, instead of 400 or more for flour or corn meal.

  1 **egg, separated**
  ½ **teaspoon salt**
1¼ **cups skim milk**
  ½ **cup yellow corn meal**
  ¾ **cup all-purpose flour**
  ¼ **cup low-fat soy flour**
  1 **tablespoon baking powder**

Put the egg white and salt in a mixing bowl and beat until stiff but not dry. Set aside. Combine the yolk with all the other ingredients in the blender and whir until smooth. Pour the corn batter into the beaten egg white and gently fold together. Spoon into an 8-inch square or round nonstick cake pan. Bake in a preheated hot (425-degree) oven for 20 minutes, until golden brown. If not served immediately, remove from the pan to retain crispness. *Sixteen servings, 49 calories each.*

VARIATIONS

Low-Cholesterol Cornbread: Use a second egg white in place of the egg yolk. *47 calories each.*

Northern-Style Cornbread: Add sugar substitute to the batter equal to 3 tablespoons.

Corn Muffins: Spoon the batter into 12 muffin cups. Bake for 15 to 20 minutes at 425 degrees. *Only 65 calories each.*

Cornsticks: Spray a cornstick pan with vegetable coating for no-fat baking. Add the batter and bake at 425 degrees for 15 to 20 minutes. *Fourteen cornsticks, 55 calories each.*

⋖ COTTAGE CORNBREAD ⋗

When added to corn meal, cottage cheese provides a farm-fresh, dairy-rich flavor and helps reduce the calorie count, rather than add to it. Because cottage cheese is so generous with body-building protein, a normally starchy food such as this is better nutrition, too. There's only a minimum of butterfat in this recipe, and it is lower in cholesterol than it would be if made with sour cream. (Heart-smart cooks can further lower the cholesterol by using two egg whites in place of the whole egg called for in the recipes.)

1 **cup corn meal**
¾ **cup skim milk**
½ **cup low fat creamed cottage cheese**
1 **egg**
1 **teaspoon salt**
1 **teaspoon baking powder**
½ **teaspoon baking soda**
   Sugar substitute equal to 1 tablespoon sugar (optional)

Combine all the ingredients, stir well, and spoon into an 8-inch round nonstick cake pan. Bake in a preheated 425-degree oven for 20 to 25 minutes. Cut into wedges to serve. *Sixteen servings, 43 calories each.*

⋖ QUICK RAISIN BRAN BREAD ⋗

3 cups all-purpose flour
1 teaspoon salt
4 teaspoons baking powder
   Sugar substitute equal to ¼ cup sugar
1 cup whole bran
6 tablespoons raisins
2 eggs
1 cup skim milk

Sift the flour, salt, and baking powder together, then stir in the sugar substitute and whole bran and raisins. Beat the eggs and milk together and stir into the batter only until mixed. Pour into a nonstick bread pan and bake in a preheated 375-degree oven for 50 minutes. *Twenty slices, 99 calories each.*

⋖ IRISH SODA BREAD ⋗

This is one snack you won't have to pass up. Our Slim Gourmet soda bread recipe, in addition to being easy, is also low in calories and cholesterol because we make it with no fat or sugar.

But that's not all: our soda bread is extra rich in protein because we replace part of the wheat flour with low-fat soy flour. Soy flour is milled from the soybean, richest source of vegetable protein that grows on God's green earth. By combining soy with the self-rising wheat flour, we increase the protein value of the flour by 44 percent.

There are no eggs in this recipe, either, which makes it an ideal snack bread for cholesterol watchers as well as calorie counters. A slim slice, lightly spread with polyunsaturated margarine or diet orange marmalade, makes a nice dessert or TV time treat.

Buttermilk, despite its name, contains no butter. In fact, it's virtually fat free. At 88 calories a glassful, this low-calorie dairy drink has the same calorie count as skim milk, and the same good dairy nutrition. If you have no buttermilk, you can prepare this recipe with sour skim milk. To make fresh skim milk sour, simply add a tablespoon of lemon juice or vinegar. Plain yogurt (not the sugared-up kind) can be used, although its calorie count is somewhat higher, about 130 calories an 8-ounce cup.

2½ cups self-rising flour
 ½ cup low-fat soy flour
 ¼ cup granulated sugar substitute (optional)
  1 teaspoon baking soda

1½ **cups buttermilk, sour skim milk, or yogurt**
  5 **tablespoons raisins**

Combine all the ingredients except the milk and raisins in a mixing bowl; stir well to blend evenly. Stir in the raisins, then stir in the milk. Scrape the batter out of the bowl and pile in the middle of a nonstick cookie sheet. Rub a little salad oil into your hands so the batter won't stick, then pat and shape the batter into a smooth, round loaf. Bake in a preheated 350-degree oven for 45 minutes. Serve warm or cool. To serve, cut the loaf in half, then slice thin. Freeze the other half, if you wish. *Forty slices, about 39 calories each.*

20
CAKES

If you're an infrequent cake baker, or normally only use mixes, keep these tips in mind: assemble all your ingredients before you begin. Use measuring cups and spoons. Preheat your oven when you start. Use nonstick baking pans. And no peeking in the oven until near the end of the baking period.

Golden-crusted home-baked cake, what could be better? A cake that's only half as fattening, that's what!

ONE-BOWL GOLD CAKE

Our Slim Gourmet One-Bowl Gold Cake is only 125 calories a slice, compared with most store-bought or cake-mix cakes at 250 calories or more! And best of all, our cake is easy to make.

To make this cake recipe, you'll need cake flour, not all-purpose flour. It isn't necessary to sift it, however. Simply measure out 1½ cups, and stir the baking powder into the flour until it seems reasonably distributed.

  5 eggs
  ½ cup skim milk
  2 teaspoons vanilla extract
  ½ teaspoon salt
 10 tablespoons granulated sugar
    Sugar substitute equal to ½ cup sugar

2 teaspoons grated orange peel
1½ cups cake flour
1 tablespoon baking powder

Combine the eggs, milk, vanilla, salt, sugar, sugar substitute, and orange peel in a mixing bowl. Mix on high speed with an electric mixer.

Measure the flour and stir in the baking powder. Add to the mixing bowl and mix on slow speed until thoroughly blended. Scrape the sides of the bowl with a spatula, then beat for 1 minute on medium speed.

Pour the batter into a nonstick 9 × 5-inch loaf pan and bake for 45 minutes in a preheated 350-degree oven until golden and crusty. The cake is done when a knife inserted in the center comes out clean. *Twelve servings, 125 calories each.*

Homemade Sponge Cake for Lo-Cal Fruit Dessert

A slice of sponge cake piled high with strawberries and crowned with just the scantiest squiggle of whipped topping looks and tastes like a million calories. But our sponge cakes are a skimpy 65 or 75 calories a slice, barely a fraction of what you'd "pay" for layer cake or apple pie. That's because sponge cake is one of the lowest-caloried cakes there is—no fat, a minimum of sugar and flour, and lots of protein-rich egg yolks and egg whites to give texture and height. (For an even higher cake at very few calories more, add one or two additional egg whites.)

And best of all, our sponge cakes are easy, and simpler still if you have both a blender and a mixer.

◆§ SPONGE CAKE I ধ

1 cup cake flour
1½ teaspoons baking powder
3 eggs, at room temperature, separated
1 cup confectioners' sugar
¼ cup boiling water
1½ teaspoons vanilla extract
¼ teaspoon grated orange rind
¼ teaspoon salt

Stir the flour and baking powder together and set aside.

In blender or mixer, beat the egg yolks until lemon colored. Add the sugar and beat until smooth. Add the water, vanilla, and orange rind and beat. Uncover the blender and beat in the flour, a little at a time, until smooth.

In a mixing bowl, beat the egg whites and salt until stiff peaks form. Fold the batter into the egg whites, gently but thoroughly, using a rubber scraper or the mixer at lowest speed.

Spoon into 2 8-inch cake pans and bake in a preheated 325-degree oven until done, about 25 minutes. Cool thoroughly before removing from pans. *Sixteen servings, 65 calories each.*

NOTE: Spread the layers with crushed sliced strawberries or with Winter Strawberry Topping (see below) for a two-layer company shortcake. Or, put one layer in your cake box and the other in your freezer. For a dieter's portion, slice the cake layer into 8 wedges. Top with lots of fruit, unsugared, or sweetened with sugar substitute. If you're fresh out of fresh fruit, try it with canned peaches packed in juice.

Winter Strawberry Topping: Defrost 2 cups loose-pack unsweetened whole berries and add 3 tablespoons water, 1 tablespoon granulated sugar, and no-calorie sweetener equal to 2 tablespoons sugar. *Only 6 calories per tablespoon.*

⤐ SPONGE CAKE II ⤏

6 **eggs, at room temperature, separated**
¾ **cup confectioners' sugar**
   Sugar substitute equal to ½ cup sugar
¼ **cup hot water**
1 **teaspoon orange extract**
¼ **teaspoon salt**
1 **teaspoon cream of tartar**
1¼ **cups cake flour**

Put the egg yolks in a deep bowl and beat until very thick. Add half the confectioners' sugar and beat well. Add the sweetener and hot water, a little at a time, and beat. Beat in the orange extract.

Put the egg whites in another (nonplastic) bowl and add the salt, cream of tartar, and remaining sugar. Beat until stiff peaks form.

Triple-sift the flour, then gradually fold it, alternately with the egg whites, into the yolk mixture, a little at a time. Spoon into a 9 x 5-inch loaf pan and bake in a preheated 350-degree oven for 50 minutes. Remove from oven and cool for 1 hour. *Sixteen servings, 75 calories each.*

⤐ STIR-CRAZY CHOCOLATE CAKE FOR LAZY LO-CAL COOKS ⤏

Here it is, waistline watchers, a low-calorie version of the easiest cake of all. This chocolate-rich snack cake is even simpler to prepare than a packaged cake mix because it creates no dirty dishes at all. Not even a mixing bowl or blades. All you do is dump all the ingredients in your cake pan, then simply stir and bake. It's as easy as that.

But work-free preparation is only one of its advantages. We've taken the basic recipe and eliminated the superfluous fat and sugar calories, thereby cutting the total calorie count in half, without any significant change in taste or texture. The cake is deep, dark, and dense, just the ticket for chocolate fans, yet only 82 calories a serving. A slice of chocolate or devil's food cake prepared from a packaged cake mix is 201 calories.

This recipe contains no eggs, milk, butter, or other animal fats. The rising action is accomplished by the dynamic meeting of baking soda (bicarbonate of soda) and vinegar. Once your cake is well stirred, get it in a hot oven immediately—and gangway!

1½   cups all-purpose flour
 ½   cup granulated sugar
      Sugar substitute equal to ½ cup sugar
  3   tablespoons unsweetened cocoa
 ½   teaspoon salt
1¼   teaspoons baking soda
  1   cup water
  1   tablespoon white vinegar
  2   teaspoons vanilla extract

Combine all the dry ingredients in a 9-inch round or square nonstick cake pan. Stir well. Pour the water, vinegar, and vanilla directly into the pan. Stir with a spoon in a circular motion until all the ingredients are well blended. Level the surface with a spoon, then place in a preheated 350-degree oven. Bake for 25 minutes, or until the cake springs back gently when pressed. Serve hot or cold, topped, if desired, with chocolate whipped cream (see below). *Twelve servings, 82 calories each.*

CHOCOLATE WHIPPED CREAM:
  1   envelope low-calorie whipped topping mix
  1   tablespoon unsweetened cocoa
  1   tablespoon granulated sugar
 ½   cup skim milk

Combine all the ingredients in a mixing bowl and beat with an electric mixer until they become the consistency of whipped cream. *Two cups, 10 calories per tablespoon.*

~§ CHOCOLATE CAKE &~

        4 tablespoons butter or margarine
       ¼ cup brown sugar
         Sugar substitute equal to ⅓ cup sugar
        1 egg
     1⅓ cups all-purpose flour
        3 tablespoons unsweetened cocoa
        2 teaspoons baking powder
       ½ teaspoon baking soda
     1½ teaspoons vanilla extract
       ½ cup skim milk

Combine the butter, brown sugar, sweetener, and egg. Beat for 2 minutes at high speed, then add the remaining ingredients and beat for 2 minutes at low speed. Spread the batter in a nonstick 8-inch round or square cake pan. Bake in a preheated 350-degree oven for 30 minutes, until a toothpick inserted in the center comes out clean. *Eight servings, 166 calories each.*

~§ CHOCOLATE PUDDING CAKE &~

If you like chocolate pudding and chocolate cake (and who doesn't?), here's a dessert that combines the best of both—chocolate pudding cake. It makes its own rich-tasting sauce right in the cake pan. Slice yourself a warm chocolate-y wedge, and underneath you'll find a smooth and creamy hot chocolate sauce just a-waiting for you to spoon it on. No icing needed.

It's easy, too. And it's only 126 calories a serving, less than half the calories of the conventional recipe.

To make this dessert superspeedy, we use self-rising all-purpose flour, the kind that already contains baking powder and salt. If you're making this cake with regular flour, add 1½ teaspoons of baking powder and ¼ teaspoon salt to the batter.

CAKE:
        1 cup self-rising flour
        1 tablespoon unsweetened cocoa
        3 tablespoons white or brown sugar
          Sugar substitute equal to 3 tablespoons sugar
        1 egg
        5 tablespoons cold water

TOPPING:

   6 tablespoons granulated sugar
   3 tablespoons plain cocoa
   Sugar substitute equal to 10 teaspoons sugar
1½ cups boiling water

Combine the cake ingredients in a mixing bowl and beat with an electric mixer for 2 minutes on medium speed. Spread the batter evenly in a nonstick 8-inch round or square cake pan.

Combine all the topping ingredients except the hot water and sprinkle over the surface of the batter. Slow-pour the boiling water onto the surface of the cake. To do this without disturbing the topping, hold a tablespoon an inch above the surface of the cake and pour the water into the spoon, letting it overflow onto the surface of the cake.

Bake in a preheated 375-degree oven for 30 minutes. The batter will rise up through the topping and liquid, creating a crusty cake layer over a thick hot chocolate sauce.

To serve, cut a wedge or square of warm cake and spoon on the hot sauce. Or refrigerate; the sauce will chill into a layer of creamy pudding. *Eight servings, 126 calories each.*

VARIATION

Coffee-Chocolate Pudding Cake: To create a coffee-spiked chocolate sauce, substitute 1½ cups hot coffee for the boiling water. Or dissolve a rounded teaspoon of instant coffee in the boiling water before pouring it on the cake.

◆§ MOCHA LADY FINGER CAKE ৡ◆

Lady fingers are definitely ladylike when it comes to calories. Of all the snacks and sweets on supermarket shelves, lady fingers are among the least fattening. They're really a sort of sponge cake, with lots of low-calorie air.

Of course, lady fingers need companionship. Crushed fresh fruit is the quickest topper and the most figure wise. Lady fingers are also very versatile, the perfect base for all sorts of chill-and-serve desserts. Here is a mocha dessert made with diet chocolate-drink mix, the kind that comes in single-serving packets. For this recipe you can use either the milkshake type that's meant to be drunk cold or low-calorie hot cocoa mix. Both work equally well.

This dessert looks and tastes like a fancy torte, the kind you might find in a good bakery or elegant restaurant. But the calorie count is 100 or less per serving.

1 envelope unflavored gelatin
2 tablespoons cold water
1 cup boiling water
1 heaping teaspoon instant coffee
3 envelopes (single serving) low-calorie chocolate-drink mix
1 tablespoon vanilla extract
2 tablespoons sugar or equivalent sugar substitute
  Pinch of salt
2 egg whites, stiffly beaten
1 cup aerosol whipped cream
9½ lady fingers
2 chocolate cookies, crushed to crumbs (optional)

Combine the gelatin and cold water in the blender. Wait 1 minute, then add the boiling water and instant coffee. Cover and blend on high speed until the gelatin is dissolved.

Add the diet chocolate-drink mix, vanilla, and sugar or sugar substitute. Blend until smooth, then put the blender container in the refrigerator until the mixture is chilled and syrupy.

Combine the salt and egg whites and beat until stiff. Combine the whipped cream and chilled chocolate mixture with the beaten egg whites, folding gently but thoroughly until the mixture is completely blended but light and fluffy; don't overmix.

Split seven of the lady fingers and stand them inside a small loaf pan, lining the two long sides. Cover the bottom with the remaining split lady fingers. Carefully spoon the chocolate filling into the middle. Sprinkle the top with chocolate cookie crumbs, if desired, and refrigerate all day or overnight, until set. Slice to serve. *Eight servings, 100 calories each with sugar, 88 calories with sugar substitute.*

⋘ BETTE GASSE'S DIET CHEESECAKE* ⋙

CAKE:
2 cups low-fat cottage cheese
3 eggs
½ teaspoon almond extract
1 tablespoon liquid sweetener

TOPPING:
1 cup cottage cheese
1 teaspoon vanilla extract
1 teaspoon liquid sweetener

---

* Submitted by Mrs. Thomas L. Gasse of Whitman, Massachusetts.

Combine the cake ingredients in a blender and beat until smooth. Pour into a nonstick pie pan and bake in a preheated 350-degree oven for 30 minutes, then remove and let cool for 20 minutes.

Combine the topping ingredients in the blender and beat to sour-cream consistency. Spread on the cake and return to the oven. Bake for 10 minutes more at 350 degrees. *Eight servings, 101 calories each.*

CINNAMON DANISH CHEESECAKE

This is not only a quick-and-easy dessert, it makes an ideal make-ahead, low-calorie breakfast for sweet eaters who'd rather gobble down pastry than take the time for proper protein fare like ham and eggs. Empty-calorie pastry has about as much appetite appeasement value as sweetened sawdust; like sawdust, the sugar and starch calories flare up and burn out quickly, leaving your tummy cold and empty till noontime. But a protein-rich breakfast hangs in there, stiffening your resistance against more glop at coffee-break time.

5 **large cinnamon graham crackers**
2 **cups low-fat cottage cheese**
4 **eggs**
1 **tablespoon vanilla extract**
   Pinch of salt
¼ **cup granulated sugar**
   Sugar substitute equal to ¼ cup sugar (optional)
¼ **teaspoon grated lemon rind (optional)**
   Ground cinnamon

Break up the graham crackers into sections. Layer the bottom and sides of a nonstick 9-inch square or 9 x 5-inch loaf pan with the graham cracker sections, cinnamon side out, to form a shallow crust. If there's a little space between the crackers it won't matter; the filling will hold the cheesecake together.

Put the cheese, eggs, vanilla, salt, sugar, and sugar substitute in your blender. Add the lemon rind, then cover the blender and whir on high speed until smooth and creamy. Scrape down the sides with a rubber spatula, then spoon the filling into the crust. Be careful not to knock over your graham cracker walls.

Sprinkle with cinnamon and bake in a preheated 275-degree oven for 1 hour. Turn off the oven and let the cheesecake cool, undisturbed, for 1 hour longer. Chill before serving. *Nine servings, 108 calories each.*

Pineapple Danish Cheesecake: Combine 1 cup low-calorie crushed pineapple, including the juice, with a teaspoon cornstarch or arrowroot and simmer over low heat until thickened. For a sweeter topping, stir in 1 tablespoon sugar or equivalent sugar substitute. After the cheesecake (see above) is baked, spread this topping over the surface. Chill. *Nine servings, 129 calories each with sugar; 124 with sugar substitute.*

⊷ COTTAGE SHORTCAKE ⊶ WITH STRAWBERRIES

Despite its low-calorie count, this dessert is a powerhouse of protein-rich nutrition. Each cottage shortcake square provides 4.7 grams of protein, more than two slices of protein toast. The strawberries add Vitamin C.

3 eggs
2 tablespoons skim milk
½ cup low-fat cottage cheese
4 tablespoons granulated sugar
  Sugar substitute equal to ¼ cup sugar (optional)
1 teaspoon vanilla extract
7 tablespoons cake flour
1 teaspoon baking powder
½ teaspoon salt
  Strawberry Topping (see below)

Separate the eggs; put the yolks in your blender and the whites in a mixing bowl.

Add the milk and cottage cheese to the blender container and blend on high speed until smooth. Add the sugar, sugar substitute, and vanilla and blend until smooth. While the blender is still running, add the flour, a little at a time. Add the baking powder last.

Add the salt to the egg whites and beat with an electric mixer, until stiff. Gently fold the blender batter into the whites, using a rubber scraper or your mixer on lowest speed.

Spoon the batter into an ungreased nonstick 9-inch square cake pan. Bake in a preheated 350-degree oven for 25 minutes, then remove from the oven and allow to cool; the surface of the cake will settle as it cools. Chill before serving. To serve, cut in 3-inch squares and top with the topping. *Nine servings, 110 calories with strawberries; 80 calories without.*

Strawberry Topping: Combine 1 quart fresh strawberries with 1 tablespoon granulated sugar; add sugar substitute equal to 6 teaspoons sugar (optional), then divide into nine equal portions.

✑ PINEAPPLE CHEESECAKE SQUARES ఴ

CRUST:

2 tablespoons diet margarine
5 tablespoons packaged graham-cracker crumbs

CHEESECAKE:

½ cup water
½ cup instant nonfat dry milk
¼ cup granulated sugar
4 eggs
½ teaspoon salt
1 tablespoon lemon juice
2 teaspoons vanilla extract
3 tablespoons all-purpose flour
16 ounces low-fat cottage cheese

PINEAPPLE GLAZE:

1 can (8 ounces) juice-packed crushed pineapple, drained
½ teaspoon arrowroot or cornstarch
2 teaspoons lemon juice
2 teaspoons liquid sweetener, or to taste (optional)

Spread the sides and bottom of a 9-inch square nonstick cake pan with the diet margarine. Sprinkle on the crumbs and press down, then shake off any loose ones.

Combine all the cheesecake ingredients in a blender; cover and blend until smooth. Pour into the cake pan and bake in a preheated 225-degree oven for 1 hour. Turn off the heat and allow to cool in the oven for 1 hour more.

Combine the glaze ingredients in a saucepan. Stir over low heat until the mixture thickens, then spread evenly on the cooled cheesecake. Chill, then cut into squares to serve. *Nine servings, 150 calories each.*

✑ KÄSE KUCHEN ఴ
(*A German Dessert Decalorized*)

One of the prettiest sights in a German bakery window is the *Käse Kuchen*, the jewel-glazed flat German cheesecake with a pretty filling of fruit. However, while the bakery *Käse Kuchen* is apt to be fattening, not so our Slim Gourmet version.

Hurry-up cooks can, by opening up a can of fruit pie filling, cheat a little on the filling without adding too many extra calories. Canned fruit fillings aren't as fattening as other convenience products because they're not very, very sweet. Look for the least-sweet brand you can find—the less sugar, the fewer calories.

CHEESECAKE:
- 3 **eggs plus 1 egg white**
  Pinch of salt
- 1 **container (12 ounces) uncreamed cottage cheese**
- 5 **tablespoons skim milk or buttermilk**
- 2 **tablespoons lemon juice**
- 2 **teaspoons vanilla extract**
- 5 **tablespoons granulated sugar**
  Sugar substitute equal to ¼ cup sugar (optional)

PEACH TOPPING:
- 2 **peaches, peeled and thinly sliced**
- ¾ **cup (6 ounces) unsweetened apple or white grape juice**
- 1½ **teaspoons arrowroot or cornstarch**
- 2 **tablespoons sugar or equivalent sugar substitute**

Separate the egg yolks into your blender and the egg whites, along with the extra white, into a nonplastic mixing bowl. Add a pinch of salt to the egg whites and beat until stiff peaks form. Set aside.

Put the remaining cake ingredients into the blender with the egg yolks and blend until smooth and creamy, then pour into the egg whites. Gently but thoroughly fold together, with an up-and-down circular motion. Don't mix the air out of the egg whites.

Spoon into a 9-inch nonstick round or square cake pan. Bake in a pre-heated 350-degree oven for 40 to 50 minutes, until a knife inserted in the center comes out clean. Cool, in the pan, before adding the topping.

When the cake has thoroughly cooled, arrange the peaches on top in overlapping rows. Combine remaining ingredients in a saucepan; cook, stirring, until thickened. Pour over the peaches and chill. *Eight servings, 128 calories each with sugar in topping; 116 without.*

⊷ APPLE PUDDING CAKE ⊷

- 2 **apples**
- 1 **cup self-rising flour**
- 5 **tablespoons granulated sugar**
- 1 **egg**
- ½ **cup cold water**
- 3 **tablespoons brown sugar**
  Sugar substitute equal to 3 tablespoons sugar
- ¼ **teaspoon apple-pie spice**
- ½ **teaspoon ground cinnamon**
- 1 **cup boiling water**

Peel the apples, then slice them into the bottom of a 9-inch round or square cake pan.

Combine the flour, 2 tablespoons of the sugar, egg, and cold water in a mixing bowl. Beat for 1 minute with an electric mixer, then spoon over the apples.

Combine the remaining granulated sugar, brown sugar, sugar substitute, and spices. Sprinkle the mixture over the batter, then pour on the boiling water in a thin stream.

Bake in a preheated 375-degree oven for 30 minutes. To serve, cut a square or wedge of cake, then spoon on the warm "apple pudding sauce" from the pan. *Nine servings, 117 calories each.*

◄§ DIETER'S BRANDIED FRUITCAKE SQUARES ఢ►

Here's a holiday dessert even dieters can enjoy: our Slim Gourmet fruitcake squares.

This delightful, easy-do "fruitcake" has an amiably moist, brandy-soaked taste and texture, without the brandy calories. The alcohol evaporates as it bakes, leaving only the tipsy flavor.

Instead of sugared, preserved fruit, we make our dieter's dessert with canned fruit cocktail, the kind that contains no added sugar. Juice-packed fruit cocktail is only 260 calories a 16-ounce can, compared with 400 calories or more for fruit canned in fattening syrup.

The base is graham-cracker crumbs, the packaged kind that are already crushed. Or, you can make your own crumbs from whole graham crackers. The easiest way is to put the crackers in your covered blender container, a few at a time, and blend on high speed until you have enough. Graham crackers can also be placed in a plastic bag and crushed into crumbs with a rolling pin. However, this is much more time consuming, because the crumbs must be rolled very fine to be used as a cake batter. Packaged crumbs are about 330 calories.

To sweeten our cake, we use a combination of honey and low-calorie sugar substitute. We prefer the granulated type for this recipe, but any type can be used (check label for equivalent).

If you are preparing your own graham-cracker crumbs from honey-flavored graham crackers, omit the honey called for in the recipe. This dessert contains no added sugar, flour, or fat.

1 egg, separated
1⅓ cups packaged graham-cracker crumbs
2 tablespoons honey
Sugar substitute equal to 2 tablespoons sugar
2 tablespoons plain brandy
½ teaspoon pumpkin-pie spice
1 teaspoon grated orange rind (optional)
¾ teaspoon baking powder
1 can (16 ounces) juice-packed fruit cocktail, undrained
½ teaspoon salt
3 tablespoons seedless raisins
3 tablespoons chopped walnuts (optional)

Combine the egg yolk, graham-cracker crumbs, honey, sugar substitute, brandy, spice, orange rind, and baking powder. Add the juice from the canned fruit and stir until smooth.

Combine the salt and egg white and whip until stiff. Gently but thoroughly fold the egg white into the batter, then carefully fold in the fruit cocktail, raisins, and walnuts.

Spoon into a small 8-inch square cake pan with a nonstick surface and bake in a preheated 350-degree oven for 35 to 40 minutes. Allow to cool thoroughly before cutting into squares. *Nine servings, 111 calories each without nuts; 126 with.*

✍ ORANGE SPICE CAKE ❧

¼ cup brown sugar
Sugar substitute equal to ¼ cup sugar
5 tablespoons soft butter or margarine
1 egg
1¼ cups unsifted all-purpose flour
5 tablespoons currants or raisins
2 teaspoons baking powder
½ teaspoon baking soda
1 teaspoon ground cinnamon
1 teaspoon orange extract
⅔ cup fresh orange juice
2 tablespoons chopped walnuts

Combine the sugar, sugar substitute, butter, and egg in a mixing bowl. Beat for 2 minutes at high speed. Add the flour, currants, baking powder, soda, cinnamon, and orange extract, and orange juice and beat at low speed for 1 minute. Pour into an 8- or 9-inch square or round nonstick baking pan.

Sprinkle the top with the nuts and bake in a preheated 350-degree oven for 25 to 30 minutes. Serve warm or cool. *Nine servings, 169 calories each.*

NOTE: You may top this cake with peeled orange slices and the following Spiced Topping, if desired.

SPICED TOPPING:

1 **envelope low-calorie whipped topping mix**
2 **tablespoons brown sugar**
½ **cup cold water**
⅛ **teaspoon pumpkin-pie spice**
1 **teaspoon grated orange rind**

Combine all the ingredients and beat according to package instructions until light and fluffy. *Two cups, 10 calories per tablespoon.*

⊷ PINEAPPLE UPSIDE-DOWN CAKE ∂⊷

TOPPING:

1 **tablespoon diet margarine**
1 **tablespoon free-pouring brown sugar**
1½ **cups drained crushed low-calorie pineapple**

BATTER:

1 **cup sifted cake flour**
1½ **teaspoons baking powder**
½ **teaspoon salt**
2 **eggs, separated**
7 **tablespoons granulated white or free-pouring brown sugar**
  Sugar substitute equal to ½ cup sugar
6 **tablespoons hot water**
1½ **teaspoons vanilla extract**
  Pinch of cream of tartar

Butter the bottom of a 10-inch cake pan with the diet margarine and sprinkle with the brown sugar. Add the drained pineapple.

Sift the flour, baking powder, and salt together. Beat the egg yolks, sugar, and sweetener until thick and light. Beat in the hot water, and vanilla, then beat in the flour mixture, a little at a time.

Add the cream of tartar to the egg whites and beat until stiff. Fold into the batter. Pour the batter over the pineapple and bake in a preheated 350-degree oven for 35 minutes. Cool for 10 minutes, then invert on a serving plate. *Ten servings, 150 calories each with all sugar; 110 with part sugar and part sugar substitute.*

ᥬ PUMPKIN BUNDT CAKE ᥬ

6 eggs, separated
10⅔ tablespoons diet margarine
1 cup plain canned pumpkin
⅔ cup firmly packed brown sugar
Sugar substitute equal to ¾ cup sugar
2 teaspoons pumpkin-pie spice
2¼ cups sifted cake flour
1 tablespoon baking powder
½ teaspoon salt
½ teaspoon cream of tartar

In a mixing bowl, combine the egg yolks, diet margarine, pumpkin, brown sugar, sugar substitute, and spice. Beat until smooth. Sift the flour and baking powder together and gradually add to the batter, beating smooth after each addition.

In another mixing bowl, combine the egg whites, salt, and cream of tartar and beat with an electric mixer until stiff peaks form. Fold the cake batter gently into the egg whites until mixed. Turn into a Bundt pan or 10-inch tube pan and bake in a preheated 325-degree oven for 1 hour. Invert the pan to cool. *Sixteen servings, 145 calories each.*

ᥬ MYSTERY SPICE CAKE ᥬ

Low-calorie canned pumpkin gives this loaf cake a delightfully moist texture and a fascinating "what-is-it" flavor that will leave your family guessing!

½ container (8 tablespoons) diet margarine
½ cup granulated white or free-pouring brown sugar
Sugar substitute equal to ½ cup sugar
2 large eggs
1 cup plain canned pumpkin (*not* pie filling)
1 teaspoon ground cinnamon
1½ cups unsifted cake flour
2 teaspoons baking powder
¼ teaspoon baking soda
¼ teaspoon salt
¼ cup raisins

Combine the margarine, sugar, sugar substitute, eggs, pumpkin, and cinnamon in a mixing bowl and beat until smooth. Stir the flour, baking powder, soda, and salt together. Add to the pumpkin mixture and beat until smooth. Stir in the raisins. Scrape out every bit of batter into a nonstick loaf pan and bake in a preheated 350-degree oven for 30 to 35 minutes. *Twelve servings, 145 calories each.*

Diet-Wise Tricks with Cake Mixes

•§ Packaged mixes will produce bigger cakes—more slices at fewer calories —if you separate the eggs called for and whip the egg whites stiff. Combine the mix, water, and yolks according to package directions. Then fold the beaten egg whites into the batter as a final step before baking. An extra egg white will make an even bigger cake.

•§ You can save 120 calories in every cake you bake from cake mix simply by omitting the egg yolks altogether—a good point for cholesterol watchers. Again, for a bigger cake, whip the egg whites stiff before folding into the batter.

•§ Try this. Combine a package of white cake mix with the water called for. Then fold in 4 stiffly beaten egg whites. You'll get an extra tall cake with two extra servings.

•§ To make an egg-free "yellow cake," add several drops of yellow food coloring to white cake mix.

•§ You'll make a bigger, more flavorful cake and provide extra nutrition by adding one of these protein boosters to a packaged mix: ¼ cup of low-fat soy flour . . . or ½ cup skim-milk cottage cheese . . . or a 3-ounce package of low-calorie "imitation" cream cheese or Neufchâtel cheese.

•§ You can make "half a cake" (half the calories and half the temptation!), simply by measuring out 1⅞ cupful of mix from any standard two-layer packaged mix. Then add 1 egg and half the water called for! Bake your snack cake in an 8- or 9-inch square cake pan for nine servings.

•§ Contrary to what you might think, chocolate cake mixes are not more fattening than yellow cakes; in fact, they're slightly lower. White cake mix is less yet!

•§ You can save 812 calories in a "butter recipe" cake mix simply by omitting the butter. However, even without the butter added, most "butter recipe" cake mixes are still more fattening than the same-flavor standard mix.

Here's a comparison of the calorie counts in typical mixes from major producers.

Cake Mixes, Prepared	Calories (Entire Cake)	Number of Slices	Calories (Per Slice)
Angel	1,600	16	100
Chiffon type	2,320	16	145
Gingerbread	1,539	9	171
White	2,280	12	190
Sour cream	2,340	12	195
Chocolate types	2,388	12	199
Lemon, orange, pineapple, etc.	2,400	12	200
Yellow	2,424	12	202
Spice types	2,460	12	205
Pound cake	2,520	12	210
Upside-down	2,430	9	270
"Butter recipe"	3,240	12	270

HAPPY BIRTHDAY CHOCOLATE LAYER CAKE

CAKE:

1 package chocolate cake mix
    Pinch of cream of tartar or salt
4 egg whites
1½ cups cold water

FROSTING:

1 package (2 envelopes) low-calorie whipped topping mix
1½ cups cold water
2 teaspoons vanilla extract
1 envelope (4 servings) instant chocolate pudding mix
    Pinch of salt
    Sugar substitute equal to ¼ cup sugar

To prepare the cake, ignore the package directions that call for two eggs. Instead, sprinkle cream of tartar or salt on the 4 egg whites and whip them until stiff peaks form. Add the water to the cake mix and beat with an electric mixer for 3 to 4 minutes. Carefully fold the egg whites into the cake batter. Divide the batter into 2 10-inch round, nonstick cake pans and bake for 25 to 30 minutes in a preheated 350-degree oven. Cool on wire racks before frosting.

To prepare the frosting, combine all the ingredients in a large bowl and whip with an electric mixer for 2 minutes. *One very large layer cake, sixteen servings—and only 197 calories each.*

⊷§   GINGER-RICH LOAF CAKE   §⊷

With our Slim Gourmet alterations to a gingerbread mix, you'll produce a richly textured, subtly spiced loaf cake with a far superior flavor. Superior nutrition, too—because this version cuts calories while boosting protein four and one-half times.

1   **egg**
½   **cup low-fat cottage cheese**
½   **cup warm water**
2   **tablespoons granulated sugar or equivalent sugar substitute**
    (**optional**)
1   **package gingerbread cake mix**

Combine all the ingredients except the cake mix in your blender. Cover and beat on high speed until smooth, then uncover and add the cake mix, a little at a time, while the blender continues to run. Turn off the blender and scrape down the sides with a rubber spatula. Turn on the blender and beat only until smooth.

Pour the batter into a nonstick loaf pan and bake in a preheated 350-degree oven for 30 minutes, until a cake tester comes out clean. May be served slightly warm or at room temperature. *Sixteen servings, 115 calories each.*

NOTE: The flavor of this cake is rich enough for it to stand alone. However, low-calorie sliced peaches, canned or fresh, make a nice dress-up. Or try this protein-rich topping:

TANGY TOPPING:
1   **cup low-fat cottage cheese**
2   **teaspoons vanilla extract**
¼   **cup skim milk**
2   **tablespoons granulated sugar or equivalent sugar substitute**

Whip all the ingredients in the blender until smooth and creamy. Chill. Spoon on individual slices of cake at serving time. (Great on fruit, too!) *Only 15 calories per tablespoon with sugar; 10 without.*

⊷§   CHOCOLATE SPICE SQUARES   §⊷

1   **package gingerbread cake mix**
1   **package (8 servings) low-calorie chocolate pudding mix**
¼   **teaspoon ground cinnamon**
1   **cup water**

Combine all the ingredients in a mixing bowl. Beat with an electric mixer for 1 minute at medium speed, scraping the sides often, then pour into a rectangular 13-inch nonstick cake pan and bake in a preheated 350-degree oven for 25 to 35 minutes. Allow to cool slightly or chill, then cut into squares. *Sixteen servings, 109 calories each.*

21
COOKIES

If you're weight-wary, your supermarket cookie aisle is enemy territory, a no-man's land of slithery tempters ready to invade your home and subvert the most steely-willed slimmers. A well-stocked cookie jar can leak countless uncounted calories into everyone's diet, because most cookies seem hardly worth bothering about. Yet, two or three can add up to more than a slice of cake.

Did you know that a fig bar is 71 calories? A chocolate marshmallow cookie is 95 calories? Or that pecan shortbread is 77 calories, oatmeal cookies are 76, and fudge cookies are 99 calories?

Are there any bargains on the cookie shelf? A few—gingersnaps at 15 calories, animal crackers at 11, vanilla wafers and arrowroot cookies at 18, chocolate wafers at 30, and small graham crackers at 17.

The best policy is to limit yourself to two, coupled with a glass of skim milk or some fresh fruit.

⋗ APPLESAUCE-RAISIN COOKIES ⋖

Raisins can add their own special sweetness to calorie-reduced snacks.

1¾ cups all-purpose flour
½ teaspoon salt
2 teaspoons pumpkin-pie spice
1 teaspoon baking soda
1 stick (8 tablespoons) margarine or butter
⅓ cup brown sugar
1 tablespoon liquid sweetener
1 egg
1 cup unsweetened applesauce
1 cup plain bran cereal
5 tablespoons raisins

Sift together the flour, salt, spice, and baking soda. Cream together the margarine, sugar, sweetener, and egg and beat until fluffy. Beat in the sifted ingredients and applesauce, then fold in the bran and raisins. Drop by teaspoonfuls, 1 inch apart, on ungreased cookie sheets. Bake for 8 to 10 minutes at 375 degrees. *One hundred cookies, 24 calories each.*

⋗ ORANGE MACAROONS ⋖

2 egg whites
Pinch of salt
Pinch of cream of tartar
2 teaspoons grated orange rind
1 can (7 ounces) flaked, sweetened coconut
2 tablespoons cake flour
¼ teaspoon baking powder

Using a nonplastic bowl, beat together the egg whites, salt, and cream of tartar until stiff peaks form.

Combine the orange rind, coconut, flour, and baking powder and mix well. Fold in the egg whites. Drop by the scant teaspoonful on a nonstick cookie sheet and bake in a preheated 350-degree oven for 15 to 20 minutes, until the edges are brown. Cool. *Two dozen macaroons, 27 calories each.*

⋗ RAISIN-CINNAMON COOKIES ⋖

The following recipe uses diet margarine; it makes the batter easy to cream, and the cookies chewy and soft rather than crisp.

2½ cups all-purpose flour
 1 teaspoon baking soda
 1 teaspoon salt
 1 teaspoon ground cinnamon
 2 eggs
 1 container (8 ounces) diet margarine
 ¾ cup brown sugar
    Sugar substitute equal to ¾ cup sugar
 2 teaspoons vanilla extract
 ½ cup raisins

Sift together the flour, baking soda, salt, and cinnamon. Beat the eggs and margarine until fluffy, then add all the other ingredients except the raisins and beat thoroughly. Fold in the raisins. Drop by teaspoonfuls, 1 inch apart, on ungreased cookie sheets and bake for 8 to 10 minutes at 375 degrees. *One hundred cookies, 27 calories each.*

MRS. REGAN'S SUGARLESS "SUGAR" COOKIES*

 ¼ cup oil
 3 tablespoons diet margarine, at room temperature
    Sugar substitute equal to 1 cup sugar
 1 tablespoon skim milk
 1 egg
 ½ teaspoon vanilla extract
 ½ teaspoon salt
 1 teaspoon baking powder
1½ cups all-purpose flour

Beat the oil, margarine, and sugar substitute together. Add the milk, egg, and vanilla and beat well. Sift together the salt, baking powder, and flour and blend in. Drop by teaspoonfuls, at least 3 inches apart, on nonstick cookie sheets and bake in a preheated 375-degree oven for 7 minutes. *Forty-eight cookies, 24 calories each.*

VARIATIONS

Almond-Lemon Sugar Cookies: Use ¼ teaspoon almond extract and 1 teaspoon grated lemon rind in place of the vanilla.

Rolled Cookies: Add an extra 2 tablespoons of flour to the recipe. Refrigerate for at least 1 hour, covered; then roll out on a flour-dusted surface. Cut into desired shapes and bake as directed.

 * Submitted by Mrs. H. L. Regan of Vancouver, Washington.

NOTE: To glaze those "sugar" cookies without sugar, just mix a few drops of food coloring with egg yolk and brush the tops of cookie cutouts before baking. They'll have shiny surface "icing." Don't forget that sugarless baked goods don't brown well, so don't overbake.

Chocolate Chip Cookies Without Lots of Calories

Of all the cookies to tempt us could-be fatties, there's nothing quite so irresistible as "chocolate chips." So, before you succumb to somebody else's fattening goodies, whip up your own.

TRIMMER TOLL HOUSE COOKIES

1 container (8 ounces) diet margarine
Sugar substitute equal to ⅔ cup sugar
1½ teaspoons vanilla extract
1 egg
¼ teaspoon salt
¼ teaspoon butter flavoring (optional)
1 cup plus 2 tablespoons all-purpose flour
2 teaspoons baking powder
½ cup semisweet chocolate bits
½ cup raisins

Beat the diet margarine, sugar substitute, vanilla, egg, salt, and butter flavoring until fluffy. Add the flour and baking powder and beat for 2 minutes. Stir in the chocolate and raisins, then drop from a teaspoon onto a nonstick cookie sheet. Bake at 400 degrees for 10 to 15 minutes. *Fifty cookies, 32 calories each.*

SUGAR-FREE CHOCOLATE CHIP COOKIES

½ container (4 ounces) diet margarine
2 tablespoons polyunsaturated oil
1 egg
1½ teaspoons vanilla extract
½ teaspoon butter-flavored salt
¼ cup nonfat dry milk
½ cup granulated sugar substitute
1 cup all-purpose flour
½ teaspoon baking soda
2 ounces dietetic milk chocolate, cut into ¼-inch pieces

Beat the diet margarine, oil, egg, vanilla, butter-flavored salt, nonfat dry-milk, and sugar substitute until fluffy. Add the flour and baking soda, then beat for 2 minutes. Stir in the chocolate pieces. Drop by teaspoonfuls onto nonstick cookie sheets and bake at 400 degrees for 10 to 15 minutes. *Fifty cookies, 27 calories each.*

HIGH-PROTEIN LO-CAL CHOCOLATE CHIP COOKIES

1 container (8 ounces) diet margarine
½ cup free-pouring brown sugar
  Granulated sugar substitute equal to ¾ cup sugar
2½ teaspoons vanilla extract
2 eggs
1 teaspoon salt
¾ cup low-fat soy flour (see note below)
1½ cups all-purpose flour
1 teaspoon baking soda
⅔ cup semisweet chocolate bits
5 tablespoons chopped dry-roasted peanuts

Beat together the diet margarine, sugar, sugar substitute, vanilla, eggs, and salt until fluffy. Add the soy flour, all-purpose flour, and baking soda and beat for 2 minutes. Stir in the chocolate and nuts. Drop by teaspoonfuls on non-stick cookie sheets and bake for 10 to 15 minutes at 400 degrees. *One hundred cookies, 25 calories each.*

NOTE: Low-fat soy flour is available in health-food stores.

CHOCOLATE CHIP–PEANUT BUTTER GEMS

3 tablespoons softened margarine or butter
¼ cup creamy peanut butter
2 tablespoons brown sugar
  Sugar substitute equal to ¼ cup sugar
2 eggs, beaten
1 teaspoon vanilla extract
⅔ sifted all-purpose flour
½ teaspoon baking soda
½ teaspoon baking powder
3 ounces semisweet chocolate bits

Beat together the margarine, peanut butter, and brown sugar. Add the sugar substitute, eggs, and vanilla and beat until fluffy. Sift together the flour, baking soda, and baking powder and add to the peanut butter mixture. Mix well. Fold in the chocolate chips. Drop by the level teaspoonful on nonstick cookie sheets and bake in a preheated 375-degree oven for 8 minutes. *Five dozen cookies, 26 calories each.*

Refrigerator Cookies

Did you ever bake just six cookies?

If you're a cookie snitch with a weight problem, that may be the only safe way. Bulging cookie jars are soon emptied, no matter how deep their capacity or strong your resolution.

Cookie recipes are easy to double, but they defy division. How do you cut an egg in half or thirds? What do you use to measure one-sixteenth of a teaspoon of baking soda? There's one happy exception—refrigerator cookies, the kind you shape into a log and then slice off and bake as many as you need (or dare!), even if it's only half a dozen, and chill or freeze the rest. The next time you get a cookie urge, simply slice off a few more and pop them in the oven.

⤙ PRUNEWHEEL REFRIGERATOR COOKIES ⤚

1 cup finely chopped pitted prunes
½ cup boiling water
1 container (8 ounces) diet margarine
¼ cup granulated sugar
  Sugar substitute equal to ¼ cup sugar
1 teaspoon vanilla extract
2½ cups sifted all-purpose flour
¼ teaspoon baking powder

Put the prunes in a small bowl. Pour on the boiling water and set aside.

Combine the diet margarine, sugar, sugar substitute, and vanilla in a bowl and beat with an electric mixer. Combine the flour and baking powder and add to the margarine mixture. Stir with a fork, then knead lightly until the mixture forms a ball. Flatten, wrap in waxed paper, and quick-chill in the freezer.

Roll the dough out on a lightly floured board to a rectangle 24 inches long. Spread the prune mixture over the surface of the dough. Roll up the long way to form a 24-inch roll, then wrap in waxed paper and chill thoroughly.

When firm enough to slice, cut off 1-eighth inch slices and place one inch apart on a non-stick cookie tin. Make only as many as you need and freeze the remaining roll.

Bake in a preheated oven at 375 degrees for 12 minutes. *Six dozen cookies, 29 calories each.*

⋖ CHOCOLATE DROP COOKIES ⋗

½ cup semisweet chocolate bits
 2 tablespoons diet margarine
 1 egg
½ cup plain yogurt
½ teaspoon vanilla extract
 1 cup granulated sugar substitute
 1 cup all-purpose flour
 1 teaspoon baking soda
   Pinch of salt

Melt the chocolate bits and diet margarine in a small saucepan over very low heat. Allow to cool.

In a mixer bowl, beat the egg at high speed for 2 minutes. Blend in the yogurt, vanilla, sugar substitute, and chocolate mixture until well combined. Stir the flour, soda, and salt together and add to the batter. Beat for 2 minutes, then drop by the teaspoonful, about two inches apart, on nonstick cookie sheets. Bake in a preheated 350-degree oven for 8 minutes, or until firm. *Forty-two cookies, 25 calories each.*

22
PIES,
TARTS,
AND
PASTRIES

❧ McINTOSH APPLE PIE ❧

Pies from cans and boxes and packaged pies from the bread counter have more starch and sugar and less fruit than you'd use yourself. And commercial pie crusts and mixes are frequently rich with saturated fats, the kind that are chosen for their long shelf life. But the pie crust pastry we use here is relatively low in fat, and the fat we use is cholesterol-low safflower oil. We use lots of McIntosh apples, and sweeten them partly with honey and partly with sugar substitute, a clever combo of calorie savers that sweetens so well you'll never miss the sugar calories. (McIntosh cook quicker than baking apples, so take note of the shortened baking time.)

FILLING:
  5 **McIntosh apples or baking apples**
  3 **tablespoons honey**
  5 **tablespoons granulated sugar substitute**
     Butter-flavored salt
1½ **tablespoons arrowroot or cornstarch**
     Pinch of lemon rind
  ¼ **teaspoon ground cinnamon**
  ¼ **teaspoon apple-pie spice**

SAFFLOWER CRUST:
  1 **cup self-rising flour**
  ¼ **cup safflower oil**
  2 **or 3 tablespoons water**

Pare and core the apples, then cut in large chunks; don't slice too thin. Combine the apples with all the other pie filling ingredients and stir well. Set aside while you prepare the crust.

Fork-blend the crust ingredients together, adding only as much water as needed. (This crust can be rolled immediately, no chilling needed!) Reserving one-third of the pastry for the top crust, roll out the remaining pastry as thin as possible on a lightly floured board. Line an 8-inch nonstick pie pan with the pastry and fill with the apple filling. Roll out the remaining pastry. Cover the pie with a full crust or, if you wish, cut the remaining pastry in strips and make a criss-cross latticework topping. Bake the pie in a preheated 425-degree oven for only 35 minutes. (Add 15 minutes if baking apples are used.) *Eight servings, 195 calories each.*

ᴥᶳ SLIM APPLE PIE FARMER-STYLE ᶜᴥ

Apple-cheese pie is what the farmer's wife made when she had more homemade cheese than apples—a tender-crusted pie with a fragrant filling that tasted like apples and cream, spiced with cinnamon and nutmeg. It called for less pastry and sugar than conventional double-crusted apple pie, so it was far lower in calories and richer in protein.

What you'll need is packaged "farmer cheese," a very low-moisture form of cottage cheese pressed into a brick shape and wrapped like cream cheese. Most stores carry it in the cream cheese and cottage cheese section of the dairy case. If you can't find it, substitute dry uncreamed cottage cheese from which you've pressed the excess moisture.

CHEESE PASTRY CRUST:
⅓ **cup sifted all-purpose flour**
¼ **teaspoon salt**
2 **tablespoons margarine or shortening**
4 **ounces farmer cheese**

APPLE FILLING:
2 **cups sliced apples**
1 **egg**
½ **cup skim milk**
4 **ounces farmer cheese**
1 **teaspoon vanilla extract**
Pinch of salt
½ **cup granulated sugar or equivalent sugar substitute or use half**
sugar and half sugar substitute
½ **teaspoon ground cinnamon**
¼ **teaspoon freshly grated nutmeg**

Have all the pastry crust ingredients at room temperature. Combine the flour and salt in a deep bowl, then cut in the shortening with two knives until the consistency of corn meal. Mix in the farmer cheese with a fork or pastry blender until no pastry sticks to the bowl. Chill thoroughly, then roll out between two sheets of waxed paper. Remove the upper waxed paper and invert the pastry on a 9-inch pie plate. Remove the lower sheet. This pastry is very soft; the waxed paper makes handling easier.

Arrange the sliced apples in the pie shell. Put the egg, milk, cheese, vanilla, salt, and sugar or sweetener in the blender. Cover and blend on high speed until smooth, then pour over the apples and sprinkle with the cinnamon and nutmeg. Bake in a preheated 450-degree oven for 15 minutes. Lower the heat to 325 and bake 30 minutes more, until a knife inserted in the center comes out clean. *Eight servings, 181 calories with sugar; 111 without sugar; 134 with half sugar and half sugar substitute.*

◆§ SHORT-CUT APPLE PIE ᠖◆

No time to peel apples? We use canned pie-sliced apples, the kind packed in water with no sugar or starchy fillers added. Check the label—you want *plain* apples, not "apple pie filling," which is sticky-sweet and more than double in calories.

> 1 **commercially prepared graham-cracker pie crust**
> 1½ **cans (30 ounces) unsweetened pie-sliced apples**
> ¼ **cup brown sugar**
> 6 **tablespoons granulated sugar**
> 2 **tablespoons lemon juice**
> 1 **tablespoon arrowroot**
> 2 **teaspoons apple-pie spice**
> ½ **teaspoon salt or butter-flavored salt**
> **Sugar substitute equal to ⅔ cup sugar (optional)**

Unwrap the packaged crust. Drain the apples well. Thoroughly combine the apples with all remaining ingredients and pile into the crust. Invert a lightweight metal pie pan over the pie to protect the apples from drying out and bake in a preheated 425-degree oven for 45 minutes. Cool completely before cutting. Serve chilled or at room temperature. *Eight servings, 196 calories each.*

◆§ MOCK MINCE TORTE ᠖◆

> 1 **commercially prepared graham-cracker pie crust**
> 1 **can (20 ounces) pie-sliced apples, drained and chopped**

1½ cups raisins
1 tablespoon cracker crumbs
2 teaspoons arrowroot
1 teaspoon cider vinegar
½ teaspoon salt or butter-flavored salt
1 teaspoon pumpkin-pie spice
½ teaspoon apple-pie spice
½ teaspoon brandy flavoring
1 teaspoon grated orange rind
    Sugar substitute equal to ½ cup sugar

Follow the preceding recipe, using the above filling ingredients in place of the apple filling: *Eight servings, 224 calories each.*

⋖ BANANA BAVARIAN PIE ⋗

LOW-CALORIE PIE CRUST:
½ cup all-purpose flour
    Pinch of salt
2 tablespoons polyunsaturated oil
4 teaspoons cold water

FILLING:
1 envelope (4 servings) vanilla refrigerator dessert mix
1 cup cold skim milk
1 envelope low-calorie whipped topping mix
¾ cup cold water
½ teaspoon cinnamon
2 small ripe bananas
    A few sprinkles of shaved chocolate

Make the pie crust first. Sift the all-purpose flour with a pinch of salt. Fork-blend with the oil and the ice water, then shape lightly into a ball and chill thoroughly. Roll out very thin on a floured board and put into a 9-inch pie pan. Prick bottom and sides well, then prebake in a very hot (450-degree) oven until just brown; cool before filling.

Put the cold milk in your mixer bowl or blender container. Add the vanilla refrigerator dessert mix and whip according to package directions. Add the cold water, whipped topping mix, and cinnamon. Whip on high speed until the mixture is creamy and thoroughly blended, frequently scraping down the sides of the bowl or blender container with a rubber spatula. Put the bowl or blender container in your refrigerator for 30 minutes, until the mixture begins to set.

Peel the bananas. Slice one banana very thinly onto the bottom of the prebaked pie crust. Spoon one-half of the vanilla mixture over the bananas and spread it to cover. Slice the second banana on top of the filling; spoon on the remaining filling.

Chill for several hours. Just before serving, sprinkle the edges of the pie with shaved chocolate. *Eight servings, 162 calories each.*

NOTE: To save work and calories, skip the crust and serve this Bavarian dessert in parfait glasses.

⋖§ DEEP-DISH BLUEBERRY PIE §⋗

Pastry for a one-crust pie
6 cups fresh or frozen blueberries, thawed if frozen
5 tablespoons granulated sugar
  Sugar substitute equal to ¼ cup sugar
1 teaspoon lemon juice
2 tablespoons cornstarch or arrowroot

Prepare the pastry and set aside. Combine the remaining ingredients and mix well, then spoon into a deep pie pan or casserole. Roll out the pastry on a floured board and fit over the top of the pie pan, using a fork to press the crust to the edges. Puncture the center with the tines of a fork to permit the steam to escape. Bake in a preheated 425-degree oven for 45 minutes or more, until brown. Serve warm or cool. *Eight servings, 169 calories each.*

NOTE: Diabetics and those on sugar-free diets can replace the small amount of sugar called for with additional non-caloric sweeteners.

⋖§ SKINNY BLUEBERRY COBBLER §⋗

At only 88 calories a cupful, even would-be skinnies can gorge on blueberries. You can even treat yourself to a modest dessert after dinner. A blueberry cobbler, for example. It is just as rich-tasting as the fattening kind, but this one has been calorie edited with skim milk and sugar substitute. This recipe can even be made completely sugarless—simply increase the sugar substitute accordingly.

3 cups fresh blueberries, rinsed and picked over
3 tablespoons granulated sugar
  Sugar substitute equal to ¼ cup sugar
2 tablespoons quick-cooking tapioca
¾ cup water
½ teaspoon vanilla extract
1¼ cups biscuit mix
½ cup skim milk

Combine the blueberries, sugar, sweetener, tapioca, and water in the bottom of a shallow 2-quart casserole. Sprinkle with the vanilla. Fork-blend the biscuit mix with the skim milk until evenly moistened and spoon on top of the berries. Bake in a preheated 350-degree oven for 30 to 40 minutes, until the biscuit crust is well browned. *Eight servings, 142 calories each.*

NOTE: The cobbler can be made with frozen or canned unsweetened blueberries as well.

◄§ BRANDIED PEACH CHIFFON PIE §►

    3 tablespoons diet margarine
    ½ cup graham-cracker crumbs
    1 envelope unflavored gelatin
    ¼ cup cold water
 1½ cups skim milk
    5 teaspoons granulated sugar
    ½ teaspoon salt
    3 eggs, separated
    2 teaspoons brandy flavoring
      Sugar substitute equal to 2 tablespoons sugar
    1 can (8 ounces) low-calorie sliced peaches

Grease a pie pan with the diet margarine. Sprinkle with the graham-cracker crumbs, then press them firmly to surface. Quick-bake the shell in a 450-degree oven for 8 minutes and cool before filling.

Soften the gelatin in the cold water. Combine the milk, sugar, salt, and the egg yolks, lightly beaten, in a saucepan or the top of a double-boiler. Cook and stir over a very low flame until mixture thickens slightly. Add the softened gelatin, brandy flavoring, and sweetener, stirring well. Chill until the mixture begins to set slightly.

Beat the egg whites until stiff and fold into the gelatin mixture. Drain the peaches and chop coarsely, then layer with the chiffon mixture in the prepared pie crust. Chill until firm. *Eight servings, 107 calories each.*

◄§ CRUSHED PINEAPPLE PIE §►

    ⅔ cup graham-cracker crumbs
 2½ tablespoons diet margarine
    1 can (16 ounces) juice-packed crushed pineapple, undrained
    1 envelope unflavored gelatin
    1 tablespoon lemon juice
    3 tablespoons granulated sugar or equivalent sugar substitute
    2 egg whites, at room temperature
      Pinch of salt

Fork-blend the graham-cracker crumbs with the diet margarine. Press into the sides and bottom of an 8-inch nonstick pie pan. Quick-bake in a hot (425-degree) oven for 5 to 8 minutes, then cool before filling.

Drain the pineapple juice into a small saucepan and sprinkle on the gelatin. Heat over a low flame until completely melted, then remove from the heat and stir in the pineapple, lemon juice, and a few drops of yellow food coloring, if desired. Cool completely.

In an electric mixer bowl, combine the egg whites and salt. Beat on high speed until thick and frothy. Continue to beat, adding the sugar or sugar substitute a little at a time, until the egg whites are stiff.

Gently but thoroughly fold in the pineapple mixture. Spoon into the prepared crust and chill for several hours. *Eight servings, 106 calories each with sugar; 89 with sugar substitute.*

◄§ MILE-HI PINEAPPLE PIE §►

⅔ cup graham-cracker crumbs
2½ tablespoons diet margarine
1 can (16 ounces) juice-packed crushed pineapple, chilled
1 envelope unflavored gelatin
2 tablespoons honey
 Sugar substitute equal to 3 tablespoons sugar
⅛ teaspoon yellow food coloring
¾ cup chilled evaporated skim milk
¼ teaspoon salt
1 tablespoon lemon juice

Fork-blend the graham-cracker crumbs with the diet margarine. Press into the bottom and sides of an 8-inch nonstick pie pan. Quick-bake in a hot (425-degree) oven for 5 to 8 minutes, then cool before filling.

Pour the juice from the pineapple into a saucepan and sprinkle on the gelatin. Wait 3 or 4 minutes, then heat over a low flame until the gelatin is completely dissolved. Remove from the heat and stir in the chilled pineapple, honey, sugar substitute, and food coloring. Set aside.

In an electric mixer bowl, combine the chilled evaporated milk, salt, and lemon juice. Whip on high speed until the consistency of whipped cream, then gently but thoroughly fold in the pineapple mixture. Mound into the prepared pieshell and chill for 5 or 6 hours. *Eight servings, 117 calories each.*

◄§ PINEAPPLE YOGURT "CREAM CHEESE" PIE §►

8 ounces low-calorie cream cheese or low-fat Neufchâtel cheese
8 ounces plain yogurt

½ teaspoon vanilla extract
6 tablespoons granulated sugar or equivalent sugar substitute
1 can (8 ounces) juice-packed crushed pineapple, undrained
1 envelope unflavored gelatin
  Pinch of salt (optional)
1 commercially prepared graham-cracker crust

Combine the cream cheese, yogurt, vanilla, and sweetener in the blender; cover and blend until smooth. Drain the pineapple, reserving ¼ cup of the juice. Sprinkle the gelatin on the pineapple juice in a small saucepan. Wait a minute, then heat over a low flame until the gelatin is dissolved. Add to the blender and blend until smooth. Stir in the pineapple by hand, then pour the mixture into the prepared pie crust and chill for several hours. *Eight servings, 182 calories each with sugar; 147 without.*

◆§ SUNNY PUMPKIN PIE §◆

Canned pumpkin (now available any time of the year) and fresh orange juice add to the nutrition of this calorie-reduced dessert. Like all yellow fruits and vegetables, pumpkin is particularly rich in vitamin A. One slice of this pie provides more than one-third of your daily requirement.

You need only half an envelope of instant pudding mix to prepare this dessert. You can save the other half to make another pie another day—or make two pies and tuck the other one away in your freezer for the future.

¾ cup orange juice
1 envelope unflavored gelatin
½ cup boiling water
1 cup plain canned pumpkin (*not* pie filling)
½ envelope (¼ cup) instant vanilla pudding mix
1½ teaspoons pumpkin-pie spice
½ teaspoon ground cinnamon
  Dash of butter salt
2 tablespoons granulated sugar
  Sugar substitute equal to ¼ cup sugar
1 commercially prepared 8-inch graham-cracker crust

Combine 2 tablespoons of the orange juice and the gelatin in your blender container. Wait a minute for the gelatin to soften, then pour on the boiling water. Cover and blend on high speed, until all the gelatin granules are dissolved. Add the remaining orange juice, and all the other ingredients— except, of course, the crumb crust. Blend until smooth. Chill for 15 minutes in the refrigerator, then spoon into the prepared crumb crust. Chill for several hours, until firm. *Eight servings, 143 calories each.*

◄§ PUMPKIN CREAM CHEESE PIE §►

LOW-FAT PIE CRUST:

½ **cup all-purpose flour**
   Pinch of salt
2 **tablespoons corn oil**
4 **teaspoons ice water**

FILLING:

8 **ounces low-calorie cream cheese or low-fat Neufchâtel cheese**
3 **large eggs**
1 **cup plain canned pumpkin (*not* pie filling)**
2 **tablespoons skim milk**
1 **tablespoon vanilla extract**
2 **teaspoons pumpkin-pie spice**
   Pinch of salt
   Sugar substitute equal to ¼ cup sugar
¼ **cup granulated sugar**

Fork-blend all the pie crust ingredients together and knead into a flat ball. Chill thoroughly before rolling. Roll very thin, then line your pie pan and crimp the edges. Set aside while you prepare the filling.

Combine all the filling ingredients in the blender and blend until smooth. Pour into prepared crust and bake in a preheated 275-degree oven for 1 hour. Chill before serving. *Eight servings, 174 calories each.*

◄§ SLIMMED-DOWN KEY LIME PIE §►

Many key lime pie recipes are made with sweetened condensed milk as their base. This sugar-rich milk is over 1,300 calories a can. But our adaptation uses evaporated skim milk—only 287 calories a can, and very little butterfat. Our recipe is also made without eggs or egg yolks, so this key lime pie is cholesterol safe.

For the best flavor, make this pie with freshly squeezed lime juice, if possible. Unsweetened bottled lime juice may be substituted. Don't be tempted to tint the filling with food coloring. Key lime pie is never served green!

This is a refrigerator-style pie, made with a packaged graham-cracker crust, available in most supermarkets. For an even lower-calorie treat, skip the crust and follow our directions for Key Lime Parfaits (page 346).

1 **tablespoon unflavored gelatin**
⅓ **cup lime juice**

1 cup boiling water
  Sugar substitute equal to ¼ cup sugar
1 can (13 ounces) evaporated skim milk, chilled
¼ cup cold water
1 envelope (4 servings) instant vanilla pudding mix
  Pinch of grated lime rind (optional)
1 commercially prepared graham-cracker crust
  Thin lime slices and prepared low-calorie whipped topping (see
    p. 366) for garnish

In the blender, combine the gelatin and lime juice. Wait one minute until softened, then add the boiling water. Cover and blend on high speed until all the gelatin granules are dissolved. Add the sugar substitute, evaporated skim milk, cold water, pudding mix, and grated lime rind. Cover and blend until smooth, then chill in the refrigerator for about 20 minutes, until the mixture begins to set.

Spoon the mixture into the prepared pie shell and chill for several hours until firm. The pie may be garnished with lime slices and prepared low-calorie whipped topping, if desired. *Eight servings, 175 calories each, without the garnish; 181 with.*

⋖ RHUBARB MERINGUE PIE ⋗

ONE-CRUST PASTRY:
½ cup all-purpose flour
  Pinch of salt
2 tablespoons polyunsaturated oil
4 teaspoons cold water

FILLING:
2 cups diced fresh rhubarb
5 tablespoons granulated sugar
2 tablespoons all-purpose flour
2 egg yolks
¼ teaspoon baking soda
1 teaspoon vanilla extract

MERINGUE:
2 egg whites
  Pinch of salt
  Pinch of cream of tartar
10 teaspoons confectioners' sugar

Fork-blend all the pastry ingredients, then knead lightly until the pastry forms a ball. Flatten and chill thoroughly, then roll out on a lightly floured board.

Line a 9-inch pie pan with the pastry and add the rhubarb. Combine the sugar, flour, egg yolks, soda, and vanilla extract and beat together. Spoon on top of the rhubarb and bake in a preheated 400-degree oven for 20 minutes.

Meanwhile, prepare the meringue topping. Combine the egg whites with a pinch of salt and a pinch of cream of tartar. Whip until thick and frothy, then beat in the 10 teaspoons confectioners' sugar, one at a time, until stiff and glossy.

Remove the pie from the oven and cool, then spoon on the meringue, making sure you touch the crust on all sides so the meringue won't shrink. Bake an additional 20 minutes at 300 degrees. Chill and serve. *Eight servings, 120 calories each.*

❧ NO-BAKE CREAM CHEESE PIE ❧

Here's a super-quickie "cream cheese pie" that's extra easy to make with your blender. It's ready in less time than it takes to defrost store-bought frozen ones, and is less than half of the 450 calories a slice those thaw-and-serve ones have.

1   **envelope unflavored gelatin**
¼   **cup boiling water**
2   **cups cold skim milk**
8   **ounces low-fat Neufchâtel cheese**
1   **envelope (4 servings) instant vanilla pudding mix**
    Juice of 1 lemon
3   **tablespoons diet margarine**
½   **cup graham-cracker crumbs**

Empty the gelatin into your blender and add the boiling water. Blend on high speed until thoroughly dissolved. Scrape down the sides of the container with a rubber spatula, then add the milk and cheese and blend on high speed until smooth and creamy. While the blender is still running, add the pudding mix and lemon juice, a little at a time, until thoroughly blended. Refrigerate until partially set.

Meanwhile, prepare the crust. Grease the inside surfaces of an 8- or 9-inch pie tin with the diet margarine. Sprinkle on the crumbs and press into the surface. Bake in a preheated hot 425-degree oven for 6 to 8 minutes, until the crust is brown; be careful it doesn't burn. When cool, fill with the cheese mixture. Serve well chilled. *Eight servings, 185 calories per serving.*

VARIATION

Sugarless No-Bake Cream Cheese Pie: If you're on a sugar-free regime you can still enjoy this recipe, using dietetic pudding mix instead of instant pudding. But the diet pudding needs precooking, so prepare your pie this way. Put the milk and water in a saucepan and stir in the pudding and gelatin. Cook and stir over low heat until the mixture simmers and thickens. Pour the hot pudding mixture into your blender and add the lemon juice and cheese. Add a pinch of salt and beat on high speed until blended. Cool before filling the crust. *Eight servings, 156 calories each.*

৺ BLENDER-EASY CREAM CHEESE PIE ৵

12 graham crackers
    Pinch of ground cinnamon
 3 tablespoons diet margarine
 2 eggs
    Juice of ½ lemon
    Small piece of lemon peel (about 1 inch square)
¼ teaspoon butter-flavored salt
    Sugar substitute equal to ½ cup sugar
 5 tablespoons granulated sugar
1½ packages (12 ounces) low-calorie cream cheese or low-fat
    Neufchâtel cheese

Blend the graham crackers in a covered blender container, a few at a time, until all are processed into fine crumbs. Mix with the cinnamon and diet margarine and press into the bottom and sides of an 8-inch nonstick pie pan. Reserve.

Wash out the blender container, then blend the remaining ingredients, covered, until smooth. Spoon into the pieshell and bake for 45 to 50 minutes in a preheated 350-degree oven. Chill before serving. *Eight servings, 186 calories each.*

৺ STREAMLINED CHEESE PIE WITH EASY BERRY GLAZE ৵

This Slim Gourmet pie is a calorie-reduced, protein-rich treat made with fresh berries and the new low-calorie "imitation" cream cheese. These high-protein cream cheese substitutes have only half the calories of ordinary cream cheese, but the flavor is practically identical.

In addition to cutting calories, we use all sorts of hurry-up tricks to ease the preparation of this busy-day dessert. We use a commercially prepared graham-cracker crust, and prepare the filling entirely in the blender.

FILLING:

1 tablespoon vanilla extract
1 envelope unflavored gelatin
½ cup boiling water
8 ounces low-calorie cream cheese or low-fat Neufchâtel cheese
3 tablespoons granulated sugar
  Sugar substitute equal to ¼ cup sugar
¼ teaspoon salt or butter-flavored salt
½ teaspoon grated lemon or orange rind
1 cup ice cubes

CRUST:

1 commercially prepared 8-inch graham-cracker crust

TOPPING:

½ envelope unflavored gelatin
¾ cup red grape juice, well chilled
1 cup sliced strawberries, well chilled
  Sugar substitute equal to 2 tablespoons sugar

Start with the filling. Combine the vanilla and gelatin in the blender. Wait 1 minute, until the gelatin granules are softened, then add the boiling water. Cover and blend on high speed until all gelatin is dissolved, scraping down the sides of the container often. Add the cream cheese, sugar, sugar substitute, salt, and lemon or orange rind. Cover and blend until smooth, then add the ice cubes and blend on high speed until all the ice is dissolved.

Spoon the filling into the prepared crumb crust; it will have started to set already. Store the pie in the freezer while you prepare the strawberry glaze.

Combine the gelatin with 2 tablespoons of the grape juice in a small saucepan and heat over a very low flame until the granules dissolve.

In a small bowl, combine the gelatin mixture, chilled berries, sugar substitute, and remaining chilled grape juice. Put in the freezer for about 10 minutes, until the mixture is slightly thickened and syrupy, then stir well and spoon over the cream cheese filling. Store the pie in the refrigerator until serving time. *Eight servings, 183 calories each.*

⋖§ CHOCOLATE CREAM CHEESE PIE §∾

Chocolate! The first cook who named it "devil's food" knew whereof he or she spoke. At 143 calories an ounce, chocolate is truly the dieter's downfall.

But there are times when a body simply must have something chocolate— rich and sweet and creamy and *chocolate!* That's the time to head for your Slim Gourmet recipes. Stripped away from this recipe are unneeded extra fat, sugar, and starch calories, while nutrition is boosted with protein—powdered eggs, milk, and cheese.

  2 **tablespoons diet margarine**
 ½ **cup graham-cracker crumbs or chocolate wafer crumbs**
  8 **ounces low-calorie cream cheese or low-fat Neufchâtel cheese**
  8 **ounces low-fat cottage cheese**
 ¼ **cup skim milk**
  3 **eggs**
  3 **level tablespoons plain cocoa**
 ¼ **cup sugar**
    Sugar substitute equal to ¼ cup sugar
  1 **tablespoon vanilla extract**
 ½ **teaspoon ground cinnamon**

Spread the inside of an 8- or 9-inch pie pan with the diet margarine and sprinkle with the crumbs. Press firmly into place. Chill or, if you prefer, quick-bake in a hot oven for 5 or 6 minutes.

Combine the remaining ingredients in the blender and beat until smooth. Pour into the pie shell. Bake in a preheated 225-degree oven for 1 hour, then chill. *Eight servings, 168 calories each.*

⊷ OPEN-FACED PEACH TART ⊶

Even convenience foods can be diet-wise in the hands of a low-calorie cook. Refrigerator rolls, for example. With dinner, they're just extra bread, sponging up butter calories. However, those handy rolls-in-a-can are a dandy stand-in for pastry, the perfect base for turning low-calorie fruit into a spectacular dessert that only seems fattening.

Here we use them to make an open-faced fruit tart—less than 100 calories a serving. A conventional slice of peach pie can be 400 or more.

  1 **can (4 ounces) refrigerator crescent rolls**
  2 **cans (16 ounces each) low-calorie sliced peaches, undrained**
  1 **envelope unflavored gelatin**
 ½ **cup cold water**
 ¼ **cup granulated sugar**
    Sugar substitute equal to ¼ cup sugar (optional)

Break open the canned rolls and unroll the dough flat. Place in a nonstick 8- or 9-inch square cake pan and spread thin with the tips of your fingers, so that the entire bottom of the pan is covered with dough. Bake in a preheated 350-degree oven for 12 minutes or more, until brown. Remove and cool.

Drain the peaches, reserving the juice. Arrange the peaches neatly in 4 rows on top of the baked crust, all slices facing the same direction.

Sprinkle the gelatin on top of the cold water in a saucepan. Heat over a very low flame until the gelatin melts. Combine the gelatin mixture, sugar, and reserved peach juice, stirring in the sugar substitute if a sweeter dessert is desired. Chill in the refrigerator or freezer for 20 to 30 minutes, until the liquid thickens slightly. Spoon this glaze over the peaches, only enough to thoroughly cover. Chill for several hours before cutting into squares. *Nine servings, 90 calories each.*

⋗ BLUEBERRY TARTLETS ⋖

The following easy-do dessert makes the most of fresh berries. Use packaged baked tart shells, the kind with a cookie-type texture. (Frozen pie-crust-type patty shells are considerably higher in calories.)

½ **jar low-sugar or sugarless apricot preserves**
1 **tablespoon water**
2 **cups fresh blueberries, rinsed and picked over**
8 **packaged pastry tart shells**

Combine the preserves and water in a small saucepan and melt slowly over low heat. Gently stir in the fresh berries until well coated. Pile the berries into the tart shells and chill thoroughly before serving. *Eight servings, 187 calories each with low-sugar preserves; 168 with sugarless preserves.*

⋗ APPLE ROLL ⋖
(*Mock Strudel*)

Strudel pastry is a Hungarian delight which calls for kneading and stretching egg dough until it's thin as a butterfly wing. The dough is liberally buttered and wrapped around a filling of sugared fruit. If you're counting calories as I mention ingredients, you're probably getting the impression that strudel is not for would-be skinnies!

Unless you're a Slim Gourmet—then you can roll out a mock strudel that's less than half the calories. And you can do it in 10 minutes or less.

DOUGH:
1 **cup all-purpose flour**
1 **small egg**
2 **tablespoons diet margarine**
1 **teaspoon granulated sugar**
2 **tablespoons water**
½ **teaspoon salt**

APPLE FILLING:
2 **cups thinly sliced apples**
5 **tablespoons granulated sugar**

¼ teaspoon salt
1 teaspoon liquid sweetener (optional; see note below)
¼ cup chopped almonds

Put all the dough ingredients in a deep bowl and fork-blend together to distribute egg evenly. Knead lightly to form a sticky dough. Roll out very thin on a well-floured board or pastry cloth, using a floured roller. Place the dough carefully on a nonstick baking sheet and reserve while you prepare the filling.

Combine the apples, sugar, and salt; add sweetener if you wish.

Sprinkle the center third, lengthwise, of the dough with chopped almonds. Place the apple mixture on the almonds, then fold the outer two-thirds dough over the apple filling, overlapping on top. Crimp or fold the ends. Bake in a preheated 375-degree oven for 45 minutes, or until well-browned and the apples are tender. Serve warm or cool. *Eight servings, 147 calories each.*

NOTE: Prepared with 5 tablespoons of sugar, this dessert is deliciously tart. If you prefer extra sweetness without extra calories, add the no-calorie sweetener. By combining real sugar and sugar substitute, you sweeten with fewer calories and no-tip-off aftertaste.

⊷ CHOCOLATE ÉCLAIRS ⊶

Actually some less-spectacular merchandise is a lot more fattening than chocolate éclairs: ordinary apple pie, for example, is 405 calories a slice, according to government food figures. Chocolate layer cake is a fat and fudgy 445. Éclairs, by comparison, are about 270 calories apiece, and rich with egg-yolk protein. But if you can't afford even 270 calories, make our fancy-looking éclairs at half the calories. The little pastry puffs are a snap to make and only 68 calories apiece, and you can fill them with fresh berries, diet pudding, or low-fat ice milk if you don't have the ambition to make éclairs.

PASTRY:
½ cup water
2 tablespoons polyunsaturated oil
½ cup sifted all-purpose flour
½ teaspoon salt
2 large eggs

CUSTARD FILLING:
1½ cups skim milk
1½ tablespoons cornstarch
¼ teaspoon salt
¼ cup granulated sugar or equivalent sugar substitute
2 egg yolks, beaten
½ teaspoon vanilla extract

CHOCOLATE GLAZE:
   2 **teaspoons unsweetened cocoa**
   5 **tablespoons confectioners' sugar**
   1 **tablespoon hot water or black coffee, more if necessary**

Start with the pastry. Put the water and oil in a saucepan and heat to boiling. Add the flour and salt and beat, then remove from the heat and beat in the eggs, one at a time.

Spoon the batter onto a nonstick cookie sheet. Shape into strips 3-inches long, about 3-inches apart, and bake in a preheated 375-degree oven for 45 minutes. Cool thoroughly while you make the filling.

Heat the milk over a high flame until a skin forms on the surface. Add the cornstarch, salt, and sugar and beat well. Remove from the heat and add the beaten egg yolks very slowly, stirring constantly. Cook over a very low flame (or in a double-boiler) until thick. Stir in the vanilla and cool.

While the filling is cooling, make the glaze. Combine the cocoa and confectioners' sugar. Stir in the hot water or black coffee, adding more, if needed, until the glaze reaches the desired spreading consistency.

Slit open the éclairs and fill; top with the glaze. *One éclair, with filling and chocolate glaze, is 135 calories with sugar; 115 calories with sugar substitute.*

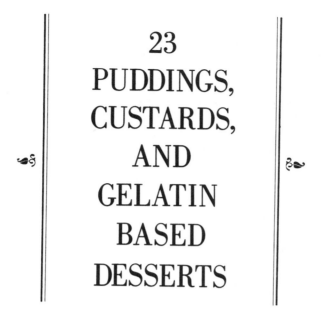

23
PUDDINGS, CUSTARDS, AND GELATIN BASED DESSERTS

◄§ CALORIE-REDUCED CHOCOLATE PUDDING §►

No-cook "instant" pudding mixes can be a boon to busy homemakers. Too bad their excessive sugar content makes them off-limits to conscientious calorie counters.

However, we've come up with a great way to str-r-r-etch those easy-do mixes so that one package serves twice as many, at half the calories. There's no niggling on nutrition, because our blender-easy method includes just as much milk—and more protein—than instant pudding prepared the usual way. Our pudding has a rich taste and soft creamy texture, and is only 97 calories a serving instead of 195 or more, prepared according to package directions.

> 1 envelope unflavored gelatin
> 2 tablespoons cold water
> 1½ cups boiling water
> 1 level tablespoon instant coffee (optional)
> Sugar substitute equal to ¼ cup sugar (optional)
> 1⅓ cups nonfat dry milk
> 2 cups cold water
> 1 envelope (4 servings) instant chocolate pudding mix

Sprinkle the gelatin on the cold water in the blender. Wait 1 minute to soften, then add the boiling water, cover, and blend until the gelatin granules are dissolved. Add the remaining ingredients in the order given to minimize risk of blender spill-over. Pour into a bowl or serving glasses and chill for several hours. *Eight servings, 97 calories each.*

NOTE: You can vary this pudding lots of ways. Use 1½ teaspoons rum, brandy or chocolate flavoring in place of instant coffee. Or, use a 1-quart envelope of sugar-free chocolate milk mix (available in some areas) in place of the nonfat dry milk. Or prepare a vanilla pudding by using instant vanilla pudding mix in place of chocolate and eliminating the instant coffee. For coffee pudding, use vanilla pudding mix and increase the coffee to two table-spoons.

⤏ CHOCOLATE POTS DE CRÈME ⤎

1 envelope (4 servings) dark chocolate pudding mix
½ cup evaporated skim milk
1¼ cups black coffee
1 egg yolk, beaten
 Few drops brandy or vanilla extract
 "Whipped Cream" (see below, optional)

Combine the pudding, milk, and coffee in a saucepan and cook, stirring, over moderate heat until thickened. Remove from the heat. Add the egg slowly to the pudding mixture, beating vigorously, then return to the heat and cook, stirring, for one minute more; stir in the extract. Pour in custard cups and chill. Top each serving with 1 tablespoon of evaporated milk "whipped cream" if desired. *Four servings, 148 calories each with "whipped cream"; 136 without.*

Sugarless Chocolate Pots de Crème: Substitute 1 envelope diet chocolate pudding mix for the regular pudding mix. Add a pinch of salt. *Only 64 calories per serving.*

"Whipped Cream": Chill evaporated skim milk in your freezer until ice crystals begin to form. Have the bowl and beaters icy-chilled, too. Whip on high speed until triple in volume. One or two teaspoons lemon juice per cup of milk will speed the whipping.

◄§ FRUIT-FLAVORED LO-CAL PUDDING §►

> 1 envelope (4 servings) any flavor low-calorie gelatin dessert mix
> 1½ cups boiling water
> 2 cups cold water
> 1 envelope (4 servings) instant vanilla pudding mix
> Fresh fruit for garnish (optional)

Empty the gelatin powder into the blender. Add the boiling water and blend on high speed, covered. Add the other ingredients, except the fresh fruit, in the order given. Cover and blend after each addition. Chill until set, then garnish with fresh fruit, if desired, and serve. *Eight servings, 93 calories each.*

◄§ HAUPIA §►
(*Hawaiian Coconut Pudding*)

> 1 envelope unflavored gelatin
> 2 tablespoons cold water
> ¼ cup unsweetened grated coconut (see note below)
> 1 cup boiling water
> 1 envelope (4 servings) instant vanilla pudding mix
> 2¼ cups cold milk
> 1 teaspoon liquid sweetener, or to taste (optional)

Sprinkle the gelatin on the cold water in the blender and let stand for 1 minute. Add the shredded coconut and boiling water; cover and blend on low speed until smooth. Add the remaining ingredients and blend, then pour into an 8- or 9-inch square cake pan and refrigerate for several hours. Cut into squares to serve. *Nine servings, 71 calories each.*

NOTE: Unsweetened grated coconut is available in health food stores.

◄§ CHEESECAKE PUDDING §►

If you'd like cheesecake flavor without cheesecake calories, treat yourself to cheesecake pudding, an extra-quick and easy Slim Gourmet dessert you can whip up with your blender.

If you like your cheesecake jeweled with fruit, vary the recipe to suit your whim by adding a layer of fresh blueberries, crushed strawberries, or drained juice-packed pineapple tidbits.

1 envelope unflavored gelatin
¼ cup boiling water
2½ cups skim milk
  1 envelope (4 servings) instant vanilla pudding mix
  1 cup low-fat, small-curd cottage cheese
  3 tablespoons lemon juice
  2 tablespoons granulated sugar or equivalent sugar substitute
½ teaspoon finely grated orange rind (optional)
  4 graham crackers, coarsely crumbled

Empty the gelatin into your blender container and pour on the boiling water. Cover and blend on high speed, scraping down the sides of the blender jar frequently with a rubber spatula. Add the milk and pudding mix and blend on high speed until completely mixed. Add the cottage cheese and all the other ingredients except the graham cracker crumbs, and blend, first on low speed, then high, to prevent overflowing.

Put the blender container in the refrigerator for about 20 minutes, until the mixture sets slightly, then swirl into 8 stemmed sherbet glasses. Top with the graham cracker crumbs and chill for several hours before serving. *Eight servings, 126 calories each.*

VARIATION

Sugarless Cheesecake Pudding: This version uses diet vanilla pudding mix, which must be cooked before it is blended with the cottage cheese. Follow these directions:

Empty a four-serving envelope of low-calorie vanilla pudding mix into a saucepan. Add the gelatin and 2 cups of cold milk. Cook, stirring, over low heat until the mixture simmers and thickens. Allow the mixture to cool slightly, then pour into your blender container. Now proceed as in the previous recipe. *Eight servings, 88 calories each.*

⋖ YOLK-FREE LO-CAL EGGNOG PUDDING ⋗

1 envelope unflavored gelatin
¼ cup cold water
  1 cup boiling water
2¼ cups cold skim milk
  1 envelope (4 servings) instant vanilla pudding mix
1½ teaspoons rum flavoring (optional)
  2 egg whites
    Pinch of salt
    Pinch of freshly grated nutmeg

Combine gelatin and cold water in the blender. Wait for 1 minute, then add the boiling water. Cover and blend until all gelatin granules are dissolved. Add the milk, pudding mix, and rum flavoring. Cover and blend until smooth, then refrigerate for 10 to 15 minutes. Beat the egg whites and salt until stiff. Gently but thoroughly fold into the milk mixture. Sprinkle with nutmeg and chill. *Ten servings, 82 calories per serving.*

⊸§ MRS. ROARK'S LEMON PRONTO* ৪৯

1 large package (5½ ounces) instant lemon pudding mix
3 cups skim milk
4 cups (2 pounds) low-fat cottage cheese
1 cup raisins

Combine the milk and pudding mix and beat until smooth. Add the cottage cheese and raisins, mix well, and chill. *Fourteen servings, 139 calories each.*

⊸§ BANANA FROMAGE ৪৯

Which is more fattening—an apple, a pear, or a banana? If you're like most calorie counters, you'll probably draw a big red circle around the banana. But a 7¾-inch banana is 60 calories, exactly the same as an average apple. And an 8¾-inch banana is precisely as "fattening" as an average pear—100 calories.

2 egg yolks
2 tablespoons granulated sugar
1 teaspoon lemon juice
1 teaspoon vanilla extract
8 ounces low-fat Neufchâtel cheese, at room temperature
3 tablespoons skim milk
4 small bananas
Chocolate curls or lemon-peel ringlets for garnish (optional)

Put the egg yolks, sugar, lemon juice, and vanilla in a deep bowl. Beat on high speed with your electric mixer until thick and fluffy, then gradually beat in the cheese, a little at a time, until smooth. Beat in the milk. Chill thoroughly.

At serving time, slice the bananas into eight pretty stemmed sherbet glasses and spoon on the chilled cheese topping. A few chocolate curls or ringlets of

* Submitted by Mrs. A. R. Roark of Ashfork, Arizona.

lemon peel really add a grand finale look to this special-occasion dessert. *Eight servings, 142 calories each.*

⋖ CURAÇAO CRÈME PARFAITS ⋗

2 tablespoons Curaçao or other orange liqueur
1 envelope unflavored gelatin
½ cup boiling water
2 envelopes (single serving each) low-calorie vanilla milkshake mix (see note below)
1½ cups ice cubes
2 tangerines, peeled, seeded, and cut in chunks

Put the orange liqueur and gelatin in blender. Wait a minute, then add the boiling water. Cover and blend until all the gelatin granules are dissolved. Scrape down the sides with a rubber spatula, add the milkshake mix, and blend until smooth. Add the ice cubes and blend until the ice is dissolved; the mixture will be cold and creamy. Layer in parfait glasses with chunks of tangerine and serve immediately, or chill until serving time. *Four servings, 86 calories each.*

NOTE: Or substitute ⅔ cup dry skim milk, ½ teaspoon vanilla extract, and sugar substitute equal to 3 tablespoons sugar.

⋖ BLENDER-EASY MANDARIN BAVARIAN ⋗

1 can (8 ounces) unsweetened mandarin oranges, undrained
2 envelopes unflavored gelatin
½ cup boiling water
Sugar substitute equal to ¼ cup sugar
1 can (6 ounces) frozen orange juice concentrate
1 cup aerosol whipped cream

In the blender, combine ¼ cup juice from the canned oranges with the gelatin. Wait 1 minute, then pour on the boiling water. Blend on high speed until the gelatin granules dissolve. Add the sugar substitute, the frozen concentrate, and remaining orange juice from the can and blend until smooth.

Pour the contents of the blender into a mixing bowl and carefully fold in the whipped cream and mandarin orange sections. Put into a mold and refrigerate all day or overnight before unmolding. Garnish with additional fruit, if desired. *Eight servings, 80 calories each.*

CHOCOLATE-WAFER
"LAYER CAKE" PUDDING

1 envelope unflavored gelatin
2 tablespoons cold water
½ cup boiling water
1 cup cold skim milk
1 envelope (4 servings) instant vanilla pudding mix
2 egg whites, stiffly beaten
21 chocolate wafers
   Crushed chocolate wafers for garnish (optional)

Combine the gelatin and cold water in the blender. Wait a minute, then pour on the boiling water. Cover and blend on high speed until all the gelatin granules are dissolved. Add the milk and pudding mix, cover, and blend until smooth.

Pour the mixture into the beaten egg whites and gently but thoroughly fold together.

Put a layer of chocolate wafers in the bottom of an 8-inch cake pan. Cover with a layer of the vanilla mixture. Add another layer of wafers, then pudding, then a third layer of wafers, concluding with the vanilla mixture on top. (Decorate with a border of crushed wafer crumbs, if you like.) Chill for several hours before serving. *Eight servings, 133 calories each.*

NOTE: With a little imagination you can easily create endless variations on the same theme. An all-chocolate or all-vanilla cake, for example, or a lemon cake with lemon pudding and vanilla (or lemon) wafers. Or an orange cake, using fresh-squeezed juice in place of the milk. Or a mocha cake flavored with instant coffee.

VARIATION

Sugar-Free Chocolate-Wafer "Layer Cake" Pudding: Use dietetic cookies and sugar-free pudding mix. However, since the dietetic pudding must first be cooked, follow our special directions:

Combine one envelope of any flavor dietetic pudding mix with 1 envelope plain gelatin in a nonstick saucepan. Add 1½ cups skim milk; cook and stir until boiling. Remove from the heat and allow to cool. Beat 2 egg whites and ¼ teaspoon salt until stiff and fold into the pudding. Layer the pudding mixture and dietetic cookies in a cake pan, according to the directions in the previous recipe. Chill all day or overnight. *Eight servings, 100 calories each.*

ᦡ KEY LIME PARFAITS ᦢ

Omit the pie shell from Slimmed-Down Key Lime Pie (page 330). Prepare the filling according to the directions, then whip 3 egg whites and a pinch of salt until stiff and fold into the prepared filling. Spoon the mixture into parfait glasses and garnish with lime slices. Chill for several hours. *Eight servings, 94 calories each.*

ᦡ SPRING PUMPKIN "CUSTARD" ᦢ

Prepare the recipe from Sunny Pumpkin Pie (page 329), omitting the pie crust. Spoon the filling into custard cups. Chill, then top with whipped evaporated skim milk, which may be flavored with vanilla and sweetened to taste with sugar substitute, if desired. *Six servings, 80 calories each.*

ᦡ FIFTY-CALORIE CHIFFON PUDDING ᦢ

This blender-easy, quick-set dessert can be made in minutes with no messy clean-up. Despite its rich and creamy taste, it's less than 70 calories a ½-cup serving—50 percent less fattening than most ordinary gelatin desserts. In addition to its ease, the nice thing about this dessert is its versatility. You can combine almost any ice milk, extract, flavoring, and fruit to create a combination that's uniquely yours—and keep the calorie count the same.

 2 envelopes unflavored gelatin
 ½ cup boiling water
 3 teaspoons chocolate extract or 2 tablespoons unsweetened cocoa
 2 teaspoons vanilla extract
 1½ cups skim milk
 3 tablespoons granulated sugar or equivalent sugar substitute (optional)
 2 cups low-fat coffee, vanilla, or chocolate ice milk

Empty the gelatin into the blender. Add the boiling water, then cover and blend on high speed, scraping down frequently with a rubber spatula, until all the gelatin granules are dissolved. Add all the other ingredients except the ice milk and blend briefly, then add the ice milk and blend until smooth. Pour into a 1½-quart serving dish or individual custard cups and chill. *Eight servings, 67 calories each with sugar; 50 without, or with sugar substitute.*

VARIATIONS

Sugar-Free: Substitute dietetic or diabetic ice cream for the ice milk. Use sugar substitute.

Cherry Vanilla: Omit the chocolate, increase the vanilla to 1 tablespoon. Use vanilla ice milk. Stir in ½ cup chopped fresh, pitted cherries.

Fresh Fruit: Omit the chocolate, reduce the milk to 1 cup. Add 1 cup cleaned fresh strawberries, blueberries, or other fruit to the blender along with the milk.

Maple Walnut: Omit the chocolate, add 2 teaspoons maple flavoring. Use coffee-flavored ice milk. Stir in 3 tablespoons chopped walnuts.

Quick Fruit: Use 2 envelopes of low-calorie fruit-flavored gelatin dessert mix—any favorite flavor—instead of plain gelatin. Omit the chocolate and sugar or sugar substitute. Use vanilla or fruit-flavored ice milk.

Yogurt Chiffon: Replace the skim milk with plain yogurt, omit the chocolate. Use fruit or vanilla ice cream. Serve with crushed berries or sliced peaches.

Pineapple: Omit the chocolate. Use 2 cups unsweetened crushed pineapple in place of the milk.

✐ ⊷ MOCHA MOUSSE ⊷

1 envelope unflavored gelatin
1 tablespoon granulated sugar or equivalent sugar substitute
1 cup hot black coffee
1 cup 97% fat-free chocolate ice milk

Empty the gelatin into the blender and add the sugar, or sugar substitute. Pour in the hot coffee and blend on high speed until gelatin is dissolved, then add the ice milk and blend again. Put the blender container in your refrigerator for 20 to 25 minutes, or until the mixture is partially set. Return the blender jar to the base and whip again on high speed until light and frothy. Pour into a 2-cup mold or a bowl and chill thoroughly. Unmold before serving. *Four servings, 61 calories each with sugar; 50 with sugar substitute.*

NOTE: For a coffee mousse, use vanilla or coffee ice milk instead of chocolate.

Egg-Rich Desserts: Ideal for Dieters

Egg-rich desserts are a dieter's delight. Rich in tummy-filling protein, eggs have an appetite-satisfying factor that's missing in empty-calorie sweets. That's because protein is slowly absorbed by the system, while quick-burning sweets and starches are quickly digested, leaving you hungry again in a few hours. Egg desserts are the ideal grand finale for calorie-light dinners.

✍ BAKED CUSTARD ಶ

Here's a basic baked custard recipe you can make three ways—with sugar, with sugar substitute, or with a combination of sugar and sugar substitute.

3 **eggs**
¼ **cup granulated sugar**
   Pinch of salt
2 **teaspoons vanilla extract**
2 **cups skim milk**

Combine the eggs, sugar, salt, and vanilla and beat well. Scald the milk, then slowly stir it into the egg mixture. Pour into 5 custard cups. Place the cups in a shallow pan of hot water in a preheated 300-degree oven. Bake for 1 hour, until a silver knife comes out clean. Chill before serving. *Five servings, 114 calories each.*

VARIATIONS

Lower-Calorie Baked Custard: Reduce the sugar to 2 tablespoons and add sugar substitute equal to 2 tablespoons sugar. *Only 96 calories per serving.*

Sugar-Free Baked Custard: Eliminate the sugar altogether; replace it with any type of sugar substitute to equal ¼ cup (check the label for equivalents). *Only 77 calories per serving.*

ಈ CUSTARD-PLUS ಶ

For extra ease and a nutrition boost, why not make your custard from one of those diet-lunch products, the kind you tear open and mix with milk for a 225-calorie lunch or breakfast? Meal-in-a-glass products are fortified with extra vitamins and protein.

2 **eggs**
1½ **cups skim milk**
   2 **envelopes vanilla diet-lunch product (Metrecal, Sego, etc.)**
      Sugar substitute equal to 1 tablespoon sugar (optional)
      Freshly grated nutmeg

Beat the eggs until yellow; add the milk and beat well. Add the diet-lunch product and sugar substitute and beat until completely dissolved. Pour the custard into 6 custard cups and sprinkle nutmeg on top. Place the cups in a shallow pan of warm water and bake in a preheated 325-degree oven for 35 to 40 minutes, until a silver knife dipped into the custard comes out clean. Chill well. *Six servings, 80 calories each.*

NOTE: For variety, try other flavors of the mixes.

NO-COOK BLENDER "CUSTARD"

2 eggs
1 envelope unflavored gelatin
½ cup boiling water
¼ teaspoon salt
½ cup nonfat dry milk
2 teaspoons vanilla extract
3 tablespoons granulated sugar
Sugar substitute equal to ¼ cup sugar
2 cups ice cubes

Break the eggs into the blender. Sprinkle on the gelatin and wait for 1 minute. Add the boiling water, cover, and blend until the gelatin granules are dissolved. Add all the other ingredients except the ice and blend until smooth. Add the ice cubes, cover, and blend until the ice is dissolved and the dessert is thick and creamy. Serve immediately. *Six servings, 93 calories each.*

SLIM ZABAGLIONE

(Italian Wine Custard)

8 eggs, separated
½ cup confectioners' sugar
½ cup sherry wine
Pinch of salt

Put the egg yolks in the top of a double-boiler, over (but not touching) boiling water. Beat the yolks and add the sugar, a little at a time, until the mixture is foamy. Add the sherry and beat until double in volume. Beat the egg whites and salt until stiff and fold into the yolk mixture. Spoon into wine glasses and serve warm or chilled. *Eight servings, at 116 calories each.*

MERINGUE-TOPPED
CHOCOLATE BREAD PUDDING

PUDDING:

  2 cups skim milk, scalded
  6 tablespoons unsweetened cocoa
  3 cups protein bread cubes
  3 egg yolks, beaten
  8 tablespoons granulated sugar
  2 teaspoons vanilla extract

MERINGUE:

     Pinch of salt
  3 egg whites
  ¼ cup granulated sugar

Combine the milk and cocoa in a saucepan; stir to mix. Cook, stirring, over a moderate flame until the milk simmers, then pour over the bread cubes in a 1½-quart casserole dish. Let stand for 10 to 15 minutes.

Add the beaten egg yolks, sugar, and vanilla and stir to combine. Set the casserole in a shallow pan of hot water in a preheated 350-degree oven. Bake for 1 hour, until a knife inserted in the center comes out clean.

Add the salt to the egg whites and beat until soft peaks form. Add the sugar, a tablespoon at a time, and continue to beat the egg whites until stiff peaks form. Pile the meringue on top of the pudding, spreading it to the edges of the casserole so it won't shrink, and return to the oven. Bake for an additional 15 minutes, until the meringue is browned. *Eight servings, 133 calories each.*

BAKED CHOCOLATE CRÈME

  2 eggs
  8 ounces low-calorie cream cheese or low-fat Neufchâtel cheese
     Pinch of salt
  1 teaspoon vanilla extract
  2 tablespoons granulated sugar
     Sugar substitute equal to 2 tablespoons sugar
  3 tablespoons skim milk
  4 teaspoons unsweetened cocoa

Combine all the ingredients in the blender and blend until smooth, then pour into 4 custard cups. Set the cups in a shallow pan of hot water and bake in a preheated 225-degree oven for 1 hour. Chill before serving. *Four servings, 179 calories each.*

⋑ NEW-FASHIONED LO-CAL RICE PUDDING ⋑

3 cups skim milk
¼ cup raw rice
¼ teaspoon salt or butter-flavored salt
6 tablespoons raisins
1 egg, beaten
1 teaspoon vanilla extract
½ teaspoon grated orange or lemon peel
   Sugar substitute to equal ½ cup sugar
¼ teaspoon ground cinnamon

Combine the milk, rice, and salt in a heavy nonstick saucepan (or in the top of a double-boiler). Cover and cook over very low heat (or over boiling water) for 1 hour. Stir in the raisins in the last 10 minutes of cooking, then remove from the heat and stir in the beaten egg. Cook, stirring, over low heat for 1 to 2 minutes. Remove from the heat and stir in the vanilla, peel, and sugar substitute. Sprinkle with the cinnamon and chill. *Eight servings, 65 calories each.*

⋑ QUICK LO-CAL RICE PUDDING ⋑

2½ cups skim milk
1 cup instant rice
¼ teaspoon ground cinnamon
6 tablespoons raisins
¼ teaspoon salt or butter-flavored salt
2 eggs, lightly beaten
¾ teaspoon vanilla extract
   Sugar substitute equal to 6 tablespoons sugar
   Freshly grated nutmeg

Combine the milk, rice, cinnamon, raisins, and salt in a heavy nonstick saucepan over very high heat. Cook, stirring, until boiling, then lower the heat to a gentle simmer and continue cooking for 15 minutes, stirring occasionally. Slowly pour the hot mixture into the beaten eggs, beating continuously. Stir in the vanilla and sugar substitute, sprinkle with the nutmeg, and chill. *Six servings, 157 calories each.*

⟨•§ GÂTEAU DE RIZ ⟩•⟩

(French Rice Dessert)

2 cups skim milk
3 tablespoons raw long-grain rice
3 tablespoons Curaçao or other orange liqueur
  Pinch of salt or butter-flavored salt
½ teaspoon grated orange rind
1 envelope unflavored gelatin
1 can (8 ounces) low-calorie fruit cocktail, undrained
3 tablespoons sugar or equivalent sugar substitute

Heat the milk to boiling in a nonstick saucepan. Add the rice, Curaçao, salt, and orange rind. Simmer, uncovered, over very low heat for 25 minutes. Meanwhile, drain the fruit, using the juice to soften the gelatin.

When the rice is cooked, stir in the softened gelatin, over low heat, until completely dissolved. Remove from the heat and stir in the fruit and sugar, or sugar substitute. Pour into a shallow dish or a 3-cup mold and chill for several hours. *Six servings, 102 calories each with sugar; 78 with sugar substitute.*

•§ SPICED CHOCOLATE RICE PUDDING ⟩•⟩

2½ cups water
3 envelopes (single serving) low-calorie chocolate milk, milkshake, or hot cocoa mix
1 cup instant rice
6 tablespoons raisins
½ teaspoon brandy or rum flavoring
½ teaspoon butter-flavored salt
½ teaspoon pumpkin-pie spice
2 eggs, lightly beaten

In a heavy nonstick saucepan, heat the water to boiling. Stir in the chocolate milk mix until dissolved, then stir in all the other ingredients except the eggs. Simmer over very low heat, stirring occasionally, for 12 to 15 minutes. Slowly pour hot mixture into the eggs, beating continually. Pour into a shallow dish and chill. *Six servings, 155 calories each.*

⪧ PINEAPPLE-STREUSEL PUDDING ⪦

PUDDING:

2 cans (16-ounces each) juice-packed pineapple chunks,
   undrained

3 eggs

2 tablespoons all-purpose flour

3 tablespoons granulated sugar substitute

TOPPING:

½ cup all-purpose flour

½ teaspoon salt or butter-flavored salt

2 tablespoons diet margarine

½ teaspoon ground cinnamon

2 tablespoons free-pouring brown sugar

2 tablespoons granulated sugar substitute

Drain the pineapple chunks and reserve ½ cup of the juice. Arrange the pineapple in a 9-inch square cake pan. Combine the reserved juice, eggs, flour, and sugar substitute and fork-whip until blended. Pour over the pineapple.

Combine all the topping ingredients, cutting the margarine in with a fork until the mixture forms crumbs. Sprinkle over the surface of the pineapple, then bake in a preheated 325-degree oven for 45 minutes or longer, until the pudding is set and the top is lightly browned. *Nine servings, 129 calories each.*

⪧ BRANDY DESSERT SOUFFLÉ ⪦

2 tablespoons all-purpose flour

¼ teaspoon butter-flavored salt

½ cup skim milk

6 tablespoons granulated sugar
   Sugar substitute equal to ½ cup sugar

2 tablespoons brandy

5 eggs, separated

Combine the flour, salt, milk, and sugar in a saucepan. Cook, stirring, until thickened, then turn off the heat. Add the sugar substitute and brandy. Stir the hot mixture into the egg yolks, lightly beaten.

Beat the egg whites until stiff peaks form, then fold into the egg yolk–brandy mixture. Pour into a soufflé dish. Set the dish in a baking pan filled with 1 inch of hot water and bake for 1 hour at 325 degrees. Serve immediately. *Five servings, 157 calories each.*

⋖ SANGRÍA JELLO I ⋗

2 envelopes unflavored gelatin
¼ cup cold water
1½ cups boiling water
1 can (6 ounces) frozen orange juice concentrate
3 tablespoon granulated sugar
  Sugar substitute equal to ⅓ cup (optional)
1 cup dry red wine
1 cup ice cubes

Combine the gelatin and cold water in the blender. Wait for 1 minute, then add the boiling water and blend, covered, on high speed until all the gelatin granules are dissolved. Add the frozen orange juice, sugar, and sugar substitute and blend until smooth. If the blender container isn't large enough to accommodate the remaining ingredients without spilling over, pour the contents of the blender into a large bowl. Stir in the wine and ice cubes until the ice melts, then pour the mixture into 8 wine glasses or stemmed dessert dishes and refrigerate. The dessert will form its own foamy topping. *Eight servings, 86 calories each.*

⋖ SANGRÍA JELLO II ⋗

2 envelopes (4 servings each) regular or low-calorie orange gelatin
    dessert mix
2 cups boiling water
1 cup dry red wine
1 can (16 ounces) water-packed fruit cocktail, drained

Stir the regular or dietetic orange gelatin dessert into the boiling water. Add the dry red wine and chill until syrupy. Stir in the drained fruit cocktail and pour into a mold. Chill all day or overnight. Unmold before serving. *Eight servings, 121 calories each with regular gelatin mix; only 48 with sugar-free gelatin.*

⋖ GROWN-UP GRAPEFRUIT GELATIN ⋗

3 grapefruit
  Water, if necessary
2 tablespoons granulated sugar or equivalent sugar substitute
½ cup white wine
1 envelope unflavored gelatin

Cut each grapefruit in half. Using a grapefruit knife or serrated spoon, scrape the grapefruit pulp into a bowl, juice and all. You should have 3 cups; add water if needed. Stir in the sugar or sweetener.

Combine the wine and gelatin in a saucepan over low heat. Stir until the gelatin granules are completely dissolved, then stir into the grapefruit. Pour into 4 stemmed glasses and chill. *Four servings, 116 calories each with sugar; 93 without.*

NOTE: For a colorful variation, use pink grapefruit, and substitute red wine for white.

↭ LAYERED STRAWBERRY DESSERT MOLD ↝

> 2 envelopes (4 servings each) regular or low-calorie strawberry
>   gelatin dessert mix
> 1½ cups boiling water
> 2 cups ice cubes
> 1 cup sliced fresh or frozen strawberries, defrosted if necessary
> 1 envelope low-calorie whipped topping mix
>   Whole strawberries for garnish (optional)

Dissolve the first envelope of gelatin mix in ¾ cup of the boiling water. Stir in 1 cup of the ice cubes until melted. Stir in strawberries, then pour into a 5-cup mold and refrigerate until set.

Meanwhile, prepare the second envelope of gelatin mix with the remaining boiling water and ice cubes in a separate mixing bowl. Refrigerate.

Prepare the whipped topping mix according to package directions. Fold the topping into the second gelatin mixture until light pink and fluffy. Spoon this pink mixture on top of the red fruit layer in the 5-cup mold. Refrigerate for several hours or all day, until firm. Unmold and garnish with additional whole berries, if desired. *Ten servings, 97 calories each with regular gelatin mix; only 35 with diet gelatin mix.*

↭ STRAWBERRY CHAMPAGNE MOLD ↝

> 1 envelope (4 servings) low-calorie strawberry gelatin dessert mix
> 1 cup boiling water
> ½ cup champagne or any white wine
> ¼ teaspoon salt
> ½ cup ice cubes and water
> 1 cup fresh sliced strawberries
> 1 small ripe banana, peeled and diced
> 3 tablespoons flaked, sweetened coconut

Dissolve the gelatin in the boiling water. Add the champagne, salt, ice cubes, and water and stir until the ice is melted. Refrigerate until partly set, then fold in the strawberries, banana, and coconut. Pour into a 3½-cup mold, individual molds, or loaf pan and chill until firm. Unmold before serving. *Six servings, 67 calories each.*

◄§ GRASSHOPPER DESSERT ◊►

1 cup boiling water
1 envelope (4 servings) low-calorie lime gelatin dessert mix
¾ cup cold water
3 tablespoons green crème de menthe liqueur
1 envelope low-calorie whipped topping mix
1 egg white
1 pint fresh strawberries, sliced and sweetened to taste

Stir the boiling water into the gelatin mix until dissolved. Stir in the cold water and crème de menthe, then chill in the refrigerator or freezer until syrupy. Meanwhile, prepare the topping mix according to package directions.

Add the egg white to the syrupy gelatin mixture and beat with an electric mixer until fluffy and double in volume. Fold in the prepared topping, then spoon into 8 footed cocktail glasses and chill until firm. At serving time, top with the sliced fruit, sweetened to taste with liquid sweetener. *Eight servings, 64 calories each.*

◄§ ARLENE NEWOHR'S COTTAGE PARFAITS* ◊►

2 envelopes (4 servings each) any flavor low-calorie gelatin
    dessert mix
1 cup low-fat cottage cheese
2⅔ tablespoons flaked, sweetened coconut

Prepare the gelatin according to directions and chill. When good and syrupy, beat until fluffy. Add the cottage cheese and beat well. Spoon into 8 parfait glasses and top with the coconut. *Eight servings, 47 calories each.*

* Submitted by Mrs. Arlene Newohr of Holland, Pennsylvania.

24
FRUIT
DESSERTS

Fresh Fruit: The Real French Finale

Everyone knows how to snack on fruit, but how do you manage it amid a setting of crystal and candlelight? The new Dione Lucas (the most formidable of American "French" chefs) cookbook suggests that whole fresh fruit may be attractively presented in a basket or bowl, with a dessert plate and dessert knives and forks for each guest. Most fruit, except bananas, should be chilled.

CHERRIES, GRAPES, PLUMS: May be eaten with the fingers.

BERRIES: Leave whole; serve in small bowls with dessert spoons.

PEACHES, NECTARINES: Serve whole, skins on, with plates and forks. Guests may peel them, or not. To slice, place stem down on a plate, anchored with a fork. Slice off-center to avoid the pit.

APPLES, PEARS: Anchor with a fork and slice in half, then quarters. Then cut out the core and cut each quarter crosswise into slices. May be peeled or not.

BANANAS: Peel them whole, then cut into bite-sized pieces.

ORANGES: Anchor with a fork, then cut off a slice of rind at top and bottom. Stand the orange on end, still anchored, then cut downward to slice off the rind. Cut the peeled orange in half horizontally and cut out each section with the tip of your knife.

WATERMELON: Serve in wedges. Run a knife between the flesh and rind, then cut fruit at right angles into bite-sized pieces. Remove the seeds with your fork.

⋖§ QUICK LO-CAL APPLESAUCE §⋗

Regular canned applesauce is 120 calories a ½-cup serving; this easy homemade variety is only 80 calories a serving.

1 can (20 ounces) unsweetened pie-sliced apples, drained
¼ cup cold water
¼ cup granulated sugar
¼ teaspoon vanilla extract (see note below)

Put the apples, sugar, and water in a saucepan and bring to a boil. Simmer, covered, over a low flame until the apples are very tender. Stir with a fork, remove from the heat, and blend in the vanilla. *Four servings, 80 calories each.*

NOTE: Why the vanilla? A few drops added to applesauce tends to heighten the effect of sweetness without adding any calories. For best results, vanilla should be added after the cooking is complete.

⋖§ FRESH BLENDER APPLESAUCE §⋗

For a change of pace, try fresh applesauce. You can make it jiffy-quick in your blender, and it needs no extra sweetening.

4 apples
¼ cup cold water
**   Ground cinnamon (optional)**

Peel and core the apples and cut into quarters, then into eighths. Put the water and three or four of the apple wedges in your blender. Whir on high speed, then add the remaining apple chunks, a few at a time, and blend. Add a touch of cinnamon, if you like. *Four servings, about 80 calories each.*

⋖§ SHERRY-BAKED APPLES §⋗

4 apples
2 tablespoons golden raisins
2 teaspoons brown sugar
**   Sugar substitute equal to 1 tablespoon sugar**
½ cup dry sherry wine

Carefully core the apples without cutting through the bottom, then stand them in a baking dish just large enough to hold them. Fill the centers with the raisins, sugar, and sugar substitute, then pour in the wine. Bake in a preheated 350-degree oven for 30 to 45 minutes, basting frequently, until the apples are tender but not mushy. Serve warm or chilled. The wine forms a delicious sauce. *Four servings, 105 calories each.*

⋅§ STIR-AND-BAKE APPLE CRUMBLE ε∾

¾ cup plain pancake mix
¼ cup brown sugar
  Sugar substitute equal to ⅓ cup sugar
1½ teaspoons ground cinnamon
 1 can (20 ounces) unsweetened pie-sliced apples, undrained
 1 teaspoon grated lemon rind
 2 tablespoons diet margarine

Combine the pancake mix, brown sugar, sugar substitute, and cinnamon and stir well. Set aside.

Empty the apple slices, liquid and all, into a 9-inch square cake pan and sprinkle with the lemon rind. Measure out ¾ cup of the pancake-cinnamon mixture and add to the apples. Stir until completely blended.

Add the diet margarine to the remaining pancake-cinnamon mixture and blend with a fork until crumbly. Sprinkle the crumbs over the surface of the apples and bake in a preheated 400-degree oven for 30 to 35 minutes. *Nine servings, 98 calories each.*

⋅§ PÊCHES AUX VIN ROUGE ε∾
(Peaches in Red Wine)

Instead of slicing fresh peaches onto a sponge cake, French homemakers slice them into a shallow bowl of chilled red wine, just before dinner. By dessert time the slices have achieved just the right degree of "spirited" chill. Allow 1 large peach per person, and serve your "peaches in red wine" in stemmed glasses. *About 70 calories a serving.*

NOTE: On those days when skinning a peach seems unreasonably laborious, use well-drained diet-packed or juice-packed peach halves.

⋅§ PEACH OR NECTARINE CRISP ε∾

FRUIT BASE:
 4 cups ripe peeled, sliced peaches or nectarines
   Sugar substitute equal to 5 tablespoons sugar

TOPPING:

½ cup quick-cooking rolled oats
3 tablespoons free-pouring brown sugar
¼ cup granulated sugar substitute
1 tablespoon arrowroot or cornstarch
¼ teaspoon ground cinnamon
2 tablespoons diet margarine

Stir the sliced fruit and sweetener together in the bottom of a nonstick pie pan. Stir the dry topping ingredients together in a bowl, then cut in the margarine until the mixture is crumbly. Shake the crumbs over the fruit and bake in a preheated 350-degree oven for 50 to 60 minutes, until brown. Serve warm or chilled. *Eight servings, 78 calories each.*

⋖§ BLUSHING PEARS ៛⋗

1 can (16 ounces) low-calorie or juice-packed pear halves, undrained
½ cup dry red wine
½ cup orange juice
   Pinch of ground cloves
   Pinch of ground cinnamon
   Pinch of grated lemon or orange rind
3 tablespoons granulated sugar

Drain the fruit and reserve the juice. Arrange the pears in a pretty crystal bowl, or in 4 individual stemmed glasses.

Measure out one-half of the reserved juice from the can and pour it into a saucepan. Add all the remaining ingredients and bring to a boil, then simmer, covered, for 10 minutes. Allow to cool enough so you don't shatter your serving dish, then pour the warm wine mixture over the pears. Chill thoroughly before serving. *Four servings, 95 calories per serving.*

VARIATION

Sugarless Blushing Pears: Substitute 1 teaspoon cornstarch for the sugar. After the wine has simmered, stir in sugar substitute equal to 3 tablespoons sugar. *Only 62 calories per serving.*

⋖§ VERY-SLIM RHUBARB ៛⋗

Rhubarb is barely 62 calories a pound; however, it takes so much sugar just to sweeten it up to a tangy sourness that most cooked rhubarb is nearly

400 calories a cupful. But if you're a Slim Gourmet cook, you won't need a whole sugar bowlful to de-sour rhubarb. A pinch of baking soda and some vanilla extract will let you do the job with a lot less of that white stuff.

2 **pounds rhubarb, cut in 1-inch pieces**
1 **teaspoon vanilla extract**
5 **tablespoons water**
5 **tablespoons granulated sugar**
   Pinch of baking soda
   Liquid low-calorie sugar substitute (optional)

Combine all the ingredients in a saucepan. Cover with a tightly fitting lid and simmer over a very low flame for 10 minutes or more, until just tender. If a sweeter rhubarb is desired, remove from the heat and stir in a few drops of liquid low-calorie sweetener. *Eight servings, 44 calories each.*

VARIATIONS

Baked Rhubarb: Omit the water. Bake, uncovered, in an ovenproof dish for 45 minutes at 300 degrees.

Sugarless Rhubarb: Omit the sugar. Add ½ teaspoon arrowroot or cornstarch to the water. Simmer until tender, then remove from heat and stir in sugar substitute to equal ⅓ cup sugar. *Only 16 calories per serving.*

Rhubarb Pineapple Compote: Omit the sugar. Combine the raw rhubarb with 2 cups syrup-packed pineapple (crushed or tidbits). Cover and simmer 10 minutes. *Only 40 calories per serving.*

Rhubarb-Banana Compote: Prepare the rhubarb according to the directions above. Combine with sliced bananas (one-half cup bananas to one cup rhubarb). Serve, well chilled, in sherbet glasses. *Only 50 calories per serving.*

⊷ SLIM STRAWBERRIES ROMANOFF ᴤᴥ

At Maxim's in Paris this is served smothered in heavy whipped cream, with half an eggshell of Cognac in the middle. It's ignited and carried to the table in a blaze of glory. The alcohol calories go up in flames but not the whipped cream, so try it this way:

2 **cups fresh strawberries** ·
½ **cup orange juice**
3 **tablespoons granulated sugar or equivalent sugar substitute**
¼ **cup orange liqueur**
½ **cup prepared low-calorie whipped topping or aerosol topping**

Wash and hull the berries and put them in a decorative glass serving dish. Stir with the juice, sugar, and liqueur and chill for one hour or more. At dessert time, spoon the strawberries into footed champagne glasses and top with 2 tablespoons of whipped topping per person. *Four servings, 139 calories each with sugar; 104 with sugar substitute.*

25
FROZEN
DESSERTS

Now it's easy to make your own ice cream without all those extra fat and sugar calories. The new ice-cream machines do their work *inside* your freezer, a vast improvement over the old-fashioned kind that needed rock salt and elbow grease.

Compact enough to fit in most freezers, the ice-cream makers have a moistureproof cord that's so flat you can close the freezer door over it. You simply mix up your recipe, load it into the machine, pop it in the freezer and plug the flat cord into a wall outlet. In an hour or so—ice cream!

If you don't have an ice-cream maker, simply freeze the mixture in a metal mixing bowl. When slushy, beat smooth. When almost frozen solid, break up and beat smooth again. The double beating prevents coarse ice crystals from forming.

As with all frozen desserts that lack commercial stabilizers, it's a good idea to let your lo-cal "ice cream" soften briefly at room temperature before serving.

ᴥ VANILLA "ICE CREAM" ᴧ

      2 egg whites
     ¼ cup granulated sugar
     ½ envelope unflavored gelatin
      3 tablespoons cold water
      1 can (13 ounces) evaporated skim milk
         Sugar substitute equal to ¼ cup sugar
         Pinch of salt or butter-flavored salt
 1½ teaspoons vanilla extract

Beat the egg whites until frothy; add the sugar gradually and beat until stiff. Combine the gelatin and cold water in a saucepan. Wait for 1 minute, then heat over a low flame until the gelatin is melted. Remove from the heat and stir in the evaporated milk, sugar substitute, salt, and vanilla extract. Carefully fold into the egg whites. Freeze in an ice-cream maker according to manufacturer's directions, or freeze in a mixing bowl and beat twice during the freezing time. *Eight servings, 65 calories each.*

ᴥ TANGY YOGURT "ICE CREAM" ᴧ

 3 cups plain yogurt
 2 teaspoons vanilla extract
 3 tablespoons lemon juice
 2 tablespoons sugar or equivalent sugar substitute (optional)
    Grated rind of 1 lemon

Combine all the ingredients and freeze in an ice-cream maker according to manufacturer's directions. Or freeze in a mixer bowl, beating twice during the freezing process. *Eight servings, 61 calories each with sugar; 49 without.*

ᴥ DIETER'S 15-MINUTE ᴧ "SOFT ICE CREAM"

      2 eggs
      2 envelopes unflavored gelatin
     ¾ cup boiling water
      1 cup instant nonfat dry milk
     ½ teaspoon butter-flavored salt
      4 teaspoons vanilla extract
      3 tablespoons granulated sugar
         Sugar substitute equal to ½ cup sugar

Break the eggs into the blender. Sprinkle on the gelatin and wait for 1 minute. Add the boiling water, cover, and blend until the gelatin granules are dissolved. Add all the other ingredients and blend until smooth. Spoon into 8 dessert dishes and put in the coldest part of the freezer for 15 minutes. *Eight servings, 76 calories each.*

⋖§ SUPER-SLIM SUNDAE ૐ৯

There's nothing like a safe sundae to beat those why-me dieting blues. But do it at home, where you can dish up a gooey delight that's under 150 calories—like one made with one-half cup of ice milk, 2 tablespoons of "Hot Fudge" Sauce, a tablespoon of whipped topping, and a half a maraschino cherry adds up to 140 calories. (Those innocuous little cherries are 8 calories apiece!) A sundae in public would probably cost you 600 or 700 calories.

½ cup 97% fat-free ice milk
2 tablespoons sauce of your choice (see below)
1 tablespoon aerosol whipped topping or Low Calorie "Whipped Cream" (see below)
½ maraschino cherry

Don't guess on the quantity of your ice cream. Ration out your ice milk with a bona-fide ½-cup measuring cup. Then pile it in a champagne glass or sherbet dish in airy little scoops to make it look like more.

Now drizzle on 2 tablespoons of the sauce of your choice—which you can make in quantity and keep on hand for crises like this. Mound a tablespoon's worth of whipped topping over the sauce, and top with half a maraschino cherry.

Slim Sundae Sauces

⋖§ "HOT FUDGE" SAUCE ૐ৯

2 tablespoons unsweetened cocoa
1 tablespoon cornstarch
Pinch of salt
1 cup skim milk
2 tablespoons granulated sugar
Sugar substitute equal to 3 tablespoons sugar
1 teaspoon vanilla extract

Combine all the ingredients in a nonstick saucepan and stir until dissolved. Heat over a low flame until the mixture simmers; the sauce will thicken as it cools. *Only 14 calories per tablespoon.*

NOTE: Vary your sauce with a little instant coffee, rum, brandy, or mint flavoring.

VARIATIONS

Sugarless Chocolate Sauce: Dissolve 1 package (4 servings) of diet chocolate pudding mix in 2½ cups cold skim milk in a saucepan. Heat, stirring constantly, until the mixture thickens. A pinch of salt and a dash of vanilla will improve the flavor. *Only 8 calories per tablespoon.*

Hot Pineapple Sauce: Drain an 8-ounce can of juice-packed crushed pineapple and simmer the fruit with ½ cup juice from the can and 1 teaspoon arrowroot or cornstarch, until the mixture thickens. *Only 7 calories per tablespoon.*

Hot Apple Sauce: Combine a 6-ounce can of defrosted apple-juice concentrate with ½ cup water and 2 teaspoons arrowroot or cornstarch. Simmer until thickened and serve hot. *Only 14 calories per tablespoon.*

⊷ LOW-CALORIE "WHIPPED CREAM" ⊷

½ teaspoon unflavored gelatin
2 teaspoons cold water
2 tablespoons boiling water
2 tablespoons nonfat dry milk
1½ teaspoons lemon juice
1 teaspoon vanilla extract
Sugar substitute equal to 4 teaspoons sugar

Soften the gelatin in the cold water, then add the boiling water and stir. Add the remaining ingredients and quick-chill in the freezer, then beat 15 minutes with an electric mixer until of whipped-cream consistency. *About 4 calories per tablespoon.*

NOTE: There's an easy-do low-calorie whipped topping mix on the market that's only 7 calories per tablespoon. Most aerosol whips, both cream and nondairy, are also 7 calories a tablespoon. The frozen whips are twice that: 14 to 16 calories per, while heavy whipped cream is 50!

⊷ CHERRIES JUBILEE ⊷

Cherries Jubilee, of course, is brandy-flamed cherries, served on vanilla ice cream. What makes it so fattening (often upward of 300 calories or more), is the butterfat-rich ice cream it's normally served on. You can turn it into a low-calorie, low-cholesterol delight by using vanilla ice milk. Be sure to choose the kind that's 97 percent fat free. And you'll serve up a spectacular dessert for 150 calories or less.

A chafing dish certainly simplifies the serving of this sauce, but you can bring it to the table in a decorative heat-and-serve saucepan. Bring the sauce to the table bubbling hot, or set the saucepan on an electric warming tray or candle server. Pour on the brandy; then allow a few seconds for it to warm to the point at which it gives off vapors.

Remember, to give food a flaming finish, you have to ignite the vapor, not the liquid, so hold your flame an inch or so above the surface. For maximum effect, ladle on the cherries while they're still flaming.

1 **quart 97% fat-free vanilla ice milk**
1 **can (16 ounces) red, tart, pitted water-packed cherries, undrained**
2 **teaspoons arrowroot or cornstarch**
2 **tablespoons granulated sugar or equivalent sugar substitute**
3 **or 4 drops of red food coloring**
¼ **cup brandy**

Before dinner, pile ½-cup servings of ice milk into 8 stemmed champagne or sherbet glasses. Store in the freezer.

Empty the cherries, liquid and all, into a saucepan and stir in the arrowroot, sugar, and food coloring. Cook, stirring, over moderate heat until the sauce simmers and becomes clear. Cover and keep warm.

At dessert time, stir the sauce and reheat to simmering. Pour the brandy on the surface of the sauce and ignite the vapors. Spoon the flaming cherries over the ice milk and serve immediately. *Eight servings, 147 calories each with sugar; 137 with sugar substitute.*

◄§ BLUEBERRIES JUBILEE ß►

1 **cup fresh blueberries**
1 **cup unsweetened grape juice**
1 **teaspoon arrowroot or cornstarch**
2 **tablespoons brandy or other hard liquor**

Combine the blueberries, grape juice, and arrowroot in a saucepan and simmer until thickened and clear. Pour the brandy over the surface of the simmering sauce and ignite the vapors with a long match. Spoon the flaming sauce over the ice cream. *Only 11 calories per tablespoon.*

⋖ LOW-CALORIE ICE CREAM SODA ⋗

¼ cup cold evaporated skim milk
1 cup diet chocolate soda
1 scoop 97% fat-free ice milk
1 tablespoon aerosol whipped topping

Combine the milk and soda in a very tall glass. Add the ice milk and top with a tablespoon of aerosol whipped topping. *One serving, 130 calories.*
NOTE: Combine any favorite flavors for interesting variations.

⋖ IRISH COFFEE FREEZE ⋗

1½ tablespoons instant coffee
1⅔ cups cold skim milk
1 envelope (4 servings) instant vanilla pudding mix
1 envelope low-calorie whipped topping mix
4 tablespoons Irish whiskey

Combine the coffee and milk in an electric mixing bowl and beat until the coffee is dissolved. Add the pudding and topping mixes and beat slowly until blended. Gradually increase the speed to the highest level and whip on high speed until soft peaks form. Beat in the whiskey, a little at a time, then freeze until firm. Remove from the freezer and allow to soften slightly before spooning. *Eight servings, 114 calories each.*

⋖ FROSTED PUMPKIN MOUSSE ⋗

1 cup plain canned pumpkin (*not* pie filling)
1 envelope low-calorie whipped topping mix
¼ cup free-pouring brown sugar
Sugar substitute equal to ¼ cup sugar
1 teaspoon pumpkin-pie spice
1⅓ cups nonfat dry milk
1 teaspoon vanilla extract
2 cups cold water
Dash of salt

Combine all the ingredients and whip until smooth. Pour into a bowl or 3-cup mold and freeze. Allow to soften briefly at room temperature before serving. *Six servings, 128 calories each.*

VARIATION

Pumpkin "Ice Cream" Pie: Prepare the pumpkin mousse as directed above and pour into a baked or packaged graham-cracker pie shell. Freeze firm. *Six servings, 191 calories each.*

ᴥᔥ EASY LO-CAL SHERBET ᘒᴗ

Add 6 or 8 crushed berries and sugar substitute (equal to 2 tablespoons sugar) to a 13-ounce can of evaporated skim milk. Freeze until slushy, then whip on high speed with an electric hand mixer. Refreeze before serving. *Four servings, about 60 calories each.*

ᴥᔥ MRS. MOON'S PINEAPPLE SHERBET* ᘒᴗ

1 can (16 ounces) juice-packed crushed pineapple, drained
5 tablespoons granulated sugar
　Sugar substitute equal to 3 tablespoons sugar
2 cups buttermilk

Combine all the ingredients and freeze until slushy. Beat on high speed with an electric mixer, then refreeze before serving. *Eight servings, 81 calories each.*

ᴥᔥ BRANDIED PEACH SHERBET ᘒᴗ

Brandy itself is pretty potent, calorie-wise, about 80 calories an ounce, so it's probably off limits as a beverage. But a few teaspoons of brandy drizzled on fruit adds barely 20 calories, and a lot more flavor punch than the calories would indicate. Now, if you ignite it, you'll light up the sky with a minor miracle—most of the brandy calories will disappear! They evaporate, along with the alcohol.

At only 7 calories a teaspoon, bottled brandy flavoring lets you add the essence of brandy without the alcohol calories and no pyrotechnics needed.

1 can (16 ounces) low-calorie peaches, undrained
1 envelope unflavored gelatin
1 teaspoon lemon juice
1 teaspoon grated lemon rind
2 teaspoons brandy flavoring
　Pinch of salt (optional)
　Sugar substitute equal to 2 tablespoons sugar

* Submitted by Mrs. F. M. Moon of Arlington, Texas.

Drain the peaches and measure out 1½ cups juice (add water if needed). Combine the peace juice, lemon juice, and gelatin in a saucepan. Cook, stirring, over moderate heat until the gelatin is completely dissolved. Put the peaches through a sieve, then combine with all the other ingredients and mix well. Pour into a shallow bowl and freeze for 1 hour. Remove from the freezer and beat with an electric mixer on high speed until fluffy, then freeze for 1 hour longer. *Eight servings, 25 calories each.*

26 BEVERAGES

DIETER'S REDDI-MIX LEMONADE BASE

2 cups fresh lemon juice
2 teaspoons grated lemon rind
3 tablespoons honey
Sugar substitute equal to ¾ cup sugar

Combine all the ingredients in a small covered jar and shake well. Store in the refrigerator and shake before using. To make a glass of lemon juice, combine ¼ cup of mix with cold water and ice cubes in a tall glass. *Ten servings, 33 calories each.*

Calorie-Safe Eggnogs to Toast the Holidays

Eggnog is nearly 350 calories a cupful, enough to take the Happy out of anybody's New Year.

And that's not even the hard stuff. We're talking about the "harmless kid stuff" the milkman delivers—liberally laced with butterfat instead of booze. Add brandy or rum, and you multiply the calories by 100 per slug.

But we don't expect you to toast the holidays with ice water, so we've concocted some calorie-safe nogs even dieters can enjoy—and even low-cholesterol dieters, because we've got a version made with the new frozen egg substitutes.

Incidentally, if you'd like to add some "spirit," add a shot or two of brandy or rum in place of the bottled flavorings. Each 1½-ounce jigger (85 proof) adds 105 calories.

◆§ SLIMMERS' FROSTY NOG §◆

2 cups ice cubes and water
2 eggs
1 cup instant nonfat dry milk
  Sugar substitute equal to 2 tablespoons sugar
2 teaspoons rum or brandy flavoring
  Pinch of butter-flavored salt
  Pinch of freshly grated nutmeg

Fill a 2-cup measure with ice cubes, then add tap water to the top. Put the ice, water, and remaining ingredients in the blender. Cover and blend until all the ice is dissolved. *Four servings, 105 calories each.*

◆§ LOW-CHOLESTEROL HOLIDAY NOG §◆

2 cups skim milk
½ cup powdered egg substitute
  Sugar substitute equal to 2 tablespoons sugar
1½ teaspoons vanilla extract or rum or brandy flavoring
  Pinch of freshly grated nutmeg

Combine all the ingredients and whir in the blender. *Three servings, 88 calories each.*

◆§ APPLE LEMONADE §◆

Lemonade, though high in sugar calories, at least has the nutritionally redeeming virtue of Vitamin C. A glass of the home-squeezed stuff offers nearly 200 milligrams of C, and other nutrients as well.

Sugar-free lemonade is simply a matter of squeezing lemon into a glass of ice cubes and water and adding liquid sweetener to taste. Or try this make-ahead mix that combines sugar substitute with apple juice. Keep it tightly capped in your refrigerator to mix up individual drinks as needed.

½ cup fresh lemon juice
¼ cup water
1 can (6 ounces) frozen apple juice concentrate, defrosted

Sugar substitute equal to 3 tablespoons sugar
Ice cubes
Club soda
Fresh mint leaves (optional)

Combine the lemon juice, water, defrosted concentrate, and sugar substitute. To prepare, put ¼ cup of the mixture in a tall glass and fill with ice cubes and club soda. Garnish with fresh mint leaves, if desired. *Six servings, 62 calories each.*

·§ STRAWBERRY-PINK LEMONADE ·

1 package (10 ounces) frozen sliced, sweetened strawberries
1 cup lemon juice
Sugar substitute equal to ½ cup sugar
6 cups cold water
Ice cubes

Defrost the berries. Combine with the lemon juice and sugar substitute in the blender, then cover and blend until the strawberries are pureed. Combine with cold water and ice cubes in a pitcher. Add fresh berries, if desired. *Six servings, 62 calories each.*

·§ CHOCOLATE MILKSHAKE ·

½ cup diet cream soda
5 tablespoons instant nonfat dry milk
1½ teaspoons chocolate extract
Sugar substitute to taste
5 ice cubes

Combine all the ingredients and whir in blender. Pour into a very tall glass and serve with a straw. *One serving, 90 calories.*

·§ COFFEE FROSTED ·

1 heaping teaspoon instant coffee
Sugar substitute to taste
½ cup boiling water
5 tablespoons instant nonfat dry milk
1 teaspoon vanilla extract
5 or 6 ice cubes

Put the instant coffee and sweetener in the blender; pour on hot water to dissolve. Add all the remaining ingredients and blend just until the ice is dissolved. Pour into tall glasses. *One serving, 91 calories.*

✑ STRAWBERRY PINEAPPLE FRAPPE ✑

1 can (6 ounces) unsweetened pineapple juice
4 or 5 large hulled strawberries, fresh or frozen
4 or 5 ice cubes
  Fresh mint leaves for garnish

Blend the pineapple juice, strawberries, and ice cubes until all the ice is crushed. Serve in a tall glass, garnished with fresh mint leaves. *One serving, about 100 calories.*

✑ EGGNOG LUNCH ✑

You wouldn't want an eggnog for every meal, or every day, especially if you're egg allergic or a cholesterol watcher. But the Slim Gourmet Eggnog Lunch is every bit as nutritious as an omelet and a glass of milk. In fact, that's exactly what it is, with a lot less bother.

And you can vary the flavor to suit yourself. One or two frozen strawberries add hardly any calories at all, and you'll think you're lunching at the soda fountain instead of dieting at home. Or try a teaspoonful of instant coffee powder or some diet chocolate syrup. A few drops of orange, lemon or banana extract can really turn on the flavor.

2 medium eggs
1 cup skim milk
½ teaspoon vanilla or brandy extract (or both)
  Pinch of freshly grated nutmeg
  Sugar substitute equal to 2 teaspoons sugar
2 or 3 ice cubes

Toss it all in your blender and *go!* When the blades stop clinking away at the cubes, you know it's ready. You'll pour out nearly 2 full, foamy, frosty glassfuls—nearly twice as much as the lunch-in-a-can. *One serving, 224 calories.*

◆§ BERRY FLIP §◆

½ cup fresh or frozen unsweetened strawberries or blueberries
5 tablespoons instant nonfat dry milk
5 ice cubes
½ cup cold water
  Sugar substitute to taste

Combine all the ingredients in the blender, cover, and blend until the ice is dissolved. Pour into a tall glass. *One serving, 112 calories.*

◆§ "CREAMY" HOT CHOCOLATE §◆

Anything that cuts down on fats and calories is a good idea for overweight, past-middle-age husbands given to occasional spurts of activity like climbing roofs or shoveling snow!

But if you've ever made skim-milk cocoa, you may have been disappointed. It was thin and watery, not at all like the creamy, fattening stuff you had as a kid. Here's a way to make it taste rich and creamy without the butterfat calories. The secret ingredient is the slight thickening action of a tiny bit of cornstarch.

2 teaspoons unsweetened cocoa
2 teaspoons granulated sugar
1 teaspoon cornstarch
  Pinch of salt
¼ cup nonfat instant dry milk
1 cup cold water
  Pinch of ground cinnamon or dash of vanilla extract (optional)

Put all the ingredients in a nonstick saucepan over low heat and stir constantly until the mixture begins to bubble and thicken slightly. Don't boil. Add a pinch of cinnamon or a dash of vanilla, if you like. *One serving, 150 calories.*

VARIATION

Sugarless Hot Chocolate: Omit the sugar and prepare as above. Before serving, stir in 2 or 3 saccharin tablets, or any type of sugar substitute you prefer. *One serving, 125 calories.*

~§ HOMEMADE HOT COCOA MIX §~

Did you know that the calories in unsweetened cocoa can range from 10 calories per tablespoon up to 27, depending on the butter-fat content? (Unfortunately, the best-known brand is one of the highest.) Once you've tried it, you might like to have your own homemade low-fat cocoa mix on hand, to use as needed. This recipe makes enough for 12 cups of prepared cocoa.

  3 cups instant nonfat dry milk
½ cup unsweetened cocoa
½ cup granulated sugar
½ cup cornstarch
1½ teaspoons salt

Mix together thoroughly and keep in a covered container. To prepare, simply add one-third cupful of the mix for each cup of water. Stir constantly while heating. *About 123 calories per ⅓ cup dry mix.*

VARIATION

Sugarless Hot Cocoa Mix: For a sugarless mix, omit the sugar and use slightly less than one-third of a cupful. Add the sweetener after heating. *About 96 calories per ⅓ cup dry mix.*

De-calorizing the Hard Stuff

DISTILLED LIQUOR: Scotch, bourbon, gin, vodka, rum, Irish whiskey, tequila, rye, and unflavored brandy all have comparable calorie counts. There's no significant difference between types of liquor, despite some people's belief that Scotch is "less fattening" than rum. What does affect calorie count is the "proof"—the concentration of alcohol. The higher the proof, the higher the calories.

LIQUOR CALORIES PER "SHOT"
(1½ ounces)

Proof	*Calories*
80	100
86	105
90	110
94	115
100	125

MIXERS: Plain and carbonated water ("club soda") have no calories, of course. Diet lemon soda and other sugar-free mixers have only a trace. But many other bitter and sour soda mixers have so much sugar they can be more fattening than the liquor you mix them with!

SODA MIXER CALORIES
(8 ounces, without liquor)

Mixer	*Calories*
Bitter lemon	128
Bitter orange	124
Club soda	0
Cola	100
Ginger ale	85
Quinine water	85
Tom Collins	85
7-Up, Sprite, etc.	96
Fresca, Tab, diet ginger ale, etc.	1

COCKTAIL WINES, APERITIFS, ETC.*
(3 ounces)

Wine	*Calories*
Dry wine	90
Sherry	120
Dry sherry	100
Sweet vermouth	100
Sangría	99
Sparkling wines	100
Sweet and "pop" wines	160 plus

* These are average; individual brands vary widely. The sweeter, the higher the calorie count.

COMMERCIAL COCKTAILS*

Cocktail	*Calories*
Bloody Mary	135
Daiquiri	180
Gimlet	150
Mai tai	180
Manhattan	155
Martini	175
Margarita	175
Old-fashioned	160
Screwdriver	185
Sour	175

* Bottled or made from mixes, including 1½ ounces 90-proof liquor. Individual brands vary; these are average.

MISCELLANEOUS OTHER DRINKS
(8 ounces)

Beverage	Calories
Beer	100
Ale	100
Malt liquor	110
Lite or lo-cal beer	65
Miscellaneous punches	175
Dairy eggnog (no liquor)	345
Alcoholic eggnog	670

Slim Mixed Drinks

The calorie counts for the cocktails that follow are for 80 proof and don't include the garnishes.

Slim Gimlet: Juice of 1 lime, 1 ounce vodka or gin, and 4 drops liquid sweetener. Shake well with ice and strain into a well-chilled glass. Garnish with lime peel. *Only 75 calories.*

Slim Sour: Juice of 1 lemon, 1 ounce Scotch or bourbon, and 5 drops liquid sweetener. Garnish with a fresh cherry. *Only 73 calories.*

Wet Martini: 1 ounce gin or vodka and 2 ounces dry vermouth. Shake with ice and strain into a cocktail glass with an olive. *Only 125 calories.*

Wet Bikini: 1 ounce gin or vodka, ice cubes, and sugar-free Fresca. *Only 65 calories.*

Lower Manhattan: 1 ounce rye or bourbon, 2 ounces sweet vermouth, and a double dash of bitters. Shake with ice and serve with a fresh cherry. *Only 149 calories.*

New-Fangled Old-Fashioned: 1 ounce rye or bourbon, 2 ounces club soda, 4 drops liquid sweetener, 2 double dashes of bitters, 2 ice cubes, 1 fresh cherry, and an orange slice. Serve in an Old-Fashioned glass. *Only 69 calories.*

Very, Very Bloody Mary: 1 ounce vodka, 5 ounces tomato juice, a squeeze of lemon, a dash of Worcestershire, and a dash of salt. Shake with ice and strain. *Only 97 calories.*

Left-handed Screwdriver: 1 ounce vodka or gin and 5 ounces orange juice. Pour over ice cubes in a 10-ounce glass. *Only 133 calories.*

Demi-Daiquiri: 1 ounce light rum, juice of 1 lime, 2 ounces club soda, and liquid sweetener. Shake with cracked ice and strain into a cocktail glass. (For a frozen daiquiri, omit the soda and add a scoop of shaved ice. Serve in a champagne glass.) *Only 75 calories.*

27
FIVE-DAY
MENUS

MONDAY'S MENU

Breakfast: 1 cup high protein cereal with ½ cup skim milk and ½ cup blueberries or strawberries

Snack: Cup of bouillon

Lunch: Hamburger (2½ ounces lean ground round) on a roll
Onion and pickle slices, catsup
Coleslaw with diet dressing
Low-calorie beverage

Snack: Hot chocolate (made with skim milk, plain cocoa, sugar substitute)

Dinner: 1 ounce 80-proof liquor with ice water, club soda,
Diet soda, tomato or orange juice
Slim Gourmet "Cordon Bleu" (see below)
Wine Sauce (see below)
Broccoli or green beans, with butter-flavored salt
Small baked potato with yogurt or cottage cheese topping
Tomato-cucumber salad with 1 teaspoon vinegar,
½ teaspoon oil
1 slice French bread, 1 teaspoon diet margarine
Coffee or tea or skim milk

379

Dessert or Snack: Pineapple shortcake (angel or sponge cake topped with crushed pineapple)

Today's Recipes

⋖§   SLIM GOURMET "CORDON BLEU"   §⋗

1¼   pounds lean veal, chicken or turkey cutlets
  3   ounces Swiss cheese, thinly sliced
  3   ounces lean boiled ham
     Chopped fresh parsley
  2   tablespoons salad oil
  5   tablespoons seasoned bread crumbs

Divide the cutlets into six equal pieces; pound thin with the edge of a heavy plate. Top each piece with a thin slice of cheese, then a thin slice of ham. Sprinkle with parsley, then roll up, with the cheese and ham on the inside.

Dip each roll first in the salad oil, then in the bread crumbs, coating lightly. Place on a nonstick baking sheet. Bake in a preheated hot (400-degree) oven for 10 to 12 minutes, until browned. Serve with wine sauce (see below), if you wish. *Six servings, 271 calories each with veal, 238 with turkey or chicken.*

Wine Sauce: Combine 1 can (13 ounces) evaporated skim milk with 2 tablespoons dry white wine, 1 chicken bouillon cube, and 1 tablespoon arrowroot or cornstarch. Cook, stirring, over moderate heat until thick. Thin to gravy consistency with boiling water, then stir in some chopped fresh parsley. *Six servings, 55 calories each.*

TUESDAY'S MENU

Breakfast: 6 ounces tomato juice
Whole-Egg French toast (see page 381)
Coffee or tea, skim milk

Coffee Break: 2 graham crackers, lightly spread with peanut butter or diet cream cheese
Coffee or tea, skim milk

Lunch: Cold roast chicken leg
½ cup potato salad with diet mayonnaise
Celery hearts
Diet soda or skim milk
Sliced peaches (sugar-free or artificially sweetened)

Snack: Blender shake (small banana, ¾ cup skim milk, ice cubes, vanilla)

Dinner: 3 ounces claret
Continental Flank Steak with Mushrooms (see below)
Green salad with Caesar diet dressing, croutons
Broccoli with butter-flavored salt
Coffee or tea, skim milk

Dessert or Snack: Sundae (scoop 97% fat-free ice milk topped with fruit or diet syrup)

Today's Recipes

∼§ WHOLE-EGG FRENCH TOAST ∽

Soak 2 slices gluten, diet, or protein broad in 1 beaten egg until absorbed. Wipe a nonstick skillet with 1 teaspoon polyunsaturated oil. Brown on both sides over moderate heat. Serve with 1 tablespoon low-sugar jam or 2 tablespoons warm low-calorie maple syrup. *One serving, 229 calories.*

∼§ CONTINENTAL FLANK STEAK WITH MUSHROOMS ∽

1¾ **pounds flank steak**
    Meat tenderizer
    Garlic salt
  2 **tablespoons water**
  1 **tablespoon all-purpose flour**
 ⅔ **cup dry red wine or beer**
 ¼ **teaspoon poultry seasoning**
  1 **can (4 ounces) sliced mushrooms**

With a sharp knife, make shallow criss-cross slashes on both sides of the flank steak. Sprinkle the steak with tenderizer and garlic salt, then put it, along with the water, in a large nonstick skillet over moderate heat. When the moisture evaporates the steak will brown in its own melted fat. Brown on both sides.

Sprinkle the steak on both sides with the flour, then add the remaining ingredients. Simmer, uncovered, until the mushrooms are heated through and the sauce is thickened. The steak should be served rare, sliced very thinly against the grain. *Six servings, 210 calories each.*

WEDNESDAY'S MENU

Breakfast: ½ cantaloupe
2 eggs, scrambled in a nonstick pan, no fat
1 ounce Canadian bacon, pan-fried, no fat
Coffee or tea, skim milk

Coffee Break: Bouillon, 2 saltines
1 tablespoon peanut butter

Lunch: Chef's salad (lettuce, onions, tomatoes, green pepper tossed with 2 ounces shredded turkey, 1 ounce ham, 1 ounce cheese)
Diet French dressing
Sugar-free soda, skim milk

Snack: ½ cup diet gelatin with fruit (sugar-free or artificially sweetened)

Dinner: 3 ounces Chianti wine
Tossed salad with diet Italian dressing
Slim Gourmet Spaghetti and Meatballs (see below)
2 breadsticks
Italian green beans or zucchini sautéed in 1 teaspoon diet margarine
Espresso coffee

Dessert or Snack: Fruit cup (sugar-free or artificially sweetened)

Today's Recipe

SLIM GOURMET
∾ SPAGHETTI AND MEATBALLS ∾

1 pound extra-lean beef round, trimmed of fat and ground
1 egg
½ cup soy granules or high protein cereal, crushed
2 tablespoons grated onion
Garlic salt and freshly ground pepper
½ teaspoon oregano or Italian seasoning
1½ cups water
1 can (10¾ ounces) onion soup, skimmed of fat
1 can (6 ounces) tomato paste
1 tablespoon freshly grated extra-sharp Romano cheese
5 cups tender-cooked protein-enriched spaghetti

Combine the beef, egg, soy granules, onion, garlic salt, pepper, and oregano with ½ cup water. Mix lightly and shape into 12 small meatballs, then brown on a nonstick cookie sheet under the broiler.

Combine all the other ingredients except the spaghetti in a saucepan and stir well. Add the meatballs and 1 cup water. Cover and simmer over low heat for 45 minutes, then uncover and continue to cook until the liquid evaporates into a thick sauce. Serve over the spaghetti, allowing ¾ cup spaghetti per serving. *Six servings, 350 calories each.*

THURSDAY'S MENU

Breakfast: "Instant" breakfast blender nog (1 egg, 6 ounces skim milk, ice cubes, vanilla, nutmeg, sweetener)

Coffee Break: 2 slices protein toast
2 teaspoons diet jelly
Coffee or tea, skim milk

Lunch: Reuben sandwich (2 ounces lean cooked ham, 1 ounce Swiss cheese on 1 slice thin pumpernickel, broiled)
½ cup sauerkraut
Mustard pickle slices
½ bottle low-calorie or low-alcohol beer

Snack: 5 ounces plain yogurt with tangerine sections

Dinner: Oven-fried Chicken with "Cream" Gravy (see below)
Coleslaw with diet dressing
Glazed carrots simmered in diet maple syrup
½ cup rice
Coffee or tea, skim milk

Dessert or Snack: High-Protein "Cream" Cheesecake (see page 384)

Today's Recipes

⌘ OVEN-FRIED CHICKEN WITH "CREAM" GRAVY ⌘

1 frying chicken (about 2 pounds), cut up
6 tablespoons seasoned bread crumbs
1 can (10½ ounces) chicken consommé
½ cup instant nonfat dry milk
1 tablespoon arrowroot or cornstarch
Minced fresh parsley
2 tablespoons dry sherry wine (optional)

Trim all fringe fat from the chicken. Shake the pieces in a bag containing the bread crumbs until lightly coated, put, skin side down, in a nonstick roasting pan. Add no fat. Bake in a preheated 375-degree oven for 30 minutes, then turn and bake an additional 30 minutes, until tender.

Skim the fat globules from the consommé, then combine with the remaining ingredients in a saucepan. Cook, stirring, over moderate heat until thickened. Thin to gravy consistency with boiling water. *Six servings, 198 calories each.*

◄§ HIGH-PROTEIN "CREAM" CHEESECAKE §►

2 tablespoons diet margarine
½ cup graham-cracker crumbs
8 ounces farmer cheese, low-calorie cream cheese, or low-fat
    Neufchâtel cheese
4 eggs
¼ cup granulated sugar
    Sugar substitute equal to ¼ cup sugar
1 tablespoon vanilla extract
1 teaspoon grated lemon or orange rind
⅓ cup skim milk
    Pinch of butter-flavored salt

Spread the inside of an 8-inch nonstick round cake or pie pan with the diet margarine. Press the crumbs into the surface. Quick-brown in a hot (450-degree) oven for 6 to 8 minutes.

Combine all the remaining ingredients in the blender and blend until smooth. Gently pour into the crumb crust and bake in a slow (250-degree) oven for 1 hour. Allow to cool in the oven with the door open for 1 hour, then chill before serving. *Eight servings, 136 calories each with farmer cheese; 152 with low-calorie cream cheese.*

FRIDAY'S MENU

Breakfast: Toasted English muffin
             2 tablespoons low-calorie cream cheese or low-fat
                Neufchâtel cheese
             Coffee or tea, skim milk

Coffee Break: Orange freeze (in blender, ½ cup orange juice,
                ½ cup skim milk, 1 scoop low-fat vanilla ice milk)

Lunch: Oriental Tuna Omelet for Two (see page 385)
             Tomato wedges with diet dressing
             Asparagus tips with Worcestershire sauce
             Chinese tea, fortune cookies

Snack: 1 apple or pear or ½ cup canned fruit (sugar-free or artificially sweetened)

Dinner: 3 ounces dry sauterne
3 slices white meat turkey with fat-free gravy
⅓ cup dressing (made with stuffing mix, no fat added)
½ cup squash or mashed turnip, butter-flavored salt
Hearts of celery
1 tablespoon low-sugar cranberry sauce
Coffee or tea, skim milk

Dessert or Snack: Topless Pie (see below)

Today's Recipes

~§ ORIENTAL TUNA OMELET FOR TWO ୫~

Spray-on vegetable coating
5 **eggs, lightly beaten**
1½ **tablespoons minced onion**
1 **can (3½ ounces) water-packed tuna, drained and flaked**
Soy sauce
Hot Chinese mustard

Spray an 8-inch nonstick skillet liberally with vegetable coating for no-fat frying. Heat over a moderate flame until a drop of water sizzles on the surface. Add the eggs all at once and do not disturb for 10 seconds.

Sprinkle the minced onion on one half. When the egg begins to set, gently lift the outer edges to permit the egg to run underneath. When nearly cooked, sprinkle on the tuna. Tip the frying pan over a heated plate and roll out the omelet. Cut in half and serve immediately with soy sauce and mustard. *Two servings, 247 calories each.*

⊷ TOPLESS PIE ⊷

PASTRY:

¾ cup self-rising flour

3 tablespoons polyunsaturated oil

2 tablespoons water

FILLING:

6 cups sliced peaches or apples

3 tablespoons honey

Sugar substitute equal to ½ cup sugar (optional)

Pinch of butter-flavored salt

2 teaspoons lemon juice

Apple-pie spice or almond extract

1 tablespoon arrowroot or cornstarch

Fork-blend the flour and oil together; add the water gradually, until pastry leaves the side of the bowl. Shape into a ball and pat out flat. Using a well-floured board and roller, roll out immediately as thin as possible. Line the bottom of a nonstick 8- or 9-inch pie pan. Trim and discard extra pastry (you should have ¼ cup left over).

You may use either fresh fruit or drained canned juice-packed peaches or unsweetened pie-sliced apples (not apple-pie filling). If using apples, season with 1 scant teaspoon apple-pie spice; peaches may be seasoned with a few drops almond extract. Combine the fruit with all the remaining ingredients and spoon into crust. Invert an empty pie pan on top of the pie, or cut an 8-inch round of aluminum foil to cover the fruit. Bake in a 425-degree oven for 30 minutes or more, until the fruit is tender. Serve warm or chilled. *Eight servings, 136 calories each.*

INDEX